W9-BPQ-531

CATHOLIC THEOLOGY
in the
NINETEENTH
CENTURY

CATHOLIC THEOLOGY
in the
NINETEENTH
CENTURY

The Quest for a Unitary Method

GERALD A. McCOOL

A Crossroad Book
THE SEABURY PRESS · NEW YORK

1977
The Seabury Press
815 Second Avenue
New York, N.Y. 10017

Copyright © 1977 by The Seabury Press, Inc. All rights reserved. No
part of this book may be reproduced, stored in a retrieval system, or
transmitted, in any form or by any means, electronic, mechanical,
photocopying, recording, or otherwise, without the written permission
of The Seabury Press, Inc.

Printed in the United States of America

Library of Congress Cataloging in Publication Data

McCool, Gerald A
Catholic theology in the nineteenth century.
"A Crossroad book."
Includes bibliographical references and index.
1.Theology, Catholic—History. 2.Theology,
Doctrinal—History—19th century. I.Title.
BX1747.M25   230'.2   76-30493
ISBN 0-8164-0339-2

To the memory of
Walter Stokes, S.J.

Acknowledgements

An expression of gratitude is due to Fordham University for the Faculty Fellowship which enabled me to spend the school year 1975-1976 in research and writing. A warm word of thanks is also due to the Reverend James Hennessy, S.J., then President of the Jesuit School of Theology in Chicago, and to Dean Joseph Kitagawa of the University of Chicago Divinity School. A visiting research professorship at the Divinity School and a scholarship in residence at the Jesuit School of Theology placed at my disposal the magnificent resources both of the University library and of the libraries attached to the divinity schools clustered around it. A formal expression of gratitude should also be addressed to Dr. Anne Carr, Assistant Dean of the Divinity School, to its faculty and students, and to my colleagues at the Jesuit School of Theology. Their encouragement and cooperation with my work had a great deal to do with its successful conclusion. Finally, a very special word of thanks is due to Professor David Tracy of the Divinity School for the indispensable stimulating help which he gave to the shaping of this book in many stimulating conversations during my stay in Chicago.

CONTENTS

INTRODUCTION

On 22 April 1870 the Apostolic Constitution on Faith, *Dei Filius*, was solemnly approved by the assembled fathers of the First Vatican Council. On 4 August 1879 the encyclical *Aeterni Patris* was issued by the Roman pontiff Leo XIII. These two dates are significant in the history of Roman Catholic theology.

Separated by almost ten years, in one of the most momentous and troubled decades in the Church's history, the two documents differed significantly in both their doctrinal content and in the weight of their authority. *Dei Filius* was an apostolic constitution, approved unanimously by an ecumenical council. It defined and clarified the Church's dogmatic teaching about the freedom and supernatural character of faith and the relation between supernatural faith and natural reason. *Aeterni Patris*, on the other hand, was a purely disciplinary document, resting upon the juridical authority of the reigning pontiff, Leo XIII. Its scope was limited to the method of philosophical instruction approved for the education of future priests in seminary and Catholic faculties. When linked together, however, in the minds of the Roman authorities and of the theologians influenced by these two documents, as in fact they were, *Dei Filius* and *Aeterni Patris* amounted to a profoundly significant concrete decision by the highest authorities of the Catholic Church.

It was a decision which profoundly influenced the history of Catholic theology. Indeed it determined the course of its development for almost a century. It also fixed the pattern of Catholic theology's understanding of its own history from the beginning of the Catholic reaction to the Enlightenment in the early nineteenth century until the publication of *Aeterni Patris*. Finally it determined the method according to which Catholic positive and speculative theology endeavored to retrieve the heritage of its own Catholic doctrinal tradition and to present that tradition to the

1

modern world in an ongoing dialogue with contemporary culture.

A good deal of the credit for these developments must be attributed to Joseph Kleutgen, the greatest of the early Jesuit neo-Thomists. Kleutgen was the theologian who drafted the final version of the Apostolic Constitution on Faith adopted by the First Vatican Council. The language of the constitution on the relation between faith and reason reflects Kleutgen's scholastic thought. The classification of disapproved positions under the opposed categories of fideists, who conceded too little to unaided human reason in relation to man's knowledge of God, and semirationalists, who conceded too much, is due to Kleutgen. Kleutgen is often credited with the principal, if not the exclusive, authorship of *Aeterni Patris*, the encyclical in which Leo XIII proclaimed the Church's official option for the Aristotelian method of St. Thomas in her philosophical and theological instruction. Finally Kleutgen's two major works, *Die Theologie der Vorzeit* and *Die Philosophie der Vorzeit*, present a masterly exposition of the German theology of Hermes, Günther, and the Tübingen School, followed by an incisive critique of their theology in the light of his own scholastic system.

Self-Interpretation of Catholic Theology

For years the generally accepted picture of the pre-Thomistic nineteenth-century theology was Kleutgen's interpretation of it. At the beginning of the century Catholic theologians had forgotten their scholastic heritage. They had attempted to restore Catholic theology by using new theological methods modeled on the philosophical method of post-Cartesian philosophy. These methods had shown that they could not handle satisfactorily the relation between faith and reason. Hence the condemnation of the traditionalist Bautain on the grounds of fideism, and the condemnation of the post-Kantian theologians Hermes and Günther on the grounds of semirationalism. In the second half of the nineteenth century a renewed Neo-Thomism had restored the Church's traditional scholastic method in philosophy and theology. Scholasticism had shown that it could handle the problem of faith and reason. In *Aeterni Patris* a grateful Church had given her official approval to the Thomistic revival. Hence the history of nineteenth-century Catholic theology was the story of its journey *ex umbris et imaginibus in veritatem*.

A century later, in another momentous and troubled decade in the Church's history, Catholic theologians are engaged in a serious reconsideration of the received interpretation of nineteenth-century Catholic theology. Catholic theology has undergone a steady internal evolution since the inception of the Maréchalian New Theology *(nouvelle théologie)* thirty years ago. The historically open, dialectical, subject-oriented theologies of Rahner and Lonergan are authentic developments of the Maréchalian New Theology of the forties and fifties. The New Theology, which we associate with the names of Henri de Lubac, Henri Bouillard, and the theological faculty of Fourvière, was the polar antithesis of the Dominican Thomism of Garrigou-Lagrange, Jacques Maritain, and the Toulouse Dominicans associated with *La Revue Thomiste*. But it also had little in common with the New Theologians' great Jesuit predecessor, Louis Billot. More than that, its distinctive theses would have won little sympathy from the distinguished Jesuit founders of the neo-Thomist movement Matteo Liberatore and Joseph Kleutgen.

The distinctive characteristics of the New Theology were its subjective starting point, a receptive attitude toward post-Cartesian philosophy, a dialectic of the subject, reminiscent of the dialectic of Fichte and the post-Kantian idealists, the grounding of the objective validity of conceptual thought through an *a priori* grasp of the absolute, and an emphasis upon an organic conception of nature and society strongly influenced by neo-Platonic and patristic thought.

But these were the characteristics that distinguished the anti-Thomistic modern theologies of the nineteenth century. The fundamental theses of the Jesuit New Theology were, in fact, the philosophical "errors" from which their neo-Thomist ancestors had hoped to "free" Catholic theology. Thus, sixty years after *Aeterni Patris* the Jesuit descendants of the early neo-Thomists had welcomed into their revised Thomistic synthesis the epistemology and metaphysics of their ancestors' theological archenemies.

And, as if to heighten the irony, the New Theologians performed their act of unfilial betrayal by exploiting the philosophical potentialities of the weapon their ancestors had used to undermine the epistemology and metaphysics on which their opponents' modern theologies were built. This weapon was St. Thomas' metaphysics of knowledge and the metaphysics of man and being which that metaphysics of knowledge required.

GEISELMANN AND THE CATHOLIC TÜBINGEN SCHOOL

At the very time that the New Theologians were carrying out their radical reorientation of Thomistic theology, Joseph Rupert Geiselmann was engaged in his historical research into the theology of the nineteenth-century Catholic Tübingen School. The Tübingen theologians had been great rivals of the scholastic theologians in nineteenth-century Germany. Neither school was destined to understand or sympathize with the other. The Tübingen theologians were noted for their strong attachment to Catholic orthodoxy and their devotion to the Church. They were also very careful scientific theologians. Consequently Tübingen theology avoided the shattering Roman condemnations which sealed the fate of other nineteenth-century theologians. Tübingen continued to function as a respected faculty of theology, justly proud of its theological tradition and of the contribution which it had made to the revival of Catholic thought in Germany. Nevertheless, in the period between *Aeterni Patris* and the middle 1930s, the theology of Tübingen's nineteenth-century representatives, Drey, Möhler, Hirscher, Staudenmaier, and Kuhn, was generally considered worthy of no more than historical interest. The theological method of the nineteenth-century Tübingen theologians was dismissed as one more nineteenth-century method which had failed the crucial test of dealing successfully with the relations between faith and reason, grace and nature.

Geiselmann's patient editing of the works of the Tübingen School has changed this negative estimation of their theological method. Geiselmann has given his readers a detailed and exact exposition of the Tübingen theology of revelation, its understanding of the development of doctrine and the role of the Holy Spirit in the Church, which is the bearer of Christ's living tradition. As the result of Geiselmann's work theologians now possess a clearer picture of Tübingen's theological method, and Tübingen theology is taken seriously again as an orthodox nineteenth-century alternative to Thomism. For Geiselmann has shown that, contrary to the commonly held belief, the Tübingen theologians did, in fact, possess a consistent and orthodox theology of faith and reason, grace and nature. It was not the failure of the Tübingen theologians to deal with these problems in a satisfactory manner which occasioned the abandonment of the Tübingen theology after *Aeterni Patris.* It was the failure of the scholastically oriented Roman theologians and their increasingly powerful disciples to understand and appreciate the Tübingen solutions.

Following Geiselmann's footsteps, younger theologians in the Tübingen tradition, Walter Kasper for example, have also turned their attention to the work of the nineteenth-century Catholic Tübingen School. Their purpose, moreover, is not simply to expound and vindicate the nineteenth-century Tübingen theology. It is rather to develop its resources as a living tradition in Catholic theology. For just as contemporary Thomism is no longer the Thomism of Liberatore and Kleutgen, contemporary Tübingen theology would not be the theology of Drey, Möhler, and Hirscher. Contemporary Tübingen theology would be a theology of the present age, whose epistemology and metaphysics have evolved through its dialogue with contemporary philosophy. Nevertheless, since Tübingen epistemology and metaphysics were fundamentally diverse from the epistemology and metaphysics of St. Thomas, a developed Tübingen theology should present itself as a distinctly different theology, a genuine and orthodox alternative to a developed Thomism. Should this occur, the debate between Tübingen and Thomistic theology would be renewed in the Catholic Church, this time, hopefully, through a calmer and more fruitful exchange of views.

RECONSIDERATION OF GERMAN NINETEENTH-CENTURY THEOLOGY

The debate between a developed Thomism, which has united St. Thomas' metaphysics of knowledge, man, and being with the major themes of Thomas' nineteenth-century opponents, and the contemporary heirs of the Tübingen theological tradition is simply one interesting example of Catholic theology's renewed interest in its nineteenth-century history as the centenary of *Aeterni Patris* draws near. A number of important studies have appeared in recent years dealing with the works of the German theologians Hermes, Günther, and Frohschammer. The Italian "ontologists" Gioberti and Rosmini have also been critically reconsidered. Several very valuable works on the history of the Thomist revival have been published in the last few years. The attitude of their authors has been almost uniformly positive toward the non-Thomistic nineteenth-century theologians; and the aim of their works has been to throw light on the possibilities which the nineteenth-century "modern" theological method held out for the development of modern Catholic theology, and which the neo-Thomist critics of the modern nineteenth-century systems failed to see. In some instances, these authors tell us, those lost possibilities have been retrieved by contemporary transcendental Thomism. Such seems to have been the case with Anton Günther, for example. Karl Rahner's systematic theology does justice to some of the key insights of Günther's speculative theology. Günther's speculative synthesis was based on the ontological relations linking together the Trinity, the Incarnation, the Holy Spirit, and the Church. Rahner has been able to link the Christian mysteries together, and, like Günther, Rahner has been able to relate his unified system of the Christian mysteries to the inner life of the human subject and the human subject's experience of his historical world of spirit and nature. But, in other instances, as perhaps in the case of Tübingen theology, Catholic theologians are being confronted with a nineteenth-century Catholic theology which has come to life again and which may represent a genuinely distinct and irreducible theology, incapable of absorption into even a highly developed transcendental Thomism.

A Genuine Option Between Thomism and Other Methods

The possibility of a genuine option between a developed Thomism and a restored pre-Thomistic nineteenth-century system could well be the result of the current historical research into Catholic nineteenth-century theology. At least two factors affecting contemporary Catholic theology give us reason to think so. The first of these is the freedom given to Catholic theologians by the Second Vatican Council to experiment with non-Thomistic theological systems. *Aeterni Patris* no longer enjoys the status of an irrevocable theological option, based on immutable dogmatic and metaphysical principles. Its theological signification has been relativized. *Aeterni Patris* must now be considered an historical moment in the dialectical progress of theological development. The second distinctive characteristic of contemporary theology is the current ferment over theological method. This means that the nineteenth-century debate over theological method, which the official option of *Aeterni Patris* seemed to have closed definitively, has been reopened. The disciples of St. Thomas and the partisans of the "new" theologies are free once more to submit their diverse theological methods to the judgment of their fellow theologians.

As a result, Catholic theologians are considering again the two major documents in which the Church's nineteenth-century decision for Thomas' Aristotelian method was expressed. Theologians are restudying the nineteenth-century debate between the Thomist and non-Thomist theologians which preceded the Church's decision. What were the dogmatic and philosophical reasons which the Thomists advanced to justify the choice of St. Thomas' theology? Are those dogmatic and philosophical reasons still valid?

Catholic theology is a systematic intellectual reflection on the historical data of Christian revelation encountered in the living tradition of the

Church and accepted through the reasonable act of faith of the Christian believer. Therefore apologetics, and positive, speculative, and moral theology must all be concerns of the Catholic theologian. Each of these disciplines must be assigned the proper place in a Catholic theological synthesis demanded by the system's proper theological method. But, in order to assign these disciplines their proper place and designate their proper function, a Catholic theological system must define the relation of each discipline to the supernatural act of faith through which the Christian believer assents to historical Christian revelation. It must also specify the character of the rational reflection which justifies the reasonableness of the Christian act of faith and leads the Christian to a deeper penetration of its content.

The relation of rational reflection to the supernatural act of faith was specified in different ways by Thomistic and non-Thomistic nineteenth-century theologians. And, as a result, the nature and function of apologetics, and positive, speculative, and moral theology differed radically in their systems. And so, in consequence, did the conception of a perduring doctrinal tradition in Catholic theology.

KLEUTGEN'S ARISTOTELIAN SCIENTIFIC THEOLOGY

The neo-Thomist theologians, of whom Joseph Kleutgen was the greatest representative, were convinced that St. Thomas' theology of grace and nature was the only theology which could accurately determine the proper relationship between faith and reason. Grace was the entitative habit inhering in the soul. Faith was an operative habit inhering in the intellect. Natural reason could prove the existence of God and the reasonableness of the act of faith. Therefore apologetics was an historical and philosophical propaedeutic to faith and reason. Consequently the traditionalism of de Lamennais, Bautain, and the Catholic Tübingen School, which made man's knowledge of the first principles of metaphysics and ethics dependent upon a primitive act of divine revelation communicated to Adam's descendants by tradition, deprived human reason of its legitimate autonomy and, by doing so, undermined the reasonableness of the act of faith. It was not surprising therefore that none of these theologians appreciated the necessity of an historical and a philosophical apologetics.

On the other hand, certain knowledge of the Trinity, the Incarnation, and the other Christian mysteries could be acquired only through the free assent of faith which proceeded from the supernatural operative habit of faith in a human intellect elevated by the entitative habit of sanctifying grace. But Rosmini, Gioberti, and the ontologist philosophers and theologians, who required an intuition of Infinite Being to ground the objectivity of human knowledge, conceded thereby to philosophical natural reason an intuition of God's own being which only grace could give. The German theologians, Hermes and Günther, claimed that unaided philosophical reason could make true and certain judgments about the Christian mysteries. Therefore both the ontologists and the German theologians were semirationalists who failed to respect the gratuitous and distinctive character of supernatural knowledge.

Positive and speculative theology could never be assigned the function of a philosophy of revelation in an orthodox Catholic method. But this was precisely what Hermes and Günther did and the Tübingen theologians did in their theological methods. If positive and speculative theology were not intrinsically different in their intellectual operations from a philosophy of revelation, that must imply that either natural reason's legitimate autonomy had been compromised by a traditionalist fideism or that the gratuity and irreducible distinctiveness of supernatural knowledge had been compromised by a semirationalist exaggeration of natural reason's power to penetrate the intelligibility of the Christian mysteries.

Thus Kleutgen's theology of grace and nature determined his Thomist theology of faith and reason. Both of these in turn demanded an Aristotelian metaphysics of substance and accident, faculty, habit, and act. An Aristotelian metaphysics of man and being required an Aristotelian theory of knowledge to ground it. An Aristotelian theory of knowledge led in turn to an Aristotelian theory of metaphysical science. And this, combined with a Thomistic metaphysics of grace and nature, led to Kleutgen's Aristotelian conception of an Aristotelian science of theology to which an Aristotelian science of philosophy was subordinated. Apologetics was a scientific propaedeutic to theology, independent of faith in the character of its natural intellectual operations. Positive and speculative theology were subsequent to faith and dependent upon the habit of faith for the supernatural character of their operations and the supernatural character and necessity of their evidence.

Catholic theology was the Aristotelian science of those truths which are believed precisely in so far as they are believed. Its first principles were the revealed truths of faith which must be assented to by the believing mind elevated by the supernatural habits of grace and faith. Therefore only a believer could be a scientific theologian. Only a believer could think like a theologian and only a believer had access to theology's necessary and certain evidence, for only the assent of faith could provide theology's certainty based on the testimony of the revealing God, and only the changeless divine truth of the revealing God could ground its immutable necessity.

Scientific theology could link revealed first principles together in explanatory syllogisms whose conclusions would provide a deeper understanding of the faith. Or the theologian could establish a theologically certain conclusion by means of a minor premise known by natural reason. The positive theologian could reassemble the elements of the developed notions employed by speculative theologians and the Church's magisterium from their dispersed and undeveloped elements in theology's historical sources. But, as a scientific theologian, he was directed in his historical research by the developed scholastic notions which it was his task to "justify" historically. Scholastic speculative theology could then relate these developed notions to each other, draw analogies to them from nature, and so enable the believing Christian to deepen his interior understanding and appreciation of them.

Moral theology was directed to human action. It was an Aristotelian practical science which directed man to the attainment of the supernatural end of his elevated nature—union with the triune God in the beatific vision. Moral theology was directed, however, in its reflections by scholastic positive and speculative theology. For the primary subject of Thomas' Aristotelian theology was God, the *alpha* and *omega,* God, the creative source, the Incarnate Redeemer and the supernatural end of elevated human nature.

Thus Kleutgen's science of theology was a science of individual nature and the eternal triune God who was that nature's source and end. There was no place in it at all for the Romantic and post-Kantian metaphysics of community and no place at all for history and the intelligible but nonlogical development of thought through the changing conceptual frameworks of suceeding historical and cultural world views. The reason was clear enough. Kleutgen associated traditional Catholic theology with its "old" scholastic method. This method, in Kleutgen's eyes, had reached its full development in the post-Reformation scholasticism of Cano, de Lugo, Vasquez, and Suarez. Once we understand that, we also understand why the restoration of Thomism which Kleutgen was trying to achieve would ultimately disappoint the hopes of the early neo-Thomists that through it modern theology would be provided with a satisfactory theological method. For, like Kleutgen himself, the post-Reformation scholastics were erudite, fair-minded metaphysicians. But they could not think historically. And so, again like Kleutgen himself, they were unaware that their Aristotelian theological method could not handle history.

Kleutgen: The Unconscious Author of Thomistic Pluralism

What connection then can there be between the developed Thomism of the New Theologians, Rahner and Lonergan, and the Thomism of their neo-Thomistic ancestor? In the last quarter of the twentieth century, Thomistic theology is characterized by its historical openness, the evolutionary character of its thought, and its sensitivity to the plurality of diverse cultural and conceptual frameworks. Nevertheless there is a connection between the historical Thomism of Rahner and Lonergan and the antihistorical Thomism of Joseph Kleutgen and Matteo Liberatore. The connection is found in the Thomistic theory of knowledge and the anthropology which Kleutgen called upon to justify his Aristotelian metaphysics of nature and supernature. The Thomistic theory of knowledge demanded a substantial union of soul and body in man. The Thomistic intellect was always an abstractive intellect. Its concepts could only deal with the Holy Mystery who is the subject of Christian revelation through the indirect and analogous concepts of a judging intellect which, as St. Thomas said so well, knew what God was not rather than what God was. Abstraction and analogy rather than direct and intuitive knowledge of God distinguished the scholastic approach to God from the approach of post-Cartesian philosophy and, despite its *rapprochement* with modern thought in the twentieth century, abstraction and analogy are still the cognitional characteristics of Thomistic metaphysics and theology.

In fact, the historicism and pluralism that characterize the contemporary Thomism of Rahner and Lonergan are grounded upon their abstractive theory of knowledge and upon the analogy of being which it permits. The distinction between the categorical universals of the conceptual intellect and sense knowledge of the singular on one hand and unobjective knowledge of Infinite Being on the other lies at the heart of Rahner's philosophy of knowledge and being. Likewise the distinction between the categorical universal and the mind's implicit grasp of its infinite goal is the epistemological ground for the metaphysical pluralism defended by Jean Marie LeBlond and the historical pluralism of conceptual and cultural frameworks defended by Bernard J. F. Lonergan. The metaphysics of abstraction through the dynamism of the active intellect, brought back to honor by Liberatore and Kleutgen in their controversy with post-Cartesian philosophy, turned out to be the necessary condition for the evolution of twentieth-century Thomism into a pluralistic and historically oriented theology.

Kleutgen himself failed to exploit these possibilities of the metaphysics of abstraction which he and Liberatore had brought back from oblivion. For Kleutgen himself was antisubjective and antihistorical in his philosophical approach. Reacting against the Cartesian subjective starting point in epistemology and metaphysics, Kleutgen stressed the sensible origin of man's conceptual knowledge. In Kleutgen's metaphysics the intentional forms represented in man's universal ideas were the correlates of the changeless forms in sensible things themselves. For Kleutgen the intelligibility of being was not grounded in the intelligible motion of the knowing mind. Neither was it grounded in an unobjective grasp of the moving mind's Infinite Goal. The intelligibility of being was grounded in the contingent intelligibility of sensible things themselves.

Thus Kleutgen unconsciously built into neo-Thomism the pluralism which would emerge again during its twentieth-century evolution. On the one hand he stressed the unity of epistemology, anthropology, and metaphysics required for a coherent defense of St. Thomas' theory of abstraction. This line of thought has been the hallmark of the subjective and historical Maréchalian tradition which now is the dominant current in Thomistic theology. But on the other hand Kleutgen stressed with equal emphasis that the intelligibility grasped in the universal is the intelligibility of the sensible singular. This is the line of thought which has characterized the Thomism of Gilson and Maritain and the theology of Garrigou-Lagrange. At the time of the New Theology controversy in the middle of the twentieth century the radical opposition between these two possible developments of Kleutgen's neo-Thomism flared into violent opposition. After the New Theology controversy Thomism could no longer be considered a unitary system of philosophy and theology. Kleutgen had made a great contribution to Catholic theology but it was not the contribution which he himself thought that he had made.

POST-KANTIAN METHOD: THE ALTERNATIVE TO THOMISM

Structuring the modern theologies of the nineteenth century which the neo-Thomists proposed to replace was a theory of knowledge, anthropology, and metaphysics that were completely different from the Aristotelian theory of the neo-Thomists. This was the theory of knowledge, anthropology, and metaphysics of the post-Kantian German idealists, and especially of Schelling.

Like Kant himself, the post-Kantian idealists divided the intellect into discursive reason *(Verstand)* and intuitive reason *(Vernunft)*. *Verstand* was restricted to the world of objective phenomena. *Vernunft*, on the other hand, was capable of intellectual intuition of *noumenal*, or metaphysical reality. This intuitive grasp took place through a two-fold process. The first stage was *Vernunft*'s passive reception of metaphysical reality *(Glaube)*. The second stage was *Vernunft*'s rigorous scientific reflection upon intuited metaphysical reality *(Wissen)*. In this type of post-Kantian metaphysics, therefore, philosophy was understood to be a science *(Wissenschaft)* of faith *(Glaube)*, or a science of revelation.

In post-Kantian philosophy, moreover, the Infinite Absolute "went out of itself" through its finite self-manifestation in the dynamic universe of nature and spirit. Furthermore, in a manner reminiscent of Plotinus' neo-Platonism, the world of nature and spirit was conceived to be an organic universe of interrelated forms or souls. And, as in the Plotinian universe, each natural species had its own specific "idea" which realized its virtualities through its embodied development in and through the individual members of the species. In the same way, each natural human community in the spiritual universe had its own specific communal idea which achieved the perfection of its realization through the free activity of individual members. And, since spiritual realities were also self-conscious, the community's formative idea manifested itself on the level of consciousness as the communal spirit or *Geist*.

But, if the communal idea must realize its virtualities through the free activities of individuals, its authentic development could be frustrated through their mistaken or malicious choices. Nevertheless, in post-Kantian philosophy, contradiction had its own dialectical intelligibility. An idea defined itself over against its opposites. A developing idea became what it was by excluding what it was not. Evil and mistaken choices raised to the level of consciousness forms of life and types of action which contradicted the authentic unfolding of the community's formative idea.

If then the communal idea was to attain its authentic perfection, the community must consciously exclude them. This the community would inevitably do, since the intelligible influence of the community was operative in the individual consciousness of every member of the community, whereas ill-informed and evil choices proceeded from the unintelligible contingency of ignorance and malice. The community's history was genuine history, since it proceeded from the free choices of individual agents. Nonetheless, that history had an intrinsic dialectical intelligibility because it was the communal history of the unfolding of a formative idea which reached its own perfection through the conscious exclusion of its opposites.

Noumenal reality manifested itself through the act of intuitive "faith" to the members of an organic community who could then make explicit the ideal system of essences which constituted its intelligible structure through its scientific reconstruction by philosophical reason. This post-Kantian model of "faith" and "reason" determined the relations between revelation, apologetics, and positive and speculative theology in the modern traditionalist systems which opposed themselves to Kantian rationalism and Hegelian pantheism in the first half of the nineteenth century. French traditionalism, the theology of the Catholic Tübingen School, the metaphysical dualism of Anton Günther, the "ontologism" of Rosmini and Gioberti were built upon it. As a result the nonscholastic theology of the first half of the nineteenth century manifested a sensitivity to the intelligibility of history, tradition, and community to which the Aristotelian neo-Thomists were singularly blind. The post-Kantian Catholic theologians also displayed an appreciation of the apologetics of immanence, based on the exigencies of the human spirit which the Aristotelian neo-Thomists, whose own apologetics was built upon the "objective signs" of miracle and prophecy, deeply distrusted. Therefore the definitive victory of the neo-Thomists over their post-Kantian rivals in the closing quarter of the nineteenth century resulted in a tension between Roman Thomistic theology and subjective, historical modern thought that led to the painful confrontation of the modernist crisis, and which Maritain endeavored to resolve through his brilliant development of the Thomism of Cajetan and John of St. Thomas before it broke out again in the controversy over the New Theology a decade before the opening of the Second Vatican Council.

REASSESSMENT OF THE NINETEENTH-CENTURY DEBATE

The major issue between the neo-Thomists and the post-Kantian modern theologians was the ability of their respective theological methods to handle adequately the Catholic teaching on faith and reason, grace and nature. To settle that issue the neo-Thomists and their rivals had to define the relation between revelation and philosophy, apologetics, and positive and speculative theology in their theological methods. And, since theological method had inevitable epistemological and metaphysical presuppositions, the neo-Thomists and their rivals also had to define the philosophy of knowledge, man, and being which their theological methodology implied.

Leo XIII's prescription of neo-Thomism as the system to be used in the philosophical and theological education of the Church's priests was based on the conviction that the Thomistic metaphysics of substance and accident could preserve the necessary distinction between grace and nature which post-Kantian metaphysics had shown itself unable to preserve, and that Thomism's abstractive theory of knowledge avoided the confusion between natural and supernatural knowledge of God which post-Kantian intuitive epistemology could not avoid. Furthermore the Aristotelian metaphysics of man and being made it easier for the Catholic theologian to defend the essential unity of man and to account for man's certain but limited knowledge of his Creator through causal arguments for God's existence and the indirect knowledge of God's nature acquired through the analogous concepts of an Aristotelian abstractive intellect. Leo XIII's commitment to Aristotelian epistemology and metaphysics in *Aeterni Patris* carried with it a parallel commitment to Aristotelian scientific method in Catholic theology.

In the last thirty-five years Catholic theology has modified considerably the nineteenth-century theology of grace and nature defended by the leaders of the neo-Thomist movement. Since Vatican II Aristotelian theological method has been abandoned by the most important theologians among the transcendental Thomists. In recent years theological pluralism has been accepted by Karl Rahner as an unavoidable reality in present-day theology and the hope of imposing a single method upon the community of theologians is no longer entertained. The definition and theoretical vindication of a modern theological method has become a major preoccupation of Catholic theologians.

It is not surprising then that Catholic theologians have begun to reassess the significance of the debate over philosophical and theological method which ran through nineteenth-century Catholic thought from the beginning of the century until Leo XIII's definitive option for Thomism in his encyclical *Aeterni Patris*. The doctrinal, methodological, and philosophical issues which were raised in that debate are being reappraised and their significance for the contemporary debate over theological method is receiving serious consideration. For in contemporary Catholic theology the relationship between apologetics, or fundamental theology, and speculative theology is as much an issue as it was in the nineteenth century. And in contemporary Catholic theology the relation between positive and speculative theology still remains a problem whose solution demands the use of a coherent system of epistemology and metaphysics.

The present volume focuses upon the two leading Jesuit neo-Thomists, Liberatore and Kleutgen, and upon the nonscholastic theological methods which were the object of their explicit criticism. It endeavors to recreate the nineteenth-century debate over theological method in the light of modern historical research and from the perspective of the contemporary debate over theological method.

From the history of the nineteenth-century contest between the "modern" theologians and the neo-Thomists to determine the method of Catholic theology and from the concluding chapter on twentieth-century Thomism a good deal can be learned about the doctrinal and philosophical issues which confront any theologian who addresses himself seriously to the problem of theological method. A fair amount can also be learned concerning the possibilities and limitations of the two basic methods of nineteenth-century theology which, albeit in greatly modified form, still influence the methods of contemporary Catholic theologians. The theologian who is well acquainted with the nineteenth-century debate over theological method will come to realize that the contemporary debate is its historical continuation. For the contemporary debate over theological method is simply another phase in the dialectical movement of Catholic theology's response to the challenge of post-Enlightenment thought from the beginning of the nineteenth century through Vatican I, *Aeterni Patris*, the modernist crisis, between-the-wars Thomism, the New Theology controversy, and Vatican II up to the present.

To understand where we are in Catholic scientific theology we must understand where we have come from and how far we have traveled in the course of the last two centuries. The contemporary quest for an adequate method in Catholic theology has a history. The better that history is known the clearer will be the theologian's understanding of his own discipline and his own scientific task. The focus of this volume is upon the nineteenth-century stage of the journey toward an adequate theological method. Our first chapter then will be devoted to the state of Catholic theology at the beginning of the nineteenth century when the quest for a modern theological method was begun in order to meet the challenge of post-Enlightenment thought.

1

THE BACKGROUND OF
NINETEENTH-CENTURY THEOLOGY

In the foreword to his *Histoire de la théologie au xixe siècle* Edgar Hocedez remarks that the most striking characteristic of nineteenth-century Catholic theology is its unity. The tension between the natural and the supernatural orders was the single theme which ran through the diverse systems of Catholic theology and served as the focus of theological controversy from the early years of the century to its conclusion. Rationalism, in its empirical or idealistic forms, was the only adversary outside the Church which Catholic theologians took seriously.[1] Rationalism made unaided human reason the sole norm of truth and certitude. Thus, since the revealed Christian mysteries are accessible only through faith, rationalism excluded positive Christianity from the field of serious intellectual discussion. The rationalism which all Catholic theologians considered their common enemy was not necessarily the philosophical rationalism of the Cartesian school. Many Catholic philosophers in fact considered Cartesianism or German idealism the only sound approach to the challenge which the empiricism of Locke, Hume, and Condillac presented to the Christian faith. The rationalism against which all the Catholic theologians aligned themselves was the Enlightenment commitment to pure reason on the basis of which the defenders of "natural religion" in France and Germany had rejected the intellectual and moral claims of positive Christian revelation. Enlightenment rationalism could take the form of Humean empiricism, Kantian critical philosophy, post-Kantian idealism, or even an unsystematic eclecticism. Its philosophical form was not important. "Reason" degenerated to "rationalism" when it claimed that its philosophical conclusions entailed either the rejection of religious belief or the confinement of religious teaching within the limits of pure

17

reason. From the early years of the nineteenth century Catholic theology took the form of a reaction against eighteenth-century rationalism. The common aim of Catholic theologians was to show that the negative conclusions drawn by the rationalist philosophers were unwarranted and that belief in positive Christian revelation was intellectually justified. Catholic theologians disagreed violently, however, about the philosophical and theological method which should be used in order to achieve their common goal.

Three Diverse Reactions to Rationalism

The most direct way to undercut rationalism was to show that unaided human reason was intrinsically incapable of reaching any true or certain conclusions about religious or moral issues. This was the approach adopted by the strict traditionalists. A less radical way of refuting the rationalists was to adapt one of the prevailing contemporary philosophies to Catholic apologetics and systematic theology. A nineteenth-century Christian philosophy of this sort could then serve a double function. On the philosophical level it could undermine the rationalist objections against the Christian faith. On the theological level it could provide the philosophical framework for a modern scientific theology through which the Christian faith and its revealed mysteries could be presented to the educated classes in a rigorous intellectual system comparable to the systems of Schelling and Hegel. Hermes, Günther, the Tübingen theologians, and the ontologists, each in different ways, exploited the possibilities of this approach which was the one most favored in the first half of the century.

A third approach was to claim that the negative conclusions which the rationalists had reached concerning the credibility of the Christian mysteries were the logical consequence of applying modern philosophy to religion and morals. This did not mean that the rationalist conclusions were true; it simply meant that they were consistent with their philosophical starting point, principles, and method. It certainly did not mean that the rationalist conclusions about religion and morals were the conclusions to which the free working of a properly instructed mind must inevitably lead. Nevertheless, they were the inevitable result of the intellectual confusion which the endless series of mutually antagonistic modern philosophies had produced in badly educated minds. None of the modern philosophies could provide a sound solution for the problem of faith and reason, and any attempt to correct and adapt them in the hope that they could do so was doomed in advance to failure. Without exception they were all vitiated by the fundamental defect of individualistic rationalism. In modern philosophy reason was individual reason, separated from the Church's authoritative communication of Christian tradition. The separation of individual reason from the Church's authoritative communication of tradition had occurred within theology at the time of the Protestant Reformation. Descartes had extended it to Catholic philosophy. Rationalism and skepticism were the inevitable results of modern philosophy's separation of itself from Catholic tradition. Therefore they could never be overcome until philosophy had been persuaded to retrace its steps, abandon the modern form which it had assumed with Descartes, and rebuild itself anew in vital continuity with the sound Christian philosophy of the scholastic period. This would be the approach which the partisans of the Thomistic revival would take in the latter half of the nineteenth century.[2] It would then become the program of a movement which, virtually nonexistent in the first half of the century, gained ground rapidly at the beginning of the second half and assumed a dominant position within Catholic theology in the closing years of the century.

These diverse responses to the challenge of rationalism engendered a prolonged controversy within Catholic theology over which of them should prevail. The debate inevitably became a debate over the limits of grace and nature. Faith and reason are natural and supernatural knowledge. The freedom of the act of faith, the distinction between natural knowledge of God and revealed knowledge of the Christian mysteries, the distinction between innate awareness of God's presence in the thinking mind and the Beatific Vision, for which grace is necessary, enter into any Catholic theology of faith and reason, or, in other words, of revelation and philosophical knowledge. In the nineteenth century the Catholic Church was defining its faith against the world view of a consciously secular society. The debate over faith and reason was far from being a purely theoretical one and, since it touched on the most sensitive and fundamental points of Catholic theology, it is not surprising that it became emotional and bitter.

In the embattled climate of the nineteenth century this theological controversy provoked a series of authoritative interventions by the Holy See, a number of which were made after the emergence of the neo-Thomistic movement in the second half of the nineteenth century. Neo-

Thomism presented itself as a reaction to the failure of the earlier nine-teenth-century theological systems to solve the problem of faith and reason without compromising Catholic orthodoxy. The sharpness of the theological polemic which it directed against the partisans of other sys-tems—traditionalism, ontologism, and Güntherian dualism—shaped its own internal development. The early neo-Thomists were above all polemicists and they clearly and consciously defined their own position in opposition to the rival systems which enjoyed the favor of the nine-teenth-century theological community.[3]

Controversy has its advantages. The neo-Thomists' repudiation of modern philosophy in all its forms obliged them to distinguish their own epistemology carefully from the rival epistemologies of Descartes, Hume, Kant, Fichte, Schelling, and Hegel. Their concerted attack on the meta-physics of Hermes, Günther, Gioberti, and Rosmini forced them to focus their attention on the metaphysical and anthropological implications of their own commitment to Aristotelian act and potency. Their campaign against the ontologists, Günther, and the traditionalists required them to clarify the connection between their epistemology, metaphysics, and nat-ural theology, on the one hand, and Catholic apologetics, on the other. Finally, since the root of their opposition to Hermes, Günther, and the ontologists was their adamant rejection of modern philosophical method in Catholic apologetics and systematic theology, the neo-Thomists were compelled to clarify the role of their own Aristotelian scientific method as the unifying structure of a coherent system embracing philosophy, apologetics, and systematic theology. Thus the requirements of their life and death struggle with their rivals for control of Catholic theology led to the rapid production of several neo-Thomistic masterpieces in which the principal theses of neo-Thomistic epistemology, anthropology, and metaphysics were exposed and their interrelation in a unified Thomistic system was sharply defined.[4] Neo-Thomistic Aristotelian scientific method was contrasted with the philosophical methods of Descartes, Kant, Schelling, and Hegel, and the implications which a choice of method contain for apologetics, and positive and speculative theology were clearly drawn. Thus, in the early years of the neo-Thomistic revival the Catholic theological community was given an opportunity to contrast neo-Thomism with the several other systems which existed in nine-teenth-century Catholic theology and to make a judgment on the merits of the neo-Thomistic argument that Thomism, and Thomism alone, could do justice to the demands of both faith and reason. Whether the nineteenth-century theologians were given the freedom to choose between them, however, is a very different question.

But controversy had disadvantages as well as advantages. The passion of the debate and the frequent recourse to ecclesiastical authority in the course of it confirmed the scholastics in their antipathy to modern philosophy and blinded them to the real advantages which their opponents had found in it. This antipathy and their deficient sense of history prejudiced the early neo-Thomists against the subjective and historical approach to reality which a number of their rivals had exploited in their theology through their contact with Descartes, Kant, and post-Kantian philosophy. As a result, the Augustianian heritage in Thomism, which was brilliantly developed in the twentieth century by Thomists in the Maréchalian tradition was neglected and viewed with suspicion for several decades.[5]

GALLICANISM AND FEBRONIANISM

The debate over grace and nature had a practical as well as a theoretical side. In its practical dimension the debate focused on the relations between Church and state, which were troubled by the conflict between the claims of the Church and the demands of national governments during the entire century. Theological controversy over the relations between Church and state was more bitter in the nineteenth century than it had been in the past but it was by no means new. In addition to the attacks of the purely secular liberals the Roman authorities had to cope with the political and theological resistance to papal authority which was rooted in the Gallicanism, Febronianism, and Josephinism of the two preceding centuries.

Gallicanism went back to the seventeenth century. Its most concise formulation can be found in the Declaration of the Assembly of the Clergy of France issued in 1682. The aristocratic Gallicanism expressed in the four articles of the declaration restricted the primacy and jurisdiction of the Roman pontiff in favor of the local bishops. The democratic Gallicanism, proposed by Richer, syndic of the Theological Faculty of Paris, asserted that Christ had conferred the power of jurisdiction on the whole ecclesial assembly. The pope and the bishops had no power of jurisdiction directly and in their own right. They exercised their authority simply as ministers of the ecclesial assembly as agents who acted in its name.[6]

Theological Febronianism dated back to 1763. In that year, Johann von Hontheim, coadjutor bishop of Trier, published his *De Statu Ecclesiae praesenti et de legitima potestate Romani Pontificis* under the pseudonym Justus Febronius. Febronianism was a development of Richer's democratic Gallicanism. According to Hontheim Christ gave the power of jurisdiction to the whole ecclesial community. Nevertheless, although individual bishops exercised jurisdiction only by title of usufruct, their authority within their own dioceses was unlimited. The primacy of the Roman pontiff was simply a primacy of honor, and, among his fellow bishops, the bishop of Rome was no more than a *primus inter pares.* The pope was subject to a general council and laws promulgated by him were valid only by the consent of the episcopacy. Papal power extended no further than was necessary for the pope to insure that the laws enacted by the general councils were enforced. Papal primacy was needed only to preserve the Church's unity. It should not be extended any further than is necessary to achieve that end.[7]

Febronianism provided the theoretical justification for the Austrian model of Church-state relations called Josephinism. In the closing decades of the eighteenth century Emperor Joseph II began his vigorous campaign to subordinate the Church to the imperial throne and make the Austrian Church as thoroughly independent of the Holy See as a Church could be without ceasing to be Catholic. The liturgy, preaching, and catechetical instruction of the Austrian Church and the education of the Austrian clergy were brought under the rigid control of the imperial bureaucracy. Although the imperial functionaries considered themselves worthy Catholics, they were strongly influenced by the rationalism of the Enlightenment. Josephinism had disasterous consequences for the life of the Austrian Church. The faith and piety of the clergy were impaired. Preaching was reduced to moral instruction in which little reference was made to the Christian mysteries. Religious practice declined. Nevertheless Josephinism remained the accepted model for the ecclesiastical policy which the Austrian and Bavarian governments followed for a considerable portion of the nineteenth century. The Holy See had to contend with the Josephinist ministers and bureaucrats in the German lands, as it had to contend with Gallican ministers and bishops in France after the restoration of the monarchy in 1815.[8]

Reaction against Josephinism was a characteristic of German theology and German church life during the nineteenth century. In the Tübingen school, for example, we observe a growing tendency to work free from the juridicism, moralism, and rationalism of Josephinist theology and to establish Catholic theology on the basis of the revealed Christian mysteries transmitted by the living tradition of a Church animated by the Holy Spirit.[9] In the other centers of the German Catholic revival we find a similar emphasis on revelation, Christian piety, mystical and religious experience. On the other hand, however, German university theology retained from its Febronian past a definite tendency to resist papal initiatives in determining doctrinal matters and to preserve the legitimate independence of the German Church. The result was a tension between German university theologians and the Holy See and an increasing effort on the part of the Roman authorities and ultramontane bishops to restrict the independence of German theologians, especially those attached to the faculties of the state universities. This tension increased when, after the revolution of 1848, the authority of the Febronian bureaucracy was weakened, and the Holy See and the German bishops asserted themselves more strongly against it.[10] The neo-Thomists, who were deeply attached to the Holy See and had close links to the Roman curia, united themselves to the ultramontane campaign against "German" university theology in the latter half of the nineteenth century. Scholasticism, as the enemy of Enlightenment rationalism, would argue that it was the most effective opponent of Enlightenment Febronianism and that its social philosophy provided the theoretical justification for a sound policy of Church-state relations.[11]

CHURCH-STATE TENSIONS

At the close of the eighteenth century the French Revolution shattered the alliance that had been the foundation of the social order in every European country, Catholic and Protestant, for centuries. The Revolution that had toppled the throne in France turned against the Church as well. The Church's property was secularized and her control over education ended. Napoleon's Civil Constitution of the Clergy was an aggressive attempt on the part of revolutionary France to bring the internal life of the Church under the control of the civil government. The revolutionary national state, secular in its outlook, anticlerical in its orientation, and guided by the naturalism and rationalism of the Enlightenment in its cultural and political aspirations, represented a new model in Church-state relations quite different from the Gallican and the Febronian models. Febronians and Gallicans considered themselves authentically

Catholic in their political thinking. They had no desire to repudiate the alliance between the throne and the altar. They merely wished to correct an imbalance in favor of the Holy See and restore the alliance to what they considered was its proper form. Revolutionary France on the other hand wanted to abolish the alliance between the throne and the altar along with the *ancien régime* of which it was a part. Rationalist in their thinking and individualistic in their social theory, the anticlerical liberals who carried the tradition of the Revolution into the nineteenth century reduced religion to a purely private concern. To their way of thinking the Church was a private society which, like every other subordinate society in a modern national state, must be subject to the control of the national government. The Church should never be accorded the status of a supernational power with which the modern national state would have to deal on equal terms and with which the modern state would have to settle its differences by formal treaties or concordats.

During the nineteenth century the Holy See was in constant conflict with Gallicanism and Febronianism on one side and with revolutionary anticlerical liberalism on the other. The restoration of the old order after the fall of Napoleon failed to restore the alliance between the throne and the altar to its prerevolutionary state. The Church emerged from the Revolution and the Napoleonic Wars considerably weakened in relation to the European national governments. The old prince-bishoprics of Germany had gone forever. The German Catholic universities had been suppressed when Church property was secularized at the beginning of the century, and the Catholic faculties of theology that remained were all located at universities controlled by the state. Millions of Catholic subjects formerly governed by Catholic rulers now found themselves under the control of Protestant monarchs.[12] From 1815 to 1830 Restoration France pursued a Gallican ecclesiastical policy with the support of many bishops who were still attached to the *ancien régime.* The government of Prussia was staunchly Protestant. The Austrian and Bavarian bureaucrats who dealt with ecclesiastical affairs were Febronian by tradition. And in all of these countries a vocal and influential segment of the bourgeoisie complained that their governments were overfriendly to the Church. The liberal bourgeoisie identified the intellectual and political world view associated with the French Revolution with scientific progress, political freedom, and cultural maturity. As the century progressed political and cultural liberalism became more widespread among the educated middle classes. It was the driving force behind the revolutions of 1830 and 1848, which seriously threatened the temporal power of the papacy and the continued existence of the Papal States. In reaction Gregory XVI and Pius IX adopted a policy of systematic opposition to political liberalism. The liberal war cries of cultural progress and representative government were equated with apostacy and rebellion against legitimate authority.

THEOLOGY AND POLITICS

It was in Italy that the liberal and nationalistic enthusiasm generated by the French Revolution made Church-state tensions most acute because in Italy the pope was a secular as well as a religious ruler. The Papal States were a clerical principality whose autocratic and inefficient government was detested by its subjects. Their clerical and authoritarian form of government offended the sensibilities of the Italian middle class, which shared the attachment of the nineteenth-century bourgeoisie to liberty and social progress. The continued existence of the Papal States stood in the way of Italy's unification as a national state. Yet neither Gregory XVI nor Pius IX was willing to relinquish his temporal sovereignty nor even modify it sufficiently to allow the papacy to assume the new relationship to the united Italy which most Italians, even the ardent Catholics, hoped would come into being. The stubbornness with which the popes clung to their temporal power thoroughly alienated the Italian liberals and, after the revolution of 1848, made the papal government increasingly dependent on the hated Austrians, who occupied the north of Italy, the decrepit Bourbon government of the two Sicilies, and ultimately upon the armed support of Napoleon III.[13]

These Church-state tensions influenced the Church's whole intellectual life during the nineteenth century. Fear of liberal revolution, especially in the Papal States, made the Roman curia a firm supporter of "legitimate" royal governments and an enemy of democratic popular sovereignty. On the other hand, although the Holy See was dependent upon Austrian support in Italy, Austrian and Bavarian Febronianism left a great deal to be desired in respect to the religious education of the laity and the intellectual formation of the clergy. To make up for its weakened diplomatic and political position in relation to the national governments the Holy See began to play a more direct and aggressive role in the political and intellectual life of the individual national Churches than it had played under the *ancien régime*. In those days a wealthy and powerful

Church dominated education, and politically powerful prelates, secure in their alliance with the throne, were an effective counterweight to papal influence.

In accordance with this new policy, the Holy See, beginning with the pontificate of Gregory XVI, began to play a dominant role in the internal direction of Catholic theology through a series of disciplinary decrees and formal condemnations.[14] The direction of speculative theology and the pursuit of the Holy See's political designs were increasingly united in the papal response to the intellectual and political challenges to the pope's authority during the embattled pontificate of Pius IX. Rome intervened in almost every serious theological controversy during the nineteenth century and, in almost every case, the intervention was influenced by the Church-state tensions. Lamennais' anti-Gallicanism had a good deal to do with his delation to Rome by a Gallican episcopate, and his espousal of representative government insured his condemnation by the reactionary Gregory XVI after the revolution of 1830. Gioberti and Rosmini were both supporters of Italian nationalism and their systems were hailed as Italian philosophies. This fact helped to provoke the antipathy which the neo-Thomists manifested toward both of them. The Jesuit neo-Thomists were staunch supporters of the pope's antinationalist policy after 1848, and, as Italian nationalists, Rosmini and Gioberti were objects of suspicion, even though Rosmini remained a devoted and saintly priest until the day of his death. The theological controversies that raged in Germany during the latter half of the nineteenth century were linked to the struggle between the Holy See and the bishops on one side and the universities and civil authorities on the other over the intellectual formation of the Catholic clergy.

This active intervention by the Holy See in the affairs of their national Churches was encouraged by the growth of devotion to the Holy See among European Catholics during the nineteenth century. For many European Catholics the pope was the only effective leader to whom they could turn for direction in their fight against secularism and irreligion. These Catholics, called "ultramontanists" by their opponents in northern Europe, promoted the growth of papal authority and influence.[15] Despite the opposition of Gallicans, Febronians, and liberals, the pope's authority within the Church increased progressively during the nineteenth century until it reached its apogee in the definition of papal primacy and infallibility at Vatican I. The increase in papal prestige and influence promoted by ultramontanist piety caused a strong reaction from the opponents of papal centralism inside and outside the Church.

Opposition to the centralizing trend manifested itself most strongly in the German lands where the Febronian tradition remained alive and even orthodox theologians were disturbed by the effect on theology of disciplinary decrees issued by curial congregations in the highly charged political atmosphere of Rome. The misgivings which a number of German bishops expressed about the advisability of defining papal infallibility were justified when it intensified the *Kulturkampf* between the Prussian government and the Catholic Church and led to the apostacy of the Old Catholics.[16]

The theological controversies of the nineteenth century cannot be divorced from the Church-state tensions of the period. The relations between faith and reason and the relations between Church and state after all were aspects of the one basic problem concerning the relation between grace and nature. The defense of papal power and the defense of Catholic truth were associated in the minds of the early Neo-Thomists. The protection of theology's legitimate autonomy and a proper respect for the modern culture of the European universities were valid reasons for the opposition which the ontologists and the German theologians expressed to the growth of neo-Thomism and to the interference of the Roman curia with the orderly development of theology. It is possible to describe the emergence of neo-Thomistic philosophy and theology almost exclusively in terms of a power struggle and treat it as a classic exercise in ecclesiastical politics. To do that, however, is to underestimate the intellectual significance of neo-Thomism as a serious philosophical and theological option that consciously opposed itself to several other carefully considered philosophical and theological options in the second half of the nineteenth century and presented the philosophical and theological evidence which justified its opposition. Neo-Thomism cannot be properly appreciated as a philosophical and theological method until it is contrasted with the rival methods which it intended to replace. To do that, however, we will have to examine more carefully the intellectual climate in which these rival systems arose and define in more detail the specific form in which the problem of faith and reason presented itself to Catholic theologians in the early years of the nineteenth century.

THE DECLINE OF SCHOLASTICISM

By the beginning of the nineteenth century scholasticism had ceased to be a significant force in Catholic theology. Scholasticism was still taught faithfully in the Dominican houses of study in Spain and in the

Kingdom of the Two Sicilies but its influence outside Dominican circles was not widespread. Recent research has shown that the Italian Vincentians had made their Collegio Alberoni at Piacenza a center of Thomistic philosophy and theology in the middle of the eighteenth century.[17] Nevertheless, although this Alberonian renaissance was to play an important role in the neo-Thomist revival in later years, Alberonian Thomism was practically unknown, even in Italy, in the first three decades of the nineteenth century.

In France the turmoil of the Revolution and the Napoleonic Wars had totally disrupted the Church's system of clerical education. Lamennais, whose own philosophical and theological education was sketchy and unsystematic, lamented the lack of adequate intellectual preparation, which hampered the clergy of his generation in their apostolic work.[18] Bautain, who had received a first-rate philosophical education and taught philosophy in a Strasbourg seminary, knew very little about scholasticism although in Strasbourg, unlike the rest of France, the scholastic tradition had preserved its influence and retained its hold upon a number of the local clergy.[19]

Even before the suppression of the Catholic universities scholasticism had fallen upon evil days in Germany. During the eighteenth century German scholasticism had been strongly influenced by the deductive rationalism of Christian Wolff.[20] Its epistemology, anthropology, and metaphysics differed markedly from the philosophy of Thomas' *Summa Theologiae* and indeed from the philosophy of Thomas' great sixteenth-century commentators. The Cartesian *cogito*, Cartesian innatism, and Cartesian physics had corrupted the purity of its Aristotelian epistemology and metaphysics. Cartesian deductivism and Cartesian commitment to an ideal of mathematical certitude had distorted its philosophical method. Deductive mathematical science had replaced Aristotelian science as its ideal model of philosophical method. Eighteenth-century scholastic treatises no longer followed the Aristotelico-Thomistic division of speculative philosophy into physics, mathematics, and metaphysics that was based on the Thomistic epistemology of the three degrees of abstraction. They followed instead the Wolffian division of philosophy into ontology, cosmology, and psychology, even though the Wolffian division of the philosophical sciences was based upon a non-Thomistic epistemology and metaphysics and a non-Thomistic theory of philosophical science.[21]

These changes in its epistemology, metaphysics, and understanding of scientific method shattered the unity of philosophy and theology in eighteenth-century scholasticism. The unity between philosophy and theology in Thomas' *Summa Theologiae* depended upon his Aristotelian division of the philosophical sciences and his Aristotelian conception of scientific method. Thomas' speculative theology is an Aristotelian metaphysical science whose necessary first principles come from revelation and, unlike philosophical first principles, cannot be justified by natural reason. Aristotelian science, which rests on the Aristotelian abstractive theory of knowledge and its necessary first principles derived by the human intellect from sense experience, provides the intelligible link between philosophy and theology in Thomas' *Summa Theologiae.* Revelation provides theology's first principles. Then a scientific speculative theology can link the principles together and draw deductive conclusions from them by the application of Aristotelian logic and metaphysics to the data of Scripture and tradition.

The rationalist scholastics of the eighteenth century no longer possessed a unified system of philosophy and theology. Their Wolffian epistemology undermined the coherence of their philosophy. Their deductive notion of science, based on intuitive first principles and modeled upon the Cartesian ideal of necessary certitude and apodictic evidence, was no longer the notion of science upon which St. Thomas had modeled his speculative theology. Their misunderstanding of the central place of Aristotelian abstraction in Thomas' division of scientific knowledge led to an inevitable misunderstanding of the intelligible connection between philosophy and theology in St. Thomas' scientific exposition of revelation.

Thus, even though scholasticism managed to survive in a few scattered places after the eighteenth century, its own internal unity had been lost through its contamination by Wolffian Cartesianism. It would not become a coherent unified system again until after the neo-Thomistic revival.[22] Nineteenth-century scholastics therefore were not necessarily neo-Thomists. The difference between a traditional scholastic and a neo-Thomist lay precisely in the neo-Thomist commitment to Thomism as a unified Aristotelian science comprising philosophy and theology and built upon an Aristotelian epistemology, anthropology, and metaphysics.

The suppression of the Society of Jesus in 1773 removed the most influential supporter of scholasticism in eighteenth-century Europe. Toward the end of the century Joseph II suppressed the diocesan seminaries in his empire and replaced them with theological centers in Vienna, Prague,

Pest, Pavia, and Freiburg. The professors who taught at these centers and their sub-branches were appointed by the state and often they were chosen for their Febronian and rationalist tendencies. Official textbooks were imposed which, since they had to have the approval of the governmental authorities, reflected the juridicism, moralism, and rationalism of the approved Josephinist theology. The Josephinist theological centers were later accused of undermining the faith of their theological students rather than deepening and strengthening it.[23] These accusations are due in part to the strong reaction against Josephinist rationalism among German theologians at the beginning of the nineteenth century, and we cannot forget that good and even saintly men were forced to teach under the Josephinist system and struggle against the limitations which it imposed on them. Nevertheless the generation of theologians who taught in the German lands under Austrian control from the time of the suppression of the Society of Jesus until the theological revival in the early years of the nineteenth century had no contact with the scholastic tradition, even in its eighteenth-century Wolffian form. They were forced to rebuild anew and to use the resources which their own education and their cultural milieu placed at their disposal. It was only natural therefore that they should derive their model of systematic theology from the great idealist systems of the Romantic period whose creators, like themselves, were reacting against the individualism and the rationalism of the German Enlightenment.

The Restoration of Catholic Theology

The first three decades of the nineteenth century were a period of rebuilding of Catholic institutions, Catholic life and Catholic theology after the shattering impact of the French Revolution and the Napoleonic Wars. Although the effect of the Revolution upon the German Church had been profound, the damage to its inner life and external structure had been less severe than in Latin Europe. As a result, the revival of Catholic theology occurred in Germany sooner than it did in the rest of Europe. The first three decades of the nineteenth century were the period in which the Romantic movement, the flowering of post-Kantian idealism and the inauguration of scientific historical study created a widespread and sympathetic interest in religion in the German educated classes. The intellectual climate stimulated and supported creative work in theology.[24]

Catholic intellectuals shared in the Romantic reaction against the individualism and rationalism of the *Aufklärung*. An enthusiastic group of distinguished Catholics, including Anton Günther, gathered around St. Clement Mary Hofbauer in Vienna. A similar group gathered around the Princess Galitzin in Münster. The new Catholic faculties of theology began to assert their influence. Bonn became an important theological center under the direction of the pious Canon Hermes. In 1817 the Catholic faculty of theology at Ellwangen established itself beside the distinguished Protestant faculty of theology at the University of Tübingen. King Ludwig of Bavaria, a former student of the saintly Catholic theologian, Johann Michael Sailer, founded the University of Munich in 1825 and invited Schelling to join its faculty of philosophy. Here Schelling continued to exercise the remarkable influence on Catholic theology which he had exerted from the early years of its revival. A Catholic faculty of theology was established at Munich to which von Baader, Görres, and Döllinger were appointed and to which Möhler came to spend the last years of his life in 1835.

None of these philosophical and theological centers were scholastic in their orientation, although, as we would expect in the Romantic period, they all displayed a friendly and respectful interest in medieval and patristic thought. There was, however, one important center of traditional scholasticism in early nineteenth-century Germany. This was the diocese of Mainz. During the Napoleonic occupation of the Rhineland Joseph Ludwig Colmar, a former pupil of the Jesuits, had been appointed bishop of Mainz with the French emperor's approval. Colmar was a friend of Bruno Liebermann, a firm supporter of the traditional Strasbourg scholasticism. Colmar invited Liebermann to come to Mainz and reorganize his seminary along Tridentine lines. Liebermann made Mainz a stronghold of traditional scholasticism.[25] His own *Institutiones theologicae dogmaticae* was widely used in the Catholic seminaries of Germany, France, Belgium, America, and even Rome during the 1820s. His colleague, Andreas Räss, who had accompanied Liebermann from Strasbourg to Mainz, founded the influential review *Der Katholik* in 1820. In the latter half of the nineteenth century the traditional scholastics of Mainz would ally themselves with the neo-Thomistic attack on Hermes, Günther, and the Catholic Tübingen School. *Der Katholik* and *Civiltà Cattolica* would become the two most powerful organs of the neo-Thomistic movement. In the early years of the century, however, Mainz' influence was limited. The inspiration and the leadership of the neo-Thomistic revival would come from Rome. Mainz would follow; it would not lead.

In Latin Europe the revival of Catholic theology was considerably slower. The French Catholic faculties of philosophy and theology were intellectually inferior to their German counterparts. University philosophy in France was eclectic rather than systematic and, as Bautain discovered, French philosophy was not particularly useful for Catholic apologetics or Catholic systematic theology. The dominant movement among French Catholics during the restoration period was traditionalism, which openly professed its distrust in unaided human reason and, with the exception of Bautain, the French traditionalists were literary men rather than professional philosophers or theologians.

The reestablishment of the Society of Jesus in 1814 and the return of the Roman College to its control in 1824 created an important center of traditional scholastic theology in the Eternal City. The theologians of the Roman College made their presence felt throughout Europe within a decade after the restoration of the college to Jesuit control. Philosophy at the Roman College was eclectic not scholastic and remained so until the pontificate of Leo XIII. Gioberti and Rosmini could not be considered important philosophers until the 1830s, and Italian neo-Thomism was not a significant force in Catholic thought until after 1850.[26]

Problems Confronting Catholic Theology

The theologians of the Catholic renaissance addressed themselves to two major tasks. The first was the defense of the Catholic faith against the rationalism and the religious skepticism of the Enlightenment. The second was the presentation of positive Christian revelation in a coherent, unified system that could stand comparison with the systems of Fichte, Schelling, and Hegel without compromising the supernaturality and the unique, historical character of positive Christian revelation.

The rationalists of the Enlightenment had rejected Christianity because of its claim that it was a unique historical religion based on positive divine revelation. Such a positive religion, the rationalists insisted, was incompatible with "natural religion" because the intellectual principles and moral precepts of natural religion were derived from the general principles of unhistorical, mathematical "human reason." Hume's critique of universal ideas and Kant's restriction of theoretical reason to the world of appearance had shaken the foundations of the "natural religion" professed by the Wolffian rationalists. Nevertheless the reason which

Kant supported in his defense of a "religion within the limits of pure reason" retained many characteristics of Enlightenment reason. The speculative reason of Kant's *Critique of Pure Reason* and the practical reason of his *Critique of Practical Reason* were necessary *a priori* unifying functions of human consciousness. Their unification of experience, of necessity, always occurred in the same way. Speculative reason was the *a priori* ground of the world of appearance and of the necessary laws of its deterministic physics. Practical reason was the *a priori* source of the necessary moral postulates to which every free agent must assent through faith. These postulates must be admitted. Otherwise the moral demands of the categorical imperative could not be integrated into the coherent intelligible universe of necessary thought. Faith in the postulates of practical reason was required for the coherence of rational thought. Therefore the refusal of faith in the postulates of practical reason was a logical impossibility.

Revealed religion can have no place in Kant's necessary and universal intellectual world. Religion cannot exceed the bounds of speculative and practical reason. Religion's only source and justification is found in the moral postulates to which philosophical "faith" must assent in order to integrate the moral demands of practical reason's categorical imperative into the coherent world of necessary and universal reason. Thus the reason of the Enlightenment, which dominated European philosophical thinking in its Kantian form, presented a difficult problem of "faith" and reason to Catholic philosophers and theologians. Theologians found themselves caught between the corrosive skepticism of English empiricism that undercut all religious faith and Kantian rationalism, which reduced religion to philosophical moralism. Unless they wished to seek refuge in pure fideism, Catholic theologians would have to show how religious faith and human reason, revelation and philosophy, could be reconciled in the believing Christian's intellectual experience.

This meant that Catholic theologians would have to show how, in the light of Kant's critique of human knowledge, an act of faith, in the Catholic meaning of that term, remained possible. The act of faith, as Catholics understood it, was an intellectual assent to an historical word of revelation made under the illuminating influence of grace. Far from being imposed as a demand of logical necessity, the act of faith was free. Furthermore, since the act of faith was supernatural in character, its refusal could not entail an implicit denial of the intrinsic intelligibility of the physical or the moral order. In other words, the Catholic theologian who set out to defend the possibility of the act of Christian faith against the objections raised by Kant's critique of knowledge would have to vindicate its status as an authentic and distinctive act of intellectual cognition which could neither be invalidated by Kant's critical philosophy nor equated with an act of purely philosophical reasoning.

The second problem that challenged Catholic theologians was how to show that positive Christian revelation could enter into a rigorous explanatory system without compromising its historical and supernatural character. This problem was not the Kantian problem concerning the cooperation of faith and reason in making the original assent of Christian faith. It was rather the problem of the cooperation of faith and reason in acquiring a scientific understanding of the historical data of Christian revelation by means of a systematic theology. It was, in other words, the problem of relating tradition and positive historical theology to speculative theology. This is the basic problem that challenges every theologian who believes that a single speculative system, embracing all theology, is possible. For the German theologians, who were challenged by the great speculative systems of the German idealists, it was the theological problem *par excellence*. The first problem was primarily a problem for apologetics and the theology of the act of faith. The second problem was a problem about the nature and method of scientific theology, the *fides quaerens intellectum* of the Augustinian and Anselmian tradition. In the land of Hegel it became the problem of how a speculative system of positive Christian revelation was possible. Hegel himself did not believe that such a system was possible. To enter into a speculative system, positive revelation must be "sublated" and absorbed into the higher synthesis of philosophy. You could have either positive revelation or systematic knowledge, since religion and philosophy operated upon different levels of intellectual consciousness. But you could not have both simultaneously. That would involve a contradiction. All through the nineteenth century Catholic theologians would be trying to show that Hegel was wrong and that a synthesis of positive revelation and speculative thought was possible. In the first half of the century Catholic theologians would attempt to effect the synthesis on the basis of post-Kantian scientific method. In the second half, under the influence of the neo-Thomists, they would revert to the Aristotelian scientific method of St. Thomas.

Faith and Kantian reason, the tradition of positive Christian revelation and Hegelian speculative system: these were the antitheses which the philosophers and theologians of the Catholic revival had to try to reconcile. They could reject Kantian reason and speculative system and reduce Christianity to faith, revelation, and historical tradition. At times some of the extreme traditionalists seemed almost willing to opt for that approach. They could attempt to show that the act of Christian faith was really not incompatible with Kantian critical reason. This, in its main lines, was the thrust of Hermes' apologetics and positive theology. Or they could attempt to reconcile revelation and faith with philosophical system in such a way that Christian philosophy became in essence a "philosophy of revelation," which was the antithesis of Hegel's rationalistic speculative system. This, in principle, was the program of the moderate traditionalists, whose greatest representatives in the 1830s were Bautain in France and the theologians of the Catholic Tübingen School in Germany. And, despite the accusation of semirationalism leveled against him by his neo-Thomistic critics, it was also the program of the Viennese theologian, Anton Günther.

In the following chapters we will see how the French traditionalists, Hermes, and the Tübingen theologians attempted to meet the challenge of reconciling faith and reason through the use of their modern nineteenth-century theological methods. The neo-Thomists criticized each of these methods. Each one of them, according to the pioneers of the neo-Thomistic movement, had proved itself incapable of reconciling faith and reason in an adequate and orthodox speculative system. Furthermore the neo-Thomists presented their critique of the modern nineteenth-century theological methods not simply to justify the skeptical attitude toward the new systems adopted by the traditional scholastics of the Roman College, but to argue that the confusion produced in Catholic thought by the plurality of the modern systems was clear evidence of the need for a single unified system in Catholic philosophy and theology. Furthermore the inadequacy of all the modern systems, which the neo-Thomists claimed that they had established, was an irrefutable argument that only one system of Catholic theology was possible. This system was neo-Thomism. The inadequacies of the modern methods were due to their dependence upon a post-Kantian scientific method which rested upon a defective epistemology and metaphysics. The adequacy of the scholastic Aristotelian scientific method was vindicated by the sound epistemology, anthropology, and metaphysics of the Angelic Doctor which the post-Kantian philosophers and theologians had discarded.

In the early years of the nineteenth century the traditionalist form of the Romantic reaction against Enlightenment rationalism was the leading movement in the Catholic philosophy and theology of the French restoration period. In our second chapter we will give a brief sketch of French traditionalism, paying particular attention to the Christian philosophy of its greatest theological representative, Louis Bautain.

2

FRENCH TRADITIONALISM

The core of the traditionalism associated with the names of Joseph de Maistre, Louis de Bonald, and Félicité de Lamennais can be expressed in three fundamental theses. Individual human reason, when left to itself, is incapable of reaching any certain knowledge concerning moral or religious matters. Thus the moral and religious truths which the human race actually possesses have not been acquired by the use of unaided individual reason. On the contrary, they were communicated to the human race by a special act of divine revelation. Tradition infallibly transmits the content of this primitive divine revelation to succeeding generations. Consequently the common consent of the human race to these basic moral and religious truths, which is explained by their transmission to each succeeding generation through tradition, is the criterion of certitude in religious and moral matters.[1]

JOSEPH DE MAISTRE

De Maistre was the first of the French traditionalists. He was neither a philosopher nor a theologian by profession. He was a diplomat and a man of the world whose literary ability made him a persuasive apologist.[2] De Maistre was a fervent royalist with a passionate hatred of the French Revolution. He was also an ardent Catholic who was utterly convinced that a renewed alliance between the throne and the altar provided the only hope of restoring the social order which the Revolution had shattered. Nothing else could reestablish the cohesive unity of culture, religion, and authority required for the existence of a healthy and stable society.[3]

De Maistre's traditionalism reflects the reaction against the mechanism

37

and individualism of the Enlightenment that is characteristic of the Romantic period. Human reason as we find it in the real world, de Maistre argues, is the socialized reason of concrete historical man. It is not the abstract, individual reason idolized by the Englightenment philosophers. In the concrete historical order, human reason is incapable of reaching religious or moral truth if it is left to its own devices. Individual men can only discover religious and moral truth through the help of the society in which they live. Concrete society forms each individual mind through its language and its cultural institutions. Language can only be learned through its communication by another intelligent being, and, until it has been formed by language, the concrete human mind is incapable of religious, moral, or social thought.[4]

De Maistre's model of society is the Romantic, organic model. The individualistic, mechanistic model of society proposed by the Enlightenment philosophers is not the society in which man actually lives. There is no such thing as an isolated, individual "human reason" whose thought is independent of its inherited historical language, social forms, and cultural institutions. Individual minds do not form society. Society forms individual minds. Neither can there be such a thing in reality as a "separated" human reason that can philosophize with no regard to revealed religion. Organized society could never have been formed unless God first revealed to primitive man the fundamental religious and moral principles on which all society must rest. No society could endure unless God's primitive revelation was transmitted to its members by tradition. For just as unaided human reason is incapable of discovering the basic moral principles on which society's existence depends, human reason is unable to preserve its knowledge of them by its own unaided power. Divine revelation, transmitted through tradition, is the indispensable foundation of organized society. Individual reason does not create religion. On the contrary, revealed religion, transmitted by tradition to human society, creates individual reason. It was inevitable therefore that once the "separated" individualistic reason of the Enlightenment had cut itself off from the influence of revealed religion, its erroneous philosophy would lead to the social chaos of the French Revolution.[5]

In the spirit of the Romantic period, de Maistre attacked the empiricism and mechanism of Enlightenment philosophy. His *Examen de la philosophie de Bacon* severely criticizes the English philosopher for abandoning final causes in his philosophical explanation of world events. Bacon's empiricism encouraged the Enlightenment thinkers to ignore divine providence and to reduce the events of natural and human history to the necessary operations of a mindless world machine. There was no place for God's freedom and for his divine providence in their mechanistic universe. Neither was there any place for the dignity of human freedom or for the tragic history of its abuse through original and personal sin.[6]

In de Maistre's opinion, Locke's empiricism was the philosophical ancestor of Enlightenment materialism and determinism. His *Soirées de Saint-Pétersbourg* argues against Locke's epistemology on the basis of Cartesian and Leibnizian innatism. Since sensation alone cannot account for the origin of our universal ideas, man must possess innate ideas. Nevertheless, these innate ideas were obscured by Adam's sin and fallen man can no longer acquire the moral and religious truths required for social life without the aid of a primitive revelation mediated by tradition. Consequently the social order cannot preserve its stability without the constant support of revealed religion of which Catholicism is the only authentic form. It follows then that in the concrete historical order, no individual man can attain intellectual and moral maturity unless he lives in a concrete society which is kept in existence through its inherited language and cultural institutions. The stability of each concrete society can only be preserved through the religious and moral tradition transmitted to it by the Catholic Church.[7]

In the individualistic, mechanistic model of society favored by the Enlightenment plurality is prior to unity. The many produce the one. In the organic model of society favored by the Romantics unity is prior to plurality. In society, as in every living being, one vital principle vivifies, forms, and preserves the many members of the organism. One basic principle of unity is the causal ground of the vital order among the parts. De Maistre's argument for a restored alliance between the throne and the altar in his *Du Pape* presupposes the Romantic organic model of society. Since an organic society can only be ordered through one vital governing principle, the pope is the principle of unity in the Catholic Church and the king is the principle of unity in civil society. The unity of the religious order can only be preserved through the unimpeded influence of the unitary principle of government represented by a strong pope. Likewise the unity of the civil order can only be assured through the unimpeded influence of the unitary governing principle represented by a strong king. Finally the unity of the concrete social order can only be preserved by an effective working alliance between a strong king and a strong pope.[8]

Thus de Maistre's organic model of society lent theoretical support to his antidemocratic monarchism and his fervent ultramontanism. His traditionalism was anti-Gallican and anti-Febronian in its ecclesiology and antidemocratic in its political theory.

LOUIS DE BONALD

De Bonald lacked de Maistre's literary talent and breadth of outlook. He was a dialectician cast in the Cartesian mold, despite his rejection of Descartes' "separated" philosophy. Pages of relentless analysis and deduction make his books tiring reading today.[9] Taking a line which Catholic theologians would continue all through the nineteenth century, de Bonald argued that modern philosophy's arrogant confidence in individual reason was a disastrous heritage from the Protestant Reformation. Protestantism, which rejected tradition and authority, made private judgment its norm of truth. The Protestant commitment to private judgment was imitated in modern philosophy by the Cartesian commitment to individual reason. Just as Protestantism divided Christianity into a collection of quarreling sects, modern philosophy produced an unstable succession of antagonistic systems. Between them Protestantism and modern philosophy engendered the intellectual confusion and social disintegration that reached their climax in the French Revolution. History has shown that Protestant and Cartesian individualism leads to atheism and anarchy. Individual reason must admit its religious and philosophical incapacity and submit itself to the authority of general reason and tradition.[10]

The First Principles of Thought Acquired through Language

In *Les Recherches philosophiques sur les premiers objets des connaissances humaines* de Bonald argues that the Cartesian *cogito*, the *fons et origo* of deductive rationalism's commitment to human reason, is contradicted by the most fundamental evidence of human experience. Who ever heard of a discursive reason which could begin to operate without having acquired the first principles from which discursive reasoning must proceed? But man's fundamental ideas, on which first principles are based, can only be acquired from an historical community by means of language. Who ever heard of a concrete man who could perform the act of thinking without clothing his thought in some concrete human language? The human mind is radically incapable of thinking for itself until the fundamental ideas and the first principles required for discursive reasoning have been communicated to it by another mind in the words of a concrete language. Discursive reason depends on a prior revelation.

Language must exist before the mind can begin to think—and not the Cartesian *cogito ergo sum*—is the primary truth from which all other truths follow. Furthermore, if no human mind can begin to think until it has been taught to think by language, then the collection of individual minds that constituted the first human grouping could not have invented language. Language, of necessity, must have been revealed to primitive man by a superhuman mind and, together with language, the necessary moral principles required for society's existence. Language and society are dependent upon a superhuman revelation.[11]

De Bonald was a more consistent traditionalist than de Maistre. He realized that his account of the relation between language and the first principles of discursive reason could not be squared with the admission of actually innate ideas, even though de Maistre had claimed that intuited innate ideas were required in order to account for human thought.[12] "The knowledge of the moral truths which are our ideas," he explains in *La Législation primitive*, "is not innate in man. It is innate in society."[13] In other words, the individual mind acquires its knowledge of fundamental moral principles from the society to which they have been transmitted by tradition. The human mind's dependence on revelation and tradition is intrinsic and metaphysical and not simply extrinsic and historical. Metaphysical dependence can never be overcome no matter how culturally developed an individual mind may be. The mind's virtually innate ideas must be brought to a state of actuality through the revealed word communicated by society. In that case, de Bonald's argument continues, tradition must always remain the operative instrument through which God's primitive revelation is communicated to the human race. The individual mind cannot think until it learns the first principles contained in primitive revelation from society, and there is no effective instrument through which primitive revelation can be preserved in society except tradition.[14]

This conclusion led de Bonald to a further conclusion, which he expressed most concisely in his *Defense de Lammenais*. Since individual human reason cannot acquire the first principles required for moral and religious reasoning, individual human reason is incapable of passing any judgment on their validity. It follows then that the only valid criterion of truth and certitude in religious matters is the universal consent of the human race. For the universal consent of all societies is an infallible sign that a moral or religious affirmation is not an erroneous conclusion of aberrant individual reason but that it can really be derived from the primitive revelation transmitted by tradition.[15]

God's Existence Known by Faith

Belief in revealed first principles does not lead to universal skepticism. As a philosophical position it commits its holder to the proposition that human reason is not independent; but a human reason which keeps a firm hold on the first principles that it has received through revelation and tradition can make sound and accurate deductions. De Bonald's own writings are models of rigorous deduction, and his critique of the Cartesian *cogito* is intended to be an epistemological reflection on the relationship between language and thought. Nevertheless, de Bonald is emphatic in his declaration that individual human reason is intrinsically incapable of reaching the basic truths which govern man's religious and moral life. The most fundamental of these truths is the existence of God, the author of the primitive revelation. De Bonald will no more admit de Maistre's assertion that human reason can prove God's existence than he will accept de Maistre's postulation of innate ideas. Knowledge of God's existence, like knowledge of the first principles of religious and moral reasoning, can only be derived from God's primitive revelation and, like all the fundamental moral and religious truths, it must be mediated through language and tradition.[16]

Revelation is known through faith and not through philosophical reasoning. Faith then is the source of our knowledge of God's existence, as faith is the source of our knowledge of the fundamental principles of religion and morality. "Separated" individual reason is incapable of passing any valid judgment on them. By his argument that the first principles of discursive reason can only be derived from revelation through tradition de Bonald undercut Cartesian rationalism without challenging the Cartesian model of rigorous deductive science. Descartes' great mistakes had been to separate his philosophy from revelation and to claim that reason could function individually. De Bonald's reflection on the relationship of language to thought challenged both of these Cartesian assumptions. Reason cannot begin to argue discursively without deriving its first principles from revelation. Reason cannot argue deductively from its first principles to its conclusions without clothing its thought in a concrete human language. Therefore, in order to be able to operate effectively, Cartesian reason must remain in contact with the religious and social tradition through which the primitive revelation is transmitted by language.[17]

Thus de Bonald's critique of individualistic Enlightenment reason was made in the context of Cartesian deductive science. Indeed its main point was that the first principles of a deductive science are not actually innate ideas but virtually innate ideas actualized by revelation. In that sense, a true philosophy must be a "science of revelation." This line of argument, as we shall see, for all its effectiveness against Enlightenment rationalism, is not free from ambiguity in its understanding of grace and nature. De Bonald is not clear and sharp in his account of the relationship between God's primitive revelation and the historical act of revelation made by God in Christ. If all religious and moral first principles are known by all men through faith, how can that universal faith be supernatural? If all the basic religious and moral truths are known through divine revelation, what is unique and distinctively supernatural about positive Christian revelation? These questions would recur time and again during the nineteenth century as Catholic theologians endeavored in various ways to reconcile historical tradition as the vehicle of God's revelation with philosophy as a deductive science proceeding from intuitive first principles.

FÉLICITÉ DE LAMENNAIS

The first volume of Lamennais' *Essai sur l'indifférence en matière de religion* appeared in 1817. It continued de Bonald's attack on individual reason. Individual reason cannot find truth. Left to itself, it inevitably ends up in skepticism. The history of philosophy from Descartes to Hume is proof of that. Yet the skepticism of individual reason is contradicted by the dictates of the practical common reason on which the members of human society must live their lives. Any man who lives in a concrete society discovers that he must inevitably give his assent to a number of truths. He cannot avoid doing so, if he is to make the moral decisions which practical social life imposes on him. Nature itself compels these practical assents and, by doing so, nature makes the theoretical skepticism of individual speculative reason a practical impossibility. Only a fool would question the religious and moral certitudes on which our whole society is built and which are supported by the universal consent of men.[18]

Universal human consent is our criterion of truth and certitude. This consent is the basis for our certain knowledge of God's existence. It is impossible to deny the fact of God's existence without calling into question the validity of the common reason which we must all trust in order to live our daily lives. The common consent of men, which makes it impossible for us to doubt God's existence, also assures us that God's existence was manifested to man in the primitive revelation which human society has preserved. Furthermore, the language of the human society which mediates God's primitive revelation to individual minds calls forth in them the idea of God, the infinite Revealer.[19]

The idea of God can then become the first principle of a reflective philosophy through which the fatal error of Descartes' rationalism can be exposed. Reflection upon the idea of God enables the individual mind to understand why it cannot find truth within its own finite intellect, as Descartes had claimed that the individual mind could do in his *cogito ergo sum*. Confronted with the idea of God, the individual intellect realizes that it is utterly dependent upon the Infinite Being. God, who is the mind's creator, is the necessary ground of the truth which the human intellect discovers within itself. Changeless truth, the apodictic ground of certainty, can only be found in God. Thus, if the human mind wishes to find the truth, it must turn to God, its infinite creator.[20] If, on the contrary, the human mind turns away from the universal reason, which is found in God as the creator of all minds, and encloses itself within its own individual reason, the human mind is acting against its own nature as a created intellect. No intellect which acts against its own nature can find the truth or acquire certain knowledge of reality. It follows then that individual reason is ultimately doomed to error and skepticism.

Yet, even though it acts against its nature, a spiritual reason can never utterly destroy itself. For the creator who has revealed to it the first principles of knowledge in the idea of God has also revealed the language necessary for the expression of human thought. The common consent of the human race to the fundamental truths of morality and religion is rooted in an inbuilt impulse of human nature to assent to them. That impulse in turn is rooted in the nature of the human mind as a created intellect which must turn to the creating and revealing God to find the necessary first principles on which human thought depends.[21]

There is an obvious similarity between Lamennais' account of God's relation to the individual mind and the Augustinian metaphysics of divine illumination. This similarity facilitated the blending of traditionalism and ontologism later in the century. For the ontologists too would propose a deductive philosophy whose necessary first principle was either the idea of God or, at least, the divine ideas. The association of creation with revelation is a commonplace in neo-Platonic theologies, and that association would facilitate the assimilation of traditionalist theses by the Tübingen theologians and by Günther. Lammenais himself, however, was not a very coherent metaphysician. He was content simply to associate God's creative communication of reason's necessary first principles with the primitive divine revelation. Once this association had been made, the mind's dependence upon God's activity for its knowledge of religious and moral truths could be transformed into a dependence upon revealed ideas and revealed language both of which were transmitted in an act of primitive divine revelation. The common consent of men to the basic truths of religion and morality could also be transmuted into an assent of faith.

Lamennais' position, however, is somewhat inconsistent. If the common consent of men is an act of faith, then the moral and religious knowledge derived from it must also be faith knowledge. Yet Lammenais had also claimed that this common consent was due to a natural impulse of the created intellect. He resolved the problem of reconciling these seemingly contradictory claims by the assertion that faith is our nature. Furthermore, since the common consent of men is the ultimate criterion of truth, reason can neither criticize nor vindicate it. Once we know, however, that common consent rests upon the natural impulse of our created nature, we are certain that to reject its testimony means intellectual self-destruction. Skepticism is therefore a practical impossibility and, since the only alternative to skepticism is faith, man has no choice but to live on faith.

The early reaction to Lamennais' traditionalism was overwhelmingly favorable. Gradually, however, criticism of his failure to distinguish between faith and reason began to arise. Lamennais replied to it in his *Defense de l'essai sur l'indifférence* published in 1821. Again the immediate response was favorable. Lamennais' troubles really began when he applied his traditionalism to political theory. His outspoken anti-Gallicanism provoked the opposition of a number of influential bishops, and his disillusionment with the Restoration monarchy transformed him from an ultramontane monarchist into an ultramontane liberal. His *Des Progrès de la Révolution,* published in 1829, proposed that French Catholics withdraw their support from Charles X and rally behind the liberal democrats who were seeking to replace the Restoration monarchy with a parliamentary democracy. *L'Avenir,* which Lamennais founded in 1830, became the pioneer organ of Catholic liberalism in France.[22]

The time was not ripe for Catholic liberalism. The Revolution of 1830 brought the anticlericals to power in France and led to revolution in the Papal States. Gregory XVI and his secretary of state, Cardinal Lambruschini, reacting to the events of 1830, vigorously condemned political liberalism and rejected its demand for representative government.[23] French conservatives linked Lamennais' apologetics to his politics and began an attack on his whole system. At the suggestion of the conservative Cardinal de Rohan, Jean Louis Rozaven, S.J., published a telling criticism of Lamennais' epistemology in 1831, and in the same year a list of fifty-six censured propositions, taken from the works of Lamennais and his disciples Rohrbacker and Gerbet, was drawn up, approved by sixty-three French bishops, and sent to Rome for confirmation.[24]

Gregory XVI did not wish to condemn a man who had rendered outstanding service to the Church. On the other hand he wished to express his disapproval of the political liberalism which he feared and hated. Rome attempted a compromise. On 15 August 1832 the encyclical *Mirari Vos*[25] condemned Lamennais' political ideas without mentioning his name. Lamennais, who had sincerely, but quite unrealistically, believed that he could win Gregory XVI over to his own political liberalism, was shocked at the condemnation and at the political maneuvering which went on before and after it. He published a bitter reply in his *Paroles d'un croyant*. Gregory XVI responded in another encyclical, *Singulari Vos*, on 25 June 1834. Lamennais' political liberalism and his epistemology of common consent were both condemned. This was the end of Lamennais' traditionalism as a Catholic apologetics and political philosophy. Lamennais renounced his priesthood and left the Church never to return. It was not the end of traditionalism as an option in Catholic theology and philosophy however. Traditionalism would remain a vital force for several decades, and Lamennais' ideas would be repeated in the works of other traditionalist authors.

Louis Bautain

At the time of Lamennais' final condemnation another controversy about faith and reason was attracting public attention in France. On 15 September 1834 Jean François Marie Lepappe de Trévern, bishop of Strasbourg, addressed an *Avertissement* to the clergy of his diocese which he also communicated to the rest of the French episcopate and to the Holy

See. The *Avertissement* concerned the unorthodox opinions of Abbé Louis Bautain about the validity of Catholic apologetics. The bishop had been disturbed by Bautain's views about faith and reason and, on 30 April 1834, he had asked the abbé to clarify them by submitting his written answers to a set of six questions. The answers had proven so unsatisfactory that the bishop felt that it was his duty to alert his own clergy and the bishops of France to Bautain's unorthodox teaching and the dangerous effect which it could have on Catholic apologetics.[26]

Unlike the other traditionalists, Bautain had received a professional training in philosophy. He had been one of Victor Cousin's most brilliant students and before his conversion he had been a professor at the faculty of letters at Strasbourg. The influence of pious friends and his own meditative reading of the Scriptures had restored his lost faith and, after his conversion, Bautain became a zealous and brilliant apologist.[27]

Personal acquaintance with university philosophy had destroyed his confidence in the ability of discursive reason to vindicate the intellectual and moral principles on which religion and morality are based. Kant's critical idealism had undermined the epistemological foundations of Cartesian rationalism and the common sense of Reid and the Scottish School. Cousin's eclecticism could not establish a firm criterion of truth and certitude. The sensist empiricism of Locke and Condillac led to religious and moral skepticism.

The melange of Cartesianism, empiricism, and eclecticism which passed for philosophy in the Catholic seminaries was even less satisfactory. Scholasticism had survived in a few seminaries, but, even though the Romantic movement had revived interest in it and Cousin viewed it sympathetically, Bautain shared the low opinion of scholasticism prevalent in Catholic circles during the early years of the nineteenth century. To him scholasticism was another form of rationalism; it was simply another philosophy of discursive reason which endeavored to subordinate Christian faith and Christian tradition to the judgment of the individual understanding.[28]

No discursive philosophy, which claimed to be independent of faith in the acquisition of its evidence, could establish God's existence. Neither could it vindicate the fundamental principles of the moral law. Only faith could do that. Faith alone put the human intelligence in contact with ontological reality. The reason whose reflection was subsequent to a prior act of faith was the only reason which could transcend the order of sensible appearance.[29]

When Bautain published his philosophical opinions in *De l'enseignement de la philosophie en France au xixe siècle* in 1833,[30] the result was a resounding controversy concerning the certainty of the preambles of faith. What, if anything, must be known by human reason before Christian revelation can be accepted as credible? Under the influence of Bruno Liebermann Strasbourg had become a stronghold of scholasticism, and a number of Liebermann's disciples reacted violently to Bautain's critique of discursive reason and of the traditional Catholic apologetics which rested upon discursive arguments for the credibility of Christian revelation. After Lepappe de Trévern's *Avertissement* the controversy over Bautain's fideism spread to France and Germany. The theological faculties of Bonn and Tübingen followed the affair with interest and Möhler sent a letter of advice to Bautain in 1835.[31]

The publication of Bautain's *Philosophie du christianisme* in 1835 increased the violence of the controversy. Basing himself on Kant's critique of knowledge, Bautain denied that discursive reason could make any valid metaphysical statements about extramental reality. Kant's critique of natural theology had undermined all the discursive arguments for God's existence. Kant's critique of their epistemological foundations had invalidated the discursive apologetical arguments for the credibility of revelation based on signs and miracles. These arguments were intended to convince unbelievers; but only believers, who had already accepted the existence of God through faith, were capable of recognizing the presence of God in these historical events.[32]

Reason and Intelligence

Bautain, who had a solid knowledge of German philosophy, had taken over Jacobi's distinction between *Verstand* (lower discursive reason or understanding) and *Vernunft* (the higher principle of intuitive reason) and made it an important element of his own philosophy of religion. According to Jacobi, Kantian understanding could not transcend the level of sensible reality. The supersensible order of metaphysical reality could only be grasped through the immediate intellectual intuition of *Vernunft*. *Vernunft*'s intuition of metaphysical reality was an act of "faith," a *Vernunftglaube*. Since God belonged to the higher order of metaphysical reality, God too could only be known by an act of intellectual intuition, an act of "faith."[33] No discursive proof of God's existence, proceeding from the sensible world to its creator on the level of *Verstand* in the scholastic manner, was possible. God was known through God.[34]

In other words, God was the object of immediate intuition. His existence could not be proven by discursive Aristotelian arguments. Nevertheless it could be "shown." For any man who rejected this fundamental datum of immediate intuition had cut himself off from an important element of human experience and, if we could get him to examine his own experience, it would be possible to show him that. Or, to put it another way, we could bring him to discover God within himself.

Bautain combined Jacobi's anthropology of *Verstand* and *Vernunft* with Augustinian neo-Platonism to create his own philosophy of religion.[35] Reason, or the Kantian *Verstand,* was an abstractive faculty which derived the content of its notions from the data of sense experience. Notions, which were acquired by abstraction, were not ideas. Ideas were acquired through intellectual intuition. Reason, which was confined to the level of notions, could not transcend the level of phenomena.[36] Although it could argue to the necessity of supersensible reality, it could obtain no real knowledge of God. God could only be known through immediate intellectual intuition. He was not proved by reason. He was known by "faith," i.e., the immediate intuition of the intelligence, the name which Bautain gave to the faculty which Jacobi called *Vernunft.* For intelligence alone gave access to the metaphysical world of the divine ideas. Only intelligence then can grasp the first principles of the metaphysical order. Intelligence alone can gain an insight into the intelligible order of the organic universe. Reason can deal with the individual objects of the phenomenal order but intelligence alone can grasp reality as an intelligibly interrelated universe. From this it follows that neither God's existence nor the first principles of metaphysics or morals can be "demonstrated" by discursive reason. They can only be "shown," or, more accurately, allowed to reveal themselves immediately to intelligence. In its initial encounter with intelligible reality intelligence is primarily a receptive faculty.[37]

The ideas first manifest themsleves to the intelligence in a dim and undeveloped form. They are intelligible virtualities, "seeds" of the more fully developed ideas which the intelligence will possess when it permits these "intelligible seeds" to unfold their virtual content. This unfolding, however, requires active cooperation on the part of the intelligence. The intelligence must turn its gaze to the ideas and allow them to develop and clarify themselves through a process of continuing illumination. The passive reception of faith is thus succeeded by the intelligence's cooperation with the divine illumination in a process of active intellectual reflection. When the ideas have been allowed to manifest themselves through this process of reflection, the intelligence will discover within itself the evidence which it requires for a reflex act of scientific certitude. Faith will have been transformed into the reflex certitude of knowledge. The passive and active moments of Jacobi's explanation of *Vernunft*'s acquisition of metaphysical knowledge have been identified by Bautain with the Augustinian metaphysics of the mind's passage from faith to understanding under the influence of the divine illumination.[38] In this transformation, however, the fundamental ambiguity of Bautain's philosophy of Christianity remains. What is the precise distinction between the "faith" which is post-Kantian *Vernunft*'s intuitive grasp of metaphysical reality and the "faith" which is the believing Christian's assent to the word of God's historical revelation?

Bautain's Traditionalism

Furthermore, Bautain's Augustinian ontologism was blended with French traditionalism. Bautain accepted the Romantic organic model of society and, as a Platonist, he believed that an organic society was an analogue of the human being. Society was "man writ large." The human child passes through several stages in the course of his intellectual development. No child can clarify his ideas all at once. Likewise the human race has passed through several cultural epochs in the course of its intellectual and moral development. The human race did not clarify its ideas all at once. Undeniably it has undergone an intellectual, moral, cultural, and social evolution. The individual child is dependent upon the education which he receives from society in order to effect his own intellectual development. If the child were separated from his fellow men at birth, even if he survived, he could not develop his intelligence on the human level. Culturally he would remain a brute. When a society is cut off from its intellectual and moral leaders and from its cultural tradition, that society lapses into barbarism. There must be a metaphysical explanation for this universal phenomenon.

Bautain argued that it could be found in the distinction between the reason and the intelligence which he had taken over from Jacobi. Since reason can never transcend the phenomenal order, reason can never grasp ideas. Only the intelligence grasps ideas, and the intelligence does so through its immediate intuition of the divine ideas which are identified with the divine reality. Furthermore, we have already seen that the intelligence does not clarify the content of its imperfect, virtual ideas by turning its attention to the world of sense. On the contrary it must do so by turning its gaze to the intellectual world of the ideas. The intelligence is a drive to infinite intelligible reality. The goal and end of its natural appetite is intelligible, spiritual reality, not corporeal reality, and only the goal of a natural appetite can move a natural appetite to action. Therefore the intelligence cannot begin to act, cannot move from utter passivity to actual thought until it has first been moved to action by being brought into cognitive contact with another intelligible reality. Another intelligible being must communicate its reality to the intelligence and the intelligence must receive it before the intelligence itself can be stirred to think and to reflect. Consequently Bautain's metaphysics of the intelligence confirms the fundamental traditionalist thesis affirming the necessity of a primitive revelation. The mind cannot begin to reflect actively until the divine ideas have been communicated to it through an act of divine self-revelation.

Knowledge of God and of the first principles of speculative and moral reasoning depends upon an act of primitive revelation received by the intelligence through "faith." Prior to that revelation and its passive reception, no mind can think. After its reception, the mind can actively cooperate with God in the development of revelation's virtualities. Thus, drawing on a notion which goes back to Lessing, Bautain, like the Tübingen theologians, argues that God is the great educator of the human race.[39] God communicates the first principles of speculative and moral knowledge and God cooperates with man in their development. But in an organic universe even animals are educated through society. Brutes acquire the knowledge they need to survive by learning their basic skill from the adults of their species. Knowledge is acquired through a social process of education. Likewise, in an organic world, human intelligence cannot be the individualistic reason of the Enlightenment. Intelligence is socialized intelligence. It is stirred to action and developed through its social contact with other intelligences in the process of education. Material reality can never move the mind to think. Contact with intelligible reality, ideas and other minds, is needed to do that. Contact with other minds, however, in an organic universe, can only occur through the medium of language, the common linguistic bond of a concrete society. Thus the human intelligence comes into contact with divine revelation in two ways. It does so directly through immediate intuition of the divine ideas; and it does so indirectly through contact with other human minds in which the divine ideas have already been received and developed. But since intelligence must be moved to think through the words of a human language, contact with other human minds in a concrete society is a necessary condition for human thought.[40]

As an educator, society enables its individual members to share in the clarification and development of the divine ideas already accomplished by its intellectual, moral, and spiritual leaders. Thus society makes possible a communal and historical development of God's primitive revelation by transmitting it to each succeeding generation through tradition. Tradition brings each individual member of society into contact with the basic truths of metaphysics, morals, and religion and enables him to continue their development. Tradition, communicated by society and received through "faith," is required for the individual's knowledge of the first principles and for acquisition of the intellectual and moral discipline demanded for active reflection upon them. The man who has been educated by society, however, will be able to clarify the ideas which he has received through "faith" and so acquire the explicit intellectual evidence required for certain knowledge. Bautain was not a strict traditionalist like Lamennais. As an Augustinian ontologist he believed that the divine ideas manifested themselves to reflective intelligence and provided the evidence needed for certain knowledge.[41] Society was indispensable, however, for the speculative and moral education of reflective intelligence, and society educated its members through tradition. Knowledge was not acquired by abstracting ideas from sensible reality by the individual Aristotelian "reason." Knowledge was acquired by a reflective clarification of the ideas passively received through "faith" from the tradition of an educating society.

Bautain's Apologetics

Bautain's ontologism and traditionalism determined his approach to apologetics.[42] The Church is the supernatural organic society to which Mosaic and Christian positive revelation has been entrusted.[43] The supernatural self-manifestation of the triune God and the divine ideas connected with that manifestation are communicated to individual intelligences by the language of Catholic tradition and above all by the inspired words of Sacred Scripture. The educative society of the Church and its tradition are the only sources from which the ideas contained in God's supernatural self-manifestation can be received through "faith." If then the unbeliever will take these ideas from the Church's tradition through a preliminary act of faith—in which they are accorded no more than the status of an hypothesis—

the ideas will have been communicated to his intelligence. If, in addition, the unbeliever is willing to turn to these ideas in the deeper faith of willing acceptance, their radiation will illuminate his intelligence. If, following the moral and ascetic discipline taught him by the society of the Church, he meditates upon the words of tradition and, above all on the words of Sacred Scripture, the intrinsic intelligibility and beauty of the divine ideas contained in Christian revelation will manifest themselves more fully. Their goodness will excite his love and the intelligible evidence of their truth will move him to assent to their certainty. His first act of "hypothetical faith" will be transformed, through the influence of God's supernatural illumination, into the supernaturally certain act of Christian faith.[44] Aristotelian abstractive "reason" does not lead to faith.[45] Hypothetical faith educated by Christian tradition leads the faithful intelligence to the reflectively certain knowledge of its Christian revelation which justifies the definitive act of Christian faith. Hypothetical faith leads through reflective knowledge to definitive supernatural faith.

On the other hand scholastic apologetics, which relies on Aristotelian discursive reason, is committed to the position that Aristotelian reason prepares the way for faith by proving the credibility of Christian revelation. But scholastic apologetics, Bautain argued, cannot possibly succeed in its purpose. Scholastic apologetics employs discursive arguments for God's existence, but discursive reason can know nothing about God. God's existence is not proved by causal arguments from God's material creation. God's existence is shown by an immediate intuition of his own uncreated spiritual reality.[46] Scholastic apologetics seeks to convince the unbeliever that revelation is credible by discursive arguments based on the signs and miracles which testify to it; but only the believer, who already knows of God's existence by faith, can recognize miracles as signs of God's revealing power.[47] How then are we to address the unbeliever? If the unbeliever is a simple man, we should preach the gospel to him simply with sincerity and love. If he turns to the words of tradition and Scripture with the humility and love of faith, the triune God will manifest Himself to him. If the unbeliever is an educated man consciously committed to his religious skepticism, we must make him realize that his human intelligence is moved to seek the truth by its innate need of the infinite. Man's longing for truth, goodness, and beauty cannot be satisfied until his intelligence comes to rest in a satiating intuition of the triune God. We must make the unbeliever see that the drive to truth and goodness which he finds in his own experience raises questions about the meaning of his human life to which only Christian revelation has the answer. If we do that, the unbeliever will be willing to make the first act of "hypothetical faith" and turn to tradition and Scripture in a spirit of open receptivity. After that, God's supernatural self-revelation through the words of Scripture will do the rest.[48]

Bautain's apologetics was an early nineteenth-century version of Augustine's apologetics of the restless heart.[49] Sixty years later that Augustinian apologetics would appear in a late nineteenth-century version in Maurice Blondel's "apologetics of immanence."[50] Its reception by most scholastic philosophers and theologians then would be as hostile as the reception given to Bautain's apologetics by the Strasbourg scholastics.

Reaction Against Bautain

The reaction against Bautain both in Strasbourg and beyond its borders was so vigorous that Bautain was advised by Lacordaire to go to Rome and explain himself in person to the Roman authorities. Bautain was prudent enough to take Lacordaire's advice and, armed with a warm letter of recommendation from the conservative Jesuit preacher Félix de Ravignan, he left for the Holy City. At Rome Bautain followed the lectures of the leading Jesuit theologian, Giovanni Perrone, at the Roman College and conferred amicably with the Roman officials. Contact with Perrone seems to have convinced Bautain that his traditionalist apologetics was theologically untenable, and, after a friendly interview with Gregory XVI, in which the pontiff informed him that he had sinned "by too much faith," he returned to Strasbourg with the recommendation that he make his peace with his bishop.[51]

Upon Bautain's return, Andreas Räss, who had returned from Mainz and was now coadjutor bishop of Strasbourg, requested him to sign a series of propositions which amounted to a retraction of his fideistic apologetics.[52] In 1844, when Bautain applied for papal authorization to establish a religious congregation, the formal condition required for granting it was that he sign a number of promises. He would never teach that human reason could not establish God's existence, the spirituality of the soul, or the fundamental principles of metaphysics. He would never teach that human reason cannot acquire true and full certitude about the motives of credibility, i.e., the evidence on which the credibility of Christian revelation is based. Specifically these motives of credibility were miracles and prophecies, especially the resurrection of Jesus Christ. This was the end of the Bautain affair as far as the Church authorities were concerned. Bautain was never condemned by Rome and none of his books was ever placed on the Roman Index.[53]

Bautain was the most profound of the French traditionalists. In his apologetics and philosophy of religion traditionalism was united to Jacobi's cognitional metaphysics of *Verstand* and *Vernunft* and to the Augustinian metaphysics of divine illumination. Like de Maistre and unlike Lamennais, Bautain united his traditionalist epistemology to an intuitive theory of innate ideas. He specifically linked it to the Augustinian theory of divine illumination. That connection made him both a traditionalist and an ontologist and, in this, he resembled the moderate traditionalists of the Catholic Tübingen School who shared his commitment to Jacobi's metaphysics of *Vernunft* and *Verstand*. Later in the nineteenth century the ontologists would incorporate most of the traditionalist theses into their own system and continue the tradition of Bautain. On the other hand, the pure or strict traditionalists, who were hostile to the ontologists, rejected innate ideas and continued the tradition of de Lamennais.

Bautain's linking of his traditionalism with Jacobi's metaphysics of *Vernunft* and *Verstand* associated his traditionalism with the traditionalism of the Tübingen theologians, whose Christian philosophy of revelation was built upon the same distinction between discursive reason and intuitive intelligence. The great traditionalist themes—God's primitive revelation, the role of an organic society in the education of the human intellect, the historical transmission and development of revelation through tradition, faith, the cognitive and affective response to the tradition mediated by society, as the starting point of knowledge, reflective knowledge which begins with a grasp of the divine reality and moves to certain knowledge through an intellectual unfolding of the virtual content of the divine ideas, denial that discursive knowledge can reach metaphysical reality through the notions which it abstracts from sense experience—are all found in Bautain. These themes would constantly recur in the nineteenth-century systems of the Tübingen theologians, Günther, and the ontologists. Traditionalist ontologism, in its German and Latin form, united the Romantic organic view of society and intelligence to a neo-Platonic metaphysics of man and being. The union of these two elements made early nineteenth-century philosophy and theology intuitive in its theory of knowledge, organic and historical in its view of

nature and history. As the individual mind developed the implications of
the intuited divine ideas through a reflection that must begin with faith,
society developed the intelligibility of the primitive revelation through
its historical tradition. There was an intelligible necessity in social and
intellectual history whose explanation was the expansion of the primitive
ideas communicated to mankind in God's original revelation.

MODERATE TRADITIONALISM AND THEOLOGICAL METHOD

Bautain was the greatest representative of French moderate traditionalism, a philosophical orientation which retained its influential position
in Catholic theology until after the First Vatican Council. In moderate
traditionalism, as we have seen, Jacobi's metaphysics of *Vernunft* and
Verstand was united to the Augustinian epistemology and metaphysics of
divine illumination. In the Augustinian tradition of moderate traditionalism, theological reflection was equated with the intellectual progress
from a primitive act of faith to a philosophical understanding of its
content. The metaphysical structure of the act of faith, however, was
determined by the structure of post-Kantian *Vernunft*'s receptive intuition of noumenal reality. Scientific philosophical "understanding" of
faith was equated with the post-Kantian scientific explicitation of the
intelligible complexus of interrelated ideas originally disclosed in *Vernunft*'s "act of faith," i.e., its receptive intuition of noumenal intelligibility. Thus scientific understanding was metaphysically posterior to the
intuitive act of faith, *Vernunftglaube*, and systematic philosophy was metaphysically dependent upon the revelatory self-disclosure of noumenal
reality in the mind's intuitive act of faith. Without noumenal reality's
primitive act of self-revelation to the receptive human intellect the mind
would not possess the first principles which it required for its subsequent
discursive reasoning. Neither could it have any knowledge of the intelligible ideas which it linked together in the ideal systems of its philosophical science.

This moderate traditionalist conception of the relation between "faith"
and philosophical "reason" remained the dominant conception in Catholic theology during the first half of the nineteenth century. French moderate traditionalism, especially in the highly developed form which it
assumed in Bautain's philosophy of Christianity, was very close to the
traditionalism of the Catholic Tübingen School. But whereas Bautain
had confined his attention almost exclusively to problems of apologetics,

the Tübingen School created a scientific theological method which not only embraced apologetics but extended its scope to positive, speculative, and moral theology as well. The ontologism of Rosmini and Gioberti shared with moderate traditionalism a number of fundamental philosophical presuppositions and a post-Kantian conception of scientific method.

In the middle of the 1830s two rival philosophical and theological methods explicitly contested the validity of moderate traditionalism. The first rival method was the semirationalism of Georg Hermes, whose stronghold was the theological faculty of the University of Bonn. The second rival method was the scholasticism centered at Strasbourg, Mainz, and the Roman College, a heritage of eighteenth-century Jesuit scholasticism.

Moderate traditionalism vehemently rejected Hermes' theological method. In the eyes of Bautain and of the Tübingen traditionalists Hermes' theological method was a survival of eighteenth-century Enlightenment rationalism. Hermes' commitment to individual reason was expressed in the Kantian form which the post-Kantian philosophy of Fichte and Schelling had transcended. Moderate traditionalism also rejected Aristotelian scholasticism as another form of eighteenth-century rationalism because of scholasticism's reliance upon Aristotelian discursive reason or *Verstand*. Moderate traditionalists rejected the scholastic proofs for God's existence whose starting point was sense experience. Given their post-Kantian theory of knowledge this was the only consistent position which they could take. In addition, they rejected as invalid the scholastic apologetical arguments for the reasonableness of the act of faith based on signs and miracles. They also refused to accept the validity of the scholastic distinction between the apologetical arguments accessible to natural reason and the theological arguments whose evidence and certitude could not be grasped prior to the placing of a supernatural act of faith whose objective correlate was historical Christian revelation. Given their post-Kantian understanding of the relation between faith and reason these moderate traditionalist positions were quite coherent and consistent.

The first major clash between moderate traditionalism and scholasticism on a purely theological issue occurred when the controversy between Bautain and the Strasbourg scholastics erupted. The issue between the two schools was not clearly resolved on that occasion mainly because both Bautain and the great scholastic apologete Giovanni Perrone were eager to work out an amicable and diplomatic reso-

lution of the controversy. Bautain, although he was a professional philosopher, was not a professional theologian. He had made a very favorable impression upon the Roman authorities during his stay at Rome
and once Perrone had discovered that Bautain was prepared to retract
his assertion that the scholastic apologetic arguments were invalid, his
prime concern was to effect Bautain's reconciliation with his bishop
and assure the continuation of the Strasbourg philosopher's valuable
service to the Church. Hermes' theological method and the political
agitation of Hermes' contentious disciples appeared at the time to be far
more dangerous to Catholic theology than the well-intentioned impreci-
sion of the pious and conciliatory Bautain.

Later in the century the differences between traditionalist and scholastic method in philosophy and theology would not be settled so easily and
amicably. The Strasbourg scholastics and the scholastic theologians of the
Roman College would no longer be the leading representatives of scholastic thought. The leadership of the scholastic movement would be taken
over by the aggressive group of Jesuit neo-Thomists who were making
their first—and unsuccessful—moves toward the restoration of Thomism
as a unitary system of philosophy and theology at the very time when
Bautain was engaged in his own unsuccessful struggle with the Strasbourg scholastics. The neo-Thomists would not be as tolerant of moderate traditionalism as Perrone had shown himself to be. The battle
between the post-Kantian method which moderate traditionalism had
introduced into Catholic theology and the Aristotelian method of scholasticism would be fought to the finish in philosophy, apologetics, and
dogmatic and moral theology. In the third decade of the nineteenth
century, however, that battle was still in the future, and Bautain's difficulties at Strasbourg and Rome did not seriously compromise the theological position of moderate traditionalism which remained an important
movement in France, Italy, and Germany.

Thus, until the definitive condemnation of Georg Hermes removed his
theological method from serious contention, the battle for domination
within Catholic theology remained a three-sided one. Hermes' semirationalism and Tübingen traditionalism were the two most organized and
coherent theological methods in German Catholic theology. Scholasticism was beginning its renascence at the Roman College and, much more
modestly, at the scattered centers of neo-Thomism in Italy. It is to
Hermes, Tübingen, and renascent scholasticism, therefore, that we must
turn our attention in our study of the quest for a unitary method in
nineteenth-century theology.

3

HERMES, DREY AND RENASCENT SCHOLASTICISM

GEORG HERMES

Georg Hermes encountered the philosophy of Kant and Fichte during his student days at Münster. The encounter left his Catholic faith badly shaken. The torment of the religious doubts provoked by German idealism impelled the pious young student to devote several years to personal reflection on the rational justification of the act of faith and the soundness of theology's claim to be a valid source of knowledge. He hoped in this way to arrive at a personal solution to the two-fold problem raised by Kant's philosophy. This two-fold problem was the validity of the act of faith in Christian revelation and the possibility of a scientific theology In the context of post-Kantian idealism, science meant *Wissenschaft*, objectively certain and necessary knowledge, grounded upon immutable principles. How could there be a science whose object was the contingent historical facts of Christian revelation?[1]

Kant's *Critique of Pure Reason* and his *Critique of Practical Reason* vindicated objective knowledge through the *a priori* forms and categories of speculative reason and the categorical imperative and postulates of practical reason. For Kant therefore certain and objective knowledge was a timeless grasp of the absolute and universal; it was not historical knowledge of positive contingent facts. Science and history were mutually exclusive. The validity of objective knowledge was established through the absolute inability of the human mind to doubt or deny it. The operations of the discursive intellect were determined by the *a priori* functions of unification which governed the operations of the discursive intellect as such and so contained implicitly the intelligible structure of all possible objects. The mind could no more deny the existence of these *a priori* functions of unification than it could deny, as a thinking subject, that it was confronted with a world of objects. Were the mind to do so, it would contradict itself in its very act of thinking and destroy the very possibility of thought itself. Kant's vindication of objective knowledge therefore rested on the absolute inability of the discursive mind to refuse its assent to the objects of its thought and to their *a priori* conditions without destroying thought itself. Logical inability to withhold assent was the apodictic sign of objective certitude.

But, if Kant's vindication of objective certitude were correct, how could an act of faith in Christian revelation be valid rational knowledge? And how could Catholic theology be a science? The act of faith was a free assent to a contingent fact revealed by God. Catholic theology had contingent historical revelation as its object. Science and history were mutually exclusive according to Kant. Yet, ever since the Middle Ages, Catholic theology had defined itself as a scientific discipline which moved from its revealed first principles to its conclusions according to the norms of a scientific method.

Hermes devoted his career to solving the difficulties which Kantian philosophy had raised against the rationality of the act of faith and the scientific status of Catholic theology. His first work, *Untersuchungen über die innere Wahrheit des Christentums* (Investigations into the Inner Truth of Christianity), published in 1805, was favorably received, and he was appointed Professor of Dogmatic Theology at Münster two years later.[2] After the publication in 1819 of his *Philosophische Einleitung,* the first part of his *Christkatholische Theologie,*[3] he was invited to join the theological faculty at the University of Bonn. Hermes' career at Bonn was even more brilliant than it had been at Münster. His reputation as a scholar and teacher and his salutary influence upon his students won the admiration and respect of Archbishop Spiegel of Cologne, who appointed him to a number of sensitive positions in the archdiocese.[4] The *Positive Einleitung,* the second part of Hermes' *Christkatholische Theologie,* appeared in 1829. The three volumes of his major work on dogmatic theology, *Christkatholische Dogmatik,* were published posthumously between 1834 and 1836.[5]

Hermes' orthodoxy was never seriously challenged during his lifetime, although, even in his Münster days, a number of theologians had questioned the soundness of his opinions. After his death in 1831, however, the objections raised against his teaching became more frequent and serious and his work was finally delated to Rome. Rome's unexpected condemnation of Hermes' works, which were placed on the Roman Index, raised a storm of protest in Germany.[6] Hermes' disciples and the Prussian government waged a long and bitter campaign to force a reversal of the Roman condemnation. Gregory XVI and his secretary of state, Lambruschini, adamantly refused to reconsider the case and the long series of protests and diplomatic maneuvres ultimately proved fruitless. Even after his condemnation, however, Hermes' ideas remained influential in Germany.[7]

Hermes followed the main lines of the Kantian critique of knowledge. Reason was divided into speculative and practical reason. Speculative reason was capable of apodictic knowledge about the objective world of sensible experience. Practical reason was capable only of "faith" in the postulates which it was obliged to make in order to meet the unconditional moral demands of the categorical imperative. Unlike Fichte and the other post-Kantian idealists, Hermes did not unite speculative and practical reason in a single faculty. He did, however, concede to *Vernunft*, the higher intuitive use of reason, a speculative grasp of metaphysical reality which Kant had denied to it. Like Bautain, Hermes distinguished in man's intellectual powers a discursive faculty *(Verstand)* and an intuitive faculty *(Vernunft)*. Although Kant had conceded only problematic knowledge of the metaphysical order to *Vernunft* in its speculative use, Hermes made *Vernunft* a faculty of metaphysical intuition through which the judgments of *Verstand* could ultimately be grounded in the real. Thus, although Hermes remained essentially Kantian in his philosophy, his metaphysical conception of *Vernunft* freed him from the speculative skepticism of Kant's critical idealism.[8]

Hermes' Method of Universal Doubt

On the basis of his reformed Kantianism, Hermes believed that he could overcome the Kantian difficulties against the act of faith and the scientific status of theology. His method, as he describes it in his *Philosophische Einleitung* of 1819, was a method of rigorous universal doubt. Hermes' reading of Kant and Fichte and his personal struggle with his own religious doubts had convinced him that ruthless doubt was the only road to apodictic certitude. Any proposition which could be doubted must be doubted, and the doubt must continue until the mind can no longer withhold its assent. For Kant had shown that objective knowledge was universal and necessary knowledge. Therefore objective certitude must be apodictic certitude. That proposition alone is certain which the mind must affirm as necessarily true. For certitude it does not suffice that a proposition be known as true in fact. Its contradictory must be known to be impossible.[9] Hermes' ruthless doubt reminds his modern reader of Husserl's *epoche*. Despite the great difference between Hermes and Husserl, the aim of both was the same, to acquire the apodictic certitude which both of them associated with scientific knowledge *(Wissenschaft)*.

In his *Philosophische Einleitung* Hermes insisted that the Christian's moral obligation to seek the truth required him to apply rigorous methodical doubt to all his beliefs, including his religious beliefs, with ruthless disregard of every consideration other than the attainment of certainty. But how is the Christian to acquire this type of apodictic certitude about historical Christian revelation? Certainly not through the use of speculative reason. Speculative reason can tell us nothing about contingent historical facts. Historical facts can never be known with apodictical certitude. An historical fact could have been otherwise; its contradictory was not an impossibility. Therefore speculative reason can never provide certain knowledge of the historical facts on which Christian revelation rests and which furnish the evidence for the Christian's rational act of faith.[10]

Practical reason, however, might be the source of the certitude for which the Christian is looking. Improving a little on Kant, Hermes proposed his own formulation of the categorical imperative. "Establish and preserve human dignity in yourself and in others." This universal moral command imposed on every man an absolute and unconditional obligation to use each and every means known to be absolutely necessary for its fulfillment. Adequate knowledge of the conditions of moral action and of the circumstances which surround it is clearly required for the fulfilment of Hermes' categorical imperative. Therefore Hermes could deduce a second categorical imperative from his first. "Use your intelligence and your experience. In general, use all the experience which is absolutely necessary to fulfill a possible moral duty whether you already possess this experience yourself or must acquire it from others." It could well be that the knowledge you acquire must remain doubtful to speculative reason. Nevertheless, practical reason will demand that you accept it as true and certain, if the acceptance of its truth is absolutely required in order to fulfill a moral obligation imposed by the categorical imperative. In that case, practical reason commands the moral agent to disregard the uncertainty of speculative reason and assent to a proposition as true and certain. The moral agent can be absolutely certain that the proposition is true in fact. For, if it were not, practical reason, in commanding him to assent to it, would be commanding him to act irrationally, and this, as we know, is absolutely impossible.[11] Hermes was by no means anticipating the pragmatism of William James. He was simply following out the implications of the fundamental Kantian presupposition that practical reason is intrinsically rational. According to Kant, the intrinsic rationality of speculative and practical reason is a necessary condition for rational thought. Its denial is unthinkable. Denial of the intrinsic rationality of speculative and practical reason would make coherent thought impossible. It is a logical impossibility.

Hermes was on firm ground then in his claim that he could establish an objective basis for the judgments which practical reason must "accept as true" *(Fürwahrannehmen)* as well as the judgments which speculative reason must "hold as true" *(Fürwahrhalten)*. Nevertheless, there was an important distinction between these two classes of judgments. Judgments were "held as true" by speculative reason when the mind perceived the evidence for the necessary link between subject and predicate. In that case the mind could not withhold its speculative assent; it was physically obligated to give it. In judgments which practical reason was obliged to "accept as true," the mind did not see the intrinsic reason for the link between subject and predicate. The mind simply saw that it was obliged to admit that the link was there. Otherwise practical reason could not fulfill an unconditioned demand of the categorical imperative. Practical reason therefore was not physically required to make assents of this sort; it was simply morally obligated. Assents of this sort were practical judgments of "faith," in the Kantian philosophical sense of "faith." And Kantian judgments of "faith" were freely made.[12]

Once these distinctions had been made, Hermes could argue that contingent historical facts could be known with apodictic objective certainty. Historical judgments fell into the class of judgments which were "accepted as true" by practical reason. In other words they were assents which practical reason was obliged to make because they were absolutely necessary to fulfill an unconditional moral demand of the categorical imperative. The categorical imperative commanded moral agents to make whatever judgments were necessary to fulfill absolute moral obligations whether the evidence on which they were based could be derived from the agent's own experience or had to be taken on authority from the experience of other men. On occasion this meant that moral agents must have recourse to history and assent to the truth of contingent historical facts on the authority of historical tradition and its records. Practical reason must accept the facts of history as true in the measure in which that was necessary to fulfill the demands of the categorical imperative.

Granted that line of argument, Hermes could then move on to his next deduction. The categorical imperative required that practical reason "accept as true" the historical facts of Christian revelation. For the admission of these facts was absolutely required in order to fulfill a number of unconditional demands of the moral law.[13]

Hermes' Apologetics

Through this series of deductions Hermes had laid the groundwork for a Kantian Catholic apologetics. His *Positive Einleitung,* the second part of his *Christkatholische Theologie,* proposed how this sort of apologetic could be used in practice. The goal of Hermes' *Positive Einleitung* was similar to the goal of other works of Catholic apologetics. Hermes intended to argue that Christian revelation rested on positive historical statements whose truth could be known with certainty and that the Catholic religion was the religion proposed by those statements. Hermes' apologetics differed radically from the scholastic works of Catholic apologetics, however, by its refusal to use any of the usual arguments from speculative reason. Speculative reason could not be a source of objective certitude about historical facts or of the truth of historical statements. The knowledge of physical nature derived from speculative reason could justify no certain knowledge about the signs and miracles through which the supernatural character of Christian revelation was to be authenticated. None of the proofs proposed by Catholic apologetics through its use of speculative reason were apodictically certain. Each one of them could be doubted, since the contradictory of their conclusions was not impossible; and, according to the ruthless demand of Hermes' philosophical method, whatever *could* be doubted *must* be doubted.[14]

Practical reason, however, could provide apodictic certitude both for the fact of Christian revelation and for the claim that the Catholic religion was the form of religion proposed in it. In a long series of deductions Hermes argued that practical reason required the acceptance of Christian revelation as true because assent to its historical occurrence and to the propositions proposed by it was required for the fulfillment of the unconditional demands of the moral law. Therefore the historical reality and the positive content of Christian revelation must be accepted as true by practical reason. Consequently the act of Christian faith was a rational and certain judgment of practical reason. Kantian practical reason guaranteed both the rationality and the freedom of the act of faith. For judgments of practical reason were both rational and free. They were judgments of "faith" and, as such, they were morally but not physically necessary.[15]

Hermes' Speculative Theology

Hermes' *Christkatholische Dogmatik,* published between 1834 and 1836, tackled the second difficulty posed by Kantian idealism, the possibility of scientific theology, i.e., necessary knowledge of positive revelation in the form of scientific *Wissenschaft.* Hermes' *Einleitung in die christkatholische Theologie* had already argued, as we have seen, that the propositions of Christian revelation could only be "accepted as true" by practical reason. Speculative reason could never acquire any knowledge of the intrinsic reason why they were true. Therefore the Christian mysteries, "accepted as true" by practical reason, remained utterly impenetrable to speculative reason. The Christian believer had no knowledge at all of *why* they were true. All that Catholic speculative theology could be expected to do therefore was to establish, through its method of ruthless doubt, that the content of each individual Catholic doctrine was necessarily contained in the propositions of the Christian revelation which practical reason was obliged to "accept as true," and to show that these propositions in no way contradicted the demands of practical and speculative reason. For the categorical imperative forbids us to accept as true any proposition which is in opposition to the demands of reason. This was Hermes' negative rational norm of Catholic revelation. No proposition could be accepted as true on the basis of revelation which contradicted the rational demands of reason.[16]

Hermes' theological method thus reduced speculative theology to the status of a Kantian form of positive theology. All that scientific theology could do was to show that the positive propositions of historical revelation must be accepted as true by practical reason. Hermes was willing to admit into his speculative theology propositions which were conclusions from two premises, each of which must be accepted as true. Further than that he would not go. Speculative theology of any sort, whether it was the scholastic speculative theology which argued from revealed first principles through minor premises derived from natural reason to its theological conclusions, or whether it was the speculative historical theology of the Tübingen School, were excluded by his method of rigorous doubt and its requirement of apodictic necessary certitude.[17]

Hermes' theological system was an heroic effort to meet the Kantian demand for apodictic certitude in his Catholic apologetics and dogmatic theology. Meeting those demands required him to make radical changes in the method and norms of evidence employed in both those disciplines. The scholastic apologetics, based on the authentication of Christian revelation through signs and miracles, was rejected as cognitively invalid. The Christian act of faith was equated with the philosophical faith of Kantian practical reason. Dogmatic theology was reduced to the status of positive theology.

The most criticized element of Hermes' system was his theology of the act of faith.[18] Catholic theology requires that the act of faith be a free supernatural assent whose motive is the authority of the revealing God. In Hermes' theology the motive of the assent of faith is no longer the authority of the revealing God but the moral demands of a Kantian categorical imperative. Hermes himself admitted as much, and endeavored to answer the objection that his assent of faith did not transcend the limits of the philosophical order and of natural knowledge. His way of handling the difficulty was to make a distinction between the mind's intellectual assent to the propositions of Christian revelation and the "living faith" which expresses itself in the moral resolve to live one's life in conformity with the demands of Christian revelation. The supernatural act of faith is the act of living faith. To meet the demands of Catholic theology, however, the assent of faith itself must be supernatural, and it must transcend the limits of natural knowledge and the philosophical order. Hermes' distinction therefore did not really meet the major difficulty against his theology of the act of faith.[19]

Hermes' endeavor to arrive at apodictic necessary certitude about the positive historical contents of Christian revelation, as we have seen, reduced his speculative theology to positive theology. His method was one of many attempts to solve the problem of establishing a necessary science of Christian revelation. The only necessity which it could discover in historical revelation was the necessity of its individual propositions. The Tübingen theologians discovered another necessity in Christian revelation but it was not the static necessity of its isolated individual propositions. It was the necessity which governed the dialectical evolution of the idea of the Kingdom of God, the supreme idea which penetrates the intelligible system of revelation and unfolds itself through the historical development of living tradition in Christ's Church. In the Tübingen theology Romantic traditionalism joined hands with post-Kantian idealism. Hermes' individual reason was replaced by the socialized reason of the traditionalists and the post-Kantian idealism of Schelling. The result was an approach to the reasonableness of the assent to Christian revelation that had more in common with the traditionalist ontologism of Bautain than with the rationalist apologetics of Hermes, and a conception of the relationship between positive and speculative theology that was the antithesis of the relationship between them proposed in Hermes' *Christ-katholische Dogmatik.*

Johann Sebastian von Drey

Johann Sebastian von Drey, the founder of the Catholic Tübingen School, was professor of apologetics and dogmatic theology at Ellwangen until 1817 when that faculty was transferred to the University of Tübingen, where he continued to teach until 1846. Drey's most distinguished students at Tübingen were Johann Adam Möhler, Johann Baptist Hirscher, Franz Anton Staudenmaier, and Johann Evangelist Kuhn. Möhler was professor of church history at Tübingen from 1825 to 1835 and then at Munich from 1835 until his death in 1838. Staudenmaier began his career as professor of dogmatic theology at Giessen. He remained there until 1837 and then went to Freiburg, where he taught until 1856. Hirscher was professor of moral theology at Tübingen from 1817 to 1837 and then continued his career at Freiburg from 1837 to 1863. The youngest of the four was Johann Evangelist Kuhn. Kuhn began his career as professor of New Testament at Giessen and then spent forty-five years between 1837 and 1882 as professor of dogmatic theology at Tübingen.

Möhler was the most famous member of the Catholic Tübingen School. His *Die Einheit in der Kirche* and his *Symbolik* were popular successes in Germany and caught the imagination of Europe. Their organic, historical exposition of ecclesiology and doctrinal development appealed to the sensibilities of the Romantic period through exploitation of the Romantic notions of community, historicity, and vital organic totality. Möhler's influence lasted well beyond his own century. His two theological masterpieces helped to inspire the metaphysical and communitarian model of the Church as the mystical body of Christ which supplanted Bellarmine's juridical model during the first half of the twentieth century. Along with Newman, Möhler is credited with the introduction of the intuitive and historical approach to the development of doctrine, which replaced the scholastic endeavor to account for doctrinal development during the same period.

Until Joseph Rupert Geiselmann began to produce his brilliant series of studies on the Catholic Tübingen School, Möhler was the only member widely known in theological circles outside of Germany.[20] Today, however, thanks to Geiselmann, the whole theological community has been made aware of the historical and doctrinal significance of the School as a whole. Geiselmann has given us a clearer and more accurate understanding of the theological method which Drey's disciples derived as a common heritage from the teaching of their master. For Drey, the founder, was the inventor of a new and powerful theological method which enabled the early Tübingen School to meet the challenge of Kantian and post-Kantian philosophy by drawing upon the possibilities of German idealism.

Drey's theological method was inspired by Schelling's *Vorlesungen über die Methode des Akademischen Studium* (Discourses on the Method of Academic Study). One of the important elements of Schelling's idealism was its philosophy of revelation. Inspired by Schelling, Drey created a theology of revelation that enabled him to do justice to some of the basic insights of the traditionalists.[22] Drey's theology of revelation contained within it a theology of tradition, an ecclesiology and a theology of doctrinal development.[23] At its heart was a new theological method in which history and scientific system, philosophy and theology were united in a way that was radically different from the way in which they were united in Hermes' Kantian theology or in the Aristotelian scientific theology of the scholastics.

The main lines of Drey's theological method can be found in his programmatic article "Revision des gegenwärtigen Zustandes der Theologie" (Revision of the Present Status of Theology), published in 1812,[24] and in his *Kurze Einleitung in das Studium der Theologie* (Brief Introduction to the Study of Theology), published in 1819. Drey reacted vigorously against the Enlightenment separation of science from history which, as we have seen, reduced Hermes' speculative theology to a Kantian positive theology. This type of theology might establish that the individual doctrines of Christian revelation were true and certain. But it could establish no organic connections between the individual doctrines themselves. Much less could it establish any intrinsic intelligibility in the historical process of their temporal emergence and development. In Hermes' Kantian speculative theology, for example, each revealed doctrine was timelessly true and certain. There was no place for an intrinsically intelligible and authentic development of dogma. Each doctrine was established individually. The doctrines were not intrinsically related to each other as parts of one intelligible system. It was no wonder then that Enlightenment theology was often reduced to a moralistic positive theology. It was incapable of being anything else. Even Hermes' theology, despite the piety and orthodox intentions of its author, was not free from that sort of reductionism.

Schelling and Drey

Schelling's idealism provided the philosophical solution to the problem of science and history which Enlightenment philosophy had created. In Schelling's system of identity, the Absolute, the transcendent unitary ground of the universe, contains in its infinite identity the contradictory opposites which exclude each other in their finite manifestations within the world. In the Absolute, nature and spirit, freedom and necessity are one and the same. The Absolute, moreover, manifests itself in its finite realizations through the two-fold order of nature and spirit. Since it is the manifestation of a spiritual, unitary Absolute, the universe is a living, organic whole. The universe is a vital cosmos made up of intrinsically interrelated members. Furthermore, the living cosmos is not only characterized by the intrinsic relationship between each of its members and their relation, as members of the finite universe, to the universe's Absolute Ground, it is also characterized by an intrinsic, goal-directed drive to self-development. In Schelling's idealism, the model of a living organic whole replaced the mechanistic world model of the Enlightenment, in which the world's atomic elements had no intrinsic relation to each other and in which the elements were devoid of intrinsic dynamism.

Furthermore, in Schelling's idealism, life is not a blind reality of the purely biological order. Life is essentially spirit, and spirit is self-conscious. Schelling's organic cosmos therefore is an intrinsically interrelated, self-conscious, self-developing universal world process. In Schelling's universe an intelligible process of intrinsic growth and development belongs to the essence of the finite cosmos and to the essence of each of its intrinsically interrelated members.[25] The individual members of Schelling's cosmos are organically subordinated members of larger natural or spiritual units. The self-development of individual members and of the larger units to which they are intrinsically related is directed from within by intrinsic intelligible principles or "ideas," in a manner analogous to the way in which, in the metaphysics of Aristotle and Plotinus, the vital, goal-oriented self-development of plants and animals is directed through the causal influence of the intrinsic principles which Aristotle and Plotinus call their souls. For Schelling, the "ideas" which inform the natural and spiritual unities are intrinsic principles which can "become" and unfold their virtualities through a process of intrinsic self-development. This process can occur within the individual intelligence; it can occur within the living beings of the natural order; it can occur within the natural species; or it can occur within the spiritual unities that constitute human societies.[26]

Furthermore, the unified process of cosmic self-development is the process of the Absolute's self-manifestation through its "becoming" in the cosmos in the dual order of nature and spirit. It was possible for Drey to adapt Schelling's philosophy of the Absolute and the Absolute's "becoming" in the cosmos to meet the needs of a Catholic theology of creation and revelation. God's continuous act of creation could be transformed into God's "becoming" in the interrelated world of organic nature. God's manifestation of his reality to man's intuitive *Vernunft*, which Jacobi had shown was only moved to action by contact with another spirit, could become the traditionalists' primitive revelation. The divine ideas, received in the primitive revelation, could "become" as they unfolded their virtualities through the active reflection upon *Vernunft*'s ideas, the post-Kantian process of reflection on *Vernunftglaube* (intuitive philosophical "faith"), which we have already encountered in Bautain's philosophy of Christianity, and which Drey had also taken over from Schelling. Independently of Bautain, Drey had found in Schelling the foundations for his own traditionalist theology of revelation. Drey's traditionalism, however, had a metaphysical foundation whose unity and coherence were firmer than the metaphysical foundations of Bautain's philosophy of Christianity.[27]

The life process of a universe in which life is essentially spirit must ultimately arrive at the stage of self-development in which spirit becomes conscious. Spirit must emerge and, in an organic universe, unitary spirits must be related to each other as members of larger spiritual wholes. Unity, however, is due to the intrinsic metaphysical influence of an internal spiritual principle. Individual spirits therefore are related to each other as members of a spiritual community that is informed, preserved, and directed in its authentic self-development by its own intrinsic community "idea." Each individual member therefore is related to the spiritual cosmos through his membership in his own ideal community. And the spiritual world, its communities and individuals, is intrinsically related to the world of nature and nature's species and individuals.[28]

The Idea of the Kingdom of God

Every genuine community therefore, every authentic society, has its own intrinsic spirit or *Geist*, which is the conscious expression of its formative "idea." As the formative idea unfolds its virtualities and achieves its authentic development through the activity of the individual members of the community, the evolution of the formative "idea" manifests itself on the conscious level through the intellectual and moral evolution of the "community spirit." Thus it is only on the communal level, in the cultural tradition through which the community spirit expresses itself, that a genuine knowledge of the community's formative idea can be obtained.

On the basis of Schelling's philosophy, Drey was able to argue that the Catholic Church was an organic spiritual community informed by one fundamental idea. This formative idea achieved its development through the activity of the Church's individual members and manifested itself through the spirit of the Catholic community whose conscious expression was found in the living tradition of the Church.[29] The formative idea of the Christian community, which came to expression in her tradition, was the idea of the "Kingdom of God." This idea existed in the Christian community because it had been communicated by God to the human race through an act of divine revelation.[30]

As we have already seen, Drey, along with Bautain, accepted the metaphysical principle that *Vernunft*, man's faculty of intellectual intuition, could only be moved to action through contact with another spiritual reality. Drey also drew from that admission the same traditionalist conclusions. Material creation could never bring man to a knowledge of God or of metaphysical reality. God must reveal himself directly, if God is to be known. Or failing that, the idea of God must be received in man's intuitive intelligence through the spoken word of another man in whose mind the idea of God has already been received. The man who has never heard the name of God will never come to know him. Our human knowledge therefore must begin with an act of primitive revelation which introduces the intellect to the metaphysical order and supplies discursive reason with its first principles.[31] God, however, as a free and provident creator, has his free purposes which he intends to achieve through the historical development of the human race. His eternal plan for mankind exists in the changeless infinity of his own mind. But in his providence God has determined to reveal his own reality and manifest his providential plan for mankind's salvation in gradual stages. Part of that plan was communicated in the primitive revelation to our first parents. More was communicated to the patriarchs and prophets of the Old Law by the divine inspiration which infused divine ideas into their receptive intellects. They in turn communicated these ideas to the members of their community through the instrumentality of the spoken word. God's ultimate revelation of his providential plan was made to the Word Incarnate. Then Christ communicated the ideas of this definitive revelation to his community through his oral teaching. These revealed ideas, however, form an intelligible system. They are all formed into a single intelligible whole by one directive, architectonic idea, the idea of what God intends to "become," through his free self-communication in revelation and through the gracious designs of his providence, within the community of the Church. The overarching idea of God's eternal decree for the human race, which is to manifest itself to men in time, is the idea of the Kingdom of God. This is the formative idea that unites all the subordinate ideas communicated by the words of Christ's teaching into a unitary intelligible system of Christian revelation.[32]

The idea of the Kingdom of God is the formative idea of the community which is the bearer of that revelation. And the idea of the Kingdom of God has been received by the Christian community in faith and exists as an idea within the consciousness of the Church's communal spirit. The idea of the Kingdom of God therefore comes to conscious expression in the tradition of the Church, and the words of that tradition will communicate it to the intellects of the Church's members.[33] Schelling's ideas, moreover, are not only received in the intellect or *Vernunft*. They develop their intelligible virtualities through the process of active reflection that follows upon their reception. This is true in community spirits as well as individual spirits. Consequently the virtualities of the intelligible system of revealed ideas informed by the architectonic idea of the Kingdom of God will evolve within the consciousness of the Church. This means that there must be an intelligible process of historical evolution in the tradition of the Church.[34]

Drey's Historical Dialectic

At first glance this metaphysics of development would seem to require a linear process of increasing intelligibility in the Church's awareness of Christian revelation. Human freedom, error, sin, and heresy would seem to be excluded. Drey's theology of historical revelation would seem to have acquired its ideal intelligibility at the cost of the contingency and freedom which are essential to genuine history. Schelling's idealism, however, insisted upon the freedom of each individual will. Each individual spirit could either conform freely to the intelligible ideas which came to consciousness in the community spirit or it could turn away from them and take refuge in the individualism of its own "subjectivity." The interrelationship between the individual and communal spirit and Schelling's dialectic of opposites gave Drey the clue which he needed to work out a theology of historical tradition in which ideal necessary intelligibility could be combined with contingency, freedom, and heresy in the development of Christian doctrine.[35]

Within a system of interrelated intelligibilities each idea requires its opposite and each idea reaches its full self-determination by progressively defining itself over against its opposites. This is required by the general principle which the German idealists took over from Spinoza that every determination is a negation. According to that principle every virtual idea must achieve its positive self-determination by excluding all that it is not from the intelligible essence that makes it what it is. Full self-determination, achieved by excluding all its opposites, is required for the perfect development of an idea. If then the full self-development of an idea must occur through the idea's historical unfolding, the process of its negative self-determination must be accomplished through an historical dialectic of opposition.

This historical dialectic of opposition reconciles the apparent contradiction between genuine history and scientific necessity. The directing idea which informs each organic spiritual community unfolds its virtualities by directing the community's growth in spiritual self-possession and guiding the community's progressive realization of its genuine communal values and potentialities. The formative idea does this, as we have seen, through the intellectual and volitional action of the communal spirit or *Geist*. This communal *Geist*, the objective spirit of each community, is mediated to the "subjective" spirit of each individual member. Such mediation is consistent with the neo-Platonic metaphysics of Schelling's idealism. For in the metaphysics of Plotinus the Universal Intellect or *Nous* is present and operative in each individual intellect and the Universal World Soul (whose necessity Schelling admitted) is present and operative in every individual soul. Yet, since each individual spirit is free, its "subjective" choice may contradict the synthetic values through whose revelation the communal spirit realizes on the conscious level the virtualities of the communal idea. The judgments which individual spirits make, under the influence of free choice, may contradict the authentic judgments of the communal spirit. "Subjective" error will then oppose itself to "objective" truth. The subjective unintelligibility, born of man's misuse of his personal freedom, will oppose itself to the intelligible necessity of the order of ideas.

In an intelligible universe, however, this subjective error has a necessary place in the development of an ideal system. The progressive self-determination of the community's guiding idea, carried out through the judgments and choices of individual members, is a conscious historical process. The self-determination of an historical idea, as we have seen, can occur only through a process of negation. Negation excludes the false, distorted "possible unfoldings" of its own essential virtualities as they successively present themselves on the level of consciousness. As the communal spirit actively and consciously excludes these "false virtualities," the community's formative idea consciously "becomes what it should be." For it is precisely by excluding the false "possibilities for development" which contradict its own intrinsic intelligibility that the communal idea consciously develops its own ideal reality in time.

But how do these "false possibilities of development" arise on the conscious level? They arise through the dynamic interaction of the communal spirit and the free spirits of the individual members of the community. The communal spirit, in Schelling's neo-Platonic metaphysics, expresses itself in and through the individual spirits. When the free false choices of individual spirits are made or the false judgments of individual spirits are pronounced through their misguided use of their intellect and will, these "false possibilities" are raised to the level of consciousness. They become options for thought and action presented to the other members of the community. Yet even though the occurrence of these "false possibilities" is due to the freedom of individual spirits, they occur *necessarily*. They *must* arise. Otherwise communal ideas cannot reach their full development through a conscious negation of their opposites. Error, due to freedom, contingency, and "subjective" unintelligibility, is a necessary constituent of the dialectical process of ideal self-determination. History, precisely as history, has its own ideal necessity. History is the intelligible process by which the architectonic idea that informs a spiritual community realizes its virtualities through the dialectical process of negation.[36]

But how can the communal idea overcome the opposition represented by "false possibilities" within a community of free spirits? It can do so through the influence of the communal spirit upon the individual spirits to which it is mediated. "False possibilities" are either individual judgments or individual free decisions made by "subjective spirits" acting individually. But since they are errors and aberrant choices, they lack the intrinsic intelligibility of the ideal order. Thus, as their consequences reveal themselves in time, their intrinsic lack of intelligibility must manifest itself to other intelligences. The individual intelligences of the other members of the community have an intrinsic natural desire for the intelligible. Furthermore they are directed in their individual thinking by the influence of the communal spirit present and operative within them. The combined influence of their natural desire for intelligibility and of the communal spirit is far more extensive and deep rooted than the attraction of the "false possibilities" proposed by the aberrant "subjective" judgments made by individual members of the community. Ultimately therefore the members of the community will reject them. Thus Schelling's dialectics reveals the metaphysical necessity which underlies Lamennais' criterion of truth and certitude, the common consent of the human race.[37]

Scientific Reconstruction of History

It is possible therefore for a human knower who has acquired an accurate knowledge of the events which constitute the empirical record of a spiritual community's history to grasp the necessary intelligibility of that historical process. Careful reflection upon the empirical events of that history enable *Vernunft* to intuit the necessary ideas which inform the interrelated members of that historical organic whole. Intuition of the necessary ideas will then be followed by a dialectical investigation of the ideas' historical self-determination through the process of negation by which they exclude their opposites. This dialectical investigation enables the inquirer to identify the course of an idea's authentic self-determination through the process of its self-realization in history.[38] Dialectical investigation leads to a scientific reconstruction of the whole complex development of the interrelated system of ideas which achieve their self-development through the empirical events which constitute the observable history of an organic community. For this interrelated system of ideas is the ideal expression of the unitary architectonic idea which informs the intelligible totality that constitutes a spiritual community. The ordered self-development of each of these ideas, in harmony with the ordered self-development of every other idea in the system, is in fact the authentic intelligible self-development of the unitary architectonic idea which informs the whole and "comes to be" in and through the whole.[39] The process of scientific reconstruction is a reflexive grasp of the relation of each of the subordinate ideas to the architectonic unitary idea which has directed their dialectical self-development as members of an intelligible system. Once that relationship has been seen, the reflective mind understands why the authentic historical development of that system of ideas through the dialectical process of negation had to be exactly what it was. The reflective mind, in other words, has grasped the necessary intelligibility of a genuinely historical process. Scientific knowledge of history has been acquired.

Drey was now ready to construct his scientific theology of historical Christian revelation. The unitary architectonic idea which informed the subordinate ideas of Christian revelation was the idea of the Kingdom of God. All the truths which God intends to reveal for the education of the human race and all the free decisions which God in his providence has made concerning the orders of its creation and redemption are expressions of this unitary idea. Through Adam, the patriarchs, the prophets, and Christ, God has progressively revealed this idea of mankind with increasing perfection. Different communities have been the bearer of the idea of the Kingdom of God, the family, the clan, the Jewish people, and finally the Catholic Church. God's definitive communication of the idea of the Kingdom of God was made through Christ.[40]

The Catholic Church is the bearer of that idea in the definitive form in which it was communicated to man by Christ. Thus the dialectical self-realization of the idea of the Kingdom of God becomes the living, dynamically self-communicating tradition which develops historically in the successive periods of the Church's life. The Church then is a living community formed by the unitary idea of the Kingdom of God.[41] Her outer form, cult, discipline, and hierarchical organization are visible expressions of that idea. Her doctrinal tradition is its manifestation in the form of language. Since ideas must unfold their virtualities in history, the Church's tradition must undergo doctrinal development. And since an idea's self-development must occur through the process of dialectical negation, doctrinal development, under divine predestination, must occur through the community's rejection of "false possibilities" proposed in the form of heresies by individual members. *Opportet haereses esse.* Heresy and its rejection in doctrinal development can culminate in the firm certitude of a dogmatic definition.[42]

Method and Divisions of Theology

Drey's theology therefore will follow the method which, following Schelling's *Discourses on the Method of Academic Study,* he had proposed as the means through which the intellect can acquire a scientific grasp of the intelligible necessity that directs a genuinely historical process. Theology will be a philosophy of historical Christian revelation. The divisions of theology set down in his *Kurze Einleitung in das Studium der Theologie* follow the stages of that method. Theology is divided into two distinct disciplines, historical theology and dogmatic theology.[43] Both theological disciplines have as their object the history of Christian revelation contained in the tradition of the Catholic Church. For reflection on Christian revelation must begin with a reflection on its spiritual ideas as conveyed to the individual intellect by the words of Christ's educative community. Historical theology has for its task the establishment of the factualness of the historical content of Catholic tradition. It will use the method of historical studies. Dogmatic theology, on the other hand, is a scientific theology in the strict sense of the word. Its task is to grasp through intellectual intuition the ideal essences contained in the factual content of Christian tradition. It is ideal, not factual, in character. Its aim is to grasp the intelligible relation of each essence to all the other essences within the ideal system of Christian revelation informed by the architectonic idea of the Kingdom of God.[44]

Dogmatic theology is concerned with intelligible ideal necessity, not factualness. Whatever has actually been taught in the history of the Church is historically true. Therefore errors and heresies are historically true. They are positive facts contained in the experience of the Church. But they are not dogmatically true. That alone is dogmatically true which is an authentic development of the intelligible system of ideas informed by the architectonic idea of the Kingdom of God. Nevertheless errors and heresies have their ideal value since errors and heresies are the opposites which the ideas of Christian revelation have to negate in order to achieve their own authentic self-development. Therefore dogmatic theology has a positive function. It can show the intelligible meaning of each significant error and heresy as a necessary stage in the historical self-determination of the idea of revelation and thus provide a scientific vindication of the authentic development of revealed doctrine through the dialectic of history.[45]

Dogmatic theology can then turn its attention to its speculative or philosophically constructive function. It can show that the individual essences manifested through the various revealed doctrines are linked in one ideal system. By a process of rigorous deduction dogmatic theology can then establish that the system of ideal essences is an intelligible, necessary, orderly, and progressive self-expression of the one architectonic idea of the Kingdom of God. The rigorous deductive process which establishes the exact intelligible relation of each ideal essence in the system of Christian revelation to the architectonic idea of the Kingdom of God is an ideal reconstruction of the historical process of development in Christian tradition.[46]

Apologetics was not simply a part of dogmatic theology. It was a separate discipline with its own proper scientific method. Drey's three-volume *Apologetik* gives a brilliant illustration of how that method worked in practice.[47] Drey did not base his apologetics upon a philosophical vindication of God's existence and attributes as a scholastic apologist would have done. As a traditionalist Drey believed that isolated individual reason could not argue to God from material creation. God must be known from the idea of God passively received in the human intelligence. The idea of God therefore must be communicated through words by another human being in whose intelligence the idea of God already exists. In the concrete order men were incapable of grasping God's existence unless the intellectual, moral, and religious education which they received from their community developed in them the mental capacity and moral freedom needed to recognize and ratify man's proper relationship to God. Isolated from his community, and thus deprived of its educational influence, no concrete man can acquire any real knowledge of his creator. And, since all communities from Adam down have been bearers of one of the forms of historical revelation, the communal experience which educates the minds and wills of their individual members must contain the living divine tradition. In the real order then a concrete mind can only come to know God through contact with God's historical revelation mediated by one or another of the different religious communities. The only real apologetic questions therefore are What concrete, historical religious form is the authentic expression of God's definitive revelation, and What concrete religious community is its bearer?

As a scientific reflection on concrete, historical revelation, apologetics too will be a philosophy of revelation. As such, it will seek out the ideal relation between the ideas that are intuitively grasped in the concrete events of religious history. Since it is a Christian philosophy, apologetics will be a theological discipline. Christian faith has no need for a philosophical foundation outside itself. Christian tradition contains its own necessary system of ideas. Scientific theology, which grasps their necessary structure, is therefore a philosophy in itself.

Apologetics is a scientific reflection upon the Christian religion and the living tradition of which it is the bearer. Its aim is to show, through its intuitive grasp of its intelligible ideas and through a deductive exposition of their relationship, why the Christian religion must be divine. The first volume of Drey's *Apologetik* establishes the necessary relation between the ideas of religion and revelation, and the necessary relationship between the idea of a revealing God and the idea of a free recipient of revelation. From those relationships the necessary criteria for the verification of divine revelation by a human mind inevitably follow. Signs and miracles for example must occur. The second and third volumes of the *Apologetik* carry out a series of further deductions whose starting point is the idea of religion. From the idea of religion Drey endeavors to demonstrate that Christianity alone is the perfect religion. The history of religion furnishes the empirical data in which the essences of the various other forms of religion can be grasped intuitively. Once these essences have been grasped, Drey can demonstrate that none of them can realize the idea of the perfect religion. They are not just incomplete realizations of that idea. They are aberrant developments. The perfect religion is a religion of salvation. It promises a salvation which can only come from God. It brings salvation through a savior who can only be God himself. The perfect religion is the divinely revealed religion of the Incarnation. Therefore it must be Christianity.

Theology for Drey was a philosophy of revelation. Drey agreed with the traditionalists in their assertion that God could be known only through the revealed ideas received in the intuitive intelligence or *Vernunft*. Together with Schelling and Jacobi, Drey considered *Vernunft* a faculty which must first intuit ideas through an act of receptive faith before it could clarify them sufficiently through reflection to acquire certain scientific knowledge *(Wissenschaft)* of their necessary intelligibility. Like the traditionalists Drey believed that only contact with another spiritual reality could move *Vernunft* to the act of intuitive faith that led to the process of scientific reflection. Again, like the traditionalists, Drey believed that the ideas of primitive revelation must be communicated to the individual *Vernunft* through the written and spoken words of historical and communitarian tradition.

Therefore Drey's apologetics and his dogmatic theology were both scientific reflections on living tradition and the communities which were its bearers. Apologetics, through its scientific reflection upon the ideas contained in divine revelation, demonstrated that only the Catholic Church could be the bearer of that revelation in its authentic form. Only Catholic tradition was free from aberrant development of the intelligible virtualities of the idea of the Kingdom of God. Dogmatic theology disclosed the necessary dialectic of negation which is the intelligible law directing the historical evolution of Catholic tradition. Its philosophical reconstruction of that history as the intelligible self-expression of the idea of the Kingdom of God enabled the theologian to determine with apodictic certitude why historical revelation possesses the intelligible structure that it does and why its historical development necessarily followed the course that it took. Faith was transformed to reason, and history manifested its scientific system in Drey's philosophy of revelation.

The distinctiveness of Drey's theology was due to its exploitation of Schelling's idealism.[48] Drey's metaphysics of an intelligible system of ideas informed by a unifying architectonic idea was taken over from Schelling. The metaphysics of the idea's intelligible self-development through a dialectical process of negation was borrowed from Schelling too. Without Schelling's metaphysics Drey's dialectical development of living tradition within the community of the Church would be deprived of its intelligible necessity and his reflective reconstruction of historical revelation would not possess the apodictic evidence which grounds its scientific certitude.

There were problems with Drey's theology of course. The principal problems concerned the relation of faith to reason. Was the primitive revelation an act of natural knowledge? If so, on what basis could its later development through positive revelation be supernatural? Were not all these revelations intelligible developments of the one architectonic idea of the Kingdom of God? On the other hand, if the act of primitive revelation was a supernatural act, did that not mean that human intelligence could have no natural knowledge of God? Another serious difficulty raised against Drey's theology was its lack of clarity concerning the relation of grace to nature.[49] Scientific reflection on ideas received through faith occurred when *Vernunft* directed its attention to them. Reflective use of *Vernunft* always required man's use of freedom. But was that free response within the power of unaided nature? If it was, was the free response to Christian revelation a natural assent? And, in that event, had not Drey fallen back into Hermes' semirationalism? Yet, if the free assent to God's primitive revelation was not within the power of unaided nature, was not then all human knowledge a work of grace? These were the difficulties which the scholastic theologians raised against Drey's post-Kantian traditionalist theology from the viewpoint of their own Aristotelian metaphysics of grace and nature. Despite these difficulties— which, given Drey's metaphysics of the idea of the Kingdom of God, are far from being unanswerable—Drey's theological method proved to be a brilliant invention that showed its fruitfulness in the theology of the Catholic Tübingen School and whose possibilities for Catholic theology are far from exhausted. In the latter half of the nineteenth century, however, the leading German neo-Thomist, Joseph Kleutgen, would launch a full-scale attack on Drey's theological method in his critique of the moral theology of Drey's disciple, Johann Baptist Hirscher.

RENASCENT SCHOLASTICISM

Drey's programmatic article "Revision des gegenwärtigen Zustandes der Theologie" was published in 1812. In 1814 the Society of Jesus was restored to the universal Church. The Catholic faculty of theology moved from Ellwangen to Tübingen in 1817. Georg Hermes was appointed professor of dogmatic theology at Bonn in 1819. In 1824 Gregory XVI restored the Roman College to the Society of Jesus and Father Luigi Taparelli d'Azeglio was appointed rector.[50] Giovanni Perrone of the Roman College had been a member of the Roman committee which, after their detailed examination, had recommended the condemnation of Hermes' works.[51] When Hermes' disciples Braun and Elvenich came to Rome to protest his condemnation in 1837, the papal secretary of state, Cardinal Lambruschini, referred them to Johann Philip Roothan, the general of the Society of Jesus. This learned Jesuit, the cardinal informed the infuriated Germans, could explain to them in their own language the theological reasons that had led to their master's condemnation[52] in 1835. Louis Bautain arrived in Rome shortly after the visit of Braun and Elvenich. His docile and courteous approach made an excellent impression on the Roman officials and theologians whom he had come to see, and the contrast between his piety and courtesy and the stormy language and aggressive behavior of the Germans became a topic of Roman conversation. Moreover, Bautain found it advisable to attend the lectures of Father Perrone and to consult with him so that he could correct the deficiencies in his own theology.[53]

By the mid-1830s then the Jesuit theologians of the Roman College had become a power in the Church. The Gregorian University of the Roman College was a pontifical university. Its theologians had already acquired the influential positions in the Roman congregations which they would occupy for the rest of the century. These were the congregations to which complaints about unorthodox teaching were referred for pontifical determination. Perrone had played an important role in Rome's official reaction to the complaints concerning both Bautain's traditionalism and Hermes' rationalism. His approach had been to steer a middle course between the two opposed positions. As Rome's reaction to Bautain and Hermes showed, Perrone was unwilling either to deny natural reason's ability to establish the existence of God and the credibility of revelation by means of discursive arguments (the traditionalist position), or, to admit that natural reason could make the supernatural assent to faith through a judgment of Kantian practical reason (Hermes' position). As far as apologetics went, Perrone believed that the scholastic position concerning both the ability of natural reason to acquire certain knowledge about the revealing God and the limits of that ability should be upheld. Otherwise the distinctions between faith and reason and grace and nature might be dangerously blurred.[54]

Taparelli was no longer at the Roman College when Hermes' disciples and Bautain had their interviews with Roothan and Perrone. Taparelli had relinquished his rectorship in 1829 to become provincial of the Jesuit province of Naples. In 1833 he was removed from this position by a visitor sent to Naples by the Jesuit general. The main reason for Taparelli's removal was the turbulence created in the Neapolitan scholasticate by the vigorous campaign to introduce neo-Thomism there. Taparelli had been the initiator of that campaign and he had to take the consequences of the hostile reaction which it had provoked.[55] Perrone and Taparelli are two significant names, both of which appear in the early history of the Roman College. Both were scholastics in their own fashion. Perrone was a scholastic by tradition, but, like the eighteenth-century scholastics, he no longer looked upon scholasticism as a tightly organized, intrinsically articulated theological system structured by one coherent philosophy of knowledge, man, and being. Taparelli, on the other hand, was a neo-Thomist who believed that scholasticism was an articulated system. Perrone and Taparelli were two very different types of scholastic. Both were founders of schools, and the struggle between these schools would determine the course of Catholic theology for over a century.

Perrone was essentially a positive theologian with little interest in scholastic speculation. Although he played a part in Hermes' condemnation, he had no prejudice against German theology as such. In fact he publicly praised Möhler's *Symbolik* in an address before the Academy of the Catholic Religion in 1837.[56] Perrone's two great disciples and future colleagues Carlo Passaglia, S.J., and Johannes Baptist Franzelin, S.J., who later became a cardinal, were also positive theologians.[57] Passaglia was familiar with St. Thomas but he was an eclectic rather than a scholastic in his personal philosophy. In his speculative reflection he was drawn chiefly to the post-Tridentine theologians Petau and Thomassin and, through them, to the Greek Fathers. Passaglia, like Perrone, admired Möhler, who strongly influenced his own ecclesiology. His interest in German theology was even greater than his mentor Perrone's, and his interest was sympathetic.[58] Franzelin too was essentially a positive theologian with a profound knowledge of oriental languages. As a Tyrolese, he was a German by race and culture. Franzelin too showed a sympathetic interest in German theology and used the works of Drey, Denziger, Hergenröther, and Döllinger in the formation of his own theology.[59] Neither Passaglia nor Franzelin could be called scholastic theologians in the neo-Thomistic sense. Indeed, one could say that, if the term is taken in the sense in which the promoters of the Thomistic revival understood it, the first scholastic theologian at the Roman College was Louis Billot, S.J., the future cardinal. But Billot was not appointed to the faculty of the Gregorian University until 1885, six years after the publication of *Aeterni Patris*.[60]

The theologians of the Roman College were eclectic in their scholasticism. They often wrote in Latin and they used the scholastic style of expression in their writings. They were papalists in their ecclesiology, and the German College, whose students attended the classes at the Gregorian, was the pope's counterweight to the influence of the German governments upon the education of the Catholic clergy through the faculties of the German universities. The distinction between Roman and German theology was a real one, and the rivalry between the German College and the German university faculties of theology was an important fact of life in ecclesiastical politics. Nevertheless, the theologians of the Roman College had no interest in creating a unified speculative system of theology to rival the German speculative systems. Their own conception of the relationship between positive and speculative theology was quite unclear and their own interest in scholastic speculation was moderate, to say the least. Their colleagues on the faculty of philosophy at the Roman College were actively hostile to scholasticism, which they dismissed as an outmoded form of thought. The Roman College never shared the vision that inspired Taparelli and the initiators of the neo-Thomistic movement. On the contrary, from the inception of the movement until its resistance was crushed by Leo XIII after *Aeterni Patris*, the attitude which the faculty of the Roman College adopted to the Thomistic revival was an attitude of frank hostility.[61]

The impetus for the neo-Thomistic movement came from Taparelli and another Italian Jesuit, Serafino Sordi, neither of whom was in favor at Rome in the 1830s. Serafino Sordi had been a fellow novice with Taparelli in 1816.[62] He was already an ardent Thomist and his vision of Thomism as an integrated system of philosophy and theology converted Taparelli to Thomism. A few years later when Taparelli became rector of the Roman College he was distressed by the lack of coherence and order in its teaching of philosophy. The discontent among the students of philosophy confirmed his conviction that philosophical education was ineffective unless a single coherent system was presented to the students. Since the philosophy of St. Thomas was the only philosophy which could structure a sound system of philosophy and theology, the philosophy of St. Thomas should form the basis of the philosophical instruction offered at the Roman College. Taparelli endeavored to secure the appointment of Sordi to the faculty to help him accomplish this purpose but the resistance of the philosophical faculty to the appointment of a Thomist was so vehement that the appointment could not be made.[63] Taparelli, however, made two converts among his students, each of whom would play a crucial role in the history of neo-Thomism. The first was the young Jesuit scholastic Carlo Maria Curci, the future founder of *Civiltà Cattolica*,[64] the other was the young seminarian Gioacchino Pecci, who later became cardinal archbishop of Perugia and who, as Leo XIII, committed the Church to neo-Thomism as the one recommended system of ecclesiastical education.[65]

The province of Naples had its own scholasticate and when Taparelli became provincial in 1829 he renewed his attempt to make Thomism the core of a coherent systematic philosophical education. To help him achieve this purpose he secured the appointment of Father Domenico Sordi to the faculty of his scholasticate. Domenico, like his brother Serafino, had studied at the Vincentian Collegio Alberoni, the Thomistic center at Piacenza, and, like his brother, he was an ardent Thomist.

Domenico unfortunately lacked his brother's discretion and political ability. His belligerence and indiscretion raised a storm in the scholasticate. By 1833 he had been dismissed, Taparelli had been removed from office, and the short-lived neo-Thomistic movement at the Neapolitan scholasticate had been brought to a halt.[66]

Nevertheless, Taparelli had set forces in motion that would lead to unexpected consequences within three decades. Curci, who had come with him to Naples, had become a convinced convert to Serafino Sordi's vision of Thomism as a unitary system of philosophy and theology. Young Matteo Liberatore was a student at the scholasticate at Naples. And, although he would not become a Thomist for many years, he was a friend of both Taparelli and Curci.[67] Naples was more friendly to Thomism than Rome had been. A Thomistic tradition still existed among the Neapolitan Dominicans. The famous eighteenth-century Thomist Salvatore Roselli, O.P., had been a Neapolitan and his six-volume *Summa philosophiae ad mentem Angelici Doctoris Thomae Aquinatis* (1777–1783) was used with great success in Spain and Naples.[68] In 1840 Gaetano Sansaverino founded the review *La Biblioteca Cattolica* at Naples. He founded a second review the following year, called *La Scienza e la Fede*, which in many respects became a model for *Civiltà Cattolica*. In 1846 Sansaverino founded the first academy of Thomistic philosophy in Italy.[69] During the period in which his brother was creating turmoil in the scholasticate at Naples, Serafino Sordi was professor of philosophy at the Jesuit college at Modena. Among the Jesuits there was the young Giuseppe Pecci, the brother of the future Leo XIII. Sordi converted Pecci to his vision of a unified Thomistic system as effectively as Taparelli had converted his brother Gioacchino.[70]

After 1850 this scattered series of events led to completely unexpected consequences. Gioacchino Pecci had become bishop of Perugia. He removed the eclectic professors of philosophy from his diocesan seminary and replaced them with Dominicans, one of whom was Tommaso Zigliara, the future cardinal, whom Pecci himself ordained to the priesthood. Zigliara was to become one of Leo XIII's great collaborators in the restoration of Thomism during his pontificate. In 1851 Giuseppe Pecci left the Society of Jesus and went to teach at the seminary at Perugia. The two Pecci brothers then collaborated to make Perugia an active center of the Thomistic revival.[71] By 1852 Serafino Sordi was provincial of Rome and Curci, Taparelli, and Liberatore were collaborating in the editing of the new Jesuit review *Civiltà Cattolica*. Liberatore was a friend of San-

saverino and Joseph Kleutgen, who had been appointed to the faculty of
the Roman College in 1843 and was appointed consultor to the Congregation of the Index in 1851. Kleutgen was in friendly contact with the team
on *Civiltà Cattolica.* The scattered centers of neo-Thomism were all in
contact with each other.[72]

By 1850 the intellectual force of the Romantic movement had been
spent and the influence of German idealism was on the wane. The revolutions of 1848 had turned Pius IX against modern movements in social and
religious thought. The climate was favorable for an aggressive attack on
modern philosophy and upon the theological systems structured by it.
Kleutgen and the team on *Civiltà Cattolica* would soon be ready to launch
it. In the early 1850s the politically conservative officials of the Roman
curia and the promoters of the neo-Thomist movement were troubled by
the success of two philosophical and theological movements which had
emerged from the post-Kantian approach to philosophy and theology
inaugurated by moderate traditionalism. The first of these was ontologism which, in the systems of Rosmini and Gioberti, had assumed the
ascendancy in Italian Catholic thought. The second was the metaphysical
dualism of Anton Günther. Matteo Liberatore would be the great adversary of the ontologists among the Jesuit neo-Thomists. Kleutgen would
be Günther's great opponent. Kleutgen's attack, however, would not be
restricted to Günther's theology alone. It would be extended to the post-
Kantian traditionalism of the Tübingen theologians and to Hermes'
semirationalism as well. Modern neo-Thomism would be invented in the
debate between Thomism on the one hand and ontologism and German
theology on the other which the Jesuit neo-Thomists began in 1853.
Liberatore and Kleutgen would structure the constellation of theses in
epistemology, anthropology, and metaphysics that form the core of the
modern neo-Thomistic synthesis. Kleutgen would define and attempt to
vindicate the Aristotelian scholastic method in theology through its application to apologetics, and positive, speculative, and moral theology.
The philosophical and theological method of the Jesuit neo-scholastics
cannot be properly appreciated until it is seen in contrast with the contemporary methods to which it was proposed as an alternative. The most
interesting of these methods is perhaps the metaphysical dualism of
Anton Günther. Unlike the theology of the Catholic Tübingen School,
Günther's theological method may no longer be a live option in Catholic
theology. Nevertheless its similarity to contemporary scholastic systems,
like the system of Karl Rahner, for example, which are very live options

indeed, is startling. Understanding Günther, we can understand why Kleutgen's scholastic theological method took the form which it did and we can also understand—and regret—the rich possibilities for development which Kleutgen's hostility to post-Kantian method in Günther's dualism and in Tübingen theology excluded. In our next chapter then we will turn our attention to the philosophical and theological method of Anton Günther.

4

ANTON GÜNTHER'S DUALISM

Anton Günther was born on 17 November 1783 in Lindenau in northern Bohemia. The home life of a poor but extremely pious family created in him the profound personal piety which remained one of his striking characteristics until his death. While still quite young Günther decided that he had a vocation to the priesthood. The rationalistic atmosphere of the University of Prague, however, provoked troubling doubts about the faith in the mind of the young student. These doubts became so intense that in 1806 he abandoned the thought of ordination and devoted himself to the study of law. He pursued the study of law at the University of Prague for the next three years and, during that time, acquired a solid understanding of Kant, Fichte, and Schelling. In 1810 Günther accepted a position as tutor in the home of Prince von Bretzenheim. This was the first of a series of tutoring positions through which Günther supported himself during the next decade. The contact with the upper levels of the Austrian nobility which these positions gave him was to prove useful in later years. One of his former students, Friedrich Cardinal Prince von Swartzenberg, proved to be one of his most loyal and influential defenders in the difficult period which culminated with the condemnation of his teaching in 1857.[1]

Vienna became Günther's home for the rest of his life, and it was to be the scene of his whole scholarly activity. In the capital of the Austrian Empire the young scholar made the acquaintance of Adam Müller, from whom he learned the distinction between the concept and the idea which later became the key element of his own system of dualistic metaphysics.[2] He was also accepted into the brilliant circle of Catholic intellectuals which had gathered around St. Clement Mary Hofbauer. Their influence overcame his intellectual difficulties and rekindled his early desire to devote his life to the service of the Church. Finally, eleven years after his arrival in Vienna, Günther was ordained to the priesthood at the age of thirty-seven.

After his ordination Günther felt called to the religious life. He first considered entering the Redemptorists but changed his mind and entered the Society of Jesus instead. After a year in the Jesuit novitiate, however, both he and his Jesuit superiors came to an amicable agreement that his vocation was to work alone. He spent the remainder of his life as a private scholar in Vienna. Although the University of Munich and the University of Bonn invited him to accept professorships, Günther declined the invitations. Quite possibly he might have accepted a professorship at the University of Vienna but Vienna never made the offer. Günther remained an intellectual free lance, supporting himself by his writings and by his modest salary as a censor of books for the Austrian government.

Nevertheless, Günther's private status did not lead to obscurity. His publications made him a dominant figure in mid-century German Catholic theology. His disciples held professorships in Vienna, Bonn, Breslau, Bamberg, Augsburg, Trier, and Tübingen. Among his patrons and protectors were two influential German-speaking cardinals, his former student Friedrich Cardinal von Swartzenberg, archbishop of Salzburg and later of Prague, and Melchior Cardinal Diepenbrock, archbishop of Breslau. His opponents, however, were also influential and they included not only the conservative archbishop of Cologne, Johann Cardinal Geissel, but also Joseph Kleutgen, who was consultor to the Congregation of the Index at the very time when Günther's books were delated to Rome. The complaints of Günther's critics finally brought about Günther's condemnation and his books were placed on the Roman Index in 1857. Günther accepted the condemnation, which meant the destruction of his life's work, in a spirit of faith but with profound inner anguish. He died piously, as he had lived, on 24 February 1863.[3]

A Post-Kantian Philosophy of Religion

Günther was a prolific writer. His first major work, *Vorschule zur spekulativen Theologie des positiven Christentums* (Propaedeutic to the Speculative Theology of Positive Christianity) (1829) was a two-volume exposition of his general system. His other major works were *Peregrins Gastmahl* (Peregrine's Banquet) (1830), *Süd- und Nordlichter am Horizonte spekulativer Theologie* (Southern and Northern Lights on the Horizon of Speculative

Theology) (1834), *Der letze Symboliker* (The Last Symbolic Thinker) (1834), *Janusköpfe für Philosophie und Theologie* (Janusheads for Philosophy and Theology) (1834), *Thomas a Scrupulis* (1835), *Die Juste-Milieus in der deutschen Philosophie gegenwärtiger Zeit* (The Golden Mean in Contemporary German Philosophy) (1838), *Eurystheus und Herakles: Metalogische Kritiken und Meditationen* (Euristheus and Heracles: Metalogical Critical Reflections) (1843), and *Lentigos und Peregrins Gastmahl* (Lentigo's and Peregrine's Banquet) (1857). From 1849 to 1854 Günther edited the philosophical journal *Lydia*, in which a number of his important articles appeared.[4] In addition to these major works Günther published a long series of critical reviews, which were often extended essays, during the course of his whole career. The modern reader feels rather overwhelmed at the bulk of Günther's extensive *corpus*. More intimidating, however, is the challenge of its unattractive style. Günther had a penchant for the philosophical dialogue, a literary genre which had become outmoded even in his own day, and there is a sharpness of tone in his critical writing which the modern reader finds unpleasant. These difficulties, and the comparative inaccessibility of Günther's works partly explain the neglect into which his theology had fallen until the recent critical studies of Wenzel, Pritz, and Beck[5] rekindled interest in Günther's dualism, by calling attention to the analogies between Günther's systematic theology and some contemporary speculative systems, in particular that of Karl Rahner.[6]

Like Hermes and the Tübingen theologians, Günther was preoccupied with the problem of faith and reason. Like them he considered the problem essentially a problem of harmonizing historical Christian revelation and the demands of necessary scientific knowledge or *Wissenschaft*. When understood in these terms, the problem of faith and reason became the philosophical problem of harmonizing *Glaube* (faith) with *Wissen*, the necessary and apodictically certain knowledge demanded by Kantian and post-Kantian philosophy. Faith was a presupposition for the mind's reception of historical revelation *(Offenbarung)*. Science, or *Wissenschaft*, was the necessary scientific knowledge acquired by active reflection upon the revelation received through faith. If *Glaube* were to become the object of *Wissen*, positive revelation would have to be transformed into necessary, systematic knowledge by the process of active intellectual reflection. The active reflection which led to necessary, systematic knowledge was philosophy. If then *Glaube* were to be transformed into *Wissen*, Catholic theology would have to become a philosophy of revelation.[7]

Günther's conception of the Catholic theologian's task is strikingly similar to Drey's understanding of the role of the dogmatic theologian. This was because both Günther and Drey were working in the context of post-Kantian idealism in which the passage from faith to knowledge was achieved through the passive and active functions of *Vernunft*. Faith, passive intuitive reception, provided the intelligible object for the active reflection which led to knowledge, and, since *Vernunft* was endowed with freedom, both of its functions, the passive and the active, were intrinsically influenced in their operation by *Vernunft*'s free response to the intelligible reality that confronted it in its act of intuition. In Günther's epistemology, moreover, *Verstand*, or discursive reasoning, was restricted to the world of phenomenal appearance whose data were subsumed under its universalizing categories. Only *Vernunft*, intuitive intelligence, had access to the world of metaphysical reality. God's existence could not be established nor could his attributes be known through the discursive argumentation of *Verstand*. If then there was to be a philosophy of revelation, that philosophy could only operate on the level of *Vernunft*.[8]

Günther therefore rejected scholastic theology because its philosophical armature was Aristotelian epistemology and metaphysics. Aristotle's philosophy was a philosophy of the discursive *Verstand*. Consequently Aristotle could not provide the philosophy of revelation which was required to solve the problem of faith and reason.[9] Yet this problem was the most urgent problem which the Church faced in modern Europe. Theologians could not ignore it. The educated classes of modern Europe had been trained to unify their intellectual and cultural experience by means of philosophy. Modern culture, the achievement of the modern universities, was the outcome of that unification. A scholastic theology, built upon Aristotle's epistemology of the discursive reason or *Verstand*, could never unify the experience of an educated believer through a sound and adequate philosophy of revelation. Hegel's attempt to integrate Christian revelation and post-Kantian philosophical reason had ended in pantheism. Nature and spirit, thought and reality were identified in Hegel's impersonal Absolute Idea. A post-Kantian philosophy of revelation then could easily lead to pantheism. Nevertheless post-Kantian philosophy did not lead to pantheism because pantheism was the necessary consequence of its discursive logic whereas Aristotelian epistemology and metaphysics did so for that very reason. Hegel's philosophy had ended in pantheism not because of an intrinsic flaw in the very nature of post-Kantian epistemology and metaphysics but because Hegel had identified the idea with the concept in his speculative system.[10] Hegel's error could be exposed and corrected in an epistemologically coherent post-Kantian philosophy of revelation.

The major threat to Christian faith among educated Germans was pantheism. Pantheism had replaced the personal God of historical revelation with its impersonal Absolute Idea. The greatest proponent of modern pantheism was Hegel and the most urgent task which confronted Catholic philosophers and theologians in Germany was to expose and correct the errors of his system.[11] To Günther Hegel was the enemy *par excellence,* and it was against Hegel that the main thrust of his system was directed. The roots of Hegel's pantheism, Günther was convinced, lay in his metaphysics of knowledge. Hegel's Absolute Idea was really a speculative concept or *Begriff.* Subject and object were ultimately united in its impersonal intelligibility. The personal God ceased to be the supreme reality in Hegel's intelligible universe, and nature and spirit were identified in Hegel's Absolute *Begriff.* Hegel's intelligible system of nature and spirit was a dialectical pantheism in which the impersonal Absolute first identified itself with the *cosmos* by emanation and the *cosmos* in return identified itself with the Absolute through the dialectical ascent of nature to spirit and the dialectical ascent of spirit to the Absolute Idea.

This pantheism was inevitable, Günther believed, because no philosophy whose model of the supremely real being was a conceptual idea or *Begriff* could avoid monism. Since the supreme idea or *Begriff* was an impersonal Absolute, in which all thought and reality were identified, the Absolute's metaphysical communication of its reality to the finite world must take the form of a necessary emanation. This was the case whether Hegel's Absolute Idea identified itself with the finite world of nature and spirit through its dialectical self-expression in them, or whether Plato's Idea of the Good communicated its reality to the ideal world, which in turn communicated its ideal reality to the world of sense through "participation."[12] The ineluctable pantheism of the *Begriff-Idee* infected the philosophy of Plato and Aristotle as thoroughly as it infected Hegel's dialectical pantheism. And, since scholasticism was fundamentally an Aristotelianism, scholasticism too was incurably pantheistic. Only the personal piety and the philosophical naiveté of the scholastic doctors had saved them from explicitly professing the pantheism which was the theological consequence of their Aristotelian epistemology and metaphysics.[13]

Descartes' philosophy, however, provided the means through which the danger of pantheism could be overcome.[14] In his *cogito ergo sum* Descartes made a number of vitally important discoveries. His first discovery was epistemological. Absolute certainty was found in the human knower's intellectual intuition of his own spirit or *Geist. Cogito ergo sum.* Therefore the starting point from which certain and necessary knowledge must be derived was the self-awareness of the human spirit. Human self-awareness was the source from which *Vernunft* could acquire its intellectual intuition of noumenal reality, not the physical world of sensible appearance subsumed under the categories of *Verstand.* Descartes' second discovery was metaphysical. He was a *res cogitans.* He was a human spirit, and spirit was essentially different from matter. Consequently the self-conscious spirit was not and *could not be* either a product or a conscious expression of the physical world objectivized by *Verstand.* Descartes' third significant discovery brought him into the realm of philosophical theology. He was a doubting spirit. Therefore he was a limited, restricted, and imperfect spirit. But a spirit's awareness that it was imperfect contained implicitly the simultaneous awareness of the Absolutely Perfect Being. For limited perfection can be known only in terms of its necessary correlate, Absolute Perfection. Negations are intelligible only in terms of the perfections which they negate. Therefore the starting point of philosophy was not simply the finite spirit's self-awareness. The starting point of philosophy was the limited spirit's self-awareness together with its concomitant awareness of the Infinite Being which it could never be.[15]

THE EGO-IDEA

These fundamental Cartesian intuitions cut the ground from under monistic pantheism. No finite spirit could possibly be the product or the conscious expression of nature. Yet in Hegel's pantheistic idealism the finite spirit was asserted to be a conscious expression of nature, and, through the dialectical ascent of the finite spirit, the finite universe of nature and spirit identified itself with the Absolute Idea. Descartes' fundamental intuition, however, made it evident that the Absolutely Perfect Being was an essentially different reality with which the finite spirit was not and could never be identified. Metaphysical dualism, not metaphysical monism, expressed the fundamental structure of reality. Dualism was the fundamental law of being which the finite spirit intuited with apodictic certainty through its own self-awareness.

Descartes' fundamental intuitions had more profound consequences for philosophical method than Descartes himself had realized. The reflecting subject who intuitively grasps his own intelligible reality is not an object or "thing," even though Descartes had spoken of himself as a *res cogitans*. The reflecting subject is an *Ich* or Ego and, when the *Vernunft*, through an act of active reflection, thematizes the data of its own self-awareness, it thematizes it in an *Ich-Idee*, or Ego-Idea. The human knower's most fundamental idea therefore is not an impersonal Hegelian *Begriff*. The Ego whose reality is thematized in the Ego-Idea is a person. The Ego not only receives the intelligibility of his own reality and of other beings through its act of passive intuition; the Ego thematizes this received intelligibility through its active reflection upon it. Both passive reception and active reflection, however, demand the cooperation of human freedom through the whole course of their operation. The knowing Ego therefore is a free self.[16]

Therefore to say that human knowledge begins with the *cogito* is equivalent to saying that knowledge begins with an act of *self*-awareness. All other metaphysical reality is grasped in and through the human Ego's awareness of its own self. All apodictic certitude is grounded in the human Ego's intuitive certainty of its own existence as a free self. A free self cannot be thematized as a non-self. Therefore the thematization of the Ego can never be made through the Hegelian *Begriff*, in which self and non-self, subject and object are identified. The Idea through which the fundamental intuition of the *cogito* is thematized is an *Ich-Idee*, an *Ego-Idea*. The *Ich-Idee* is the reflexive thematization of the self, and, since all reality is grasped in and through the self, all the other ideas appear reflectively in and through the thematization of the *Ich-Idee*.[17] But, since the self can never be "sublated" into an impersonal Hegelian *Begriff*, the fundamental presupposition of Hegelian pantheism is proven to be false.[18] Even though Descartes spoke of himself as a *res cogitans*, the intuitive content of the *cogito* gives us apodictic certitude that the self is not a "thing" or an objective impersonal idea. The self is a subject, a spirit or *Geist*. The apodictically certain thematization of the *cogito* through the *Ich-Idee* therefore is the starting point of metaphysics.[19]

THE METAPHYSICS OF CONTRAPOSITIONAL DUALISM

The Ego-Idea, through which *Vernunft* thematizes the self's intuitively grasped intelligibility as a free subject, contains within itself the Ego's essential relation to the Non-Ego, the *Nicht-Ich*. Therefore the human subject does not embrace all reality; it is a limited, restricted spirit. Moreover the subject, whose intelligibility is grasped intuitively through self-awareness, is related to its world of objective thought, the phenomenal physical world structured by the categories of the *Verstand*. The Ego, as subject, is essentially related to the phenomenal world of nature as its Non-Ego, the world with which it must deal but which it itself is not. Therefore the noumenal intuitive spirit, or *Geist*, knows its world of physical objects only through its dynamic relationship of opposition to its metaphysical contradictory, the Non-Spirit, the non-self. Furthermore, in the same intuitive awareness of its limitation, the Ego becomes aware of the cognitional correlate of limitation, Unlimited Reality. Since the fundamental experience of the *cogito* gives the Ego apodictic certitude that its own reality is not only essentially different from the impersonal world of nature but essentially higher, the Ego is simultaneously aware that Unlimited Reality cannot belong to the lower impersonal world of nature. Unlimited Reality must also be a spirit or *Geist*. Thus in the *cogito* the limited Ego discovers that it is related to a spiritual Non-Ego, the Infinite Person whom it can never be; and this awareness too is thematized in the Ego-Idea.[20]

Thus the essential relational structure of the universe thematized in the Ego-Idea is a relationship of opposition between unlikes, between the infinite and finite spirit, between the intuitive self-consciousness *(Selbst-Bewusstsein)* of the noumenal spirit or *Geist* and the phenomenal object-oriented consciousness *(Bewusstsein)* of the *Verstand*, between the world of spirit and the world of nature. These diverse realms of reality are *contraposed* to each other.[21] They manifest themselves as contradictories whose irreducible opposition to each other can never be overcome through Hegel's dialectical process of sublation *(Aufhebung)*. The ideal system of the noumenal universe is therefore a system of contrapositional dualism, i.e., of irreducible opposition between contradictory principles. In this ideal system both finite spirits and the Infinite Spirit must always retain their personal existence.[22] They can never be sublated into the impersonal intelligibility of Hegel's Absolute *Begriff*. The intelligibility of personal self-manifestation through an historical act of positive revelation can never be sublated into the impersonal conceptual world of Hegel's system of logic. A philosophy of revelation must always preserve the personal uniqueness of the revealer and the historical and personal uniqueness of his act of revelation.

Günther's Metaphysical System

On the basis of his contrapositional dualism Günther worked out his theory of knowledge and his metaphysics of man and nature. In Günther's post-Kantian philosophy *Vernunft* was the faculty which intuitively grasped the world of noumenal reality. Thus it was *Vernunft* which intuitively grasped the absolutely unconditioned ground, the noumenal first principle, on which the intelligibility of both the noumenal and phenomenal worlds depended. *Vernunft* then was the faculty through which the necessary principles of identity and sufficient reason were intuitively grounded. Identity and sufficient reason were the principles on which the necessary scientific knowledge *(Wissenschaft)* of philosophy depended.[23] *Vernunft*'s intuitive grasp of these principles occurred through the finite spirit's intuition of its own intelligibility in the fundamental act of self-consciousness or self-awareness. The Ego's grasp of its own noumenal reality, in the apodictic certitude of the *cogito*, grounded the principle of identity. *Cogito ergo sum.* The Ego's grasp of its own self as a limited and conditioned identity of thought and being grounded the principle of sufficient reason. No limited, conditioned intelligibility could be the necessary, unconditioned ground of universal intelligibility. Only the Infinite Reality, which manifested itself to the limited Ego as its unlimited Non-Ego, could be the absolutely unconditioned ground of universal intelligibility. Self-consciousness therefore provided the apodictically certain proof of God's existence.[24]

The same proof established that God was the creator of the finite universe. Since God was the Infinitely Other, he could not identify himself with the world through a pantheistic process of emanation. God was infinite intelligibility and infinite self-consciousness. But awareness of unlimited consciousness necessarily entailed consciousness of its cognitive correlates, non-conscious being and limited conscious being. Therefore God's self-awareness required that God possess in his own intellect the idea of a finite universe whose possible constituents must be the conscious and unconscious realities of the natural world and the limited intelligences of the spiritual world. Furthermore the idea of a possible universe which exists in the mind of the infinite necessary being must be the idea of a universe of which God himself must be the ground. And, since the Infinitely Other cannot ground the universe by pantheistic emanation, he can only do so by producing the world from nothing through an act of free creation. God then by necessity is the possible free creator of a finite universe of spirit and nature. Actuation of that possibility, on the other hand, is not a metaphysical necessity. God's actual creation of the world, which did not have to happen, must occur through an act of divine freedom.[25]

The created spirit's response to God, his free creator, must also be made through an act of freedom. *Vernunft* was not just an intellect which responded to intelligible truth; it was also a freedom which responded to intelligible good. Consequently Günther could argue that the response to God demanded by the human spirit's reflection upon the Ego-Idea (in which the intelligible structure of the dualistic universe was contained) must be a moral and religious one. *Vernunft's* response to the intelligible universe contained in the Ego-Idea was a free response to the world of values and to that world's personal ground. Human freedom had a profound influence upon man's ability to grow in his understanding of the intelligible system of the universe.[26]

Although the Cartesian distinction between the mind as *res cogitans* and matter as *res extensa* grounded Günther's dualistic metaphysics of spirit and nature, Günther totally rejected Descartes' mechanistic physics. Post-Kantian idealism and the Romantic organic conception of nature caused Günther to consider the interrelated universe of nature as a living being. Günther's world of nature was a cosmic animal, animated by its own world soul, the *Naturseele*. Like the neo-Platonic World Soul, Günther's *Naturseele* emanated the individual souls, or animating principles of singular composites, into the world of nature. The world of nature was not a homogeneous mass of disparate lifeless atoms. It was a vital organic universe, whose individual beings were divided into different genera and species by their specifically different animating principles. Furthermore, again in accordance with the metaphysics of post-Kantian idealism, the organic world of nature was an evolving one. Life was impelled by the natural appetite imparted to it by the world soul to ascend through the hierachically ordered stages of its embodiment until it reached the level of consciousness. Then sensation ascended to the level of imagination. Imagination in its turn ascended to the level of *Verstand. Verstand* was the highest form of natural life. The genera and species of its categorical concepts were the conscious self-expression of the genera and species incarnate in the living world of nature.[27] *Verstand,* however, could never move up to the level of *Vernunft.* For while *Verstand* belonged to the world of nature, *Vernunft* belonged to the world of spirit. *Vernunft* possessed intuitive knowledge of the intelligibly real. Discursive *Verstand* was restricted to structured objective knowledge of phenomena. It could never attain to certain knowledge of the phenemenal world's noumenal ground.[28]

Man, however, possessed both the noumenal knowledge of *Vernunft* and the phenomenal knowledge of *Verstand*, imagination and sensation. Man belonged to the world of spirit and to the world of nature.[29] As a composite of spirit, soul and body, man was the dynamic union of two essentially opposed principles. He was made up of a spiritual ego and a living, knowing corporeal composite animated by its own natural soul. Since nature could never produce spirit, man's spiritual ego was directly created by God. His natural soul, on the other hand, was produced through emanation by the world soul. As a living union of spirit and nature, man was the center and compendium of the universe. Held in being by the mysterious interaction—the "marital union"—of spirit and animated body, man was essentially a mystery. He was, to use Günther's own phrase, "the world sphinx." As a member of a natural species man was an individual. As a free, self-conscious spirit, man was a person. The Infinite Spirit was the unitary ground of the spiritual and natural universe. The human spirit, which joined itself to the world of nature through its "marital union" with its animated body, was God's contrapositional "image" *(Gegenbild)*, in and through whom the whole universe opposed itself to the God with whom it could never be identified.[30] In man the universe of nature and spirit consciously realized its relationship to God. This relationship could never be expressed through the discursive logic of Aristotle. Aristotle's logic was a logic of the *Verstand*. As such, it was applicable only to the categories of phenomenal appearance. The relationship between nature and spirit, finite spirit and God was expressed through a metalogic of the *Vernunft*, whose epistemological foundation was the Ego's insight into the fundamental relations of the universe intuited in its primordial act of self-awareness and thematized in the Ego-Idea.[31]

GÜNTHER'S DOGMATIC THEOLOGY: THE FIRST AND THE SECOND ADAM

Günther's metaphysics of man and nature enabled him to construct a dogmatic theology in which a number of familiar traditionalist theses received a systematic metaphysical justification.[32] Christian revelation was an historical reality which the believer encountered in the Church and received through faith. Theology was a reflective understanding of the intelligibility contained in that revelation. Theology was no more a substitute for faith than *Vernunft*'s active reflection was a substitute for its passive reception of the intelligible object of reflection through its intuitive act of philosophical "faith." Revelation came from God in several stages. It was communicated to our first parents through an act of primitive revelation, augmented in Old Testament revelation and brought to its ultimate and perfect form in the revelation made by God to Christ and through Christ to his Church. Revelation was transmitted to individual intelligences through society. The Catholic Church was the society which was the bearer of God's definitive revelation. The individual believer must first receive God's revelation from Christ's community, the Church, before he can undertake his active reflection upon it as a theologian.[33]

These theses, which Günther held in common with Bautain and the Tübingen theologians, do not constitute the uniqueness and originality of Günther's dogmatic theology. Günther's uniqueness and originality is found in the metaphysical relationship which Günther establishes between the revelation made to the first Adam and the revelation made to Christ, the Second Adam, and in the metaphysical relation to human society which both Adams possess. All of these relationships are grounded in Günther's dualistic metaphysics of God, spirit, and nature.

Günther's theological synthesis was built upon His anthropology. *Vernunft* is a natural drive to intelligible reality. Consequently only contact with another spiritual reality can stir it into action. The limited *Vernunft* of the human Ego, since it is not the ground of its own activity, remains passive until it is stirred to action by its contact with another spirit. Therefore, unless God had communicated his reality to the limited intelligences of the first men, none of these intelligences could ever have begun to think at all. All human knowledge therefore was grounded in an act of primitive revelation made to the first Adam.[34]

Like every man, the first Adam was a finite spirit "wedded to" an animate body. His human body, which made Adam a member of the human species, was the metaphysical ground for the relation which linked Adam as an individual to every other individual in the human race. In Adam that relationship received its unique specification through the act of generation which, once it was performed, would link Adam to every one of his human descendants as their common ancestor, the founder of the human race. But, like every man, Adam was also a person, a created spirit, whose intuitive self-awareness was combined with certain knowledge of his creator, from whom he had received, in the act of primitive revelation, the gift of language as the necessary condition of human thought and human communication. Before his loving relationship to God had been severed by the Fall, Adam was able to reflect upon the intelligibility thematized in the Ego-Idea, and that intelligibility, as we shall see later, grounded his apodictic certainty that, as a dynamic union of spirit and nature, he was a contraposed image of a triune God.[35]

But Adam failed to use his freedom properly. He sinned and by sinning violated the intelligible order of the universe which it was his duty to preserve. Once Adam had sinned by placing himself above God in the order of his preferences, his intelligent spirit lost its domination over the appetites of his "natural" body. A love which has separated itself from the intelligible order of being and value cannot retain its control over the lower "loves." For that control is part of the intelligible order of the universe from which the aberrant love has severed itself. Thus the sinful Adam was aware that neither he nor any of his descendants could restore the shattered order of the universe. Only God, the unconditioned ground of universal order, had the power to do that. But, if Adam were to generate a race of men whose disordered natures were doomed to inevitable frustration, his action would have been unintelligible and immoral. Therefore God could not have given to the sinful Adam the divine command to "increase and multiply" which made him the father of the human race unless God had also promised Adam a redeemer. This meant that one person of the triune God would unite himself to the nexus of spirit and nature in man and, by doing so, reestablish the shattered order in man which no human power could restore. God's promise of a Second Adam, made to the first Adam when he was ordered to "increase and multiply," has been transmitted to all of Adam's descendants in some form or other, as the history of religions testifies.[36]

Christ, the Second Adam, is the second father of the human race, the restorer of the human spirit's lost liberty. In Christ the Divine Logos united himself dynamically to Christ's finite human spirit and Christ's animated natural body.[37] In a supreme manner Christ became the center and compendium of all reality. As a bodily individual Christ is organically related to every member of the human race. Through Christ, as an individual, the restoring grace brought by the Logos reaches every other individual among Adam's descendants. Christ's finite spirit moreover was immediately united to the Word of God. And so Christ's human consciousness had special access to the divine ideas and to the free decrees of divine providence. Christ's human consciousness therefore became the source of privileged knowledge about God and God's relation to the worlds of nature and history which no other finite spirit could possess. Through Christ's revealing word Christ's privileged knowledge and its intelligible content was transmitted to other human spirits. Finite human spirits can receive Christ's revealing word in faith, actively reflect upon it, and transmit it to other human spirits through the medium of language.[38]

Thus Adam and Christ were metaphysically related to the human race as its first and second founders. The intelligible order of the universe demanded that if the fallen Adam were to become the father of the human race, Christ must come as the Second Adam who would redeem it. The intelligence of the first Adam was the recipient of God's primitive revelation. The intelligence of Christ was the recipient of God's definitive revelation. The words of the human community of the two Adams were the medium through which revelation has been transmitted from Adam's primitive revelation through Christ's definitive revelation up to the present. Theology was a reflection upon the revelation of the first and the Second Adam in the community of the first and Second Adam. The intelligible structure of the universe was metaphysically grounded in the two Adams. An adequate reflection upon that intelligible structure must be a reflection upon the revelation of the two Adams received in faith.[39]

Through Christ's human spirit the saving power and truth of God are communicated to the human race. Since there is only one Second Adam, there can be only one community of grace and revelation. This is the historical community to which Christ's definitive "second revelation" is communicated by the words of its sacred books and of its preaching. The Second Adam is not related to the individuals to whom he is the metaphysical source of grace and revelation as one isolated atom to another. The Second Adam is related to them as organically interrelated members of a living body animated by the Holy Spirit. As the Second Adam Christ continues to live and act in this redeemed community.[40]

The revelation which proceeds from Christ's self-consciousness enters the self-consciousness of the individual believer through the community to which the Second Adam communicates his life of grace. This community is Christ's Church. Animated by Christ's Holy Spirit, the Church is an organic society. It is endowed with the orderly divisions and hierarchical structure which an organic society must possess. The Church communicates the grace of the Logos through its sacraments, and it communicates Christ's revelation through the authoritative teaching whose truth is guaranteed by the living presence of the Holy Spirit.[41]

ANTHROPOLOGY AND THE INTELLIGIBLE NECESSITY OF THE CHRISTIAN MYSTERIES

The first revelation, made to Adam, manifested the intelligible order of the natural and spiritual worlds. Christ's second revelation manifested the intelligible order of redemption, to which the human spirit has access through its explicit act of Christian faith. Nevertheless in both revelations the Infinite Spirit has communicated his intelligibility to the finite spirit. If then the finite spirit reflects on its own reality as God's contraposed image *(Gegenstand)*, the human Ego should be able to penetrate more deeply into these two intelligible manifestations of its infinite Non-Ego.[42]

Christ, the Second Adam, is the Word made flesh. Unquestionably therefore the God who manifests himself in the revelation made through Christ is the triune God of Christianity. Nevertheless the human spirit's philosophical reflection on its own noumenal intelligibility manifests that the second revelation, made through Christ, is an intelligible unfolding of the first revelation, made to Adam, and which Adam, in the untroubled purity of his spirit before the Fall, was able to understand.[43]

The human spirit must achieve its actual self-consciousness through a dynamic process. In the first moment of that process the spirit is simply a "substance." It has not yet attained the ontological status of a self-conscious "subject." In order to become a "subject," the "substance" must determine itself to the state of being a knower and lover. But to be able to know and love, the undifferentiated substance must first differentiate itself. In other words, it must emanate from its own undifferentiated reality the two dynamic functions or faculties, receptivity and active response, which constitute free *Vernunft*. In doing so, the substance "passes over" into its two faculties. When these faculties are stirred to action through contact with another spirit, *Vernunft* becomes aware of the noumenal spirits which it intuits and of the phenomenal objects brought to consciousness by *Verstand*. The human spirit is thus enabled to define itself as an Ego, a knowing subject, over against the Non-Egos presented to it in its act of knowledge. In that very act *Vernunft* can intuit its own reality in the *cogito*. Consciousness of Non-Egos gives rise to self-consciousness. Substance has become a subject.[44]

The necessary process through which the undifferentiated substance determines itself into a subject follows the three stages of the Hegelian dialectic. The substance first exists in its undifferentiated state (thesis). It then passes over into its differentiations, *Vernunft*'s dual faculties of passive receptivity and spontaneous reaction (antithesis). Finally it reunites these faculties with itself in its act of self-awareness, which is an act of intuitive self-possession (synthesis).

God, the finite spirit's unlimited Non-Ego, is also a self-conscious spirit. Therefore, even though God is infinite and eternal, God too must have determined his substance to the status of self-conscious subjectivity through a timeless triadic process. But whereas the limited spiritual substance achieved self-consciousness by first knowing what it was not, God can only "begin" the timeless process of self-determination by knowing his own reality. For dependence upon another being to achieve self-knowledge is the characteristic of a limited and conditioned knower who is not the sufficient reason for its own act of knowledge. But God is the unconditioned ground of universal intelligibility. Therefore God's knowledge of other beings must be the epistemological correlate of his prior knowledge of himself.

Nevertheless, self-consciousness is the term of a necessary process of emanation through which an undetermined substance determines itself to self-awareness. The origin of this process within the divine self-knowledge is the Father. The Father knows himself and, in knowing himself, emanates the Son as his objectivated image. The Son therefore is an objective, apodictically certain knowledge of Being *(Überzeugung)* and, as objective certain knowledge *(Überzeugung)*, the Son is the term of an act of intellectual generation *(Zeugung)*. Since the act of intellectual generation, however, is an act of objective knowledge, Father and Son are opposed terms, knower and known. They are related to each other through the opposition of thesis and antithesis. Thus the opposition between them must be sublated by a subsequent act of knowledge in which the being of the Father and the being of the Son is seen to be identical. This subsequent act of knowledge is the Holy Spirit which, as the known identity of Father and Son, the knower and the known, proceeds intelligibly from both. Through the procession of the Holy Spirit God becomes aware of himself. He knows his unitary essence *(Wesen)* through the intelligible emanations which constitute the processions of the Trinity. Therefore a self-conscious God must be triune.[45] In the untroubled consciousness of his innocence before the Fall, Adam could understand that. For Adam was aware that the unlimited Non-Ego, whom he grasped intuitively in his own act of self-awareness, was an infinite self-conscious Spirit. But what Adam could understand, Hegel could not. That is why Hegel thought that the Absolute had to produce the world by necessary emanation in order to achieve its own self-awareness. Consequently Hegel's misunderstanding of the metaphysics of the divine self-consciousness prevented him from seeing that the origin of the world was due to an act of free creative love.

If Hegel had understood the metaphysics of contrapositional dualism, he would never have proposed his pantheistic identity in being between the Absolute and the finite universe. The finite universe is God's Non-Ego. Therefore the finite universe must be what God is not. The term of God's creative transient activity is not identical with God. On the contrary, it is the finite negation of God. There can be no identity in essence between man, who is the image of the Trinity, and the Trinity itself. The Trinity consists of three persons or "formalities" identified with a single essence *(Wesen)*. In man, the contraposed image of the Trinity, there are two irreducibly opposed substances, his spirit and the natural body which is animated by man's natural soul. Nature and spirit are opposed to each other in man as distinct essences. They are united only by the form—the striving toward consciousness—which is found in both. Striving toward consciousness attains its formal unity in human knowledge through the "marital union" between spirit and animated body in the cognitive operations of the human knower. Man is a trinity of body, soul, and spirit unified by the form of striving toward consciousness. He is the contraposed image of the Trinity because he is the compendium of the natural and spiritual universe, the universe which the triune God opposes to his own infinite self-consciousness as its cognitional correlate, God's finite Non-Ego.[46] Totally different in essence, man and God are alike only in their common dynamic striving toward consciousness.

Thus Günther's metaphysics of self-consciousness vindicated the intelligibility of a triune God as the necessary ground of the intelligible order of the natural and spiritual worlds. Günther's anthropology could also show, to some degree at least, the intrinsic intelligibility of the Incarnation. The Son of God was required to unite himself to the nexus of nature and spirit in man in order to restore the shattered harmony between them which no man could reestablish. By doing so, the Word of God restored the form which made man the image of the Trinity and enabled the striving toward consciousness, the unitary bond of spirit and nature, to achieve its goal. The Word of God, as the redeemer, restored the order of the *cosmos,* and so the order of nature and the order of history are understandable only through the continuing influence of God as its creator and redeemer. To the impersonal pantheism of Hegel Günther opposed an intelligible personalism in which the Trinity was the free personal ground for the order of creation, the Incarnate Logos was the personal ground for the order of redemption, and the order of creation was united to the order of redemption by the metaphysical relation of the universe to Christ, the Incarnate Logos and the Second Adam.[47]

SIMILARITIES TO THE TÜBINGEN THEOLOGIANS AND RAHNER

As the Tübingen theologians did, Günther accepted the traditionalist thesis concerning the necessity of a primitive revelation as the condition for the operation of man's discursive reason. Like Möhler among the Tübingen theologians Günther believed that contact with other human spirits through the mediation of language in society was a metaphysical condition for the spirit's first act of thought.[48] Again, like Möhler, Günther believed that contact with the living tradition of the hierarchical Church, which is animated by the Holy Spirit, is a prerequisite for contact with the Second Adam.

As Pritz has pointed out, there are also striking similarities between Günther's theology and the theology of Karl Rahner.[49] Both theologies begin as theological anthropologies which develop into Christologies. In both systems the theologies of the Trinity, the Incarnation, and the Church are systematically related to each other to establish the intelligible pattern of God's self-manifestation through the orders of creation and redemption.[50] In both theologies the Incarnate Word, as person and individual, is related, by means of a metaphysics of nature, spirit, and society to every man who has lived or will live upon the earth. The influence of Christ's grace and Christ's revelation stretches from Adam until the Second Coming.[51] In both theologies Christ and the Trinity are the personal grounds of the concrete order of the universe. In both systems the metaphysics of self-awareness in God and man explains why this is so. In both theologies a metaphysics of divine "revelation" is the condition of possibility for human thought. And in both theologies there is an intrinsic connection between this metaphysical revelation and God's historical revelation of himself in Christ. Both Günther and

Rahner can then argue on the basis of their theological anthropology that, if the philosopher-theologian reflects upon the revelation of the Second Adam, which he encounters in the living tradition of Christ's definitive society, he can show the unbeliever the explanatory value of the Christian mysteries. Christ and the Trinity ultimately explain why man's concrete experience of the universe—the created and redeemed correlate of God's act of knowledge and free love—must necessarily be the experience which in fact it is.

But we must remember that resemblance is not identity. There are significant differences between the theologies of Günther and Möhler, and the differences between the theology of Günther and the theology of Karl Rahner are even more significant. More important still, resemblance should not be mistaken for historical dependence. No scholar has ever suggested that Rahner's theology has any historical connection with the theology of Günther.

Günther's Theological Method

Like the Tübingen theologians and unlike Hegel, Günther never allowed the intelligibility of the spirit, thematized in the Ego-Idea, to be absorbed into a system of impersonal concepts or *Begriffe*. Because he did not, he was able to defend a relationship between faith and reason which prevented positive revelation from being absorbed into the impersonal logic of an Hegelian philosophy. In Günther's philosophy, as we have seen, faith or *Glaube* was *Vernunft*'s passive reception of ideal intelligibilities. *Wissen*, or scientific knowledge, was the result of *Vernunft*'s active reflection upon the intelligibility received in faith. In *Wissen* the intuited intelligibility was thematized through an orderly system of ideas. The metaphysics of the Ego-Idea, however, precluded the possibility of "sublating" either God or the finite spirit into the identity of thought and being which constituted Hegel's speculative idea or *Begriff*. The spirit and its personal self-expression retained their irreducible identity. They always retained a unique intelligibility which could be intuited but never completely systematized. *Wissen* was never more than the outcome of a speculative reflection upon an intuited intelligibility which always preserved its cognitional priority to *Vernunft*'s act of self-reflective thematization.[52]

Thus, even in the philosophical order, reason or knowledge was always dependent upon a prior act of faith. Philosophical faith was the intuitive reception of the intelligibilities of the spirit, nature, and God. Philosophical faith therefore was the necessary source of the intelligibilities of the natural order which God revealed to Adam in the first revelation. Christ's second revelation communicated to his disciples the intelligible fullness of God's supernatural self-manifestation. God's personal self-manifestation in Christ perdured in the living tradition of the Catholic Church. *Vernunft* could intuit the intelligibility of that concrete revelation through a higher act of Christian faith. And, once that intelligibility had been intuited, *Vernunft* could thematize it, through a subsequent act of reflection, in an orderly system of ideas. Consequently there could be *Wissen*, necessary, scientific knowledge, whose object was the revealed intelligibility intuitively received through the Christian act of faith. This *Wissen*, or philosophy of the supernatural intelligibility of the second revelation made through Christ, was dogmatic theology.[53]

But the method employed in philosophy remained the same whether the object of its reflection was the natural intelligibility communicated to Adam in the first revelation or the specifically supernatural intelligibilities manifested through Christ's second revelation. The difference between philosophy and theology therefore had nothing to do with their method. It was purely and simply a difference between two types of intuited intelligibility. Or, in other words, it was a difference between the objects toward which their philosophical reflection was directed. Considered as a scientific discipline, philosophy was in no sense the handmaid of theology. Both disciplines were equal partners engaged in a cooperative endeavor to systematize the natural and supernatural intelligibility communicated to man by the first and second revelations. As disciplines philosophy and theology were completely independent of each other.[54] Integration of philosophical and theological knowledge could not be achieved by subordinating philosophy to theology as a subalternated science according to the scholastic model. The synthesis of philosophy and theology could only be achieved within the intelligence of each individual thinker. It was the responsibility of each individual thinker to make his own personal synthesis of philosophical and theological knowledge.

Günther's conception of theology as a philosophy of revelation was similar to the conception of theology proposed by the Tübingen theologians. Like the Tübingen theologians, Günther was able to work out a theology of doctrinal development on the basis of his philosophy of revelation. Günther's theology of doctrinal development, however, was to prove more startling to his contemporaries than the theory of doctrinal development proposed by the Tübingen theologians. We have already seen how Günther's theological reflection disclosed the intelligible connection between the first revelation and the second. Nevertheless, although Christian theologians have no difficulty today in seeing how the revelation of the triune God was already contained in God's primitive revelation to Adam, since they are reflecting upon a developed religious experience, the ignorant and sinful pagans who lived in the ages between Adam and Christ could not clarify the content of the first revelation sufficiently to see that. Clearly then, Günther affirmed, the philosophy of revelation is not a timeless, unhistorical deduction of obvious conclusions from first principles which are equally evident to all men at all times. Philosophy must progressively increase the content of the intuitions given to intelligence in its receptive act of faith, and it must progressively clarify their content through reflective systematic thematization. The passage of time and society's growth in scientific knowledge and culture profoundly influence the depth and extent of intelligence's receptive intuitions and the clarity, rigor, and coherence of their reflective thematization.[55]

Christ's positive historical revelation is not a collection of pre-given ideas. It is the concrete intelligible self-revelation of Christ's inner experience. Christ's experience is transmitted to the intelligences of Christian believers through the concrete language of their Christian tradition. Since this is so, there will be a development in theology, as cultural and scientific development increases *Vernunft*'s ability to intuit and thematize the intelligibility incarnate in the words of Christian tradition. Christians of every age and culture will always reflect on the same revelation. But, given the reality of scientific and cultural development, Christians of different ages cannot have the same theology. The urgent concern of the Church must always be that in each generation the Christian faith is thematized through a theology whose breadth of vision and systematic rigor can meet the demands of contemporary culture.[56]

If nineteenth-century theologians were to achieve that goal, Günther insisted, theology must be given greater freedom by the Church's *magisterium*. The "school," or the community of theologians, is not the *magisterium*. In the Church of Christ, which is an organic hierarchical community, the *magisterium* has the right and duty to pronounce against false doctrine. When it does so, the *magisterium* is making its own specific contribution to the legitimate development of doctrine. On the other hand, the initiative in thematizing the doctrinal content of Christ's second revelation belongs to the theologians. The unfolding of revelation's doctrinal content through scientific *Wissen* is achieved by philosophical reflection, according to the rigorous demands of scientific method, upon the intelligibilities passively received through faith. The theologians are the only members of Christ's organic community who possess the scientific training required for that type of reflection. Only the theologians are equiped to determine by a rigorous scientific method whether or not a given thematization is an authentic expression of the intelligibility contained in Christian revelation. The role of the *magisterium* is to serve as the Christian community's final arbiter in matters of faith. The *magisterium* should wait for the completion of the theologians' work before giving or denying its approval. It should not assume the initiative in the direction of theology's development as it wished to do in the nineteenth century.[57]

CRITICISM OF GÜNTHER'S SYSTEM

Günther's adversaries found a great deal of difficulty with his contrapositional dualism. His philosophy of revelation, in their opinion, led to semirationalism. Günther claimed that a reflection on the intuitive content of the spirit's self-awareness revealed that, as an infinite self-conscious spirit, God must be triune.[58] That was far more than Hermes had ever tried to claim, although Hermes had been condemned for semirationalism. Hermes had been content to argue that practical reason requires belief in the Christian mysteries as postulates which are required for the fulfillment of an absolute moral duty. Furthermore, although Hermes required the theologian to show that there was no positive opposition between the demands of necessary scientific knowledge and faith in the Christian mysteries, he had never attempted to demonstrate the positive possibility of the Christian mysteries themselves. Yet Günther's philosophy of revelation did precisely that. Günther protested that all his philosophical argument was intended to show was that the processions of the Trinity were necessary. *How* the processions occurred within God's infinite reality remained an unfathomable mystery. This distinction, however, did not suffice to avert Günther's ultimate condemnation.[59]

Furthermore, Günther's theology of creation placed unacceptable limitations upon the divine freedom. Actual creation, it was true, was still attributed to an act of divine freedom. Yet, if God were to create at all, he must create the universe represented in the divine idea of his finite Non-Ego. And this universe, according to the metaphysics of contrapositional dualism, had to be Günther's universe of spirit and nature. The neo-Thomists among Günther's adversaries were unwilling to admit that Günther's universe of spirit and nature was the universe which God actually created. They were less ready to admit that Günther's universe was the only one which God could possibly create.[60]

Günther's dualistic anthropology led to equally unsatisfactory theological conclusions. The human body, animated by its natural soul, was united dynamically to the human spirit. What sort of composite was man in this dualistic metaphysics? And how, Günther's critics asked, did Günther's metaphysical anthropology square with the teaching of the Council of Vienne that the intellectual soul was the form of the body? Günther's intellectual spirit was no soul, and it was certainly not the form of the body. The natural soul, emanated from the world soul, was the body's animating form in Günther's anthropology.[61]

Günther's metaphysics of the Trinity led to problems too. In Günther's system personality was identified with the achievement of conscious self-identity. God had to determine himself to self-consciousness through the procession of the divine persons. But were there then three centers of consciousness in Günther's Trinity and consequently three gods? Or, on the other hand, was there just one conscious center of consciousness in Günther's God and consequently only one person? Günther's dualism could lead to tritheism or to unitarianism but it was hard to see how it could lead to Catholic orthodoxy. Under these circumstances Günther's opponents could argue that this dualistic trinitarian theology was far less satisfactory than Thomas' scholastic trinitarian theology which employed the Aristotelian categories of substance and relation. Thomas' subsistent relations accounted for the diversity of persons and his substance accounted for the unity of nature within the Trinity. Thomas respected the transcendence of the Trinity as a revealed mystery. Yet his metaphysics of subsistent relations removed the dangers of tritheism and unitarianism. Günther, it would appear, had failed in both of these respects.[62]

Despite these difficulties, which were among the reasons advanced in support of Günther's condemnation, Rome was reluctant to condemn a respected and pious theologian whose supporters were numerous and influential. Günther's enemies were persistent, however, and although his case dragged on for several years after his delation, they finally prevailed. Günther was condemned in 1857 and his books were placed on the Roman Index. The theologian who prepared the official report on Günther's teaching, on which Günther's condemnation was based, was Joseph Kleutgen, consultor to the Congregation of the Index and the most powerful thinker among the leaders of the neo-Thomist movement. As we shall see in two later chapters, Kleutgen's own presentation of neo-Thomism took the form of a systematic alternative to the systems of Hermes and Günther and to the Tübingen School's dogmatic reconstruction of historical revelation as the intelligible development of the Idea of the Kingdom of God.

In the same year in which Kleutgen began to publish his philosophical and theological defense of scholasticism as an alternative to the modern German systems, his Italian colleague Matteo Liberatore began to publish his series of articles on epistemology, philosophy of man, and metaphysics in *Civiltà Cattolica*. Liberatore's major adversaries, however, were not the proponents of the German post-Kantian theological systems. The Italian neo-Thomist presented his own description and defense of Thomism as an alternative to ontologism, and, above all, to the ontologism of Gioberti and Rosmini. Unlike Kleutgen's writings, Liberatore's articles were almost exclusively philosophical in character. Nevertheless, by deliberate intent, his epistemology, anthropology, and metaphysics explicated and contrasted the philosophical presuppositions which underlay the scholastic Aristotelian and the modern post-Kantian scientific method. To understand the strengths—and the weaknesses—of the neo-Thomistic scientific method as it was presented in the works of its great innovators, a careful reading of Liberatore's philosophical writings is absolutely necessary. One cannot understand Liberatore, however, without a prior understanding of the post-Kantian Augustinian systems of philosophy and theology with which his own Thomism was contrasted. Liberatore, after all, was a polemicist. The point of his writing was to show that post-Kantian Augustinianism had failed as a philosophical and theological method and that it should be replaced with the Aristotelian scientific method of the Angelic Doctor. Our next chapter therefore will be devoted to a consideration of Italian, French, and Belgian ontologism which, as will be evident, was another form of the moderate traditionalist approach to philosophy and theology. Of the three national schools of ontologism, the Italian was the most coherent and by far the most profound. Among the Italian ontologists the greatest beyond doubt was the philosopher and theologian Antonio Rosmini Serbati. Rosmini was a profoundly holy man in his personal life, a deep and original thinker, and a devoted servant of the Church. Unfortunately, however, *odium theologicum* and the political passions fanned by the tensions of the Italian *risorgimento* prevented the papalist Jesuit neo-Thomists from appreciating his personal worth and blinded them to the promise which his thought held out for the renewal of Catholic theology.

5

ONTOLOGISM

Ontologism enjoyed great favor throughout the middle period of the nineteenth century. Italy, the home of Rosmini and Gioberti, could be called its native land, and its supporters among the Italian clergy and laity were extremely numerous. In France ontologists could be found among the theologians of the Sorbonne and in the ranks of the Sulpicians, the Benedictines, and the Jesuits. In Belgium, where Gioberti had spent ten years in exile, ontologism had a particularly strong hold. Indeed it became the official doctrine of the philosophers and theologians on the faculty of the Catholic University of Louvain.[1]

Ontologism was a general orientation in philosophy and theology rather than a single coherent system. It has been questioned in fact whether Rosmini, for example, should be called an ontologist at all.[2] Ontologism was a popular response of mid-century Catholic philosophers and theologians to the threat which empiricism and Kantian idealism posed to the metaphysical foundations of revealed religion and morality. Ontologist anthropology combined the post-Kantian anthropology of *Vernunft* and *Verstand* with Augustine's metaphysics of divine illumination. *Vernunft*'s intuitive grasp of noumenal reality could then be transformed into an Augustinian intuition of the necessary divine ideas or at least into an intuitive grasp of the Absolute Idea of Being.

Although the ontologists were fundamentally Augustinians, their approach to philosophy was shaped by the post-Kantian conception of philosophy as an ideal system of necessary knowledge. Like the post-Kantian idealists the ontologists solved the problem of objectivization by grounding the necessity of the objects affirmed by *Verstand* through the unconditioned noumenal reality intuited by *Vernunft*. And, like the post-Kantian idealists, the ontologists considered philosophy the methodical

113

unfolding of the intelligibility virtually contained in one fundamental Idea or Reality. The intuitive presence of that Idea or Reality in the human mind was required to ground the necessity of the principles of identity and sufficient reason, which are requisites for rational thought. The logical order and the ontological order were linked in one intelligible order in human thought. Philosophy must begin with a reflection on the data of self-consciousness. For there alone the unconditioned ground of thought and being could be found.

Like the Tübingen theologians and Günther, the ontologists addressed themselves to the problem of faith and reason in the context of post-Kantian philosophy, and, like their German colleagues, they incorporated a number of traditionalist theses into their own ontologistic metaphysics. The general pattern of thought which justified the subsumption of this family of diverse philosophies under the general rubric of ontologism can be seen through a cursory consideration of three representative examples. These are the ontologism of Gioberti, Rosmini's metaphysics of the Idea of Being, and the traditionalist ontologism of the Louvain School.

Vincenzo Gioberti

Gioberti applied the name "ontologism" to his own philosophy in his *Introduzione allo studio della filosofia* (1840).[3] He did so to distinguish his own theory of knowledge from Cartesian innatism, which he rejected as a "psychologism." Like Descartes, Gioberti believed that the starting point of philosophical reflection must be the mind's reflection upon its own conscious activity, and, like Descartes, Gioberti claimed that he had discovered within his own mind the idea of the perfect Infinite Being. The notion of the Absolutely Perfect Being then became the guarantee of the objectivity of knowledge in Gioberti's ontologism as it had been in Descartes' philosophy.[4]

The infinite Idea of Being, grasped through intellectual intuition, guaranteed the objectivity of other ideas. The Idea of Being, however, was not simply an ontological modification of the finite intellect, as Descartes himself had held. The Idea of Being was nothing less than the infinite divine reality itself, immediately present to the soul.[5] In essence Gioberti's epistemology and metaphysics were a modern version of Malbranche's seventeenth-century Augustinianism. And this meant that Gioberti was committed to Malbranche's claim that the necessary ideas which ground the mind's objective judgments are in God and are in some manner "seen" in God. The Infinite Being was immediately present to the human intellect from the beginning of the intellect's conscious existence. Thus the intellect's apodictically certain knowledge of the absolute order of being was derived from its intuition of the Infinite Being within it.[6]

Gioberti considered his ontologism the only effective philosophical refutation of empiricism and Kantian idealism.[7] Locke and Condillac had made it evident that sensation could not be the source of necessary and universal knowledge. Kant had shown clearly that *Verstand*, discursive understanding, possessed no necessary and universal knowledge of noumenal reality. The post-Kantian idealists had pointed the way toward a solution to the problem of vindicating the mind's necessary and universal knowledge of real being. The solution which they proposed was *Vernunft*'s intellectual intuition of noumenal reality.

The Christian philosopher therefore found himself on the horns of a dilemma. He was forced to choose between the contending claims of the empiricists and the Kantians on one side and the post-Kantian idealists on the other. He could opt for the metaphysical skepticism of the empiricists and Kant, or he could opt for the metaphysical pantheism of Fichte, Schelling, and Hegel. Aristotelian scholasticism could offer him no help in his effort to free himself from this dilemma. The content of scholastic universal ideas was obtained by abstraction from contingent sensible realities. Metaphysically considered, the universal ideas themselves were no more than intentional *species*. They were simply representations of contingent reality, spiritual modifications of a contingent mind. They were ontologically incapable of bringing the mind into contact with the unconditioned necessity of absolute metaphysical reality. Scholasticism could not overcome Kant's skeptical objections to the possibility of objective metaphysics and the subjectivism to which that skepticism led.[8]

The Christian philosopher could find a way out of his dilemma, however, through the Augustinian anthropology in which God's immediate presence to the mind justifies its apodictic certainty that there is objective truth. In Augustine's epistemology and metaphysics, as Gioberti interpreted them, the mind's awareness of the infinite necessary Truth as the "light above the mind" is nothing less than a grasp of the divine reality itself. The idea of God was God himself, Gioberti insisted in his *Degli errori filosofici di Antonio Rosmini* (1841).[9] Any intentional reality less than God himself would be contingent and conditioned, and no conditioned

idea could be the intelligible ground of absolute, necessary, unconditioned objective truth. It would not bring the mind into contact with
absolute objectivity. For objectivity demands the strict universality
which comes from unconditioned necessity. And thus the mind would
still remain a prisoner of its contingent subjectivity. Metaphysical skepticism would not have been overcome.[10]

Since the mind's intuitive grasp of the absolute and necessary Idea of
Being is an immediate intuition of the divine reality, the logical order of
our knowledge and the ontological order of metaphysical reality are
identical. Metaphysics would not be possible unless they were. Therefore
the starting point of metaphysics must be the mind's reflection upon the
necessary Being which guarantees the identity of both orders as their
common intelligible ground.[11]

Gioberti's Traditionalism

Metaphysics therefore is a systematic reflection upon the intelligibility
of the Infinite Necessary Being immediately present to the mind. Gioberti's philosophy, like the metaphysics of Augustine and the philosophy of the German idealists, is a reflection upon the relation between the
infinite and the finite, between the necessary unconditioned Absolute
and contingent, conditioned spirit. Reflection raises to explicit awareness
the intuition of the Necessary Being that was always implicitly present
in consciousness. Once the idea of being has reached the level of explicit
philosophical awareness the reflective mind cannot refuse to admit its
absolute necessity. Metaphysical reflection is forced to make its primordial explicit judgment: Being exists necessarily. Yet since the mind has
grasped the identity of the logical and ontological order in that very
judgment, it is also aware that the Idea of Being is a self-revelation of Real
Unconditioned Being.[12] Being is the divine reality revealing its presence
to man's finite intelligence. Therefore a more accurate expression of the
implicit content of the Idea of Being would take the personal form: I exist
necessarily For the Idea of Being, as the self-communication of an Infinite Spiritual Absolute, is the self-revelation of a person.[13]

Gioberti's ontologism, like the metaphysics of Günther and the Tübingen theologians, unites the intelligible manifestation of Being to the finite
intelligence with the traditionalists' "primitive revelation." It continues
its traditionalist line of thought with the further claim that, given the
intelligible relation between the Necessary Being and the contingent
human intelligence, God must supplement the "primitive revelation,'

made through the Idea of Being, with the further revelation of language or the "word." For the implicit intelligibility of Being can only be determinately explicated through the use of judgments. But determinate judgments cannot be made without the use of words.[14] Since language is a necessary condition for the formulation of any determinate judgment, language is the necessary expression, the "reflex revelation" of the Idea of Being. Consequently the Infinite Being, who is the source of the necessary intelligibility of the logical and ontological orders, could not have left the choice of the linguistic sign through which the "first revelation" of Being must be expressed to the contingent haphazard choice of individual minds. It follows then that the Creator himself must have invented language as a "second revelation," or more exactly, as the "primordial revelation clothed with a form by the Revealer himself." Both the primordial idea of philosophy and its linguistic form of expression are the necessary expression of a primitive divine revelation.[15]

Philosophical reflection upon this divine revelation is the explication of the intelligibility grasped intuitively through the presence of the Infinite and Necessary Being to the contingent existing mind. The intelligibility of Being grounds the first philosophical principle. This principle, which embraces both the ontological first principle (the first reality, the ontological ground and origin of all other realities) and the psychological first principle (the first idea, origin and ground of all other ideas), can be expressed in the judgment, Being creates existents.[16] The similarity between Gioberti's first philosophical principle and Günther's proof of the creative God from self-consciousness is evident. The reason for the similarity is obvious. Both Günther and Gioberti were strongly influenced by post-Kantian idealism. Carlo Maria Curci, one of the leaders of the neo-Thomistic movement, remarked sarcastically that Gioberti's formula, "Being creates the existent," was simply another way of expressing Schelling's pantheistic formula, "Being transforms itself into the existent."[17]

Once we understand Gioberti's metaphysics of Necessary Being's self-communication to the contingent existing mind, his association of his philosophical first principle with Augustine's metaphysics of illumination is quite understandable. In Augustine's metaphysics of creation, the Necessary Divine Intelligible "forms" the contingent spiritual intelligence and "makes" it a mind. Augustine was strongly influenced by the metaphysics of Plotinus, and in his own philosophy "creation," illuminative "formation," and "revelation" are identified in God's metaphysical communication of his necessary intelligibility to the contingent mind. Illumination, which makes the mind a mind, accounts for the Necessary Truth above the mind that rules its judgments. Gioberti therefore was not without justification when he identified his own metaphysics of consciousness with the metaphysics of St. Augustine. Without the divine illumination contingent minds could neither exist nor think. Thanks to the divine illumination, contingent minds have intuitive knowledge of the necessary principles of identity and sufficient reason without which objective discursive knowledge would be impossible. For Augustine, as well as for Gioberti, "Being creates existents" is the first principle of thought and being.[18]

Like Günther's proof of the creative God, Gioberti's philosophical first principle is presented as a metaphysical refutation of pantheism. The contingent existent cannot necessitate a Necessary Being. Therefore creation is a free act through which the Infinite Being produces existents from nothing. Therefore when the contingent human knower reflects upon his own self-awareness, he finds the whole universe within it. The mind finds God within itself and it finds itself within God as its creative cause.[19] And it finds the sensible universe within itself as a dynamic capacity for knowledge and love. Being creates existents and existents return to Being through the knowledge and love of the contingent human spirit. Gioberti can then claim reasonably that the metaphysics of illuminative creation-revelation is the foundation for all of man's metaphysical reflection.[20]

The Spirit's Need of the Supernatural

Metaphysics, in short, is a scientific reflection upon the intellect's primitive intuition of the Necessary Being. Nevertheless, Gioberti argues in his *Teorica del sovranaturale* (1838),[21] a purely philosophical reflection upon this primitive intuition is incapable of satisfying the intellect's innate desire to understand the intelligible unity of the world of being. Man's primitive intuition of Necessary Being manifests that the human spirit is a drive to know unlimited truth and to rest in unlimited good. The same intuition, since it establishes God's existence as the ground of an intelligible order of being, manifests that the spirit's drive is itself intelligible. Nevertheless man is a limited, incarnate knower. His senses cannot intuit intelligible being. His intellect cannot experience sensible reality. There is a link between sensible and intelligible reality in an intelligible universe but man's divided powers of knowing cannot discover it. Man has an innate appetite to understand the world but reality is ultimately incomprehensible to him.[22]

Being surpasses the capacity of the human mind. For man Being is a superintelligibility. Yet in an intelligible universe man's desire to know and love cannot be doomed to ultimate frustration. Man's experience of Being therefore makes him suspect that there is a further source of knowledge through which he can come to know unlimited truth and to enjoy unlimited good. There arises in man a desire for supernatural knowledge and for the beatitude which must come from a loving intuition of unlimited truth and goodness. Man's experience of Being ultimately awakens in him a desire for the beatific vision. This desire prepares him to welcome the historical revelation which explains to him the meaning of his longing and offers him the means of satisfying it through the Christian life of faith that leads to heaven. Gioberti's ontologism thus provides the Church with an apologetics of exigence that explains the reasonableness of the Christian act of faith by showing its aptitude to satisfy the immanent needs of the human spirit.[23] As Blondel maintained at the close of the nineteenth century, Gioberti argued in 1838 that philosophy, if carried to its logical conclusions, raised questions and provoked desires which only supernatural revelation could satisfy. And, like Blondel, Gioberti contrasted this apologetic to the extrinsicist scholastic apologetic which argued to the reasonableness of faith through arguments derived from signs and miracles.

In the turbulent period after the revolutions of 1848 Gioberti broke with the Church and became a cabinet minister in the anticlerical government of Piedmont. His political career was very brief and he died an exile in 1852. According to some of his commentators Gioberti's posthumous works indicate a definite drift toward pantheism. Other commentators vigorously deny this. Our account of his ontologism is taken from his early works in which his ontologism, even though it was later condemned, still appeared a viable option for Catholic philosophy and theology.[24]

ANTONIO ROSMINI

Antonio Rosmini Serbati was undoubtedly the greatest Italian philosopher of the first half of the nineteenth century. He was also a theologian of considerable merit, a spiritual writer, the founder of a religious congregation, and a cultural leader of prodigious influence. The *Edizione na-*

zionale of his works, whose publication was begun at the centenary of
Rosmini's death in 1959, will eventually embrace sixty volumes. Rosmini
was one of the earliest Italian scholars to show an interest in the philosophy of St. Thomas. Shortly after his ordination to the priesthood he
founded an academy for the study of St. Thomas near his home at
Rovereto. He was by no means a Thomist in the sense of the neo-Thomistic revival, however, and the theory of knowledge proposed in his *Nuovo
saggio sull'origine delle idee* (1830)[25] was closer to the philosophy of St.
Augustine than to the philosophy of the Angelic Doctor. The neo-Thomists later denounced his theory of knowledge as a form of ontologism.
But Gioberti in his fierce attack on Rosmini, *Degli errori filosofici di Antonio
Rosmini* (1841) criticized Rosmini severely for failing to adopt the ontologist solution to the problem of knowledge. Scholars today consider the
classification of Rosmini's philosophy as an ontologism inaccurate. Unlike Gioberti, Rosmini did not identify the essences which ground our
necessary judgments with the divine ideas.

Rosmini's "Ideal Being"

The starting point of Rosmini's philosophy was the mind's reflection
upon the notion of Being. Being, and Being alone, is the common element
which is found in every act of knowledge. Being is implied in every
judgment. All certain knowledge rests upon the primitive, self-guaran-
teeing, immediately evident intuition: Being is. Being is immediately
intelligible; it manifests itself to the mind with the essential attributes
which characterize it.[26] The Being which reveals itself immediately to the
knowing mind is necessary and universal, eternal, uncreated, infinite,
immutable, simple, self-identical, and homogenous. These are the attributes required to ground the necessary universal intelligibility of thought
as such.[27]

Furthermore Being is objective. Being manifests itself to human consciousness as a reality which is at once independent of contingent conditioned intellects and relative to a thinking intellect. An object is an object
for a mind, but an unconditionally necessary object cannot derive its
intelligibility from a contingent mind, even from the *a priori* categories
of Kant's individual—and therefore subjective and contingent—reason.[28]
Being, as the necessary object that is the ground of objectivity as such,
manifests itself as relative to an infinite, unconditioned, eternal, and
necessary mind. Being, in other words, manifests itself as relative to
God's mind. Being is the thought of God, for, in God, thought and being

coincide. As the objective thought of God, Being manifests itself as essentially ideal.[29]

God thinks himself from all eternity. His divine thought produces an absolutely necessary object. The divine operations, however, are absolutely perfect. Therefore the divine word, the divine objective thought, produced by the divine act of thinking, must be the absolutely perfect intellectual reproduction of God's infinite reality. God's objective thought must be the Divine Word as a subsistent Person.[30] Nevertheless, within the objective term of its operation the divine act of thinking can distinguish an intelligible matter and an intelligible form.[31] For in Saint Augustine's metaphysics of objective thought, derived from Plotinus' metaphysics of the intellectual "formation" of the subsistent eternal *Nous,* objective thought is the result of the formation of potential "spiritual matter" by an intelligible form. Thus the divine act of thinking can distinguish in the infinite object of its thought the "form" of the subsistent Person and the "intelligible matter" which is the pure possibility of Being. Then, through an operation of the divine will, the divine act of thinking can abstract and represent in a divine idea the pure possibility of Being.

This pure possibility of Being is not the Word of God. It is the content of a divine idea acquired through a process which makes its ideal representation a pure abstraction. Nevertheless, without being God, the pure abstract possibility of Being, the divine "intelligible matter" is "something divine." As the "spiritual matter" actuated by the "form" of the Word, it is "something of the Word," a "dependence on the Word." Therefore when the "pure possibility of Being" is objectivized in a divine idea which is related to the divine mind as the term of a divine act of thinking, the ideal representation of the "pure possibility of Being" participates in the divine attributes of necessity, eternality, simplicity, and immutable self-identity. This representation of the "pure possibility of Being" is the Ideal Being that manifests itself to the human mind as an ideal intelligibility whose normative necessity is grounded in its relation to the divine act of thinking. This "ideal pure possibility of Being" is Rosmini's Idea of Being.[32]

The Idea of Being must be the term of an immediate intuition. For the Idea of Being is the necessary condition of every judgment.[33] Being is the unconditioned ground of the necessary principles of identity and sufficient reason which must be presupposed in order for a judgment to be possible. Knowledge of Being then must be prior to the act of judging.

It cannot be derived from experience. Knowledge derived from experience presupposes the process of objectivization accomplished through the judgment. But the possibility of the judgment requires a prior knowledge of Being. The intuition of Being, Rosmini claims, is the condition of possibility for the very exercise of thought; and, again drawing upon Augustine's metaphysics of intellection, Rosmini calls the intuition of Being the "form of our understanding" and the "light of our intelligence." God's communication of Ideal Being to the finite intellect makes it an intelligence in act. Therefore, since man possessed intelligence only in potency before the communication of the Idea of Being, the Idea of Being can be called the "form" of our understanding.[34]

Rosmini's metaphysics of the Idea of Being in the divine and human intellects is clearly an adaptation of Augustine's metaphysics of the divine illumination. Plotinus' metaphysics of the "formation" of the *Nous* by the One, adopted by Augustine, and Augustine's own metaphysics of "creation—formation—illumination" are its intellectual ancestors. And, like the metaphysics of Augustine, Rosmini's metaphysics of the Idea of Being links the necessary principles on which the possibility of thought depends to the Word of God as the subsistent term of a divine act of thinking.

Rosmini differs from Gioberti in his contention that the Idea of Being is the only innate idea which the human intellect possesses. Man's knowledge of sensible reality is derived from sense experience. It is acquired through the judicial act of affirmation in which the mind applies the form of being to a datum of sense in order to make it an object of experience. This process of objectivization, which Rosmini calls intellectual perception, is the function of the faculty which Rosmini calls reason. Rosmini's metaphysics of knowledge makes a distinction between reason, the abstractive discursive intellect, and understanding, the intuitive faculty through which the intellect acquires its immediate grasp of the Idea of Being. Despite Rosmini's original and confusing nomenclature, the distinction is the familiar distinction between *Verstand* and *Vernunft*, which was a commonplace in post-Kantian philosophy. It also corresponds to the distinction between *ratio* and *intellectus* which the scholastics had inherited from St. Augustine.[35]

The acquisition of all other ideas is dependent upon the Idea of Being. Other ideas are either contained within the Idea of Being, and therefore derivable from it by analysis, or they are derived from experience by applying the Idea of Being to the data of the senses in an objective judgment.[36] As an Augustinian, Rosmini was not particularly troubled by the problem of whether the senses came into cognitive contact with external bodies. Rosmini was not preoccupied with the existence of the corporeal world or the reliability of the senses. His problem was the Kantian problem of objectivization. How can necessary objective judgments be made about the sensible world under the principles of cognition, contradiction, substance, and cause? For, if they cannot, the mind can have no real knowledge about the world of its experience.[37]

Rosmini's Ethics

The Idea of Being was not only the necessary condition for man's objective knowledge; it was the source of man's dignity as a moral person. Man's encounter with the self-revealing Infinite through the Idea of Being was the source of moral obligation and also, as Rosmini endeavored to show through an Augustinian argument, the ground of the soul's immortality. The Idea of Being therefore was the foundation of the moral order of rights and duties.[38] Man's moral goodness or malice depended upon his free response to its illuminating light for, as Augustine had also shown, man can freely choose to respond to the objective universal order of being, truth, and value which is grounded in the Idea of Being, or he can reject this order in favor of an arbitrary subjective order of his own choosing whose ground is his own individual satisfaction.[39] Charity knows the universal truth, Augustine says; concupiscence is deluded through its individual misguided judgments. Charity is the authentic form of freedom. Concupiscence is the selfish abuse of freedom.[40]

Problems with Rosmini's "Ideal Being"

The most disputed element in Rosmini's epistemology and metaphysics was his metaphysics of Ideal Being. This was the point on which Gioberti criticized him most severely. Ideal Being, according to Rosmini, is not God; it is simply objective possible being, the object of an act of thinking. Nevertheless, it shares in the divine attributes. Ideal Being is a thought in the human mind. Still it transcends the human mind. How can this be? Unless the Idea of Being is God himself, Gioberti argued, it can neither provide the absolutely necessary ground of truth nor account for the necessity of our objective judgments. His ontologism alone, Gioberti concluded, could ground objective truth. If Ideal Being is something other than God, something less than God, then it is a limited, conditioned reality. It is still in the contingent subjective order. If Rosmini's Ideal

Being is not more than an act of individual thought, Gioberti objected in
his *Degli errori filosofici di Antonio Rosmini,* then Rosmini is simply a skep-
tic. If on the other hand, Rosmini identifies his Ideal Being with a universal thought, and that thought is not identified with the infinite
transcendent God, then Rosmini is a subjective pantheist.[41]

Rosmini replied to these objections in *Vincenzo Gioberti e il panteismo*
(1847) and in *La teosofia* (1845).[42] Ideal Being, he explained, was a primitive
and undetermined reality, and the intuition of Ideal Being was simply an
intuitive insight into that activity. The Idea of Being, in other words, is
an immediate insight into the intelligible act of creation-illumination
through which God reveals himself to the human intellect as the Necessary Being and imparts to the intellect the form which makes it an
intellect in act. It was not an intuition of God himself; it was simply an
intuition into God's creative action operative within its contingent term,
the conditioned human intellect. The action which is intuitively grasped
in the Idea of Being is a universal action. Although it presupposes God,
it is not God himself. It must be admitted that the language which
Rosmini uses in his *Teosofia* reminds his reader at times of Hegel's language. Nevertheless his metaphysics of intellection was essentially
Augustinian. Rosmini, like a number of contemporary Thomists, especially Karl Rahner, saw the similarity between Augustine's linking of
God's creating action to the procession of the Word and Hegel's metaphysics of the Trinity in which the procession of the Word is continued
in the movement in which the Infinite Absolute "goes over" into the
finite universe. In that context, the procession of the Word and the
creative illumination of the finite intellect can be considered different
moments of a single universal action, i.e., the procession of the Word,
God's "abstraction of the pure possibility of being," creation-formation.
Despite the Hegelian language of the *Teosofia,* Rosmini's inspiration was
essentially Augustinian. He himself compared his metaphysics of intellection to the illumination of the finite intellect by the Divine Word in
the theology of St. Bonaventure. Indeed the resemblance between Rosmini and Bonaventure is remarkable. For Bonaventure's theology of the
Trinity followed the Greek model of trinitarian theology. And, according to that model, which Rahner incidentally has adopted, the dynamism
that begins with the procession of the Word is carried on into the action
of creation-illumination. These unified moments of the divine "universal
action," to use Rosmini's phrase, explain why the Word of God is the
Divine Exemplar of creation, and why the Word of God is the first

principle in which the order of knowledge and the order of being are grounded.

Rosmini's fundamental problem was the problem of Augustinian illumination. Exactly how does one explain the manner in which Augustine's Divine Light above the mind is somehow God and yet is not God? That is still a problem for Augustinian exegetes. Rosmini did what he could with it, but, in the opinion of Rosmini's neo-Thomistic adversaries, what he did was not enough to keep him out of pantheism. Nevertheless what he did was indeed remarkable. Like Bonaventure, he pointed out that even an abstractive intellect cannot objectivize its sense experience through the judgment without an intuitive "pre-grasp" of the Necessary Infinite, and, like Bonaventure, he saw that the formation of the mind is tied, through the metaphysics of creation, to the dynamism of the trinitarian processions. Like Bonaventure, Rosmini also saw that in the intellect's intuitive grasp of its necessary thought there is somehow contained an awareness of a "universal action" which links the order of thought and being to the Trinity. Rosmini's neo-Thomistic critics, whose attitude toward him at times was determined more by the passions of Italian politics than by serene concern for the objective truth, could not rest until, many years after his death, they finally secured his condemnation. It is ironical that, almost a century after that condemnation, one of the leading Thomist theologians should build his system around the same Bonaventurian synthesis that inspired Rosmini's metaphysics of the Idea of Being. And it is even more ironical that the same philosophical ancestry, Augustine, Bonaventure, and Hegel, should manifest itself in the theologies of Antonio Rosmini and Karl Rahner.

THE LOUVAIN SCHOOL

The French ontologists were quite numerous at the middle of the century.[43] But, although ontologism had a number of distinguished representatives and could even at times be the common doctrine of an entire faculty, as it was for a while at the Jesuit faculty at Vals, French ontologism produced no systems which could vie with the systems of Rosmini and Gioberti in their scope, coherence, and originality. Neither did France produce an internationally respected school to which a number of distinguished scholars contributed their efforts. Gioberti and Rosmini had worked as individuals. The University of Louvain, on the other hand, became the home of an internationally recognized school at which for a number of years "Louvain ontologism" was the established philosophy.

Gioberti had spent a decade in Belgium as a political exile and during the nineteenth century Belgium's cultural ties with Germany were much stronger than France's. The influence of German idealism on Belgian philosophy and theology was more immediate and extensive than in France.

Between the 1830s and the 1860s Louvain became the center of a philosophical movement whose best known representatives were the apologist Nicholas Joseph Laforêt, rector of the university, the theologian Arnold Tits, and the philosopher Gérard Casimir Ubaghs. Although it was far inferior to the systems of Rosmini and Gioberti in the profundity of its philosophy and the fecundity of the possibilities for theological development which it offered, the philosophy and theology of the Louvain School give us an interesting example of how traditionalism and ontologism were blended in mid-century university theology.[44]

Louvain Traditionalism

The Louvain School's early philosophy was a fairly typical example of modified traditionalism. Man possessed innate ideas. But he also possessed notions whose content was derived from the data of sensation. Notional knowledge gave man no access to the absolute and necessary truths of metaphysics. Metaphysical knowledge came through man's innate ideas. Because the human intelligence was a drive to spiritual intelligibility, it could only be stirred to action through contact with another spirit. This contact occurred through language which God communicated to society through his primitive revelation. Education, which was acquired through man's concrete society, was absolutely necessary to stir man's intelligence to action. Therefore only education could bring man's innate ideas from their virtual condition to the state of developed actuality. Granted that our ideas were simply mental representations and that there was a problem of the "bridge" between these representations and exterior reality, this epistemological problem was not insoluble. God had made man's mind an appetite for truth. Therefore the philosopher had simply to make an act of "faith" in his intellect's ability to achieve the purpose for which God created it.[45]

The influence of Bautain's fideistic traditionalism on the early Louvain philosophy is obvious. Nevertheless, the Louvain philosophers made it clear that their "act of faith" in the mind's ability to know reality was not to be taken as a supernatural act of faith. It was no more than a philosopher's confidence in the mind's ability to know. The evidence on which that confidence was based was the philosopher's knowledge of the mind's finality and of the mind's relation to God as its creator.

Louvain Ontologism

But how can God be known through innate ideas which are no more than mental representations? How can unconditioned noumenal necessity be found in innate ideas which are simply finite conditioned modifications of the mind? This was the fundamental objection which Gioberti leveled against Descartes' "psychologism." It was the basis for his argument that subjectivism and skepticism could only be overcome through his own ontologism. The noumenally real could only be grasped by an immediate intuition of divine ideas which were in some way identified ontologically with God himself.

Gioberti's argument made sense to the Louvain professors and, after 1850, they accepted the principal thesis of Gioberti's ontologism. Ideas were "seen" immediately in God. God was the Truth who communicated ideas to the human intellect through the light of his divine illumination. As Augustine had said in his *Confessions,* God was the changeless Truth above the mutable finite mind. When the mutable mind turned to the necessary ideas which rule its discursive thought it was turning to God.

Nevertheless language and education were still necessary conditions for human thought. Contact with another spirit was necessary to move the mind to action. Language in society was the prerequisite for contact between the individual intelligence and other finite intelligences. Through society each individual was able to share in the intelligible experience of his fellow men. The tradition of each concrete culture made it possible for the individual intelligence to join in a communal development of the virtual intelligibility contained in God's primitive revelation of his divine ideas. Since Gioberti himself had blended ontologism with traditionalism, it was not difficult for the Louvain philosophers to incorporate Gioberti's ontologism into their own version of modified traditionalism.[46]

The Louvain ontologists were not radical pioneers. They were highly talented schoolmen rather than theological innovators. There are scarcely any new ideas in their philosophy. The Louvain School is important, however, because it represents the best syntheses of traditionalism and Augustinian ontologism created by a university faculty and incorporated into its academic textbooks. Louvain ontologism gives us some idea of what a good "school course" in ontologist philosophy and apologetics looked like. And, since the blending of traditionalism and ontologism, in some form or other, was characteristic of French and Belgian ecclesiastical education in the middle of the nineteenth century, the Louvain textbooks give the historian some idea of how that approach to philosophy and theology worked out in the classroom.

Apart from the neo-Thomists, the only determined adversaries of that approach were the strict traditionalists like Bonnetty and Ventura.[47] To the strict traditionalists any form of Giobertian ontologism or Rosminian metaphysics of knowledge was rationalism. All our ideas were communicated through God's historical, positive act of primitive revelation. The content of that primitive revelation was communicated to the individual intellect by the language and tradition of his community. Faith alone, and not an immediate intuition of Gioberti's divine ideas or of Rosmini's Idea of Being, was the source of knowledge and certitude. Although ontologism was the dominant philosophy in France and Belgium during the 1850s, the attacks of the strict traditionalists and the neo-Thomists brought about the condemnations of 1861 and 1866,[48] which led to the demise of ontologism as an important influence in Catholic education. For by the end of the 1850s Roman intervention in theology and the counterattack of the neo-Thomists against the moderate traditionalist movement and post-Kantian philosophical and theological method in all its forms had begun to change the current in Catholic thought. Post-Kantian scientific method would gradually yield ground until the definitive triumph of scholastic Aristotelian method would be assured through the publication of *Aeterni Patris* in 1879. The history of Rome's intervention and of the neo-Thomist counterattack will be the theme of the subsequent chapters in this volume.

6

THE SCHOLASTIC REACTION

Roman Intervention in Theology

During the two decades between 1846 and 1866 Pius IX and the Roman congregations intervened repeatedly to influence the course of Catholic theology. Pius' encyclical *Qui Pluribus,* issued at the beginning of his pontificate (9 November 1846), was a defense of human reason's ability to recognize the credibility of Christian revelation and affirm the reasonableness of the assent of faith which the Christian was obliged to make to it. The encyclical was a reaffirmation of the Church's teaching concerning the interrelation of faith and reason.[1] It was directed principally against the growing rationalism and agnosticism among European intellectuals. Toward the middle of the next decade a series of sharp measures were taken by the pope and the pontifical congregations. This time, however, they were provoked by the teaching on faith and reason found in the works of contemporary Catholic philosophers and theologians. The authors in question considered their teaching orthodox but official Rome judged it unsound and dangerous.

In 1855 the Congregation of the Index submitted four propositions to the traditionalist philosopher Auguste Bonnetty and required him to subscribe to them.[2] The propositions, which the Congregation considered normative for sound Catholic teaching about faith and reason, ran as follows:

1. There was no conflict between faith and reason.
2. Discursive arguments could prove God's existence, the spirituality of the soul, and human freedom with certainty. Faith was posterior to reason. Therefore faith should not be invoked to prove God's existence, the spirituality of the soul, or human freedom.

3. The use of reason preceded faith and led to faith with the help of revelation and grace.
4. The method which St. Thomas, St. Bonaventure, and the scholastics employed did not lead to rationalism. This method was not the cause of contemporary rationalism and pantheism.

On 15 June 1857 the papal brief, *Eximiam tuam,* addressed to Johann Cardinal von Geissel, archbishop of Cologne, specified the grounds on which the Congregation of the Index had condemned the works of Anton Günther on 20 February 1857. Günther had been guilty of serious doctrinal errors in his metaphysical account of the unity and trinity of God and in his theology of the unity of person and duality of natures in the Word Incarnate. Furthermore he had gone against traditional, and perhaps defined, Catholic teaching by denying that the intellectual soul was the substantial form of the body. Finally his understanding of the proper relation of philosophy to theology contradicted the Catholic position that philosophy, understood as an intellectual discipline, was subordinated to the discipline of theology as its handmaid.[3]

On 30 August 1860 the apostolic letter *Dolore haud mediocri,* addressed to Melchior Cardinal Diepenbrock, archbishop of Breslau, denied the validity of the arguments which Günther's disciple, Canon Johann Baptist Baltzer, had advanced to prove that Günther's dualistic anthropology was orthodox. Günther's teaching, the letter repeated, contradicted the common teaching of the Church's doctors that the rational soul was the form of the human body. His anthropology was not orthodox as Baltzer claimed.[4]

On 18 November 1861 a decree of the Holy Office proclaimed that seven propositions, attributed to unspecified ontologists, could not be safely taught in Catholic schools.[5] These propositions were:

1. Immediate knowledge of God, at least habitual immediate knowledge, is so essential to the human intellect that without this knowledge nothing can be known. For this knowledge is the very light of the mind.
2. The Being *(Esse)* which is in everything and without which we know nothing is the divine being *(esse).*
3. Real or noumenal universals *(universalia a parte rei)* are not really distinct from God.
4. Innate knowledge of God, under the aspect of being as such *(con-*

genita Dei tamquam entis simpliciter notitia), contains all other knowledge in an eminent way. Consequently all being, whatever be the aspect under which it is knowable, is contained implicitly in our innate knowledge of God.

5. All other ideas are simply modifications of the idea by which God is known under the aspect of being as such *(tamquam ens simpliciter)*.

6. Created things are in God as parts in a whole, not indeed as in a formal whole, but as in an infinite and most simple whole which places its parts outside of itself without any division or diminution of its own being.

7. Creation can be explained in the following way. God produces a creature by the unique and peculiar act *(ipso actu speciali)* through which he knows and loves his own being insofar as it is distinct from a determined creature, such as a man for example.

On 11 December 1862 the papal brief, *Gravissimas inter* condemned the rationalism of Jacob Frohschammer,[6] and on 8 December 1864 Pius IX's *Syllabus of Errors* once more condemned Günther's thesis that philosophy, as an intellectual discipline, had an independent status in relation to theology.[7] The *Syllabus* also condemned Günther's proposal that the scholastic method be abandoned in theology because it could no longer measure up to the demands of modern science.

Finally, on 2 March 1866, a decree of the Holy Office condemned Gérard Casimir Ubaghs' *Theodicea* and *Logica*. The Louvain professors had first been accused of traditionalism. They defended themselves successfully, and Cardinal d'Andrea, prefect of the Congregation of the Index, dismissed the charge which had been brought against them. His decision was challenged, however, and the case was appealed to the Pope himself. In the course of the continuing controversy between the Louvain professors and their opponents an additional charge of ontologism was brought against the professors. Ubaghs argued in their defense that the 1861 condemnation of ontologism had been aimed at pantheistic ontologism. It did not touch the ontologism of the Louvain School. A special congregation, consisting of the members of the Congregation of the Index and the members of the Congregation of the Holy Office, was set up by the pope to adjudicate the matter. The decree which its president, Cardinal Patrizzi, prefect of the Congregation of the Holy Office, communicated to Cardinal Sterckx, archbishop of Malines, forbade the use of Ubaghs' books in Catholic schools. Ubaghs' books, Rome declared, not only contained the traditionalist errors against which Rome had taken a stand in 1855, they also contained a number of the ontologist errors which had been condemned in 1861. Ubaghs submitted to Rome's decision and, although the Louvain professors, who understood the political maneuvering behind the decree, cherished no illusions about the wisdom or the justice of its content, they realized that Louvain traditionalism and ontologism were finished. True or false, they could no longer be taught in Catholic universities or seminaries.[8]

Thus, in the eleven years between 1855 and 1866, traditionalism, ontologism, Günther's dualism, and Frohschammer's rationalism had all been condemned. Seldom, if ever, had as massive a Roman intervention in the development of theology occurred in so brief a time. Rome had condemned Lamennais, Hermes, and Bautain during the pontificate of Gregory XVI. But Rome's intervention earlier in the century had been clearly directed against individual theologians. Its impact had been limited and, although Hermes' theology did not survive its condemnation, traditionalism remained a vital force. The traditionalist theses had become a central element in Catholic theology. They could still be found either in their pure form, blended with ontologism in Latin Europe, or incorporated into Tübingen theology or Günther's dualism in German-speaking lands. This time Rome's intervention was far more effective and considerably further reaching.

It was effective, for Rome prevailed. Louvain might be unhappy, even cynical, about the condemnation of its professors. Nevertheless, Louvain submitted. German theologians might protest openly against Rome's interference in their affairs. They might even complain that it was uninformed and unenlightened as Döllinger did at the Munich Congress in 1863.[9] But Rome was determined to carry through the course of action that it had undertaken; and, in the momentous years between 1855 and 1870 the majority of the bishops and the mass of pious Catholics stood behind Rome and the pope. Rome's intervention was also amazingly far-reaching. Almost every major force in Catholic theology had been condemned except scholasticism.

Part of the explanation both of Rome's intervention in theology and of its success is clearly political. From 1848 until an easing of tension occurred under Leo XIII the Church was militantly on the defensive. Italian nationalism and liberalism, which had become increasingly anticlerical as papal intransigence continued to bar the way to national unity, was a continual threat to the autocratic and unpopular government of the

Papal States. The France of the Second Empire was an ambiguous ally. Without the support of the French emperor the Papal States would collapse under the pressure of popular discontent. But Napoleon III was primarily concerned with his own interests and he had always to remember that many of his Bonapartist supporters in France were far from being clericals. The upheaval of 1849, which had driven him from Rome, changed Pius IX from a moderate liberal to a reactionary in his political opinions and ended his earlier sympathy for the aspirations of the Italian nationalists.

The events of 1848 had changed the social and political structure in the German lands. Wilhelm Emmanuel von Kettler, who became bishop of Mainz in 1848, launched the program of social and political action which would make the Catholic Center Party a powerful force in Prussian politics. The Church in Prussia would no longer look for support to the Prussian government.[10] It would find its strength in popular movements that followed the line of the political opposition. A new base of Catholic power was emerging, the mass movements of loyal and ultramontane Catholic farmers, workers, and middle-class professionals who were still deeply influenced by the Catholic bishops. The old centers of power, the state bureaucracies concerned with religious matters, became less important. Rome was more interested in securing a doctrinally sound ultramontanist education for the priests who would be the spiritual leaders of the loyal Catholics of the lower and middle classes than it was in developing a sophisticated university theology aimed at the aristocracy and the upper bourgeoisie.

Kettler's way to break the hold of the state bureaucracy over theological education was to ignore and, if need be, to challenge it, with the strength of organized Catholic opinion to lend force to his challenge. Another way to break the hold of government bureaucracies over theological education was the use of the concordat. A striking example of the effectiveness of the concordat was the concordat signed between the Holy See and the government of Emperor Franz Joseph in 1855. The old Josephinist régime had collapsed in the tumult of 1848, and the young emperor, who had almost lost his throne in the revolution, was no friend of liberalism or the Enlightenment. The 1855 Concordat recognized the bishops' right to oversee the religious instruction given on every level of Austrian education. The control of the old Josephinist bureaucracy over theological education was broken. Josef Othmar Rauscher, who had been appointed archbishop of Vienna in 1853, was a political, although not a theological, ultramontanist.[11] Just before the signing of the concordat, which he had helped to secure, Rauscher was elevated to the cardinalate. Rauscher was one of Günther's resolute opponents, and it was no coincidence that the stalwart defender of theology's scientific independence was condemned in 1857.[12] That very year Rauscher secured the appointment of Passaglia's colleague and confidant Schrader, and the Dominican scholastic Guidi to the faculty of theology at the University of Vienna. The appointments were a sign of another significant shift of power. Two ultramontanist scholastics had been appointed to the faculty of a Germany university at the initiative of an archbishop. Kettler's method of pressure and the method of the concordat would place an increasing number of Roman-trained theologians on the faculties of the German universities.

It was significant also that by 1857 Cardinal Rauscher and Cardinal von Geissel of Cologne were ultramontanists. Since the pontificate of Gregory XVI Rome had taken pains to secure the appointment of bishops who were Roman rather than Febronian or Gallican in their ecclesiology. By the middle of the nineteenth century this policy had radically altered the attitude of the episcopate toward Rome and changed its conception of Rome's place in the direction of the Church. Bishops as well as pious Catholics became increasingly ultramontane in their sympathies. The pressure of ultramontanist popular opinion, the increasing use of the concordat, and the loyalty of simple Catholics to a pope under attack made it increasingly difficult to resist Roman direction in the name of intellectual freedom or the autonomy of national culture. In the hostile atmosphere of the middle nineteenth century that sort of conduct looked very much like "going over to the enemy." And, as the German theologians who took that line before and after Vatican I soon found out, the mass of militant ultramontane Catholics refused to listen to it. A Church at war with anticlerical liberalism needed control over the training schools from which its leaders came. The pope was the only one strong enough to secure it. The pope and the bishops were the only ones strong enough to organize a national Catholic opposition. The Holy See was the only power which could make a government recognize the rights of Catholics in a concordat.

As the Holy See replaced the bishops and the governmental bureaucracies in the control of theological education, the role of the Roman congregations, especially the Congregation of the Holy Office and the Congregation of the Index, became vitally important. These congregations were the tribunals established to adjudicate the orthodoxy of disputed doctrines. The influence of the Roman theologians attached to them was enormous. Among these theologians was Joseph Kleutgen, one of the early leaders of the neo-Thomist movement. Kleutgen played a significant role in the condemnation of Günther, the ontologists, and the Louvain School. The Jesuit theologians and the Jesuit writers on *Civiltà Cattolica* also exerted a powerful and continuous influence upon the pope and the papal entourage. There is little question that the Roman condemnations of Günther, ontologism, and the Louvain School reflected their attitude toward modern philosophy and toward the Catholic theologies whose methods had been determined by it. The influential position which these Jesuit theologians and philosophers acquired during the pontificate of Pius IX placed remarkable power over the development of Catholic theology in the hands of an incredibly small body of men. They were perhaps the most influential advisers to the Roman curia at the very moment when the papacy was resolutely determined to shape the course of Catholic theology by an unprecedented use of the authority which the curia had acquired in the centralized nineteenth-century Church. At least one historian has implied that the real explanation of neo-Thomism's triumph over its rivals in the nineteenth century was an unscrupulously brutal use of its authority by a clerical establishment.[13]

Use of power there was, and nineteenth-century Rome was accustomed to ruthless politics. Nevertheless, there was more to the neo-Thomist movement than reaction and the use of power. The Italian neo-Thomists were reactionary in their politics and extremely ultramontane in their ecclesiology. They were far from opposed to the use of force to implement their ideas. None of them claimed to be a democrat. But they did have ideas which possessed genuine intellectual merit. These ideas turned out not only to be interesting but actually fruitful in philosophy and theology.

THE NEO-THOMIST PROGRAM

The Jesuit philosophers and theologians at Rome were united in their opposition to the systems of Gioberti, Rosmini, and Günther. There were many reasons for this opposition. Some of the reasons were political, as, for example, the opposition between the papalist Jesuits and the nationalist followers of Gioberti and Rosmini on the issue of Italian unification.[14] Other reasons were methodological. The positive theologians of the

Roman College looked with suspicion on grandiose systems of the German type which, certainly in Hegel's case it was generally believed, culminated in pantheistic rationalism. Other reasons were more strictly theological. The newer theological systems, which were inspired by post-Kantian philosophy or Romantic traditionalism, took an approach to faith and reason, nature and grace which was confusing, to say the least, to theologians who had been trained to deal with these topics through a model of nature and supernature constructed upon the Aristotelian categories of substance and accident. Finally, Perrone, the veteran theologian of the Roman College, was an enthusiastic apologist and controversial theologian. The traditionalist approach to apologetics, which had made him uneasy when he encountered it in Bautain's works, could still be found, either in its pure form or mingled with some form of intuitive grasp of God's reality, in all the new theologies. There was reason enough, from the conservative Roman point of view, to be chary of them all.

The approach to the new theologies taken by the Jesuit writers on the *Civiltà Cattolica* was much more radical than the approach which the conservative theologians of the Roman College took. The program adopted by *Civiltà Cattolica* was not cautious reserve toward "novelty" and "excess." That was the approach of Perrone, who was neither a methodologist nor a speculative theologian. Perrone made no secret of his lack of interest in all systems, including the scholastic system.[15] The approach of the Jesuits on *Civiltà Cattolica* was positive. It was nothing less than a proposal to replace all the existing systems of Catholic theology with a single system: neo-Thomism.

Civiltà Cattolica had been founded in 1849, over the opposition of the Jesuit General Johann Philip Roothan, at the urgent request of Pius IX himself. The papacy was in need of a scholarly review which would provide the Church with an influential voice in Italy's cultural and social life. The pope felt that the Jesuits' intellectual stature and total dedication to the interests of the papacy fitted them to edit the review he needed. The editors of the review, especially Taparelli, had access to the pope and possessed his confidence.

By 1853 the team of Jesuits associated with *Civiltà Cattolica* had launched their campaign for the restoration of Thomism as the single system of philosophy taught in Catholic schools. Thomism alone could structure a sound theology. The scholastic method of St. Thomas was the only method through which philosophy and theology could be properly related to each other. The other systems of philosophy and theology must be removed from Catholic schools completely so that they could be replaced with the one and only adequate system of Catholic philosophy and theology. In their eyes Günther's problem was not his commitment to a system; it was his commitment to the wrong one.

The writers on *Civiltà Cattolica* were totally dedicated to neo-Thomism. Carlo Maria Curci, whom Taparelli had converted to Thomism when he was a scholastic at the Roman College, was director of the review. Taparelli himself was a member of the team of editors.[16] Serafino Sordi, who had converted Taparelli to Thomism when both were novices, was provincial of Rome and therefore in a position to lend the review his powerful and continuous support.[17] The campaign launched by this group of influential Jesuits was a two-pronged one. On the theoretical level a series of articles appeared in *Civiltà Cattolica* in which the intellectual reasons in support of their position were examined. On the practical level a concerted effort was undertaken to persuade their ecclesiastical superiors to implement the Thomistic program through the use of institutional authority.

By 1853 Matteo Liberatore had joined the team of Jesuits on *Civiltà Cattolica* and Joseph Kleutgen, of the Jesuit-directed German College, was working closely with them. Taparelli's postulate that the doctrine of St. Thomas be restored as a principle of unity in the teaching of the Society of Jesus was adopted at the Society's general congregation in 1854. In 1858 Liberatore, Taparelli, Sordi, Curci, and Kleutgen prepared an *Ordinatio Studiorum*, incorporating their ideas, which the general, Peter Beckx, made mandatory for the Society of Jesus.[18] Power was certainly being used, and it would continue to be used both within the Society of Jesus and, after *Aeterni Patris*, within the universal Church.

Bonnetty's four theses were subscribed in 1855. Ubaghs' definitive comdemnation took place in 1866. In between came the condemnations of Günther (1857), ontologism (1861), and Frohschammer (1862). Kleutgen was instrumental in all these condemnations, and, at the very time when the campaign against these modern systems was under way, Kleutgen was publishing his programmatic works in defense of scholastic philosophy and theology, *Die Theologie der Vorzeit* (1853–1870) and *Die Philosophie der Vorzeit* (1860–1863). In 1853 Liberatore began the series of articles on epistemology and metaphysics of knowledge in *Civiltà Cattolica*, which were published in book form in 1857 under the title *Della conoscenza intellettuale*. Between 1856 and 1859 he published another series of articles on the metaphysics of man, which appeared in book form under the title *Del composto umano* in 1862, and, in 1874, became the first volume of his major work on the philosophy of man, *Dell'uomo.*[19] Liberatore's *Istituzioni di Etica e Diretto naturale* was published in 1865. Thus, while ecclesiastical condemnations were dealing blow after blow to its rival systems, the two most powerful speculative thinkers among the Jesuit proponents of neo-Thomism were presenting the reasoned justification of their thesis that Thomism should replace the discredited systems. Reduced to its essence, their argument made two points. The first was that traditionalism, ontologism, and the "semirationalism" of Hermes and Günther were philosophically and theologically erroneous. The second was that neo-Thomism could meet the standards of modern scientific philosophy and theology, and, as an effective modern system, could solve the problems of faith and reason which the modern scientific philosophies and theologies had signally failed to solve.

General Approach of the Neo-Thomists

The general approach of the neo-Thomists was to argue that all the modern systems were intrinsically unsatisfactory. The adverb was all important. For, if the systems were *intrinsically* unsatisfactory, they could not be corrected from within; they would have to be replaced.

The neo-Thomists argued to the *de facto* unsatisfactoriness of their rivals' systems from the confusion which they were creating in Catholic theology. Traditionalists had undercut Catholic apologetics by undervaluing the ability of natural reason to reach certain knowledge of metaphysical and ethical first principles and to establish God's existence. The ontologists, on the other hand, made an insight into the divine essence which only the beatific vision could provide, the necessary condition of objective knowledge. Günther and some of the ontologists had compromised the freedom of God's creative act.

Although the traditionalists, the ontologists and Günther related faith to scientific knowledge in different ways, all of them blurred the distinction between natural and supernatural faith in their theologies. Furthermore, the ontological distinction between nature and grace was not clearly defined in any of these systems. Again, in the natural order, the traditional Catholic teaching concerning the soul's relation to the body was implicitly or explicitly denied in all the modern systems. It was not surprising therefore that none of these systems could preserve the essential distinction between philosophy and theology. Christian philosophy was described as a scientific reflection upon a revealed intelligibility. That conception of philosophy's nature and function as a scientific discipline was bound to lead either to fideism or to rationalism. And, in addition, it failed to recognize that theology, which, unlike philosophy, must be subsequent to the supernatural act of faith, is a work of elevated nature.

The all-important second step in the neo-Thomists' general approach to modern nineteenth-century theology was to establish that the *de facto* deficiencies which had manifested themselves in the modern theologies were intrinsic to each one of these theologies because they were necessary consequences of their starting point and method. This the neo-Thomists attempted to prove by discovering a common element which distinguished the modern systems from scholasticism and which determined their starting point and method. This element obviously was their theory of knowledge. The traditionalists denied natural reason's ability to acquire certain knowledge of the first principles of metaphysics and ethics. The ontologists and Günther, who were deeply influenced by Cartesian, Kantian, and post-Kantian philosophy, required an intellectual intuition of noumenal reality through *Vernunft* to ground the necessary first principles of metaphysics and morals.

Their theory of knowledge, with its Cartesian subjective starting point and its deductive method, was the reason why the ontologists and Günther, who were also influenced by Kant, dismissed scholasticism as a philosophy and theology of *Verstand*. Their theory of knowledge, and the Cartesian and post-Kantian scientific method to which it led, was the cause of the doctrinal confusion in these modern systems of Catholic theology.

The intuition of God, which all of these systems, except pure traditionalism, required to ground the necessary first principles of their scientific knowledge, confused the natural and supernatural orders. It also compromised the freedom of man's creation and the gratuitous character of the order of grace and faith through its metaphysical unification of creation, illumination, and revelation. No wonder then that it undermined the essential distinction between philosophy and theology. In these modern systems an intuitive theory of knowledge, whose necessary starting point was a Cartesian subject's reflection on his own act of knowledge, led to a metaphysics of thinking minds separated from the world of extended bodies. The metaphysical unity of man and nature was shattered. In any coherent system, theory of knowledge, scientific method, metaphysics of man and nature must form a unitary whole. And theory of knowledge, the Thomists argued, was the determining element within the whole.[20]

But, even if the neo-Thomists could make this argument successfully, all that it would establish was that the modern systems of Catholic theology were intrinsically deficient because their method had been determined by a mistaken theory of knowledge. The neo-Thomists would not yet have established that Thomism, as a scientific theology, would prove any more satisfactory. Still less would they have shown that Thomism was the only satisfactory system. The neo-Thomists were well aware of that, and their major effort was directed toward establishing both these points.

As we might expect, their argument began with a reflection on St. Thomas' theory of knowledge. The modern theologians had dismissed St. Thomas' scholasticism as a philosophy of *Verstand. Verstand* could never ground the necessary first principles of metaphysics and morals. *Verstand* could never prove God's existence through its discursive arguments. Was that really so? Let us show you, the neo-Thomists replied, just what St. Thomas meant by his universal ideas and let us explain to you how he accounted for their abstraction from the imaginative phantasm through his metaphysics of the active and passive intellect. Then we will show you two more things. First we will show you how Descartes, Kant, Hegel, Rosmini, Gioberti, and the ontologists all took their fatally erroneous first step through their intuitive grounding of the necessity of science's first principles because they never really understood the epistemology and metaphysics of *Verstand.* After that, we will show you how Thomism, which always understood the epistemology and metaphysics of *Verstand,* can ground a necessary scientific philosophy and theology without falling into the errors of post-Cartesian philosophy or the confusions of the theologies whose methods had been determined by it.

The Cartesian thinking subject was a mind. He was not a man. Subjectivism in epistemology led to dualism in metaphysics. Thomas' thinking substance was a dynamic unity of sense and intellect. He was a man. Man's sensitive-intellectual unitary knowledge required for its explanation the metaphysical composition of body and soul, faculty and act in the human subject. The epistemology of *Verstand* as a faculty of genuine metaphysical knowledge demanded as its ontological prerequisite the metaphysics of potency and act in the thinking subject. And, since man, the thinker, was a substantial element in the contingent world of nature, the metaphysics of potency and act must be the metaphysics of the natural world.

A *Verstand* which was capable of metaphysical knowledge could establish God's existence by its discursive arguments. It could also ground a natural law ethics. A metaphysics of substance and accident could clearly distinguish between the natural and the supernatural orders. A *Verstand* which was capable of proving God's existence and of acquiring clear, although limited, knowledge of God's nature could distinguish between natural and supernatural knowledge of God and also determine the rational criteria through which the credibility of historical revelation could be determined.

Thus, the neo-Thomists argued, the theologian who knew the epistemology and metaphysics of St. Thomas could construct a necessary, certain, and critical scientific theology. A Thomistically educated theologian could identify, understand, and correct the errors of modern philosophy. For these errors were philosophical in nature. He could dissipate the confusion which the modern systems had introduced into theological method by reinstating the necessary distinction between philosophy and theology. Thomism could accomplish this task. No other philosophy could. For all the other systems were vitiated by the subjective Cartesian starting point. Their theological methods were all invalidated by the intuitionist epistemology and the dualistic anthropology and metaphysics to which Cartesian subjectivism inevitably led.

A RADICAL CRITIQUE OF MODERN THEOLOGY

The neo-Thomist critique of the other systems of theology was therefore a thoroughgoing attack on their whole philosophical and theological method. At stake was the whole approach to philosophy and theology which characterized Romantic traditionalism and the post-Kantian modern theologies. Common to all these theological systems was the distinction between *Vernunft* and *Verstand* which Jacobi and the post-Kantian idealists employed. Bautain had incorporated this distinction into his fideistic traditionalism. Hermes, the Tübingen theologians, Günther, and the ontologists relied on it to vindicate the validity of their theological method. In all of their systems a divine intelligibility, intuited through *Vernunft*, was the necessary precondition for scientific reflection. Furthermore, the all-important distinction between faith and scientific knowledge, *Glaube und Wissen*, which determined the theological method of each of these systems, presupposed the post-Kantian epistemology of the intuitive *Vernunft*. Each one of the modern theologians accepted as an established fact Kant's critical invalidation of *Verstand*'s claim to metaphysical knowledge. Each of them relegated *Verstand*'s objective knowledge to the world of contingent appearance. Abstraction alone, without the intuition of *Vernunft*, could never confer the necessity of noumenal reality upon an objective judgment.

The epistemology of *Vernunft* grounded the metaphysical distinction between spirit and nature which modern philosophy had inherited from Descartes. Blended with neo-Platonic ontology, both in Schelling's idealism and in Augustine's metaphysics of man and nature, the metaphysics of spirit and nature provided the ontological underpinning for the organic philosophy of community and the dialectical development of living tradition's revealed intelligibility, both of which were presuppositions of the theological methods employed by Gioberti, Rosmini, and the German theologians. With the notable exception of Hermes' semirationalism, which looked back to Kant, the Catholic theologies of the middle nineteenth century were part of the Romantic and post-Kantian reaction against the individual reason of the Enlightenment. Each one of the modern theologians had been influenced in his own way by Kantian and post-Kantian philosophy.

But by the middle of the nineteenth century the Romantic movement had run its course. Schelling, the last of the great post-Kantian idealists, died in 1854. In his last years he felt himself more and more out of contact with the new forces in Germany's intellectual life. Reaction against the architectonic idealistic systems had begun. Science and the objective categories of the *Verstand*, not the ideal universe of the *Vernunft*, had become the focus of philosophical attention.[21]

A turning point had been reached in Europe's intellectual history, and a new intellectual climate was already perceptible on the continent when the neo-Thomists launched their attack on Catholic Romantic and post-Kantian theology. Their attack was unerring in its aim. It went straight for the philosophical weak spot in the whole construction of post-Kantian idealism, the epistemology of *Vernunft* and *Verstand*. The neo-Thomists saw that this epistemology was the focal point *(die Schwerpunkt)* in the determination of a philosophical and a theological method.

Thus the debate over theological method turned on three different ways of evaluating the epistemological significance of *Vernunft* and *Verstand*. These were the way of Kantian criticism, post-Kantian idealism, and Thomistic abstractive realism. Each of these diverse evaluations carried with it a series of implied consequences for the metaphysics of man, nature, and God. Each of the three, albeit in a different way, determined the method of philosophy and theology, and, in doing so, also determined the relationship between the two sciences. As fundamental epistemological positions, the three were mutually exclusive, and so were the philosophical and theological methods determined by them. Despite their differences, however, Kantian and post-Kantian epistemology shared the common presupposition that Thomas' realistic epistemology of the *Verstand* had been discredited.

But now, at the very moment when post-Kantian idealism was passing out of favor, the neo-Thomists challenged the fundamental presupposition of its epistemology and metaphysics, its denial of metaphysical knowledge to *Verstand*. That denial, assumed on the basis of empirical attacks upon the speculative intellect and the Kantian relegation of discursive reason to the world of objective appearance, had been the cause of the modern theologians' uncritical dismissal of scholasticism and its method. Therefore, although they had abandoned scholasticism and constructed their new methods for philosophical reasons, those reasons had never been critically tested. If then an impartial and informed critical reflection were to establish that St. Thomas' critical realism, and not the post-Kantian epistemology of the intuitive *Vernunft*, was the epistemologically correct position, the consequences for theological method would be revolutionary.

Scholasticism was the only philosophical method built upon Thomas' abstractive realism. All the other methods, to some degree or other, depended upon the post-Kantian epistemology of the intuitive *Vernunft*. Epistemology determined anthropology and metaphysics, and, together, these three determined theological method. If Thomas were right and the post-Kantians were wrong, Catholic theology had no alternative. It had to abandon the new theological methods as unsuccessful experiments. Their *de facto* failure to avoid unorthodox confusion was now revealed to be due to an intrinsically unsound method determined by a fundamentally mistaken epistemology. Catholic theology had to go back to St. Thomas and begin its work anew, using a sound method based on Thomas' epistemology and metaphysics.

The neo-Thomists were using power in their assault on their rivals' systems. But it was by no means purely political power. The neo-Thomists had perceived the fundamental epistemological and methodological unity in the plurality of seemingly disparate modern Catholic systems. They had also identified the source of that unity. If the neo-Thomists were right, all the modern systems did have to go. If they were right, a successful system would have to be reconstructed upon the foundation of Thomas' epistemology. But what was Thomas' epistemology and what was the metaphysics which it determined? These questions seemed capable of a clear and definite answer to the neo-Thomists. But was the answer really that straightforward? The Thomists had made a telling critique of the other Catholic systems, but had they really found a unitary system themselves? The reasons that led the neo-Thomists to think that they had will emerge in the following chapters. But reasons will also emerge to show that in the unitary system of the neo-Thomist pioneers there could already be found the seeds of a future Thomistic pluralism.

7

LIBERATORE'S PHILOSOPHICAL
SYNTHESIS

Matteo Liberatore was not an early convert to the neo-Thomist movement. Liberatore had been a student at the scholasticate at Naples when
Taparelli's attempt to establish Thomism there was brought to a sudden
halt by Father Visitor Ferrari. He himself does not seem to have been a
convert to the movement. Evidently his superiors did not think so, since
he was given a teaching post at the scholasticate under the anti-Thomistic
regime established there by Father Ferrari, who had remained in Naples
as provincial.[1]

Liberatore's publications prior to 1850 show no evidence of any attachment to systematic Thomism. Liberatore was a realist in his epistemology. He opposed the empiricism of Locke and the critical idealism of
Kant. He argued against the epistemology and metaphysics of German
idealism and he declared his opposition to the systems of Rosmini and
Gioberti. Clearly then, Liberatore had not been attracted to any one of
the popular modern systems. On the other hand he did not propose any
system of his own in place of them. Neither did he see any systematic
connection between his own epistemological realism and St. Thomas'
hylomorphic metaphysics of man and nature, neither of which he held.
The imposition of a unified scholastic method on philosophy and theology had no attraction for him either. On the contrary it seemed to be an
unwarranted intrusion upon philosophy's legitimate autonomy. In short,
prior to 1850, Liberatore appeared to be a typical mid-century Jesuit
conservative: an eclectic realist in philosophy, with little sympathy for
the new philosophical and theological systems, but with no interest in
proposing another system to replace them.[2]

Then Liberatore was invited to Rome to join the team of editors on

Civiltà Cattolica. Curci, Taparelli, and Sordi explained to him their vision of a restored Thomism. They made a convert. Liberatore plunged into the text of St. Thomas and, when in 1853 *Civiltà Cattolica* launched its literary campaign for the restoration of Thomism, Liberatore was ready. His brilliant series of articles, citing St. Thomas as their sole scholastic authority, made a cogent case for the restoration of Thomism as a unitary system of philosophy.[3]

LIBERATORE'S ACCOUNT OF UNIVERSAL IDEAS

The crucial difference between the philosophy of St. Thomas and post-Cartesian philosophy was a divergent explanation of the nature and objective value of universal ideas. The errors of the post-Cartesian philosophers, Liberatore argued, were due to their ignorance of St. Thomas' metaphysics of the direct universal. The direct universal, which, unlike the reflex universal of logic, was predicated of the singular beings of the external world, could indeed be called an image *(immagine)*. It was a *species,* a similitude of the object, the object's intentional form. The *species impressa,* the unconscious intentional form impressed upon the potential intellect by the combined operation of the phantasm and the active intellect, was a spiritual actuation of the intellect itself. Because the *species impressa* was an ontological modification of the mind it could be called subjective. The term of the intellect's vital act of knowledge, however, was not the *species impressa.* It was the conscious "mental word," or the *species expressa,* which the mind produced after it had been enabled to do so by its passive reception of the *species impressa.*[4]

The mental word of the direct universal was not subjective. True enough, the *species expressa* could be called an image or an intentional similitude. But it was not a purely representative similitude, a means which *(medium quod),* indirectly and mediately, brought the mind to its knowledge of the extramental being which the subjective idea merely represented. On the contrary, the *species expressa* was an entitative image. It was an intentional formal similitude in and through which the extramental object itself became present to the mind. The mental word of the direct universal therefore was a "means by which" *(medium quo)* the physical reality of the object itself was directly and immediately grasped.[5]

Modern philosophy had lost sight of this vital distinction between the subjective being attributed to the universal, when it is considered as a formal modification of the intellect, and the objective being of the known reality itself, which is present in the universal that is its natural sign. Thus modern philosophers took for granted that what was directly and immediately known in the universal was the subjective being of the *species* as a modification of the intellect. And, since a contingent, subjective mental modification could not transcend the conditioned and limited reality of the knowing subject, the universal, as a *species*, a purely representative sign, could not possess the necessary, objective intelligibility of noumenal reality. Consequently the direct universal, which was a subjective *species*, could not account for the objectivity of human thought.[6]

That is why the ontologists required, as did Gioberti, an immediate vision of God's eternal and necessary ideas to vindicate the objectivity of moral and metaphysical knowledge. Like the Platonists who postulated subsisting universals to ground the necessity of their metaphysical judgments, Gioberti postulated his vision of the divine ideas. His general ideas, Gioberti claimed, were in the Idea, and his universals were in the Universal, and both the Idea and the Universal were ontologically identified with God himself. But Gioberti could only avoid subjectivism at the price of opting for Hegelianism. For, like Hegel, he was compelled to identify the real with the ideal and the subjective with the objective in his Absolute Idea.

Rosmini, on the other hand, by trying to avoid Hegelian pantheism fell back into Kantian subjectivism. Rosmini attempted to account for the objectification of our ideas through his intuitive Idea of Being. The Idea of Being was applied to exterior reality through Rosmini's objective judgment of intellectual perception. In that judgment the Idea of Being was united to a sensation produced in the human knower through an impulse received from an external cause. But Rosmini's account of objectification did not differ in principle from the account which Kant had given in his *Critique of Pure Reason*. In both accounts the objectivity of our ideas was explained through the union of an *a priori* formal element, whose presence in our intellect was independent of experience, and an empirical material element, i.e., a subjective impression, produced in the knower by sensation. Kant, however, was clearheaded enough to see that his cognitional composite, produced by the union of an *a priori* formal element and an empirical material element, could not transcend the world of subjective appearance. Therefore Kant restricted the cognitional validity of his objective ideas to the phenomenal world. Since Rosmini's account of objectification was the same as Kant's account of it in principle, should not Rosmini have drawn the same conclusion? If

Rosmini were consistent, he would be a Kantian idealist.[7]

There was only one way to steer a safe course between the Scylla of Hegelianism and the Charybdis of Kantian skepticism. That was to hold with St. Thomas that there was a primitive duality within the idea between its subjective and its objective being. Put more simply, that meant a real distinction between the being of the direct universal, considered as an act of human knowledge, and the physical being of the object, present in the universal as its natural sign. As an act of thought the universal idea had a necessary relation to its object. A metaphysical relation implied an opposition between its terms. An opposition between the terms of a real relation required a real distinction between the terms. Consequently the subjective and the objective being of the direct universal were really distinct from one another.[8]

Once that distinction had been recognized, it was easy enough to see that there was no need to postulate a vision of God's reality to vindicate the objective necessity of our universal ideas. The essences which existed intentionally in our direct universals were the essences which were found in their concrete singularity in the corporeal objects of sense experience. Therefore the eternity and necessity of the essences represented in the direct universals were negative, not positive, in character. The metaphysical explanation of the timeless necessity of these abstract essences was the precision from concrete actual existence effected in the process of abstraction. Actual existence was not represented in the abstract idea. Abstract essences therefore were possible essences, and, as such, prescinded from the contingency and mutability of concrete actual existence. In other words, these ideal essences were abstract, nonexisting quiddities which, if they were to exist, would be temporal and contingent. To confuse the negative necessity and eternity of the abstract nonexisting essence with the positive eternity and necessity of God's concrete existing essence was to commit a serious metaphysical mistake.[9]

St. Thomas eliminated the possibility of this metaphysical confusion by referring to Boethius' triple distinction among universal ideas. Before God's production of finite essences, their necessary exemplary ideas existed in the divine mind *(universalia ante rem)*. Once finite beings had been produced, their essences existed in the concrete singular *supposita (universalia in re)* from which they could be abstracted by the intellect and thus acquire the negative eternality and necessity of abstract essences *(universalia post rem)*.

The divine exemplary ideas were, of course, the ultimate ontological ground for the necessity of man's objective judgments. But this was because the divine ideas were the necessary exemplary cause of the concrete essences of contingently existing singulars. In the ontological order these concrete essences had to be the essences which they were because they ceaselessly participated in the necessary intelligibility of their exemplary divine ideas. Concrete essences were created *exemplata* of their divine exemplars. As such, they did not have within themselves the sufficient reason for their own participated necessity. Therefore philosophical reflection upon the participated necessity of concrete existing essences must lead the human intellect to conclude, through an *a posteriori* argument, to the existence of God's eternally necessary exemplary ideas. Nevertheless the intelligibility of the concrete existing essences, conceptualized in the direct universal, was the epistemological ground of the principles of contradiction and causality which were presupposed in that *a posteriori* argument. No insight into the exemplary ideas was required to ground these principles themselves.[10]

LIBERATORE'S METAPHYSICS OF THE ACT OF KNOWLEDGE

The ontologists were right when they asserted that the mind could not think at all, unless, in some way or other, it received a participation in the divine light. They were wrong, however, when they asserted that the divine illumination consisted in an intuition of the divine ideas or in an insight into the Idea of Being. As St. Thomas clearly saw, the divine illumination of the human intellect consisted in the natural finality which God imparted to it as a faculty of knowledge.[11]

Man was a sensitive-intellectual knower. Therefore man must be an Aristotelian corporeal nature, composed of matter and a spiritual substantial form. An Aristotelian human nature emanated its accidental faculties of knowledge from its own subsisting essence. In an Aristotelian anthropology man's cognitive faculties were emanated from man's essence according to a descending order of ontological, though not temporal, priority. The higher spiritual cognitional faculties were emanated first. The lower material cognitive faculties were emanated from man's essence through the medium of man's intellectual faculties. Aristotle's metaphysics of the faculties' emanation was akin to Plato's metaphysics of the "communion" and participation of the forms. In both metaphysics a higher principle was present and operative in a lower principle. Under the influence of an unconscious metaphysical finality, the lower principle directed its activity toward the higher as its goal. In the Aristotelian metaphysics of the emanation of the faculties, therefore, man's intellectual faculties were ontologically present and operative in his lower sensible faculties. That metaphysics explained why, in Aristotelian anthropology, man's sensible faculties were subordinated to his intellectual faculties in their natural operation. Because they were, their own natural finality as cognitive faculties was subordinated to the natural finality of man's higher intellectual faculties. Therefore, in Aristotelian man, sense and intellect cooperated in a single, causally unified process of knowing. Together, sense and intellect constituted a unified dynamic tendency whose natural goal was the objective knowledge of being which the intellect attained in its judgment. This was the reason why Thomas could assert, with full metaphysical justification, that the participation in the divine light that made man's objective knowledge of being possible was the natural finality which God imparted to man's abstractive intellect.[12]

The finality of man's abstractive intellect accounted for its ability to make objective judgments without recourse either to innate ideas or to an intuitive insight into the divine reality. As soon as man's exterior senses perceived the diverse sensible qualities of corporeal realities, man's interior senses, linked to his exterior senses through their common unitary finality, organized the senses' disparate data into the unity of the aperceptive image. Then, because man's sensitive and intellectual faculties were directed in their operation by a unified natural finality, man's unconscious active intellect immediately proceeded to "elevate," spiritualize, and universalize the concrete form of the sensible object unified in the phantasm by his inner senses. The phantasm and the active intellect then actively cooperated to "impress" the "elevated" intellectual form of the sensible object upon man's passive, receptive "possible" intellect. This passively received universalized form was the *species impressa.* Prior to its reception of the *species impressa,* the "possible intellect" had been an undetermined, purely potential knower, a *tabula rasa.* But once the possible intellect had been "determined" by the intellectual form of the *species impressa,* it was able to elicit its own proper act of knowledge. The possible, or potential, intellect could utter its mental word. When it did so, the possible intellect produced its first conscious act of knowledge. This was the *species expressa,* the direct universal, in which the abstract form of the sensible object was immediately known.[13]

Yet, because sense and intellect constituted a single, metaphysically unified process of knowledge, the intellect, in its very act of knowing, could not fail to reflect upon its own act of knowledge and upon the operation of the imagination with which its own elicited act was in immediate metaphysical "continuity." This reflection upon the cooperative activity of the two faculties in their unitary act of knowledge revealed that the universal essence represented in the direct universal and the concrete essence represented in the sensible phantasm were ontologically identical.[14] The intellect's awareness of their ontological identity was then expressed in a second mental word. This was the judgment, in which the universal predicate was affirmed of its singular concrete subject, e.g., "Peter is a man."

Thus St. Thomas' metaphysics of knowledge destroyed the epistemological foundations of post-Cartesian philosophy. The whole man, sense and intellect together, was the source of the unitary cognitional act which culminated in the objective judgment. Therefore ideas were not intuited by a separated mind. Neither did the intellect's finality require any intellectual contact with another mind to stir it into action, as the traditionalists mistakenly believed.[15] The negative necessity represented in the universal's abstract essence contradicted both the empiricism of Locke and Condillac and the *a priori* subjectivism of Kant.[16] The intellect's natural tendency toward a cognitional grasp of being and the dynamic "continuity" between the universal and the concrete aperceptive image explained the common consent of men to fundamental religious and moral truths and their habitual use of linguistic signs. But common consent was not the cause of true and certain knowledge, nor were arbitrary linguistic signs the cause of man's ideas as the traditionalists asserted. For, as St. Thomas' metaphysics of knowledge showed conclusively, the origin of man's ideas must be attributed to the intelligibility of concrete sensible essences and to the natural finality of man's metaphysically unified cognitional faculties.

LIBERATORE'S EPISTEMOLOGY OF FIRST PRINCIPLES

The metaphysics of knowledge which Liberatore defended in his *Della conoscenza intellettuale* led to the reflection on the first principles which is found in the same series of essays and also in Liberatore's Latin text, *Institutiones Logicae et Metaphysicae*, published in 1860.[17]

The intellect's first act of knowledge was the simple apprehension or the idea. The simple apprehension, however, was an incomplete act which, by its nature, demanded its completion through the judgment. The intellect first referred the universal, represented in the idea, to the concrete form, represented in the phantasm. By doing so, the intellect could refer a universal predicate to a concrete sensible subject in a synthetic judgment of experience, e.g., "This grass is green," or "I have a pain." Man's exterior and interior senses had emanated from his Aristotelian nature as its cognitional faculties. Since the act of knowledge was their intrinsic natural goal, it would be unintelligible to consider the senses essentially fallacious in their deliverances. Consequently, if the human knower critically tested and evaluated their data, he should acquire true and certain knowledge of contingent empirical facts through his experiental synthetic judgments. Critical testing of sense knowledge was in order, but there was no justification for a Cartesian invalidation of internal and external sense experience through a philosophical method of real and universal doubt.

The intellect was able to relate each of its abstract universal ideas to every other idea. The idea of man, for example, could be compared with the idea of fish. If that were done, it became immediately evident that the idea of man necessarily included the idea of animal in its own intelligible content but that the idea of man necessarily excluded the idea of fish. Thus the comparison of universal quiddities, effected in such immediately evident analytic judgments, constituted a second source of true and certain knowledge. Thirdly, judgments could be related to other judgments through a process of discursive ratiocination. Nevertheless, the primordial act of knowledge was the simple apprehension. Judgments, whether analytic or synthetic, were subsequent to and dependent upon abstracted ideas. Discursive ratiocination was subsequent to and dependent upon judgments.

In St. Thomas' metaphysics of knowledge the origin of certain and evident first principles was attributed to the causal influence of the active intellect. With a little reflection, Liberatore argued, the meaning of St. Thomas' observation could be readily understood. Thomas' first principles were immediately evident analytic judgments. Furthermore, the evidence required to perceive the necessary relationship between the two quiddities affirmed in an immediately evident principle (*principium per se notum*) was furnished by the very act of abstraction itself. In other words, the content of the two ideas which the judgment compared in a *principium per se notum* had not been derived from other ideas by a process of deduction. Neither had it been derived from a process of induction based on the principle of causality. On the contrary, the content of the ideas that were compared in a self-evident principle had come directly from concrete sensible reality through the abstraction of their universal essences under the causal influence of the active intellect. In other words, analytic judgments of this type were *principia* because their ideas were independent of other ideas in their origin. They were *per se nota* because the evidence of the necessary relation between their ideas was seen in an act of immediate intellectual perception. Thus each *principium per se notum* was epistemologically independent of every other analytic principle. Abstraction alone provided the evidence which justified its apodictic certitude. Abstraction, which prescinded from actual existence, accounted for its universality and its negative necessity.

In St. Thomas' epistemology there were many such epistemologically independent first principles. The necessary conditio for the existence of a *principium per se notum* was fulfilled each time hat the necessary relationship between two quiddities, directly abstracted from experience, manifested itself to the mind without the need for discursive ratiocination. Such was the case, for example, in the proverbial adage that every whole must be greater than its parts.[18] Metaphysical reflection upon the fundamental structure of reality resulted in the abstraction of a number of fundamental concepts. Some of these, for example, were "act," "potency," "cause," "effect," "substance," "accident" and "relation." Once these concepts had been abstracted, the mind was able to perceive immediately the necessary relationship between the quiddities represented in each of them. Comparison of the quiddity "substance" with the quiddity "accident," for example, manifested with immediate apodictic certainty the relation of dependence between "accident" and "substance," the latter being the former's subsisting material cause. Comparison of the quiddity "cause" with the quiddity "effect," manifested with equally immediate and apodictic certainty the necessary relation of dependence between every effect and its proper cause. The immediately evident principle through which this necessary relation of dependence was affirmed was the principle of causality.

The principle of causality provided the epistemological justification for inductive generalization. Effects were dependent upon their cause. Therefore constant identity in observed effects required constant identity in their cause. Consequently from the constancy of observed effects one could argue to the essential characteristics of the nature which was their metaphysically constant cause. And so, from singular and contingent events, inductive generalization could arrive at universal and necessary conclusions about their cause. This was the epistemological justification of induction. Inductive generalizations and immediately evident first principles then furnished the multitude of major premises from which deductive arguments proceeded. There was no need for a single principle from which all other principles must be derived by deduction. On the contrary, St. Thomas' epistemology and metaphysics of knowledge excluded the possibility of such a principle.

One principle, however, was presupposed in every other judgment and therefore exercised a regulatory role in human thinking. This was the principle of contradiction: "a thing cannot be and not be at the same time." But, since judgments were necessarily posterior to the idea upon which they depended, this primordial judgment must itself be posterior to a prior primordial idea, which was contained implicitly in every other idea. The prior primordial idea on which the principle of contradiction depended was the idea of Being.

Every idea, St. Thomas said, implicitly referred to its contradictory in the cognitional act through which it was known itself. It is interesting to observe how Liberatore here referred to the authority of St. Thomas to justify his own interpretation of the axiom: Every determination is a negation. Liberatore's interpretation of the axiom, moreover, was quite different from the interpretation employed by the post-Kantians in their dialectical metaphysics of the idea's progressive self-determination. Being, according to Liberatore, was the most fundamental essential note which could be represented in a concept. Being excluded neither act nor potency, substance nor accident, cause nor effect. Being could be affirmed of everything which existed or could exist, since quiddities were possible essences and, as such, prescinded from actual existence. The content of the idea of Being therefore was pure not-nothing. Being defined itself over against the only idea which it excluded from the positive content of its quiddity, i.e., the idea of Non-Being or Pure Nothing.[19]

Thus, once the idea of Being had been abstracted, the mind could compare it immediately with the negative idea of Non-Being over against which Being must define itself. Through that very comparison the necessary relation of exclusion between them must become immediately apparent. Thus the primordial idea of Being was the source of the objective evidence which justified the primordial analytic judgment: Being is not Non-Being; a thing cannot be and not be at the same time. This primordial analytic judgment was the principle of contradiction.

The principle of contradiction affirmed the fundamental law governing the relation of each essence to every other essence. Each defined quiddity was related to its contradictory opposite as a definition to its defining negation. If then the principle of contradiction were to be denied, no essence could be related to another. Affirmative and negative judgments would become equally impossible. For, if nothing could be excluded from the intelligible content of an essence, nothing could be definitively affirmed about that essence either. This did not mean, however, that the other immediately evident principles must be deduced from the regulative principle of contradiction, Liberatore repeated, for the evidence which vindicated the certitude of each self-evident principle was the intellect's immediate insight into the intelligibility of the quiddities represented in the universals directly abstracted from the singular corporeal realities of sense experience.[20]

LIBERATORE'S PHILOSOPHICAL METHOD

Liberatore's rediscovery of St. Thomas' epistemology and metaphysics of the abstractive intellect had revolutionary consequences for philosophical method. St. Thomas' vindication of the validity of sense knowledge manifested the arbitrary nature of the Cartesian starting point. Descartes had made the *cogito* the starting point of philosophical reflection by invoking his real universal doubt in order to invalidate every other source of knowledge. But, since St. Thomas' epistemology had vindicated the essential reliability of the senses, Descartes could be fairly charged with unreasonable arbitrariness in his philosophical procedure.[21] For Descartes' real universal doubt demanded that the philosopher disregard the testimony of his senses, even though philosophical reflection could provide objective evidence of their validity. Furthermore St. Thomas' metaphysics of abstraction clarified the status of the universal's negative necessity and thus cleared up the metaphysical confusion which led to the ontologists' belief that an intuitive grasp of divine reality was required to ground it. Thomas' metaphysics of the intellect's "conversion to the phantasm" also explained why the Idea of Being which Rosmini employed to account for the objectivity of universals could not overcome the subjectivitism of Kant's critical idealism. And, in addition, Thomas' metaphysics of the judgment showed why Rosmini's primordial judgment, "Being is related to the intellect," which Rosmini invoked to manifest his Being's "ideal" character, was not, in fact, the mind's primordial

judgment. The mind's primordial judgment was the principle of contradiction, which Rosmini's supposed primordial judgment implicitly contained. For if it did not, Rosmini's ideal Being could be related and not
related to the intellect at the same time.[22]

Furthermore, the intelligibility of Being, affirmed in Rosmini's primordial judgment, could be known with certainty only through the
evidence which the intellect acquired by a metaphysical reflection on its
own act of knowing. However, that reflection revealed the ontological
identity between the abstract essence reflected in the universal idea and
the concrete essence presented to the imagination in the phantasm. Since
it did so, that reflection exposed the falsity of Rosmini's account of objectification. For Rosmini had attempted to explain the objectivity of universal ideas by an application of his Idea of Being to objects of sense in the
judgment of perception. Reflection on the act of knowledge, however,
made it plain that the potential intelligibility of concrete essences and the
natural finality of man's concrete active intellect were ontologically prior
to the conscious emergence of the idea of Being in the human intellect.
Therefore it was the concrete essences and the finality of the human
intellect which accounted for the objectivity of Being. The idea of Being
did not account for the objectivity of concrete intellects and essences as
Rosmini claimed in his metaphysics of the judgment of perception. In
fact the innate idea of the "ideal Being," which Rosmini claimed was the
objective term of a divine act of knowledge, did not exist. Neither was
there any necessity to postulate the existence of such an idea in order to
account for the objectivity of abstract universals.

The confusion in modern philosophy could be traced to the philosophical method which modern philosophy had inherited from Descartes. The
Cartesian universal doubt, the Cartesian *cogito*, the Cartesian procedure
of deducing judgments from a unitary first principle had been incorporated into the method used in modern metaphysics. Gioberti, Rosmini,
the ontologists, and the post-Kantian idealists made the Cartesian *cogito*
the common starting point of their metaphysical systems. All of them
acceded to Descartes' demand for apodictic certitude in their first principles. All shared Descartes' unwarranted distrust of sense knowledge.
Nevertheless, their own conviction that the subjective Cartesian innate
idea could not ground the apodictic certitude and necessity required for
their first principles led these later philosophers to postulate some sort
of intuitive insight into the divine reality as the objective necessary
ground which their principles required.[23]

Hence their synthetic philosophical method in which the descending logical order of deductive thought was identified with the descending ontological order of being. An intuitively known divinity became the exemplary cause of human knowledge and the exemplary cause of extramental being in the same direct immediate way. Knowledge no longer began with God's creation in order to ascend to God. Knowledge began with God in order to descend deductively to God's creation. This synthetic Cartesian method was what really defined a metaphysical system as "modern," and it was this method which distinguished "modern" metaphysics from the metaphysics of St. Thomas.

For St. Thomas' epistemology and metaphysics demanded a completely different method in philosophy. The concrete sensible singular must first be "analyzed" into its "elements," the phantasm and the direct universal, before it could be "synthesized" again in the judgment.[24] St. Thomas' epistemology of abstraction required the existence of a multitude of epistemologically independent first principles, including the principle of causality. The possibility of "synthesizing" all reality through a deductive system proceeding from one first principle was automatically eliminated. Metaphysics must first "analyze" the world of sense experience into its metaphysical "elements:" its material, formal, final, efficient, and exemplary causes. And then, once these causes disclosed that they did not have within themselves the sufficient reason for their own causality, Thomas' five-fold *a posteriori* argument, from motion, subordinated causes, contingency, grades of being, and the order of finality, established God's existence through the application of the principle of causality.

God was surely first in the order of being. But God was by no means first in the order of human knowledge. Epistemology, anthropology, and metaphysics of nature must first "analyze" reality into its constituent elements. That analysis was effected through the abstractive intellect's reflection on the world presented to it through sense experience and upon its own intellectual activity. Only when God's existence had been proven by *a posteriori* arguments founded upon this analysis could an imperfect, analogous knowledge of the divine nature be obtained through the concepts abstracted from sense experience. Only then could the philosopher attempt to acquire a synthetic knowledge of God's creation by following the order of its descent from God.[25]

St. Thomas was by no means opposed to the effort of philosophy to arrive at such a synthetic understanding of reality. But he knew quite well that in philosophy the ascending order of invention *(ordo inventionis)*, which mounts from creatures to their cause, is logically prior to the descending order of deductive explanation *(ordo judicii)*, which descends from the creative cause to creatures. St. Thomas neither began with the *ordo judicii* nor did he follow it in the exclusive fashion that was the hallmark of modern metaphysics. Thomas began with the *via inventionis* and followed it with a *via judicii.* His method was neither exclusively analytic nor exclusively synthetic.[26] It was an analytic-synthetic method. Thomas' epistemology and metaphysics could vindicate the validity of his analytic-synthetic method on the basis of objective evidence. The same could not be said of the exclusively synthetic method employed in "modern" metaphysics.

LIBERATORE'S ANTHROPOLOGY AND ETHICS

The metaphysics of knowledge which Liberatore presented in *Della conoscenza inteilettuale* was an Aristotelian metaphysics of act, potency, and the four causes. It depended upon an Aristotelian anthropology of soul, faculty, and act. Man's was an Aristotelian nature, composed of prime matter and the unitary substantial form that was his spiritual soul.[27] The substantial form of the sensible singular was individuated by quantified prime matter *(materia prima quantitate signata).*[28] That is why once its form had been "freed" from its quantified prime matter through its "elevation" by the active intellect, it could exist as a universal form in the intellect.[29] Liberatore's Aristotelianism forged the metaphysics of knowledge of his *Della conoscenza intellettuale* and the anthropology of his *Del composto umano* into a single coherent system. Thomas' Aristotelian metaphysics of potency and act linked Liberatore's metaphysics of the unitary act of sensitive-intellectual knowledge to Liberatore's metaphysics of man as a unified composite of matter and spirit. Thomas' Aristotelian metaphysics of nature was a metaphysics of unity. Cartesian metaphysics, on the contrary, was a metaphysics of duality. Hence the cleft between spirit and nature in the anthropology and metaphysics of all the modern systems.

Man's unity in knowledge and being in no way compromised the immortality of his substantial form. The human intellect, which could conceive universal ideas and "turn back" completely upon itself in its reflections upon its own cognitional activity, clearly transcended the restrictions of "extended matter" in its operations. Therefore the intellect was a spiritual agent, and, as such, the intellect—which, as a faculty, was an Aristotelian accident—must inhere in a spiritual substantial form. But, if the human soul was spiritual, it must also be immortal. For a being which was spiritual, and therefore simple or uncomposed, could not cease to exist through a process of corruption; and a soul which was intrinsically independent of matter in its action must also be intrinsically independent of matter in its being. Therefore the soul must continue to exist even after its separation from matter at death.[30]

Neither did the union of man's spiritual soul with matter compromise man's freedom. For, in addition to his intellect, man possessed another intellectual faculty, his will. But, unlike his intellect, man's will was free. For the object of the will was the good, precisely as it presented itself to the human agent through his intellect. The will, as a natural appetite, had indeed to love its satiating end or goal with natural necessity. However, since the capacity of the will, as an intellectual appetite, was coequal with the capacity of the intellect itself, nothing short of the infinite good could be that satiating end. For the range of the intellect was as wide as the range of being, and, since nothing positive could be excluded from the realm of being, this meant that the capacity of the intellect was infinite. Nevertheless, if the will must desire the beatitude of its infinitely satiating end with natural necessity, the same natural necessity could not be attributed to its love of contingent finite objects. For, although these contingent finite objects were certainly means toward the attainment of the will's satiating end, none of these contingent objects was necessarily connected with that end. And so, since every one of them was contingent and imperfect, every one of them must present itself to the rational agent with reasons militating for and against its choice. The will's choice of these objects therefore could not be predetermined through the necessary connection of any one of them with the goal of the will's natural appetite. This meant that the will's rational choice of any contingent object could only be determined by its own act. In other words, in its rational choice of contingent objects the will was free.[31]

Thomas' epistemology and metaphysics therefore laid the necessary groundwork for the Thomistic ethics of Liberatore's *Istituzioni di Etica e Diretto naturale*, which was published in 1865.[32] Man's was an Aristotelian nature. He was a unified composite of body and soul whose natural end was the beatitude to be achieved through the union of his intellect and will with the truth and goodness of infinite being. Although man could not achieve this goal in the present life, he could achieve it in the next, since his soul was immortal.[33]

Moreover, man was a free agent. Therefore he must achieve the beatitude which was the goal of his intellect and will through the free choices which he made in this present life. Consequently man needed a practical science of ethics to help him discover which of his free acts would move his nature toward its goal and which would not. Metaphysics and anthropology provided the norm man needed to make this distinction between his freely chosen acts. The norm was his human nature. The unitary finality of man's human nature manifested itself through the intrinsic finality of its natural faculties. Actions which were in accordance with the finality of man's human faculties were morally right because they were conducive to the development of man's nature and therefore were conducive to the attainment of its unitary natural end, satiating beatitude. Actions which frustrated the finality of man's human nature were not conducive to the proper development of his human nature. Hence such actions were morally wrong.[34]

The "natural law," or the sum total of moral precepts which could be derived from the intrinsic natural exigencies of human nature adequately considered (i.e., considered in its concrete, dynamic relation to the other natures in the universe), might at first appear to be no more than a rule of practical prudence. It seemed to be no more than a Kantian hypothetical imperative, "if you wish to develop your human nature and reach beatitude, act thus and so." But that was not the case. For St. Thomas' metaphysics of man and nature provided the objective evidence for *a posteriori* arguments of God's existence. And God's existence changed the whole character of ethics.

God's existence, Liberatore argued, was the necessary condition for any true philosophical ethics. In fact, without God, there simply was no ethics. Once God's existence had been established, the "natural law," derived from a reflection upon man's human nature, was seen to be a participation in God's "eternal law."[35] Human nature and every other nature in the created world had to be the essences which they were because of their ceaseless participation in God's exemplary ideas. The intelligible order of interrelated natures owed its actual existence to a perduring free act of God's creating, conserving, and concurring will. The moral order, whose demands were to be realized through human action, was part of the intelligible order of creation. Therefore it was an expression of God's ideas and God's creative and ordering will. It followed then that the demands of the moral order were also an expression of the divine intellect and will. As such these moral demands possessed the character of a divine legislative act. As expressions of the divine legislative will, the demands of the moral order possessed the character of true obligation and man's response to them was a response of duty.

Thomas' metaphysical ethics exposed the shallowness of empiricist ethics, which could neither establish a natural law nor ground its obligatory character in God's eternal law. Thomas' ethics also exposed the fallacy of Kant's moral formalism and Kant's unrealistic demand for autonomy in ethics. Kant had tried to ground moral obligation through his categorical imperative of practical reason. Kant's practical reason was autonomous. Practical reason itself was the source of the demands which it imposed on the moral agent. Practical reason's demands were purely formal. They were restricted to formal rules for determining the rightness of individual moral choices. Therefore Kant's moral order was distinct from the "empirical" juridical order which governed the relations between the individual and society. Thomas' metaphysical ethics, on the contrary, because it was grounded on God's eternal law, showed that true obligation was inseparable from heteronomy. The moral demand was an expressed demand of God's legislative intellect and will.[36] Furthermore, Thomas' metaphysical ethics, grounded upon human nature adequately considered, did not exclude the juridical order from its scope as Kantian ethics did. For human nature, adequately considered, included in its scope the essential relations which linked each individual human nature both to other individuals and to the social units of the family and the state.[37] More than that, it also embraced the relations which bound the individual, the family, and the state to God.[38] Unlike empiricist and Kantian ethics, Thomas' metaphysical ethics of God and human nature did not cut itself off from man's religious relationship to God. In Thomas' ethics, in fact, religion was a social duty which social authority was not free to ignore.

Thomas' metaphysics of knowledge and his speculative metaphysics of man and nature provided the philosophical support for his practical science of ethics. Thus Thomas' ethics, which depended upon Thomas' metaphysical "analysis" of man and nature and his *a posteriori* proofs for God's existence, was posterior to the speculative sciences in the philosophical order of Thomas' analytic-synthetic method. No intuition of God's existence was needed, as Rosmini thought, to ground the unconditioned demand of moral obligation, since God's existence, established by *a posteriori* arguments, was able to do that. And Thomas' Aristotelian ethics of human nature could ground the obligatory ethics of the social order which neither empiricism nor Kantian formalism could provide. In an age of unbridled liberal individualism, Liberatore argued, both private citizens and their governments were in desperate need of the sound direction which they could receive from Thomas' social ethics.

THOMISM AS THE ONE PHILOSOPHICAL METHOD

Liberatore's philosophical system was a remarkable achievement. Liberatore began his intensive reading of St. Thomas about 1850. His *Istituzioni di Etica e Diretto naturale* was published in 1865. In that decade and a half he produced a profound epistemological and metaphysical critique of the synthetic method employed in modern Catholic systematic theology. In contradistinction to the scholastic positive theologians, who were content to confine their criticisms of contemporary theologians to individual points in their theology, Liberatore assigned himself the task of proving that the tension between traditional theology and modern theology was due to the radical difference in the philosophical method which they employed.

Theory of knowledge determined philosophical method. For theory of knowledge divided into the dualism of intellect and sense of post-Cartesian philosophy and the unity of sense and intellect in Thomistic Aristotelianism. Dualism in epistemology led to dualism in anthropology. Descartes' man was a mind linked to a mechanical body; the idealists' man was a spirit dynamically linked to a "natural composite." Neither of these men was a coherent metaphysical unit. Thomas' man, on the contrary, was a metaphysically unified sensitive-intellectual nature.

Epistemological dualism was the reason for the synthetic method employed by modern Catholic theologians. A Cartesian mind was forced to rely on the veracity of the Absolutely Perfect Being to guarantee the truth of its judgments about extramental reality. And the Absolutely Perfect Necessary Being was the content of a Cartesian innate idea. In post-Cartesian philosophy the Cartesian intuition of God joined to the Cartesian deductive method produced the synthetic method in theology. Abstractive Aristotelianism, on the other hand, did not require the innate idea of God to validate its judgments about sensible reality or to ground the necessity and objectivity of its ideas. And, in addition, the multiplicity of its epistemologically independent analytic principles eliminated the possibility of a deductive synthetic method. Thomism and post-Cartesian philosophy were irreducibly opposed philosophies. If then Thomism's philosophical method was sound, the method of post-Cartesian philosophy could not be.

As Liberatore saw it, the crucial issue between St. Thomas and the post-Cartesian philosophers was the epistemology and metaphysics of abstraction. This was the epistemology and metaphysics which exposed the arbitrariness of the Cartesian doubt and the epistemological unsoundness of the Cartesian *cogito* with its attendant innatism. Thomas' metaphysics of the active intellect resolved the problem of objectification without recourse to Kantian apriorism or to an ontological intuition of the divine reality. It invalidated the epistemology of the first principles on which the systems of Rosmini and Gioberti were built. In Liberatore's hands Thomas' epistemology and metaphysics of abstraction had become a powerful weapon of destruction.

But Liberatore also used it as a remarkably constructive instrument. Theory of knowledge determined anthropology. Anthropology required a general metaphysics. Therefore theory of knowledge not only determined a philosophical method, it also determined a whole philosophical system. The constellation of these which Liberatore organized around the metaphysics of the active intellect was a remarkable piece of philosophical construction. Individually the theses could be found in the works of the Angelic Doctor. But their systematic interrelation was the work of Liberatore. And it was precisely this systematic interrelation of epistemology, anthropology, metaphysics, and ethics which constituted neo-Thomism as a distinctive philosophical system. Neo-Thomism had become a modern system, consciously opposed to empiricism, Kantianism, ontologism, and post-Kantian idealism. It was now a modern philosophy, with a modern problematic, in conscious possession of its own peculiar philosophical method.

Liberatore believed that he had shown that Thomism could vindicate the philosophical superiority of its own peculiar philosophical method to the methods employed in every other modern system. He had achieved his purpose. He had advanced the solid philosophical reasons which justified the Thomist claim that the days of eclecticism in Catholic philosophy were now over. The intrinsic reasons for the failure and confusion of modern systematic philosophy had been exposed. Liberatore had shown that there was only one sound philosophical system and only one valid philosophical method. Both were found in the philosophy of the Angelic Doctor. Modern Thomism and modern systematic philosophy were irreducibly opposed. A melange of both was a philosophical absurdity. The method of modern philosophy had been proven unsound. Therefore only one sensible conclusion could be drawn. Catholic philosophy must return to the philosophy of the Angelic Doctor.

But had Liberatore himself returned to the philosophy of the Angelic Doctor? In the light of historical scholarship the only answer which can be given is that he had not. Liberatore's concept of Being was "pure non-nothing."[39] But this was the definition of Being given by Duns Scotus. It was not the definition of Being given by St. Thomas. Thomas' notion of Being was not the notion of a possible essence. Being for Thomas was "that whose act is existence" *(id cuius actus est esse)*. Existence was not known in the simple apprehension. Existence could only be known through the affirmation of the judgment.

The act of existence never appears in Liberatore's metaphysics. In Liberatore's interpretation of the Angelic Doctor, Thomas' metaphysics of man and Being is identified with Aristotelian hylomorphism. Liberatore's ignorance of the act of existence distorted his interpretation of Thomas' metaphysics of knowledge. The concrete form of the sensible singular was individuated by quantified prime matter. Once that form had been "elevated" by the active intellect, it could be "expressed" by the potential intellect in its first mental word, the direct universal. Then, through the possible intellect's reflection upon the phantasm, the abstracted essence could be reunited to its concrete subject in the intellect's second mental word, the judgment. Judgment, for Liberatore, was never more than the mind's recognition of the identity between essences. The synthetic judgment recognized the identity between the abstract essence of the direct universal and the concrete essence represented in the phantasm. The analytic judgment recognized the identity between the abstract essences represented in diverse direct universals.[40]

Therefore the metaphysics of knowledge and being in terms of which Liberatore criticized the other systems of modern philosophical theology was not itself Thomistic. Indeed it contained philosophical positions which later scholarship has shown were incompatible with the genuine metaphysics of the Angelic Doctor. Thus, at best, Liberatore's Thomism could be no more than a transitional Thomism whose inaccuracies and misrepresentations would have to be corrected by more accurate historical scholarship. But was it not possible that the omissions and distortions in Liberatore's account of Thomas' metaphysics were the very reason why Liberatore himself believed that Thomism was a unitary system irreducibly opposed to every one of the post-Cartesian systems of modern Catholic theology?

In the metaphysics of St. Thomas objective judgments are grounded on the intelligibility of *esse* affirmed in the existential judgment. The intelligibility of *esse* grounds the necessary principle of identity without which no objective judgment could be made. But which *esse* grounds the principle of identity? Is it the contingent *esse*, the contingent act of existence of the sensible singular? Several groups of Thomists accept that answer and they have built their philosophical and theological methods upon it. But how could the contingent act of existence of the sensible singular ground the normative necessity of the principle of identity? Can anything less than the necessary intelligibility of God's Infinite *Esse* ground the universal normative necessity of that principle? And where else can the necessity of the Divine Existence be encountered except within the human mind? These questions are strikingly similar to the questions asked by Gioberti and Rosmini. But the philosopher who asked them was the Thomist Joseph Maréchal. And he and the whole school of transcendental Thomists have built their philosophical and theological methods on the answer which Maréchal proposed to them.

The solution which Liberatore himself proposed to the problem of objectification was not a Thomistic solution. The metaphysics of existence, which Liberatore overlooked, and the epistemology of the judgment, which Liberatore did not understand, were both required to provide a Thomistic solution to the problem. Once that fact became evident the problem could not fail to emerge again in Thomistic epistemology and metaphysics. When it did, Thomists would divide into rival camps over the proper solution to be given to it. Gilsonian and Maritainian Thomists would seek their solution through the intelligibility of the contingent act of existence of sensible singulars. Maréchalian Thomists would seek the solution through the Infinite Act of Existence that was the term of the natural finality of the active intellect.

The Maréchalian solution to the problem of objectification would be closer to the solution proposed by Rosmini than it would be to the solution which Liberatore offered. The transcendental method of Maréchalian Thomism would exploit the Augustinian heritage of Thomism and reveal a kinship between the philosophy of St. Thomas and the Augustinian philosophy of Rosmini that would have startled Liberatore. A century later transcendental Thomism would create a theology of revelation which would be reminiscent of Günther's "philosophy of revelation."

Nevertheless, Thomism's debt to Liberatore was enormous. Later

Thomists would move beyond him. Transcendental Thomism would incorporate into its own Thomistic synthesis many elements of the systems which Liberatore had condemned. Nevertheless Gilsonian, Maritainian, and Maréchalian Thomism were born within the neo-Thomist movement. The unity which Liberatore forged between Thomas' philosophy of knowledge, anthropology, metaphysics, and ethics would characterize them all. Despite their disputes over theory of knowledge, and the difference in philosophical method which those disputes provoked, Thomists would continue to structure their systems around the metaphysics of the active intellect which Liberatore brought to the world's attention in his *Della conoscenza intellettuale.* Transcendental Thomism's return to the earlier theologies of the nineteenth century could occur only through the development of the intellectual movement which Liberatore had begun.

8

KLEUTGEN'S THEOLOGICAL SYNTHESIS: I. APOLOGETICS AND POSITIVE THEOLOGY

Joseph Kleutgen was the most profound and original thinker among the Jesuit neo-Thomists. He was also the most influential. As we have already seen, Kleutgen was appointed consultor to the Congregation of the Index in 1851. The memorandum which he prepared on Günther's theology for that congregation furnished the basis for Günther's condemnation in 1857.[1] Kleutgen's commentary on the condemnation of ontologism by the Holy See was universally accepted in the nineteenth century as the definitive exposition of that much debated document.[2] Kleutgen's commentary, which first appeared in the Mainz review *Der Katholik* in the summer of 1867, was published as the first volume of Kleutgen's *Beilagen zu den Werken über die Theologie und die Philosophie der Vorzeit* (Appendices to the Works on the Old Theology and Philosophy) in 1858. Kleutgen and Franzelin coauthored the draft of the Constitution on the Act of Faith adopted at the First Vatican Council.[3] It is highly probable that Kleutgen was one of the authors designated by Leo XIII to draft the encyclical *Aeterni Patris,* which became the *magna carta* of official Thomism within the Catholic Church. Certainly during the year in which the encyclical was drafted Kleutgen had been called back to Rome at Leo XIII's express desire and appointed prefect of studies at the Gregorian University of the Roman College.[4]

Kleutgen was born in Dortmund, Germany, on April 9, 1811 and died at St. Anton bei Kaltern, Austria, on January 13, 1883. After theological studies at the University of Münster in the school year 1832–33 and at the University of Paderborn in the school year 1833–34, he entered the Jesuit novitiate at Brig, Switzerland, in 1834. Following his ordination in 1837 he was appointed professor of philosophy at Freiburg, Switzerland and subsequently professor of rhetoric at Brig. In 1843 he was called to Rome, where he spent the greater part of his active life. Besides his office as consultor to the Congregation of the Index, Kleutgen held important offices at the General Curia of the Society of Jesus. In addition he was professor of rhetoric at the German College and served as confessor to its students. Kleutgen's influence upon the students of the German College, who attended class at the Gregorian University of the Roman College, was very strong. Through these students, a number of whom, like Matthias Scheeben, became distinguished professors of theology upon their return from Rome, Kleutgen helped to shape the course of German theology during the latter half of the nineteenth century.[5]

Despite his residence in Rome, Kleutgen remained very much in touch with current developments in German theology. He was, in effect, the "German expert" for the Congregation of the Index. Furthermore, since the "Germaniker," as the alumni of the German College were called, were destined to become a spearhead of Roman influence in German theological circles, their Roman mentors were concerned to see to it that these students were prepared to hold their own against their colleagues who had been trained at the German universities. Kleutgen therefore was unusually well versed in German theology and philosophy, as well as in scholastic philosophy and theology, when he undertook the series of studies on theology, philosophy, and their respective methods that appeared in his two major works, *Die Theologie der Vorzeit* and *Die Philosophie der Vorzeit*. The first volume of *Die Theologie der Vorzeit* was published in 1853, the same year in which the Jesuits on *Civiltà Cattolica* began their campaign for the restoration of Thomism.[6]

Vorzeit was a popular word in nineteenth-century Germany. In its general sense, *Vorzeit* stands for the "old times," or the "premodern" period. Romantic reaction against the rationalism, individualism, and skepticism of the Enlightenment, and Romantic attachment to the organic, religious, and mystical approach to life, which the Romantics associated with the Middle Ages, found expression in an unfavorable contrast between "former times" *(Vorzeit)* and "modern times" *(Neuzeit)*.

Kleutgen, who was no Romantic, used the popular term, *Vorzeit*, in a more restricted and technical sense. Modern philosophy, which had its own peculiar method, began with Descartes. Catholic theology, some time later, began to imitate the modern Cartesian method. By the middle of the nineteenth century, a Catholic theology which consciously rejected the older scholastic method in favor of a theological method modeled on the method of modern philosophy had become the dominant Catholic theology. Explicitly post-Cartesian in its method, this modern Catholic theology displaced the theology which, in Kleutgen's view of history at least, had been the dominant theology in the Church from patristic times to the mid–eighteenth century. For Kleutgen, therefore, *Die Theologie der Vorzeit* meant, in effect, "pre-Cartesian theology."[7]

Although Kleutgen was well aware that scholastic method as such did not antedate the twelfth century, he believed that scholasticism was the legitimate development, and indeed the mature and perfect form, of a scientific method which had originated in ancient Greece, assumed its Christian form in the writings of the Church Fathers, attained its maturity in the high Middle Ages, and continued its authentic evolution in the controversial, positive, speculative, and moral theology of the post-Reformation period. There were doctrinal differences between the schools in the "old" theology, as there were notable historical differences between its successive periods. Nevertheless pre-Cartesian theology remained in essence one and the same theology. The reason for its perduring identity could be found in the fundamental identity of its epistemology, metaphysics, and scientific method. Historical and doctrinal differences among the practitioners of the "old" theology were due to the degree of perfection or coherence with which individual theologians had developed the virtualities of its epistemology, metaphysics, and scientific method.[8]

"Modern" (post-Cartesian) theology, on the contrary, represented a radical break in the history of Catholic theology. Far from being an intrinsic, coherent evolution of the scientific method which had been employed in Catholic theology since patristic times, modern theology was a completely new intellectual creation, a theological *nova creatura*. The reason for the unbridgeable gulf between the two theologies was the radically new theological method which the "new" theology had taken over from post-Cartesian philosophy. Admittedly there were diverse and opposed schools among "modern" Catholic theologians, as there were diverse and opposed schools among "modern" philosophers. Nevertheless, the method which "modern" Catholic theology accepted as normative and on the basis of which the modern theologians proposed to resolve their differences was modeled upon post-Cartesian philosophy. In essence therefore there were only two radically different Catholic theologies, the "old" theology and the "new" theology.[9]

The "Old" and the "New" Theology

The radical opposition in method which Kleutgen claimed existed between scholastic philosophy and theology and the modern systems was admitted by the modern theologians in Germany. Hermes, the Tübingen theologians, and Günther had all severely criticized what they considered to be irreparable deficiencies in the scholastic method. The intrinsic deficiencies in its method were alleged to be the reason why scholastic philosophy and theology could not protect the Catholic faith against the inroads of the skepticism and pantheism to which so many contemporary philosophers had fallen victim. Modern theology alone could protect the Catholic believer against these dangers. Precisely because of its different method, modern theology's exposition and defense of Catholic truth could meet the modern demand for certainty, necessity, completeness, coherence, and scientific rigor which scholasticism was incapable of meeting.[10]

The issue then was fairly joined. But, by the middle of the century, Kleutgen considered, the modern theologians had been given a fair opportunity to make their case against the "old" theology, to address themselves to the major problems in Catholic theology, and to define and defend their own theological method. On the record of their achievement, Kleutgen argued, it could be shown that modern theology had failed to justify its claim that its scientific method was superior to the method of the "old" theology. Catholic theology, as taught in the nineteenth-century German schools, was divided into three major areas: dogmatic theology, practical theology, and speculative theology. The new theology had distinguished representatives in each of these areas, and in each one of them a modern theologian had argued that his method should be substituted for the scholastic method because of the latter's intrinsic deficiencies. Hermes had made the case for his own method in dogmatic theology. Hirscher had argued for the use of Drey's theological method in practical theology. Günther had given the reasons why his dialectical method should be employed in speculative theology.[11]

Kleutgen conceded that these three theologians were, without exception, pious and loyal Catholics. Unquestionably they were orthodox in intent. Their apostolic concern was laudable. They sincerely believed that their method alone could provide the effective defense against rationalism, skepticism, and pantheism which scholasticism was incapable of providing. Nevertheless, the record of their accomplishment showed that their handling of dogmatic and moral theology had been less than satisfactory. Their description of scholastic epistemology, metaphysics, and scientific method was an historical caricature. Their own scientific methods suffered from intrinsic deficiencies which, despite the good intentions of the theologians who employed them, led inevitably to errors and inaccuracies in their scientific exposition of Christian revelation. The time had come, Kleutgen felt, to set the record straight and to present a careful, extended, and historically accurate comparison between scholasticism and the three leading modern theologies in Germany. Was the scholastic method in fact the hopelessly deficient scientific method which it appeared to be in the historically inaccurate accounts of it given by the German theologians? Did their own theological methods really hold the key to the solution of the urgent problems in Catholic theology?[12]

Thus Kleutgen undertook his critique of the three leading German theologies with a three-fold aim. He had first to convince his readers that the German theologians simply did not know scholasticism and that the criticisms which they leveled against it were without historical foundation. An unwarranted prejudice against scholasticism was the basic reason for their unshakable conviction that only their own method could cope with modern theological challenges. Kleutgen's second purpose was to show that the modern theologians had failed to do justice to the demands of the Catholic faith in their theological exposition and defense of the Catholic mysteries and that the intrinsic deficiencies of their modern method accounted for their failure. Kleutgen's third and final goal was to show that, once it was properly understood, the scholastic method met the modern requirements for a rigorous scientific method while remaining free from the crippling deficiencies of post-Cartesian philosophy.

There was no reason then, Kleutgen would argue, for the Church to abandon her "old" theology in order to carry on an effective dialogue with the modern world. Theological continuity should not be confused with theological stagnation. The "old" theology could and should continue its intrinsic evolution. Patristic theology had evolved into scholasticism. Medieval scholasticism had developed into baroque scholasticism. Baroque scholasticism was capable of growing into a richer and more complex modern scholasticism. Kleutgen made it very plain that he had no axe to grind for any particular school or any historical period. He had no Romantic attachment to the Middle Ages. He was arguing for the retention of a common fundamental method which all the "old" theologians shared and basic epistemological and metaphysical positions required to undergird it. The issue between the scholastic and modern theologians, as Kleutgen saw it, was not *whether* Catholic theology should evolve and develop. The issue was *how* that necessary theological progress should be made. In the context of the nineteenth-century theological debate, the issue of *how* became the issue of choosing between the scholastic and the modern method. In Kleutgen's eyes, the issue of method was an issue of theological self-identity. Did Catholic theology evolve authentically by remaining the theological science which it had been since patristic times? Or did it evolve authentically by transforming itself into something radically different, a theological *nova creatura?*[13]

OUTLINE OF KLEUTGEN'S CRITIQUE OF GERMAN THEOLOGY

Kleutgen's three-fold purpose determined the ordering of the material presented in his two major works, *Die Theologie der Vorzeit* and *Die Philosophie der Vorzeit*. A fair comparison between scholastic theology and the three leading German theologies required an extended exposition of the scholastic teaching on the major Catholic doctrines that had become the focus of theological attention during the nineteenth century, and an exposition of the German theologians' teaching on the same doctrines. These doctrines were specifically the norm of faith, the nature of God, the Trinity, the freedom and the purpose of God's creative act, the supernatural order, grace, sin, the First Man, redemption, and the Redeemer. These "points of doctrine" *(Lehrpunkte),* as the reader will recognize, were the points on which either Hermes or Günther had drawn attention to themselves in their dogmatic and speculative theology or on which the traditionalism of Drey and the Tübingen theologians was exposed to criticism from the scholastic point of view.[14] The doctrinal thread which unified Kleutgen's treatment of these *Lehrpunkte* was the controversy over the natural and the supernatural orders that was carried on through the whole of Catholic nineteenth-century theology. In the form of the discussion about faith and reason, that controversy embraced the argument over the distinction between natural knowledge of God and the supernatural knowledge of the Trinity through the light of faith or the Beatific Vision, and the dispute concerning the function of God's primitive revelation in natural and supernatural knowledge. In the form of the discussion about the limits of grace and nature that controversy embraced the dispute over the knowledge and integrity of the first Adam, the metaphysical relation between the first and Second Adams in Günther's speculative theology, and the educative function of human and ecclesial society in the Tübingen theology of the Kingdom of God.

Three volumes of *Die Theologie der Vorzeit* were devoted to the exposition of the traditional Catholic theology on these doctrinal points and the teaching of Hermes, Hirscher, and Günther on the points concerning which they took issue with the scholastics. Kleutgen's reader was then invited to judge for himself whether indeed, on the basis of its handling of these urgent "modern" issues, the modern theology was superior to the "old" theology from the point of view of adequacy, coherence, and orthodoxy. Kleutgen was convinced that his careful and complete exposition of both theologies clearly established that the contrary was the case. An impartial reader could see for himself that the Roman theologians' opposition to Hermes and Günther was based on solid theological reasons and was not the result of obscurantism or prejudice.

The diversity between the scholastic and modern theologians on these fundamental "points of doctrine" *(Lehrpunkte)* was due, of course, to the diversity of the theological methods employed in the two theologies. Thus Kleutgen addressed himself in the second part of *Die Theologie der Vorzeit* to the urgent issue of theological method. In the first edition of *Die Theologie der Vorzeit* two volumes were devoted to this discussion.[15]

Kleutgen first presented a long and careful history of theology to provide the historical warrant for his central thesis that the "old" theology was essentially one scientific system built upon one scientific method. He then approached two fundamental questions which he considered indispensable presuppositions for an adequate evaluation of the effectiveness of a Catholic theological method. The first was the legitimacy of the use of philosophy in theological reflection.[16] The second was the question of the reasonableness, certainty, evidence, and freedom of the assent of faith.[17] Kleutgen's solution to these two questions furnished the philosophical and theological basis on which he would later determine the specific certainty of dogmatic, practical, and moral theology, and on which he would decide the specific relation which scientific theology bore to apologetics and philosophy.

Once this historical and doctrinal foundation had been laid, Kleutgen was in a position to address himself to his theoretical exposition of the scientific character of scholastic theology and to his defense of its scientific unity, certainty, necessity, and completeness. These were indeed the qualities which assured its balance, universality, and orthodoxy. In the course of this theoretical exposition and defense of scholastic theology,

Kleutgen contrasted the scholastic method to Hermes' method in dogmatic theology, Hirscher's method in practical theology, and Günther's method in speculative theology. Kleutgen's expository approach to theological method in the second part of *Die Theologie der Vorzeit* was similar to the approach which he had taken to the "points of doctrine" in the first part. He laid out the two methods side by side as he worked his way through the various points in his consideration and left it to the impartial reader to decide which of the two was the better one. Kleutgen made no pretense of neutrality himself. He was clearly an advocate of scholasticism. But the impression which he was anxious to create in his reader was that all he required to win his case was a fair and thorough hearing.

But, since the modern systems of theology depended upon post-Cartesian philosophy, the contrast between the scholastic theological method *(Lehrweise)* and the modern theological method would be incomplete unless it were extended to the philosophical roots of both methods. "Modern" method, both in philosophy and theology, began with Descartes. Descartes' epistemology, his subjective starting point, his theory of certitude, his innatism, and his mathematical deductivism were the philosophical presuppositions on which modern philosophy was built. Modern philosophical anthropology, metaphysics, and theodicy were determined by Cartesian epistemology. Modern theologians took Cartesian epistemology and the Cartesian metaphysics of man, nature, and God for granted. Their contemptuous attitude toward scholasticism was determined by their unexamined philosophical presuppositions.

The time had come, Kleutgen felt, to challenge these unexamined philosophical presuppositions by an in-depth comparison between scholastic epistemology and metaphysics and post-Cartesian epistemology and metaphysics. Therefore he addressed himself to the philosophical foundations of the two theological methods in the two volumes of his *Die Philosophie der Vorzeit*. The first volume was devoted in its entirety to theory of knowledge. The second volume was devoted to philosophy of being, nature, man, and God.

Thus Kleutgen's defense of the scholastic system comprised seven volumes, five in theology and two in philosophy. Three additional volumes of *Beilagen* (Appendices) brought the total number of volumes to ten. The first volume of *Die Philosophie der Vorzeit* appeared in 1860 and the second in 1863. A second edition, comprising both volumes, was published in 1878. In the first edition of *Die Theologie der Vorzeit* the first two volumes of Part I *(Lehrpunkte)* appeared in 1853 and 1854 respectively. They were followed by the two volumes of Part II *(Lehrweise)* of which the first was published in 1860 and the second in 1865. Kleutgen had originally considered including the published material treated in *Die Philosophie der Vorzeit* in Part II, the *Lehrweise* section, of *Die Theologie der Vorzeit* but finally decided that the extensiveness of the material required an independent work in order to do it justice. The third and final volume of Part I *(Lehrpunkte)* did not appear until 1870.

In the second edition all the volumes, with the exception of the third, appeared in their proper logical order. The first volume was published in 1867, the second in 1872, the fourth in 1873, and the fifth in 1874. Since the third volume of Part I *(Lehrpunkte)* was not published at all until 1870, three years after the second edition had begun to appear, Kleutgen saw no need to include it among the volumes of the second revised edition. Apart from additions and emendations, the principal difference between the first and second editions of *Die Theologie der Vorzeit* is that Günther's theology is not discussed in Part I *(Lehrpunkte)* in the first edition. The reason for the omission is interesting. At the time when Kleutgen's first two volumes appeared Günther's case was still under consideration by the Congregation of the Index. Kleutgen was the consultor to the Congregation who was charged with the preparation of the official memorandum on which the Congregation's discussion of Günther's theology would be based. Since the proceedings of the Congregation were secret, Kleutgen was not free, or at least did not feel free, to discuss Günther's theology in public until the Congregation had reached its official decision. Consequently he deferred his consideration of Günther's theology until the second part *(Lehrweise)* of *Die Theologie der Vorzeit,* which did not appear until after Günther's official condemnation.[18]

THE IMPACT OF KLEUTGEN'S CRITIQUE

Die Theologie der Vorzeit and *Die Philosophie der Vorzeit* made an enormous impression not only in Germany but in other European lands. Kleutgen's prodigious erudition enabled Catholic theologians, whose own knowledge of scholasticism was often sketchy, to become acquainted with the range of scholastic literature from the Victorines and Peter Lombard through Thomas and Bonaventure to Melchior Cano, de Lugo, Suarez, Vasquez, Cajetan, and the spiritual writers influenced by baroque scholasticism, Francis de Sales and Luis de la Puente. Kleutgen manifested in his volumes that, while he knew German philosophy and theology thoroughly and accurately, the German theologians did not know scholasticism at all. In a land where accusations of "scholastic obscurantism" were frequent that point went home.

Furthermore, despite their vast historical erudition, Kleutgen's works presented a clear and coherent view of the whole of nineteenth-century theology. Kleutgen had the gift of lucid and organized exposition. He surveyed the major issues in nineteenth-century Catholic theology, found their common source in the controversy over grace and nature, and traced the roots of that controversy to the confusion in method introduced into Catholic theology by modern philosophy. Kleutgen was not interested in producing a *Summa Theologiae*. He was arguing for the scholastic position in nineteenth-century theology and he never forgot his purpose for a moment. His analyses were careful, his arguments cogent, his tone confident, irenic, and serene.[19]

Kleutgen's counterattack against "modern" philosophy and theology gave heart to the ultramontanists who resented the liberal attacks on the papacy for its lack of sympathy toward modern science and modern culture. It reminded them of the cultural and intellectual power of their traditional philosophy and theology. If Kleutgen was right, the connection between modern thought and infidelity might be no accident, and the connection between tradition and sound reason could have a solid intellectual justification. Kleutgen's two major works contained concrete, detailed, documented analyses of the modern German theologies. They pitilessly exposed the specific failures of these modern Catholic systems, pointed to a defective theological method as their cause and indicated a definite practical remedy for the confusion and ineffectiveness of modern Catholic theology—a return to the scholastic method which the Church should never have abandoned. In Kleutgen's works a powerful mind was arguing with almost overwhelming reasonableness for the course of action which the Holy See would take in the last three decades of the nineteenth century.

The Nature of the "Old" Theology: Theology and Apologetics

From the time of Augustine, Kleutgen argued, theology had been considered the intellectual effort of the Christian believer to acquire a scientific understanding of his faith (*fides quaerens intellectum*). Theology was the science of faith, *scientia fidei, die Wissenschaft des Glaubes*. Every science had a principle or formal object. This was the cognitional "source," or "intellectual light," through which its self-evident truths manifested themselves. The intellectual light from which the self-evident truths of theology were derived was the free assent of Christian faith. The assent of faith had to be made by the mind elevated by grace. Thus the believer's free and supernatural act of faith and historical Christian revelation contained in Scripture and tradition were the sources of theology. Theology, in its traditional definition, was the science of those truths that are believed precisely insofar as they are believed.[20]

Theology therefore was not philosophy. The source or cognitional principle from which philosophy derived its fundamental, self-evident truths was the natural light of the intellect itself. Philosophy was a natural science. Theology was a supernatural science. Philosophy and theology differed from each other in the source of their self-evident primordial judgments and in the ontological character (elevated or nonelevated by grace) of the mind that carried out their scientific reflection.

In another meaning of the term, a science's "first principles" were understood to be its immediately evident primordial judgments. In this sense too, there was an essential difference between the first principles of philosophy and theology. Philosophical first principles were certain and necessary because the mind could clearly see that it was impossible for them to be otherwise. Furthermore the evidence of the truth and necessity of philosophical first principles manifested itself immediately to the inquiring mind. Metaphysics, for example, possessed the intrinsic evidence on which its own first principles were grounded. Theology, on the other hand, did not. Theology's first principles were the revealed truths of the Catholic faith. Revealed truths should be called immediately evident in the sense that they were incapable of philosophical "proof." But revealed truths were not self-evident in the philosophical sense of the term. Revealed truths were mediately evident from a philosophical point of view. For the believing mind assented to their truth on the authority of the revealing God. The believing mind did not itself possess the intrinsic evidence of their necessary truth.[21]

Yet the mediate character of their evidence accounted for the essentially higher certitude which theology's revealed first principles possessed. For their necessary truth was grounded on the infallible word of the revealing God himself. The essentially higher certitude of its first principles distinguished scientific theology from every other science; and, since only the believer who had made a formal and explicit act of faith possessed this essentially higher certitude, only the believer could engage in scientific theology.[22] An unbeliever could criticize the conclusions which a theologian derived from a set of postulated "credal presuppositions." But the unbeliever who did that was not himself engaged in scientific theology. Hypothetically postulated "credal presuppositions" were not theological first principles. Hypothetically postulated "credal presuppositions" were not the object of the supernatural assent of Christian faith. Hence they lacked the evidence and the certainty which only the assent of faith could mediate.[23]

Apologetics therefore was not a part of scientific theology, as Drey and the Tübingen theologians claimed.[24] The task of apologetics was to vindicate the reasonableness and the moral necessity of the act of faith. Apologetics drew upon philosophy to establish God's existence, the divine attributes through which God could be known as a possible revealer, and the possibility of signs and miracles through which God could testify to the authenticity of his historical revelation. Apologetics also drew upon history to establish the positive fact of Christian revelation and the content of the revelation contained in the historical sources of Scripture and oral tradition. Apologetics, however, could not establish the truth of Christian revelation. It could establish no more than its credibility and man's moral obligation to believe it. The truth of Christian revelation could only be known through the supernatural act of faith whose motive was the authority of the revealing God.

The historical and philosophical arguments employed by apologetics, on the contrary, derived their evidence from the light of natural reason. The first principles of philosophy and history were not theological first principles. They led up to the assent of faith; they were not themselves dependent upon it. Natural reason could grasp the evidence for its judgment of credibility in respect to Christian revelation.[25] But only supernatural reason could make the assent of faith to the truth of Christian revelation. Philosophy, history, and apologetics were no more than presuppositions for scientific theology.[26] They did not proceed from the theological first principles derived through the light of faith. Therefore they could not possess the evidence and necessity which those theological first principles provided. Apologetics, or fundamental theology, and scientific theology therefore were irreducibly distinct disciplines.

Theology, Grace and Faith

On the basis of his distinction between apologetics, or fundamental theology, and scientific theology, Kleutgen was able to define his own theological position in relation to the positions of the other important nineteenth-century theologians. Apologetics could establish historical and philosophical arguments for the credibility of revelation. Traditionalist fideism therefore was unsound, since, according to the traditionalists, the first principles in all the sciences depended on faith and revelation. On the other hand, if theological science not only proceeded from revealed first principles but required for its intellectual operations a mind elevated by grace and faith, a "philosophy of revelation," which differed from other philosophical disciplines only because the object of its reflection was positive historical revelation, could not be scientific theology. The "philosophy of revelation" which Günther and the Tübingen theologians advocated implied that unelevated human reason in principle had the ability to acquire the scientifically certain knowledge of Christian revelation which only faith and grace could provide. Furthermore, if theology was the science of the truths which are believed insofar as they are believed, a Cartesian real method of doubt could not be incorporated into the method of theology as Hermes recommended. For a real Cartesian doubt would destroy the certitude and the necessity of faith without which scientific theology was impossible.[27] The traditionalists conceded too little to unelevated human reason. Therefore they were fideists. Drey, the Tübingen theologians, and Günther conceded too much. Therefore they were semirationalists.

Significance of Kleutgen's Definition of Theology

Post-Reformation scholastic theology applied St. Thomas' method to the new problems which arose with the birth of controversial and positive theology.[28] Cano, Suarez, Vasquez, and de Lugo were among the great theologians associated with this period. When scholastic theology was confronted with the new post-Reformation problems, a controversy arose among the scholastics over the distinction between the formal object, the cognitional "source" or "light" of theology (the science of the truths which are believed), and the formal object, the cognitional "source" or "light" of the act of faith itself. For, when post-Reformation theology was challenged by the biblical theology of the reformers, scho-

lastic theologians were forced to defend the certainty and the necessity
of the theological conclusions which they had deduced from their revealed first principles through theological reasoning. Cano and Vasquez
defended the position that theological conclusions deduced from revealed
first principles with the aid of naturally known minor premises had the
necessity and certainty of faith itself. If they wished to hold that position,
they were also obliged through logical consistency to maintain that the
formal object of theology and the formal object of the act of faith were
identical. Suarez and de Lugo could not accept that claim because, in
their opinion, it could not be justified. Theological conclusions deduced
from revealed first principles were unquestionably certain. Nevertheless,
if the minor premise on which a theological deduction rested was not
known through the light of faith but through the light of natural reason,
its theological conclusion could not possess the certainty and necessity of
faith. Therefore, according to Suarez and de Lugo, there was an inadequate distinction between theology and faith. Theology included the
habit of faith in its intellectual operations in the way that a larger whole
includes one of its constituent parts. Nevertheless, as de Lugo put it,
theology, in its deductive conclusions, "added something" to the habit of
faith, i.e., philosophical reasoning.[29] De Lugo's definition of theology
therefore, which became a commonplace among the post-Reformation
scholastics, was "the science which derives its doctrines from faith with
the help of thought."[30] This definition, Kleutgen believed, was in perfect
conformity with St. Thomas' definition of theology as a science of faith.
Furthermore, there was no reason to confuse de Lugo's scientific theology with a semirationalist "philosophy of revelation." For, in a semirationalist philosophy of revelation, the philosophizing intellect did not
differ in nature from the philosophizing intellect which operated in other
areas of human knowledge. But in de Lugo's scientific theology the intellect which philosophized within theology had to be elevated by the supernatural grace of faith. Otherwise de Lugo could not have said that
theology "included the habit of faith" while "adding something to it."

   Thus Kleutgen's conception of the evidence, necessity, and certitude
of faith determined his definition of the nature of theology and his attitude toward a Cartesian doubt as part of a theological method. Kleutgen's
definition of the nature and certainty of theology determined in its turn
his classification of the other nineteenth-century theologians under the
rubric of "fideist" or "semirationalist," despite the significant differences
in their theological positions. By doing so, Kleutgen created the inter-

pretative model according to which subsequent generations read the history of nineteenth-century Catholic theology. Kleutgen's influence as a theologian at the First Vatican Council, especially upon the drafting of its Constitution on Faith, led to a classification of the theologies against which the constitution was directed as fideist and semirationalist, just as Kleutgen had defined them.[31] And, in later years, Kleutgen's extended and lucid exposition of the theologies of Hermes, Günther, and Hirscher in *Die Theologie der Vorzeit* became the prime reference source for several generations of historians. As a result, the commonly received interpretation of nineteenth-century Catholic theology became basically Kleutgen's interpretation, based on Kleutgen's own theology of grace and faith.

THE SCIENTIFIC UNITY OF THE "OLD" THEOLOGY

According to the "old" theologians theology was an Aristotelian science of faith. Although it dealt with a multitude of truths and derived its revealed first principles from the manifold sources of Scripture and tradition, theology was a unitary science. Despite the multiplicity and diversity of the individual truths with which it dealt, theology was unified by its formal object or cognitional light. For all the truths considered in theology were considered precisely insofar as they were believed in the testimony of the revealing God.

Furthermore this Aristotelian scientific theology, despite the diversity of the "questions" which it took up, remained a unified science because God himself was the supreme subject of whom its scientific judgments were predicated. Theology's scientific affirmations were affirmations about the triune God, the creator of the universe of grace and nature, the Incarnate God, the founder of the order of redemption, and the triune God who was the final goal of redeemed man's intellectual and volitional activity. Since God was the supreme subject of Thomas' *Summa Theologiae*, God, in his inner being and his exterior work of creation and redemption, could rightly be called the supreme "unifying idea" which directed the selection and ordering of the material treated in Thomas' speculative and moral theology. Thomas' theology therefore should be described as an intellectually unified, supernaturally certain and necessary, Aristotelian science of God's inner being and of God's exterior creative and redemptive work.[32]

Furthermore, Thomas' theological science was unified by its three-fold purpose. According to St. Thomas, scientific theology was directed by a triple aim. Scientific theology had to determine the exact content of Catholic truth and defend that truth against the intellectual attacks of its enemies. Scientific theology also had the responsibility to determine the rules which the Catholic faith prescribed for the Christian's moral and spiritual action. Finally scientific theology must lead the purified and reflective Christian soul to contemplation and spiritual enjoyment of the truth.[33]

The triple aim of Thomas' scientific theology embraced the theological functions which modern theology had dispersed among three distinct theological disciplines. Its clarification and defense of the Catholic faith fulfilled the function of modern dogmatic or positive theology. Its direction of the Christian's moral and spiritual activity fulfilled the function of modern practical theology. Its direction of the Christian soul to contemplative enjoyment of divine truth fulfilled the function of modern speculative theology. Dogmatic, practical, and speculative theology were distinguished in Thomas' scientific theology but they were never separated from each other. On the contrary, they were related to each other through the three-fold aim of Thomas' science of God's being and of God's exterior creative and redemptive work as the *alpha* and *omega* of the universe.[34]

Modern theologians like Hermes, Hirscher, and Günther separated dogmatic theology from practical and speculative theology. Just as post-Cartesian philosophy had shattered the unity of thought and being which the "old" philosophy had preserved, post-Cartesian theological method had shattered the intrinsic unity of dogmatic, practical, and speculative theology. The moderns claimed that these sharp divisions in their theology were demanded by the rigorous requirements of modern scientific method and by the complex problems of positive theology which the medieval scholastics had never been obliged to face. But this claim simply manifested the modern theologians' ignorance of scholasticism. Post-Reformation scholasticism had confronted the problems of positive theology. Melchior Cano's *De Locis Theologicis* was the supreme example of the application of scholastic method to the problems of positive theology. Suarez and de Lugo were excellent moralists. The post-Reformation scholastic theologians were by no means ignorant of the relation between their speculative moral theology and the more practical demands of their casuistry, and ascetical and mystical theology. Scholastics knew how to make the necessary distinctions between the diverse theological functions required by the triple aim of their scientific theology without destroying its scientific unity.[35]

Nevertheless, the modern theologians had made a number of serious complaints against the effectiveness of the unified scholastic method in its application to dogmatic, practical, and speculative theology. In all fairness, these complaints should be considered. Then a comparison between the modern methods in these three areas and the scholastic theological method would show whether or not these complaints were justified. To be fair and realistic, however, that comparison could not be confined to a contrast between modern and medieval scholasticism. It would have to be extended to the fully developed form which scholasticism assumed in the works of the great post-Reformation scholastic philosophers and theologians.

Scholasticism and Dogmatic Theology: Hermes

Kleutgen had already given his critical evaluation of the act of faith in the fourth volume of *Die Theologie der Vorzeit*.[36] He had criticized Hermes' method of Cartesian doubt and Hermes' theory of knowledge in his *Die Philosophie der Vorzeit*.[37] In the fifth volume of *Die Theologie der Vorzeit* Kleutgen gave a careful exposition of Hermes' theological method and, in contrast to it, presented his own conception of the nature of scholastic positive theology.

Hermes considered the scholastic approach to positive theology thoroughly unscientific. Scholastic theology was an Aristotelian science. Therefore its syllogistic reasoning began with a set of primordial judgments or revealed first principles. From these revealed principles it then proceeded to deduce its theological conclusions by the use of minor premises derived from natural reason. Hermes condemned the scholastic combination of revealed major premises and naturally known minor premises as scientifically unwarranted.

Theology had no revealed first principles or primordial judgments. All that theology possessed were its historical sources: Scripture, tradition, and Church law.[38] There was no logical order among the truths that could be derived from theology's historical sources. Therefore it was impossible for a speculative theologian to acquire a deeper understanding of revealed truths by arranging them in a descending series of syllogisms. The theologian must be content to confine himself to the methodical reading of theology's historical sources. His task was to go through them in order and establish with indubitable historical certainty that the individual truths of the Catholic faith were actually contained in them.[39] Scientific theology was not the deduction of speculative conclusions from first principles. It was the positive "assembling" of a body of individual truths from their historical sources.[40]

This could be done, Hermes claimed, because theology was "the essential content of the doctrines about God and the relation of the world, and man in particular, to God." Theology had its known historical sources; it had the scientific principle of theological relevance, on the basis of which a theologian could establish with indubitable certitude that a truth, identified as theologically relevant, was in fact contained in theology's known historical sources. In other words, scientific theology was positive theology.[41]

Scholastic speculative theology was not scientific theology. The analogous concepts which the scholastics derived from their knowledge of finite reality could not be applied to the supernatural realities of revelation and still preserve a coherent unity of meaning. Yet the major premise in a scholastic speculative syllogism was claimed to be a revealed truth and the minor premise frequently was known by natural reason alone. Scholastic syllogisms of this sort were vitiated by the fallacy of equivocation. Their middle term was applied to a revealed truth in the major premise and to a naturally known truth in the minor premise. Consequently the middle term could not preserve the logical unity which a middle term must possess in order to perform its function in a valid syllogism. Therefore the syllogisms through which scholastic theology argued to its theological conclusions were fallacious because they had four terms.[42]

Furthermore the scholastic method of deducing theological conclusions from revealed first principles led to an arbitrary and fantastic accumulation of useless questions in the scholastic treatises. Scholastic method had no norm for determining relevant from irrevelant material in the construction of its theology. Neither did it have any norm for determining when its catalogue of theological conclusions was complete. Hermes' scientific theology, on the other hand, did have a norm of theological relevance in the construction of its theology. If a doctrine did not pertain to God or to the world's relation to God, it was theologically irrelevant and therefore it should be omitted. Hermes' theology also possessed a norm for scientific completeness. Assemble theology's known historical sources. Go through them methodically, applying the two-fold norm of theological relevance and apodictical historical certitude. When the task was finished, the catalogue of theological truths was complete and the work of the theologian was known with certainty to be concluded.[43]

Kleutgen's philosophical critique of Hermes' methodical doubt and Hermes' epistemology of analogous concepts will be considered later. These philosophical presuppositions and Hermes' theology of the certainty of faith were, of course, the fundamental presuppositions which determined Hermes' position on theological method. In the second part of *Die Theologie der Vorzeit,* however, Kleutgen proposed to show that Hermes' denial of theology's scientific character could be attributed to his own ignorance of scholasticism. God and God's creating and redeeming activity was the supreme subject of scholastic scientific theology. Therefore scholastic scientific theology also made God and the relationship of the world and man to God its norm of theological relevance. The supreme subject and the three-fold aim of scholastic theology gave scientific direction to the selection and ordering of its materials. No one who had studied the *Summa Theologiae* with any care could call Thomas' scientific theology an arbitrary and fantastic accumulation of useless questions.[44]

But what was the relation of scholastic theology to positive theology? The modern theologians claimed that there was none and that the medieval scholastics simply had not done positive theology. This was not the case. St. Thomas and St. Bonaventure had not done a great deal of it but the positive theology which appeared in their works was careful, professional, and accurate. The post-Reformation scholastics, especially Melchior Cano, had given a great deal of attention to positive theology, and the proper relation of scholastic theology to it could be discovered from an attentive study of their work.

Scholastic positive theologians employed a two-fold method. The first was an analytic method. In this method the truths of the Catholic faith were taken in the conceptually developed form in which they were presented in the official teaching of the Church that had been shaped by the scholastic doctors. These developed Catholic doctrines were broken down into their constitutive elements, which could then be traced back to their original sources in the writings of the Fathers, the creeds, Scripture, or tradition. In this manner the positive theologian could vindicate the identity between the Church's developed doctrines expressed in her scholastic theology and the doctrines contained in the historical sources of Catholic truth.

The other method employed by positive theologians was the synthetic method. In the synthetic method the developed scholastic doctrines were not presupposed. The positive theologian went immediately to theology's historical sources from which he reconstructed the doctrines of Catholic theology by "gathering up" their constitutive elements through a positive study of their doctrinal content. This was the method of positive theology favored by the Reformers and Hermes. It was not their exclusive property however. Scholastic positive theologians used it too. Nevertheless there was an essential difference between the way in which scholastic positive theologians used the synthetic method in their positive theology and the way in which the Reformers and Hermes used it. Hermes and the Reformers really doubted that the theological doctrines formulated by the scholastic doctors and contained in the Church's official teachings could actually be found in theology's historical sources. Scholastic positive theologians did not.[45]

Scholastic positive theologians confined themselves to a methodical fictitious doubt. That meant that, although they did not presuppose the developed concepts of the scholastic doctors and the Church's official teaching in the positive study through which they assembled the elements of the Church's theological doctrines from historical sources, scholastic positive theologians did not suspend their personal belief in the correspondence between the Church's developed doctrines and the content of the historical sources of revelation. Melchior Cano, for example, expressly stated that his own study of theology's historical sources was dependent upon his scholastic theology. Cano's account of the guiding role of scholastic theology in his positive investigation of theology's historical sources was an accurate expression of the close relation between speculative theology and historical inquiry in scholastic positive theology. For, without the direction of scholasticism's clear and developed formulation of the truths of faith, the positive theologian lacked a clear goal in his historical research, and beginners in theology could easily be led into confusion and serious doctrinal error.[46]

Kleutgen's account of the relation between positive and scholastic speculative theology manifested one of his own great weaknesses, his lack of historical sense. Kleutgen approached historical texts in the same manner in which post-Reformation scholastics, like Cano and Suarez, approached them. Like Suarez, Kleutgen was scrupulously fair in his presentation of the texts of the philosophers and theologians whom he criticized and, again like Suarez, he displayed an unusually impressive historical erudition. But, once more like Suarez, Kleutgen had no real sense of historical development. Development, for Kleutgen, took the form of clarification and expansion of concepts or of deductive expansion of philosophical or theological principles. He showed no awareness of the role of cultural development or of different conceptual frameworks in the history of thought. He read the historical sources of theology carefully and intelligently but he interpreted them in terms of his own conceptual framework, which was essentially the conceptual framework of post-Reformation scholasticism.

Therefore, for Kleutgen, positive theology was simply engaged in "refinding" the developed, clear ideas of post-Reformation scholasticism in their scattered, confused, and less developed form in theology's historical sources. Clearly then, since the positive theologian who was guided in his work by scholastic speculative theology knew what he was looking for, he was more likely to find it.

History was a presupposition for Kleutgen's scientific theology. But Kleutgen did not consider history an intrinsic constituent of theology itself. Theology was an Aristotelian science of faith. The positive theologian could not abandon its certitude and necessity without ceasing to be a theologian. Kleutgen's absence of any sense of conceptual development and his blindness to the possibility of a plurality of conceptual frameworks within Catholic theology made it possible for him to entertain his vision of the "old" theology as a single, unified theology and to argue that a unified scholasticism was its mature, developed form.

Kleutgen could not accurately differentiate between positive and speculative theology because he had no conception of the role of history and of historical method within theology itself. Kleutgen's positive theology had to fit into his deductive Aristotelian science of faith, whose method was not historical. The function of Kleutgen's positive theology was simply to devise convincing controversial "proofs" for the existence of scholasticism's developed theological doctrines in the historical sources of theology. Positive theology could not lead to a revision of the conceptual framework through which the scholastic doctrines were expressed. Still less could it call into question the validity of an Aristotelian science as the ideal of a scientific theology. Kleutgen's contemporary reader, who is struck by the lack of historical sense in this erudite and careful theologian, cannot fail to see in him one of the cardinal weakness of neo-Thomistic theology—a weakness that would cause a widespread and deep-seated malaise in Catholic theology during the first half of the twentieth century.

9

KLEUTGEN'S THEOLOGICAL SYNTHESIS: II. PRACTICAL AND SPECULATIVE THEOLOGY

HIRSCHER AND THE TÜBINGEN THEOLOGY

Kleutgen's defense of scholastic practical theology took the form of a dialogue with the theology of the Catholic Tübingen School. In the first half of the nineteenth century German theology was divided into dogmatic and practical theology. Practical theology embraced the areas which scholastic theology classified under the rubrics of moral, ascetical, and mystical theology, and which would be classified today as Christian ethics and Christian spirituality. The leading representative of Tübingen theology among the practical theologians was Johann Baptist Hirscher. Hirscher was also the most antischolastic of the Tübingen theologians and one of the least acquainted with scholasticism.

As early as 1823 Hirscher had published an attack on scholastic theology, *Über das Verhältnis des Evangeliums zu der theologischen Scholastik der neuesten Zeit im katholischen Deutschland* (On the Relation of the Gospel to Recent Scholastic Theology). The target against which Hirscher's book was directed was the Mainz scholasticism of Räss and Weiss. The Mainz theologians were representatives of the narrow Strasbourg scholasticism. Their hostility to Bautain's traditionalism finally led to his condemnation.[1] At that time the Tübingen theologians, who were also traditionalists, manifested their sympathy and support for Bautain.[2] Hirscher's book, written more than a decade before the Bautain affair, is further evidence of the distrust and misunderstanding between Mainz and Tübingen which persisted throughout the nineteenth century. In Germany Mainz was the center of scholasticism. Kleutgen published his famous article on the condemnation of ontologism in the Mainz review *Der*

Katholik. Historically and psychologically an entente between Mainz and Tübingen was impossible. Both the scholastics and the Tübingen theologians were profoundly Catholic. Both schools were loyal to the Church. But, unfortunately, they were fated never to understand or sympathize with one another.

Hirscher's major work was his three-volume *Die chirstliche Moral,* of which five editions were published between 1835 and 1851. Four editions of Hirscher's *Katechetik* appeared between 1831 and 1840 and his *Katechismus* was reprinted several times between 1842 and 1860.[3] Hirscher was above all a pastoral theologian. His *Christian Ethics* was meant to be an edifying as well as a scientific work. It was directed primarily to pastors and the educated laity among whom its warm, affective style made it extremely popular. Hirscher's goal was to overcome the naturalism and moralism of German Enlightenment theology. Moral and catechetical instruction were to be made truly Christian again. They were to be centered on Christ, the Redeemer, his Church, and the Christian mysteries. The responsibility for the naturalism and moralism which had desiccated Enlightenment theology could be laid at the door of the scholastic theologians of the early eighteenth century. The cure for these evils could be found in the application of Drey's theological method to pastoral theology.[4]

As we saw in an earlier chapter, the unitary architectonic idea in Drey's dogmatic theology was the idea of the Kingdom of God. All the truths which God had intended for the education of the human race and all the free decisions which God in his providence had made concerning the orders of creation and redemption were contained in this unitary idea. Through Adam, the patriarchs, the prophets, and Christ, God had progressively revealed this idea to mankind with increasing perfection. God's definitive communication of the idea of the Kingdom of God had been made through Christ. Christ's definitive community of salvation, the Church, was the bearer of this idea.[5]

Hirscher's *Christliche Moral* was based upon the Tübingen presupposition that scientific knowledge must penetrate to the unitary idea which is the deepest ground and living force of any vital community. In the Church that idea, as Drey's dogmatic theology had shown, was the idea of the Kingdom of God. Existing in its eternal fullness in God's own mind, that idea, in its finite realization, had become the unitary living force in God's angelic heavenly kingdom and in God's earthly kingdom among men. Satan's revolt had brought about the fall of the angels.

Satan's temptation had led to the fall of Adam. Christ, the Redeemer, however, had become the principle of generation in the Kingdom of God. Moreover, Christ's Holy Spirit, acting within regenerated souls, had become the spirit of unity in the regenerated Kingdom. Therefore, the Church's Holy Spirit, which made each regenerated soul a child of God, was the supernatural principle of each soul's reintroduction into the Kingdom of God.

As the science of the Kingdom's practical realization, Christian ethics was the science of Christ's effective call to regeneration and divine sonship through his Spirit.[6] Christian ethics was the science of Christ's educational activity and the educative activity of his Holy Spirit through which the realization of the Kingdom was brought about on earth. Its goal was to trace the dialectical unfolding of the idea of the Kingdom of God both in each individual soul and in the community of the Church. By studying the vicissitudes of individual and ecclesial history Christian ethics would bring to light the interior and exterior virtues and the ethical, ascetical, and religious practices required for the realization of God's Kingdom through human action.[7]

Christian ethics was not an individualistic philosophical reflection. An objective science, in Drey's Schellingian understanding of that term, was an ideal reconstruction of intuited realities. Schelling's objective science required the intuitive grasp of a community's formative idea by an intellect informed with the community's *Geist* or "spirit" before it could attempt its reflexive reconstruction of that idea. Therefore Christian ethics must be the intellectual activity of the believer who had intuitively grasped the idea of the Kingdom of God through faith within the community of the Church. As a Schellingian objective science, Christian ethics must also be an organic science. Individual and social virtues and the practical demands of Christian moral and religious life would have to be grasped in their intrinsic relation to the architectonic idea of the Kingdom of God. Furthermore, since the Kingdom of God was a kingdom whose communal life depended on Christ's ceaseless regenerative activity, Christian ethics was fundamentally Christocentric. For it was the science of the practical demands imposed upon the soul by its vocation to regeneration in Christ.[8]

Again, since Christ's unifying and regenerating grace came to the individual soul through the vivifying activity of his Holy Spirit within the community of the Church, Christian ethics was the antithesis of an Aristotelian philosophical ethics. Christian ethics was the scientific study of the moral demands of a Christian life whose source was the Holy Spirit. Furthermore, the Kingdom of God must be realized on earth through the free response of individual Christians to the demands of God's directing providence. Thus, although the idea of the Kingdom of God was perfect and eternal within the mind of God himself, its progressive realization in the community of free, fallen, and regenerated men was historical and dialectical. Since practical theology was the ideal reconstruction of the progressive and dialectical realization of the idea of God's Kingdom among men, its method must not only be organic, it must also be genetic.[9]

The three volumes of Hirscher's *Christliche Moral* were devoted to the scientific reconstruction of the realization of the Kingdom of God. The successive volumes dealt in order with the foundation, the gradual growth, and the consummation of the Kingdom. The first dealt with the foundation of the Kingdom, or with what God had done for man at his creation and after his fall through the divine salvific dispensations of the Old and the New Testaments. The second volume examined the dialectic of the growth and vicissitudes of the Kingdom among men. The Church's healing and sanctifying work in all the stages of human life—childhood, youth, maturity, and old age—was presented in detail, and the theology of man's fall and conversion was developed. The third volume was devoted to the flowering of the Kingdom. The interior life of the children of God, especially the life of charity in their souls, was given careful attention. Then the exterior life of the Kingdom became the object of Hirscher's attention. Hirscher examined the Church's unity of faith and cult, the individual and social conduct of the children of God, the sincerity, fidelity, and justice required of them, and their relation to the Church's hierarchical authority. Hirscher's third volume then concluded with the theology of death, judgment, and the final consummation of the Kingdom.[10]

The Tübingen theology of grace and nature, which was presupposed throughout Hirscher's *Christliche Moral*, was quite different from Kleutgen's scholastic theology of the supernatural. In Kleutgen's theology sanctifying grace was an Aristotelian accident, an entitative habit, inhering in the soul as its proper subsisting subject. The theological virtues of faith, hope, and charity were operative habits inhering in the faculties of the intellect and will. Charity could not perdure in the soul that had lost faith and grace. Faith, on the other hand, could remain as an operative habit in a believing soul that had lost both grace and charity. Faith in fact served as a principle in this sinful soul's conversion.

As Geiselmann puts it in his remarkable study of the Catholic Tübingen school, Drey's notion of the supernatural was a modal one. As such, it did not depend upon the Aristotelian metaphysics of substance and accident which the scholastic theologians used in their theology of the supernatural.[11] In Drey's theology, the supernatural order was grounded upon God's ceaseless free directing activity, which was required for the realization of the idea of the Kingdom of God among men. As the Kingdom progressively realized its directing idea in the subhuman universe and in human society, the succession of events through which this realization occurred manifested itself as an order of nature. But nature was not the closed system of immanent causes which the deist and naturalist philosophers considered it to be. On the contrary God was constantly acting immediately upon the system of nature, not just to sustain it, but to intervene directly in order to produce new events whose *raison d'être* was found in God's own directing providence.

Thus, for example, in the act of creation itself God had made his primitive revelation. God had sent Christ as the Redeemer. God had raised up the prophets of the Old Law. God had inspired the evangelists. At every moment the Holy Ghost was immediately producing effects in the regenerated human soul through his divine activity that no finite agent could produce. The supernatural character of all these events was grounded upon God's uninterrupted efficient causality. Unlike the divine concurrence, which cooperated with natural agents in the natural order, God's immediate supernatural causality produced effects which were not contained in the necessary chain of nature's immanent causes. Thus, although each supernatural event was contained within the order of nature as an intramundane event, it transcended the order of nature in its ontological ground. For its ontological ground was God's immediate and free efficient causality.

Despite its grounding in God's efficient causality, Drey's theology of the supernatural was not an actualism. God's free causal interventions within the order of nature were neither haphazard nor disconnected. The occurence of each of them within the temporal sequences of events which constituted the natural order of the world was directed by the eternal idea of the Kingdom of God existing in the divine mind. For God's successive interventions were required in order for him to guide the earthly realization of his eternal divine idea to its authentic temporal realization. Furthermore, the supernatural activity of the Holy Spirit within each individual soul was identified with the Holy Spirit's fulfilment of his abiding function as the dynamic, directing bond of unity in the Kingdom of God on earth. Thus, although Drey's metaphysics of the supernatural was not Thomistic, it still allowed for a stable supernatural order. The supernatural order was an organically and genetically related series of events, which, as events, were part of the order of nature, but whose immediate efficient cause was the transcendent God. And in God's mind the eternal idea of the Kingdom directed each divine intervention. This is the meaning of Geiselmann's observation that Drey's notion of the supernatural was a modal notion. There is no place in Drey's theology of the supernatural for created sanctifying grace as a supernatural accident, an entitative habit inhering in the soul. Drey's theology did not explain the stable supernatural order through a supernatural accident (a formal cause) inhering in the individual soul as its material cause. Drey accounted for the stable supernatural order as an ordered series of events produced in a divinely free and supernatural way by an infinite agent directed by his eternal idea of the Kingdom to be realized on earth.

Hirscher's Tübingen theology of the supernatural led to his theology of the theological virtues. The activity of the Holy Spirit within the soul produced the fundamental virtues, the *Stammtugenden*.[12] These virtues were the living trunk, as it were, from which all the other virtues flowered as authentic expressions of the inner life of the regenerated child of God. Faith was the most fundamental of these "trunk virtues" or *Stammtugenden*. Faith was living knowledge of God's revealed truths. It was a profound interior conviction of their veracity combined with personal commitment to Christ, who, as Redeemer and Revealer, was the living ground of the world's salvation. Living faith could not fail to express itself in charity or love. Love was the surrender of the individual to the will of the Father and the Son, so that the divine work of salvation and regeneration might be accomplished within himself and within his brothers in God's earthly kingdom. Faith and love expressed themselves in activity. Activity was the devotion of all one's energies to the transformation of mankind into a visible Christian community of love.[13]

The three "trunk virtues," faith, love, and activity, constituted an indivisible, organic, active unity. Without activity, there was no love. Without love, there was no faith. Practical theology therefore was the necessary completion of dogmatic theology, just as activity and love were the necessary expressions of faith. Practical theology could not be separated from dogmatic theology.[14] They were successive stages in the scien-

tific reconstruction of the dialectical realization of the idea of the Kingdom of God.[15]

Hirscher's theology of the three fundamental virtues was a consistent
expression of the Tübingen theology of the flowering of the inner life of
charity into the exterior life of the Church. In this theology the order,
beauty, and love manifested in the exterior life of the Church were a
visible expression of the living presence of the Holy Spirit within the
ecclesial community. The inseparable coexistence of the three "trunk
virtues" as an actual organic operative unit was quite coherent with
Drey's active and modal conception of the supernatural. Hirscher's theology of the virtues also accounted for his understanding of the unifying
relationship that should exist among the various functions of practical
theology.

There were different psychological types among the regenerated children of God. In some men intelligence was the dominant psychological
characteristic. In other men the dominant characteristic was affectivity.
In still others the dominant characteristic was a gift for effective exterior
activity. In an organic Kingdom, whose exterior form was a visible expression of its unified inner life of faith, love, and activity, men of these
different types would be moved by the Holy Spirit to give expression to
the diverse aspects of the Church's inner life. Some members of the
Kingdom would be called to speculation. Others would be called to an
interior life of affective contemplation. Still others would be called to a
life of Christian action.[16]

Practical theology must take account of this diversity of individual
vocations within an organic Kingdom. Therefore, in addition to its
strictly scientific speculative function, practical theology must also have
its mystical and casuistic function. The aim of its mystical function was
to cultivate man's interior life of contemplation. Since its goal was the
cultivation of love and not the cultivation of speculation, mystical theology would not concern itself with conceptual analysis but with the practical promotion of affective contemplation. On the other hand, the
members of the Kingdom who were called to practical activity in order
to promote the growth of the exterior community of love also needed
specific practical direction to guide their concrete activity. The function
of casuistry was to provide this practical direction of the Christian's
exterior conduct.[17]

Nevertheless, since the casuistic and mystical functions of practical
theology were guided in their operation by its speculative function, and

since practical theology in its turn was an intellectual continuation of dogmatic theology, scientific theology was a unified intellectual system. Scientific theology was a true *Wissenschaft*. For its scientific reconstruction explained the meaning of Christian life and vindicated the demands of Christian moral action from their deepest ground, the idea of the Kingdom of God.

Scholastic theology, on the other hand, was not a unified theological science. Scholastic theology had no unifying architectonic idea to which its moral precepts could be related. Thus, since the scholastics possessed no unifying intellectual principle, their moral theology was no more than a disconnected series of precepts and prohibitions. Furthermore, scholastic theology was not Christocentric.[18] It was not centered upon man's supernatural life as a regenerated son of God. Neither was it focussed upon Christ's redemptive work nor upon the realization of the idea of the Kingdom of God.[19]

Scholasticism was slavishly dependent upon Aristotle.[20] It introduced pagan philosophy and pagan philosophical ethics into its moral reflections, although, as Drey and the Tübingen theologians had shown, theology neither required nor permitted any philosophy besides itself.[21] Scholasticism's servile dependence upon Aristotle was the reason for its kinship to the naturalism of the Enlightenment. Scholasticism's mystical theology was also pagan. Scholastic mysticism was built upon the heathen theosophy of Pseudo-Dionysius.[22] Thomas' devotion to Pseudo-Dionysius was well known. From Thomas Dionysius' pagan mysticism was transmitted to Eckhart and the fourteenth-century "German theologians." From them, it was transmitted through Jacob Böhme to the modern pantheist philosophers. The sober Christian ethics of the Tübingen theologians provided the remedy for the unhealthy Dionysian mysticism which scholasticism had introduced into Germany.

Scholasticism's lack of system also accounted for another serious flaw in scholastic moral theology: its Mosaic juridicism.[23] The medieval casuists were essentially lawyers. Their solution of cases, their commands and prohibitions were not intrinsically connected with the inner life of Christ and his Church. They were not traced back to the call of the Redeeming Christ to each of his regenerated children.[24] Thus the moral rule of the medieval casuists was a Mosaic slavery to the law. Because it was so, the Reformers were justified in rebelling against it in the name of the free individual's personal relationship to Christ. The Tübingen theology could do justice to the Reformers' legitimate demands without condoning their errors. Tübingen moral theology was a theology of self-consciousness and freedom confronted with the personal call of Christ. It was at once authentically modern and authentically Christian.

KLEUTGEN'S REPLY TO HIRSCHER

Kleutgen defended scholasticism vigorously against Hirscher's critical assault. Since Hirscher's ignorance of scholasticism was notorious, it was not difficult for Kleutgen to point out the errors, exaggerations, and distortions contained in Hirscher's historical account of it. What is significant today, however, is not Kleutgen's detailed correction of Hirscher's historical inaccuracies but the general plan of Kleutgen's defense of scholasticism and the philosophical principles on which his defense rested. For in that general plan and in that set of principles the radical divergence between the conception of theology entertained by the Tübingen theologians and the conception of theology entertained by the Neo-Thomists emerges clearly.

Kleutgen's major thesis in his defense of scholastic moral theology was that, contrary to Hirscher's allegation, St. Thomas' dogmatic and moral theology was built upon a unifying architectonic idea. In St. Thomas' theology, however, that architectonic idea was the idea of God, considered in his inner being and his exterior creative and redemptive work. St. Thomas' idea of God was the idea of the God who was related to the universe as its originative source and its ultimate end. St. Thomas' God was the triune God, who was at once man's creator and the satiating supernatural goal, to be possessed by man's intellect and will in the beatific vision which was the culmination of man's life of grace.[25]

And since in the *Summa Theologiae* fallen man's way to his supernatural final end was the way of the virtues, the Redeemer, and the sacraments, Thomas' idea of God as the *alpha* and *omega* of the universe included in its comprehension the Tübingen idea of the realization of the idea of the Kingdom of God. For what was the realization of the Kingdom of God, Kleutgen asked, except the work of fallen man's justification and sanctification? And this was precisely the work of which St. Thomas spoke in his theology of man's way to God through the virtues, the Redeemer, and the sacraments.[26]

Hirscher's Christocentricism was highly commendable but if Hirscher had any knowledge of the *Summa Theologiae*, he might well have asked himself why St. Thomas, who did not underestimate the historical role

of Christ in fallen man's regeneration and sanctification, made the triune
God the architectonic idea of his dogmatic and moral theology rather
than the Incarnate Word or the realization of the Kingdom of God. The
starting point and the conclusion of Thomas' theological synthesis was
the triune God. God, in the unity of his nature and the trinity of his
Persons, was the founder and goal of both the natural and the supernatural orders. Therefore the "fundamental ground" of Thomas' scientific
theology was far more fundamental and universal than the "fundamental
ground" proposed by the Tübingen theologians. For, as Suarez had
rightly observed, the most fundamental element in man's supernatural
life was sanctifying grace.[27]

Without sanctifying grace there could be no supernatural life at all.
Even if Adam had never fallen and Christ had never come, Adam and his
descendants would still have needed sanctifying grace to reach their
supernatural end. Metaphysically considered, sanctifying grace was an
entitative habit produced by the triune God, working *ad extra* through
his unitary nature, and received as an elevating accident in the individual
human soul. The soul's elevation to the supernatural order through the
formal causality of sanctifying grace was the metaphysical ground of
man's introduction into the Kingdom of God. The entitative habit of
grace was the indispensable metaphysical ground of man's supernatural
life as a child of God. The operative habits of faith, hope, and charity
were rooted in the entitative habit of sanctifying grace. From these three
theological virtues came man's power to persevere in his practice of the
moral virtues of prudence, justice, fortitude, and temperance.[28]

Unquestionably, in the historical order fallen man's regenerating grace
was due to Christ. Adam had sinned and, in God's merciful dispensation,
Christ, the Incarnate Word, had come as man's redeemer. In the metaphysical order, however, grace was a created gift of the triune God. In
the metaphysical order, sanctifying grace was an effect produced by the
triune God, operating *ad extra* through his unitary nature; and, in the
metaphysical order, sanctifying grace was an entitative habit elevating
the individual soul to its supernatural state. Before his fall, the innocent
Adam needed neither regeneration nor redemption. But, to attain his
supernatural end, the innocent Adam did need grace. The Tübingen
theologians had made a great deal of Christ's work of regeneration. They
should have realized, however, that rebirth means restoration to the life
that man had enjoyed before losing it through Adam's sin. Metaphysically therefore the fundamental ground of that supernatural life must be

ontologically prior to Christ's work of regeneration. Otherwise man would not have been restored by Christ to the same life which he had enjoyed before the fall of Adam. He would have been given a new life ontologically unconnected with the supernatural life of original justice. Therefore the ground of Adam's supernatural life could not have been the redeeming Christ; it could only have been the triune God working *ad extra* through his unitary nature.[29]

St. Thomas' *Summa Theologiae* preserved the all-important metaphysical order between the constitution of original justice and its restoration through the redemptive work of Christ. In the *Summa* God was first considered in his being and then in his creating and elevating activity. Only after the account of original sin and Adam's fall did the *Summa* turn to the redemptive work of Christ. Thus Thomas' theological synthesis was able to provide an adequate metaphysics of both original justice and Christ's redemptive regeneration.

Regeneration meant man's restoration to the supernatural order. Without the scholastic metaphysics of sanctifying grace, however, the uniqueness of the supernatural order could not be defended; and, unless it were, a satisfactory theory of original justice, original sin, and redemption became impossible. Without the scholastic metaphysics of sanctifying grace Adam's state of original justice became man's natural state. In that case only two options were open to the theologian. The theologian could opt for the Baian proposition that Adam's state of original justice, including his divine sonship and his vocation to the beatific vision, were due to human nature in its integral antelapsarian condition. Or, on the other hand, the theologian could deny the reality of man's divine sonship and his vocation to the beatific vision. Then, of course, the theologian became a naturalist.

Tübingen theology was notoriously deficient in its account of original justice and of the supernatural order. Hirscher's own account of Adam's original state prior to the trial of temptation, which he apparently "had to undergo" in order to make his definitive choice of God, was particularly unsatisfactory.[30] The Tübingen traditionalist anthropology with its metaphysics of a primitive revelation without which the first principles of metaphysics and morals could not be known, made Adam's state of original justice a natural state. And, in that case, Christ's redemptive work was reduced to the work of man's restoration to the perfection of the natural order, and the educative work of Christ and the Holy Spirit assumed the status of a natural causal influence. The Tübingen theologians therefore had to make their choice. They could embrace the Baianism which the Church had condemned, or they could embrace the naturalism against which they claimed their theology was directed. But, if they wished to defend the Church's orthodox teaching on the supernatural order, they would have to accept the Thomistic teaching on sanctifying grace and the Aristotelian metaphysics of substance and accident on which St. Thomas' theology of grace was grounded.

An historical genetic method had its advantages, of course. Nevertheless, it was not required, as the Tübingen theologians thought, in order to elucidate the metaphysical structure of a living "organism." Aristotle's metaphysical analysis of the fully developed organism into its essential structure of substance and accident, faculty and act was just as effective, and Aristotelian metaphysics avoided the danger of ambiguity and error in the theology of the supernatural order.[31] If Hirscher had employed Aristotle's metaphysics of substance and accident in his own theology, for example, he would have avoided the ambiguities about original justice, original sin, and the redemptive work of Christ which Kleutgen had pointed out in his critique of Hirscher's practical theology. The scholastic metaphysics of entitative and operative habits would also have enabled Hirscher to relate his theology of the virtues of faith and charity to sanctifying grace. If Hirscher had been able to do that, he would not have suffered the embarrassment of contradicting the formal teaching of the Church by his claim that faith could not continue to exist within the soul once charity had been lost.[32]

The inability of Hirscher's metaphysics to deal with the relation between the natural and the supernatural order was the reason for his inability to understand the proper relation between philosophy and theology. The entitative habit of sanctifying grace elevated a human nature which was complete in its own order. Man's intellect and will had their own natural formal objects. Man's intellectual nature had its own natural end. Therefore Thomas' metaphysics of nature and supernature enabled him to do justice to the legitimate claims of metaphysics and philosophical ethics. His use of Aristotle was not a "slavery" to pagan philosophy. It was an intellectual integration of the natural and supernatural orders of knowledge which were distinct, although not separated, within regenerated man.[33] The Tübingen theologians could not appreciate St. Thomas' work of intellectual integration because in their own theology the natural and the supernatural orders had become hopelessly confused.

Metaphysics and method went together. Thomas' speculative dogmatic theology was linked to his practical moral theology by his architectonic idea of God as man's efficient and final cause. Dogmatic and moral theology were related to each other as Aristotelian speculative and practical sciences. Man's speculative and practical intellects were distinct functions of the one human mind. Their diversity required a corresponding diversity in the methods of the theoretical and practical sciences, and therefore a diversity in the methods of dogmatic and moral theology. Furthermore, since the speculative and practical intellects, informed by the entitative habit of sanctifying grace, were faculties of an elevated human nature, man also enjoyed the speculative and practical knowledge supplied him by metaphysics and ethics. Thus Thomas' Aristotelian anthropology permitted his scientific integration of man's natural and supernatural knowledge while preserving their proper distinction.

St. Thomas' Aristotelian theory of the sciences also allowed for the application of the scientific principles of speculative and moral theology to practical cases through scholastic casuistry and scholastic ascetical and mystical theology.[34] Casuistry applied the general principles of Thomas' scientific theology to difficult and complex practical cases. Ascetical and mystical theology presented the truths of Christian revelation to pious Christians in a manner calculated to stir their affections. The aim of ascetical and mystical theology was to create love for Christian virtues, to stimulate the desire to acquire them, to purify the soul and direct it with Christian prudence to interior union with God along the three-fold path of the purgative, illuminative, and unitive ways. Therefore the relation between mystical theology and casuistry was not the relation proposed by Hirscher. In Hirscher's *Christliche Moral* mystical theology concerned itself with man's interior life of charity, and casuistry concerned itself with man's exterior activity.[35] The diversity of their aims, as Aristotelian practical sciences, and not the Tübingen progressive motion from the interior to the exterior, was the ground of the distinction between these disciplines. The aim of casuistry was to equip the pastor of souls to direct his flock intelligently in the solution of the complex moral decisions which they had to make concerning both their interior and their exterior lives. The aim of ascetical and mystical theology, on the other hand, was to inspire and direct the pious Christian soul on its personal journey toward union with God. Once again, Thomas' metaphysics of nature and end had enabled him to effect a correct distinction between the interrelated theological disciplines while Hirscher's inadequate metaphysics had caused him to confuse them.

Therefore the Tübingen theologians would be well advised to return to scholasticism. Their laudable theological aims were shared by the scholastic theologians. The Tübingen theologians would find in St. Thomas' dogmatic and moral theology the unified scientific theology which they were seeking. But St. Thomas' scientific theology was free from the disturbing ambiguities and confusions that weakened the Tübingen theology. In the scholastic ascetical and mystical theology of writers like Luis de la Puente and Francis de Sales, the Tübingen theologians would find the affective tone which they recommended for Catholic spiritual writing.[36] For ascetical and mystical theology were applied moral theology. The diversity of purpose between pure and applied moral theology required scholastic writers to use an entirely different style and tone in their ascetical and mystical theology. Nevertheless, applied moral theology was never separated from the austere scientific dogmatic and moral theology from which it derived its principles. In the end, the Tübingen theologians could find all that they were looking for in scholasticism. They opposed it only because they had never really understood it.

Kleutgen's Misunderstanding of Tübingen Theology

Kleutgen's reply to Hirscher in *Die Theologie der Vorzeit* was fair and intelligent. Given Kleutgen's theology of the supernatural, Hirscher's account of original justice, original sin, and Christ's redemptive work would have to appear ambiguous and unsatisfactory. And Kleutgen could not conceive of another metaphysics of the supernatural. The scholastic inability to do so perdured for several generations, as the disagreement between Brosch and Geiselmann in the 1960s showed.[37] Kleutgen's theology of the supernatural committed him to an Aristotelian metaphysics of substance and accident. Aristotelian metaphysics tied him to an Aristotelian theory of science and to an Aristotelico-Thomistic conception of the relation between philosophy and theology. Thus Kleutgen's theology, metaphysics, and conception of scientific theology formed a unitary whole.

Given Kleutgen's commitment to that unitary whole, it was inevitable that he should find himself in opposition to the Tübingen theologians on the major points of their theology. Tübingen metaphysics was not the Aristotelian metaphysics of nature. The Tübingen ideal of science was derived from Schelling and not from Aristotle. Tübingen theology had no place for sanctifying grace as an entitative habit. Consequently its theology had no room for the independent philosophy whose existence Kleutgen felt was a necessary consequence of a sound theology of grace and nature. The Tübingen theology of the supernatural, the Tübingen post-Kantian metaphysics, and the Tübingen conception of scientific theology were also a unitary whole. Therefore Tübingen theology was incompatible with the theology of St. Thomas, which alone, in Kleutgen's eyes, could defend the fundamental theses on original justice, original sin, and Christ's redemptive work that were demanded by a sound theology of grace and nature.

As a convinced scholastic, Kleutgen simply could not bring himself to believe that the Tübingen theological method could possibly be sound. And when Tübingen theologians like Hirscher, in all innocence, grossly misrepresented the historical teaching of the scholastic theologians, they confirmed Kleutgen in his conviction that the "unreasonable" Tübingen approach to theology must be due to the Tübingen theologians' ignorance of their own Catholic theological tradition. If the Tübingen theologians would spend as much time in the study of the scholastic theologians as Kleutgen had spent in the study of the German theologians, their eyes would be opened and their hostility to scholasticism would disappear.

This attitude, understandable as it may be, blinded Kleutgen to the possibility that there might be important elements of the Catholic tradition to which the Tübingen theology did justice while his own did not. The organic nature of the Kingdom of God, its historical realization through the vicissitudes of time, the place of living tradition within the Church, and the role of the Holy Spirit as the Church's vital source of unity were all highlighted in the Tübingen theology and virtually ignored by Kleutgen.[38] Kleutgen's preoccupation with the theology of the supernatural fastened his attention upon the Aristotelian metaphysics of individual nature. History and community had little interest for him.

In a more open climate Kleutgen's attention might have been directed to these fundamental deficiencies in his Aristotelian scientific theology through a genuine dialogue with Tübingen theology. But unfortunately Kleutgen and Hirscher were not engaged in a dialogue. They were engaged in a debate. Kleutgen's aim in writing *Die Theologie der Vorzeit* was to defend the "old" theology against the unwarranted attacks of its detractors and to prove that the method of Thomas' Aristotelian scientific theology was superior to the methods proposed in the "new" theologies. Kleutgen's polemical intent, combined with his own deficient historical sense, prevented him from entertaining the possibility that the picture of a unified Thomistic practical theology which he painted in his controversy with Hirscher might be an historically unwarranted representation. Modern historical research has shown that the unity between dogmatic, moral, ascetical, and mystical theology which Kleutgen defended against Hirscher's attacks was as illusory as the unity between scholastic speculative and positive theology which he defended in his debate with Hermes. By the time of Melchior Cano, positive and speculative theology had already fallen apart, and spirituality had begun to separate itself from scientific theology.[39] The effort which Cano and the post-Reformation scholastics made to hold these disciplines together by logical manipulation was heroic, but it was doomed to ultimate failure. Aristotle's scientific method could cope neither with history nor with the spiritual life of the human subject, as Rahner and Lonergan have shown in our generation.

The Tübingen theologians were aware of these fundamental weaknesses in Aristotelian theological method, although Kleutgen was not. Ironically, moreover, the philosophy of St. Thomas, which Kleutgen was struggling to restore to honor in the Church, contained within itself epistemological and metaphysical resources which could overcome the deficiencies of Aristotelian scientific method and go a long way toward satisfying the demands of the Tübingen theologians. But it never occurred to Kleutgen to exploit these resources because he himself had no problem with Aristotelian scientific method. Many generations would have to pass before these hidden resources of Thomas' epistemology and metaphysics would be brought to light. Thomism would have to be restored before it could be transformed and modified through the release of its own potentialities.

SPECULATIVE THEOLOGY: GÜNTHER

Kleutgen defined the role of speculative theology as the defense of the truths of faith against the attacks of unbelievers and the acquisition of a deeper understanding of these truths through a speculative consideration of their content.[40] The truths of faith could be compared with one another. Dogmatic conclusions could be drawn from a major and a minor premise both of which were truths of faith. Theological conclusions could be drawn through syllogisms one of whose premises was a truth known by natural reason alone. The body of interrelated revealed truths could be compared with the organized content of man's philosophical knowledge in order to acquire a coherent world view in which natural and supernatural knowledge would mutually illuminate each other.

Speculative theology required the use of philosophy in its operations. The analogous concepts derived from sense experience were necessary to relate the Christian mysteries to each other and to argue from the Christian mysteries as "revealed first principles" to certain theological conclusions. Nevertheless speculative theology could never be a "philosophy of revelation" of the type Günther proposed. Speculative theology's cognitive light, or formal principle, was the light of faith. That was why speculative theology possessed the certainty and necessity which only the act of faith could provide. Furthermore speculative theology was a religious activity. Its goal was not simply to defend the Christian mysteries against the accusation of irrationality and intellectual incoherence. Neither was its scope confined to a purely intellectual reflection upon the truths of faith. St. Thomas' speculative theology was an integral element of the religious soul's supernatural ascent to contemplative wisdom. It was an expression of the intellect's participation in God's own wisdom through the supernatural gifts of the Holy Ghost. Speculative theology therefore demanded the life of prayer, mortification, and moral and religious purification which the Fathers and the scholastic doctors associated with the soul's ascent to God through the stages of the purgative, illuminative, and unitive way. Otherwise the deeper understanding of the Christian mysteries which was the goal of speculative theology could not be achieved.[41]

Hermes had denied the possibility of speculative theology. Günther, on the other hand, had misunderstood its nature and exaggerated its capabilities. Günther had been correct when he asserted that Catholic theology should not confront the believer with a series of disconnected "revealed facts," as Hermes' positive theology did. Christian theology should try to understand the Christian mysteries in their relation to each other and then relate them to man's philosophical experience of himself and of his world. Günther had seen with remarkable acumen how a deeper understanding of the Christian mysteries could be achieved through a speculative reflection upon their interrelation. In Günther's philosophy of revelation the mystery of the Trinity was related to Adam's creation and God's primitive manifestation of himself. Adam's fall was related to the coming of the Second Adam and to the sending of the Holy Spirit, whose continuing presence assured the perduring activity of the Second Adam within his Church; and these interrelated mysteries were linked to anthropology, and the philosophy of nature, history, and society through Günther's speculative theology.[42]

Nevertheless Günther's speculative theology had proved to be a failure as a Catholic theology. The reason was Günther's inability to understand the supernatural character of speculative theology. Therefore Günther also misunderstood the nature of the certainty and necessity of which speculative theology was capable. Günther did not realize that the light of faith was the formal principle or cognitive light of theology. Therefore he saw no difference between the operations of the philosophizing mind and the operations of the theologizing mind. The only difference between philosophy and theology in his system was the difference between the objects to which their reflection was directed. The certainty and necessity of both disciplines were exactly the same.[43]

Consequently Günther could not preserve the proper distinction between faith and reason in his speculative theology. The human ego's self-awareness, achieved at the instant of God's act of primitive revelation, was an awareness of the triune God as the human ego's unlimited Non-Ego. When Adam failed in the test of obedience coincident with God's act of primitive revelation, his ungraced human nature still retained its knowledge of the triune God. In addition, Adam also possessed the knowledge that his own state as a fallen first Adam demanded that Christ, the Second Adam, must come as the Redeemer of Adam's sinful children.

Fallen man's self-awareness therefore accounted for his knowledge of the two central mysteries of the Christian religion: the Trinity and the Incarnation.[44] Günther himself made no bones about this point. For he attributed the religious ignorance and idolatry of Adam's descendants to their own sinful conduct and not to the inherited effects of original sin. Thus Christ's revealing work in Günther's system was practically reduced to educative influence as the Ideal Man. Günther rightly insisted that the discipline of moral purification was required to render the human subject capable of making the act of self-reflection through which the existence of the Trinity could be known with certainty. Günther also insisted that the Christian religion was needed as the educative institution through which that moral purification could be effected.[45] Historical revelation was also required in Günther's speculative theology to provide the positive data presupposed for Günther's "ideal reconstruction of the positive fact."[46] Nevertheless, Günther's "ideal reconstruction" itself was still an activity of natural reason. And, as such, Günther's "ideal reconstruction" was nothing less than an attempt to demonstrate by reason the truth of both the Trinity and the Incarnation. But, according to Catholic faith, such a demonstration was clearly impossible. The existence of the Christian mysteries could not be demonstrated. Knowledge of them could only be acquired through the act of faith whose motive was the authority of the revealing God.[47]

Günther's endeavor to transform faith *(Glaube)* into scientific knowledge *(Wissen)* through his "ideal reconstruction of the positive fact," confused the certainty and necessity of scientific theology with the certainty and necessity of post-Cartesian philosophy. Günther's Cartesian apodictic certitude of his own ego led to his apodictic certitude of the creating and revealing Trinity. His reflection upon the order of God's creation in the first Adam led with apodictic certitude to his knowledge of the order of redemption grounded upon the Second Adam. Günther was trying to apply the certainty and necessity of Descartes' *Discourse on Method* to his speculative demonstration of the Christian mysteries. Cartesian mathematical method, however, required the use of univocal concepts which could provide the human knower with a comprehensive insight into the nature of their objects. The deductions of Cartesian mathematical philosophy depended upon ideas which could meet the norms for clarity and distinction established by the mathematical and physical sciences. In that case, a Cartesian philosophy of revelation became a necessary deductive system in which there was no room for mystery or freedom In this type of deductive science the philosopher would comprehend the Christian mysteries, and God's freedom in respect to the order of creation and the order of redemption would be denied. Yet the incomprehensibility of the Christian mysteries and the freedom of both God's creative act and God's elevation of man's created nature to its supernatural state were required for an orthodox exposition of the Catholic faith.[48]

In the "old" theology, on the other hand, the theologian's understanding of the Christian mysteries was never affirmed to be more than imperfect and analogous. The scholastic speculative theologian never claimed to establish their existence nor to comprehend their nature through the analogous concepts employed in his theological reasoning. Still less did he endeavor to ground the connection of the Christian mysteries with each other through a system of necessary dialectical deductions. Scholastic speculative theology never claimed to be a necessary ideal system on the Cartesian or post-Kantian model. Günther's exaggerated and unorthodox claims for his own speculative theology were due to his Cartesian theory of knowledge. His Cartesian epistemology prevented him from understanding the nature of the analogous concepts through which man's knowledge of God was acquired and the limited knowledge of God which their analogous nature permitted. The content of theology's analogous concepts was acquired from sense data or from man's reflection on his own cognitional and appetitive experience. Far from claiming "comprehensive" knowledge of the divine being through the negative and analogous concepts of man's abstractive knowledge, St. Thomas declared that the human knower knew what God was not rather than what God was in his own proper and infinite reality. The indirect and analogous knowledge of God, which was all that man could acquire in the present life, fell far short of the perfect comprehension of the divine essence that would be required in order to establish the metaphysical interrelation of the Christian mysteries and their relation to the rest of man's experience through a certain and necessary system of philosophical reason.[49]

STRENGTHS AND WEAKNESSES OF KLEUTGEN'S CRITIQUE

Kleutgen discovered the fatal weakness in Günther's speculative theology when he criticized Günther's failure to appreciate the limits of man's analogous knowledge of God and the Cartesian necessity of Günther's theological reasoning. Speculative theology can never hope to achieve the apodictic certainty and necessity of Cartesian mathematical science. As Karl Rahner expressed it, God must always remain the "free unknown." God can never cease to be the "Holy Mystery." Man's knowledge of God can never be more than imperfect, indirect, and analogous. Speculative theology can never deduce its conclusions with the apodictic necessity of a Cartesian science.[50]

Nevertheless, Günther's acquaintance with post-Kantian philosophy had given him a profound conviction that the Christian mysteries could be linked together in an intelligible system. Günther's system was grounded upon the metaphysical relations entailed in the self-communication of the triune God to the first and the Second Adam. Like the Tübingen theology, Günther's speculative theology was Christocentric, organic, and historical. The Second Adam was linked metaphysically to the history of creation and to the history of man's redemption. The

Church became an organic community through the vivifying presence of the Holy Spirit, whose coming was an ontological consequence of the coming of the Second Adam.[51]

Günther's fruitful exploitation of his organic system of the Christian mysteries was impeded, however, both by his preoccupation with the necessity and apodicticity of his Cartesian scientific method and by his failure to appreciate the need for grace in man's knowledge of the reflection upon the Christian mysteries. Therefore the necessary deductions of his speculative theology failed to do justice to the free and mysterious triune God of Christian revelation.

On the other hand, Kleutgen's attention was focused almost exclusively upon the deficiencies of Günther's system. Kleutgen's principal endeavor was to direct his reader's attention to Günther's failure to respect the limits of man's analogous knowledge of God and to Günther's inability to preserve the essential distinction between the natural and the supernatural orders. Although Kleutgen appreciated the acumen with which Günther had linked the mysteries of the Trinity, the Incarnation, the Holy Spirit, and the Church into an organic system which he then related to human experience, Kleutgen made no great effort to argue that a similar linking of the Christian mysteries could be made by a scholastic speculative theologian.

In our own generation a distinguished speculative theologian, working in the Thomistic tradition, has produced a system of the Christian mysteries which, despite the notable differences between them, reminds his reader of Günther's speculative theology. Karl Rahner's systematic theology, however, does not suffer from the serious defects of Günther's speculative theology. For Rahner's theology, in which the triune God is the "Holy Mystery," does not attempt to link the Trinity to the Second Adam and the Second Adam to the Spirit and the Church through a set of apodictic and necessary philosophical deductions. Furthermore, Rahner's systematic theology, like Kleutgen's theology, is very careful to defend the intrinsic elevation of human nature to the supernatural order through sanctifying grace and the supernatural existential.[52] And Rahner's systematic theology is built upon a Thomistic anthropology and the metaphysics of the active intellect with which Kleutgen was familiar. One could argue therefore that if Kleutgen had only been aware of the metaphysics of existence and its significance in the Angelic Doctor's philosophy of man, he could have come up with a Thomistic "answer to Günther" which might have directed the Thomistic revival along a path of development similar to the path along which Rahner has led Thomistic theology in the second half of the twentieth century.

Historically and psychologically, however, such an event would have been practically impossible. Kleutgen's lack of feel for the historical and organic dimension in philosophy prevented him from appreciating the serious deficiencies of his own reconstructed Thomism in those areas. Kleutgen's antipathy toward post-Kantian philosophy did not dispose him toward incorporating its distinctive features into his own philosophy, particularly when he was convinced that post-Kantian historical and organic metaphysics was the basic reason for the lamentable failure of modern theology to do justice to the distinctness of the supernatural order. Above all, Kleutgen's dislike for the Cartesian method and for its subjective starting point made him shy away from anything like the transcendental method on which Rahner's speculative theology depends. Kleutgen was a brilliant epistemologist. Nevertheless, the historical and psychological limitations which the context of the nineteenth century controversy over grace and nature produced in him prevented him from seeing the theological possibilities of some of his own epistemological discoveries.

Die Philosophie der Vorzeit

Kleutgen's Thomistic philosophy was very similar to Liberatore's philosophical synthesis. Both Kleutgen and Liberatore defended the Thomistic unity of knowledge, anthropology, and metaphysics. Both developed St. Thomas' metaphysics of the active intellect and explained the dynamic unity of sense and intellect which it required in the act of human knowledge. The philosophy of man and nature in the second part of Kleutgen's *Die Philosophie der Vorzeit* is strikingly similar to the philosophy of man and nature which Liberatore proposed in *Della conoscenza intellettuale* and *Del composto umano;* and the analytic-synthetic philosophical method which Kleutgen recommended in *Die Philosophie der Vorzeit* did not differ appreciably from Liberatore's philosophical method.[53] Although Kleutgen was in no way dependent upon Liberatore, the understanding of Thomistic metaphysics and epistemology proposed by the two leading Jesuit neo-Thomists was strikingly similar.[54]

Kleutgen, however, approached philosophy as a theologian. Philosophy was an integral part of speculative theology. For philosophy, after all, was what was "added to" the habit of faith in de Lugo's definition of theology. Theological method was dependent upon philosophical method. The Cartesian starting point, the Cartesian epistemology of the universal idea, the Cartesian understanding of the role of the first principles, the Cartesian norm of certitude and evidence were all presuppositions of the "new" theological methods, especially the methods of Hermes and Günther.

One of the sharpest criticisms directed against the scholastics by the modern theologians was the alleged deficiency of the scholastic theory of knowledge. In this respect, as in respect to the criticism of scholastic theology, Kleutgen felt that he must set the record straight. Contrary to the allegations of the modern theologians, scholasticism did possess a profound and coherent theory of knowledge which could ground the principles of the scholastic metaphysics of man, nature, and God. And so, just as *Die Theologie der Vorzeit* contrasted the theologies of Hermes and Günther with scholastic positive and speculative theology, Kleutgen's *Die Philosophie der Vorzeit* contrasted the epistemology and metaphysics of their Cartesian method with scholastic epistemology and metaphysics. The first volume of *Die Philosophie der Vorzeit* was devoted to theory of knowledge and the second volume to metaphysics.

The relation of epistemology to metaphysics was similar to the relation of apologetics to theology. Apologetics established the reasonableness of the act of faith through which theology received its own first principles. Epistemology established the reliability of the faculties of knowledge through which metaphysics derived its certain knowledge of its necessary first principles. Apologetics was not scientific theology. Epistemology was not scientific metaphysics. Both were simply cognitional presuppositions for the certainty and necessity of their respective sciences. Their function was to present, in the form of an explicit scientific reflection, the cognitional grounds or motives because of which the certain assent which the theologian or the metaphysician gave to the necessary first principles of his particular science was a "reasonable" assent. Like the aim of apologetics, the aim of epistemology was to clarify the motives on the basis of which a legitimately certain assent could receive the scientific justification of its reasonableness. That was why Hermes had misunderstood the function both of apologetics and of epistemology. For Hermes required that the epistemologist, the apologete, and the positive theologian begin their investigations by bracketing their real assent to legitimately certain truths to meet the demands of the Cartesian real, methodical doubt.

This manner of proceeding was not only philosophically unwarranted, it was positively immoral.[55] By the very force of nature every man is aware that he must assent with certitude to his own existence, the existence of God, and the basic truths of the moral order. As he goes about the business of his concrete daily life the moral agent is well aware that the objects of these fundamental assents that structure the acts of meaning and value in which his moral decisions are made are not projections of his own mind. To withdraw his commitment to them in daily life until their existence has been demonstrated to the satisfaction of "philosophical reason" would not only be intellectually unreasonable; it would be sinfully arrogant.

Like apologetics and positive theology, epistemology could and should provide the reflex scientific justification for man's legitimate spontaneous certitudes by use of methodical fictitious doubt.[56] In other words, epistemology could prescind from its spontaneous certitude in order to present, through its reflex examination of man's faculties of knowledge, the motives which justify man's confidence in them. St. Thomas employed this method of fictitious doubt. Indeed, through his use of it, St. Thomas arrived at his *cogito*, or fundamental act of philosophical self-reflection. And St. Thomas' *cogito* was more accurate and more fruitful than the Cartesian *cogito* in grounding the validity of man's metaphysical knowledge.

In *De veritate* I, 9, St. Thomas had shown that the fundamental ground of the human knower's certain grasp of ontological reality was his reflection upon his own judicial act.[57] Reflecting upon this fundamental act of knowledge, the human knower became aware not only of his own act of knowledge but of the nature of his judicial act. Man's intellect differed essentially from the act of sense knowledge with which it cooperated in man's unitary act of knowledge. For, through its act of perfect self-reflection, the intellect was able to understand that its intellectual motion was directed by a natural finality which came to rest when the intellect assented to the truth. The intellect which revealed itself in Thomas' act of self-awareness was a self-reflective faculty of being. In its act of perfect self-reflection the intellect possessed the evidence through which it could know that it knew Being, why it knew Being, and that its natural finality was the reason why the object of its affirmation must be Being.

Kleutgen's discovery of *De veritate* I, 9 and his exploitation of its powerful "refutation of Descartes by Descartes" has been hailed as a sign of Kleutgen's unusual philosophical acumen. Rightly so. For none of Kleutgen's immediate successors in the neo-Thomist movement appreciated the potentialities of this profound Thomistic text, which was to become a commonplace among Maréchalian Thomists in the following century.[58] Kleutgen's metaphysics of self-reflection, coupled with his Thomistic metaphysics of abstraction, made possible his thoroughgoing critique of Cartesian philosophical method.

The human intellect was a faculty of being. But the intellect was united to sensibility in the unified act of knowledge which terminated in the direct universal and the judgment.[59] The intellect's judgments about sensible singular objects were judgments about being. The abstract essences represented in the direct universal were the essences of the sensible singulars existing in their intentional being within the human mind.[60] Therefore the objective evidence required for the certain judgments pronounced by the abstractive intellect was the intentional self-manifestation of the sensible realities themselves; and the necessity of the abstractive intellect's first principles could be explained by the negative necessity of the abstract essence represented in the direct universal.[61] An abstract essence was necessary and eternal because abstraction by its very nature required precision from existence.[62]

Thus, as Suarez had observed so aptly, metaphysics was the necessary science of possible essences. There was no such thing as a science of the existent. Existents were singular, mutable, and contingent. Metaphysics was the necessary science of Being. Therefore its object must be the real essence: that which was or could be.[63] The first principles of metaphysics were necessary and eternal because essences, abstracted through the elevating operation of the active intellect, prescinded from the contingent temporality of actual existence.

Therefore St Thomas' metaphysics of abstraction provided the cognitional basis for the all-important distinction between the metaphysical reality of possible essences and the physical reality of sensible singular essences, whose necessity was grounded proximately upon the elevating operation of the abstractive agent intellect and ultimately upon the exemplary causality of God's eternal and necessary ideas, which made existing singular essences the essences that they were.[64] Metaphysics was not the science of existents; it was the science of possible essences. For the abstract essences represented in the direct universal were possibles, and the necessary intelligibility of the divine exemplary ideas was independent of God's creative act. The divine ideas would have to have been what they were even if God had never freely decided to create existents. Therefore

God's necessary knowledge of his own eternal essence was the ultimate ground of the necessary certitude of metaphysical first principles.

Ignorance of the Thomistic epistemology of abstraction and of the Thomistic metaphysics of possible being was the root cause of the errors and confusion to which modern philosophy had fallen victim. Because Descartes did not appreciate the intrinsically intelligible necessity of Thomas' abstract essences, he had to ground the necessity of his deductive science in the veracity of the Absolutely Perfect Being. And consequently his system blurred the distinction between philosophy and theology. Kant did not understand the metaphysical necessity of abstract essences either. And so he restricted his category of the "real" to sensible existents and, through the logic of that assertion, was compelled to deny that the understanding could have any knowledge of metaphysical reality. But the philosopher who understood St. Thomas' epistemology of abstraction and St. Thomas' metaphysics of the nonexistential "metaphysically real," would not be deceived by the fallacious reasoning of Descartes or Kant. St. Thomas' epistemology and metaphysics supplied the evidence required to justify Kleutgen's claim that Aristotle rather than Descartes or the post-Kantian philosophers had the proper notion of metaphysics as a certain and necessary science of the real. For St. Thomas' epistemology and metaphysics clearly showed that the necessity and certitude of scientific principles was derived through the elevating operation of the agent intellect from the potential intelligibility of sensible singular essences.

KLEUTGEN'S SUAREZIANISM

Thus Kleutgen, like Liberatore, completely missed the significance of the act of existence in St. Thomas' epistemology and metaphysics.[65] Kleutgen's epistemology of the judgment and Kleutgen's metaphysics of Being, in fact, owed more to Francis Suarez than to the Angelic Doctor. This was understandable. Kleutgen's ideal of a unitary Thomistic synthesis was derived from the great post-Reformation scholastics. Post-Reformation scholasticism was really the "old" theology which Kleutgen was anxious to restore. Suarez was the greatest Jesuit representative among the post-Reformation scholastics. For Kleutgen, as for Pedro Descoqs and many another Jesuit as late as the twentieth century, Suarez' interpretation of St. Thomas was identified with authentic Thomism.

In the light of contemporary historical scholarship the "unified theology of the Angelic Doctor," which Kleutgen defended so brilliantly, must be dismissed as an historically unwarranted illusion. The epistemology and metaphysics of the Angelic Doctor presented in *Die Philosophie der Vorzeit* has also been shown to be a misrepresentation of St. Thomas' philosophy.[66] Nevertheless, despite the historical inaccuracies which later research has brought to light, Kleutgen's significant contribution to the Thomistic revival should not be minimized. Kleutgen's *Die Theologie der Vorzeit* restored Thomism to theological respectability and won credibility for his vision of a unified system of Thomistic theology. Kleutgen's *Die Philosophie der Vorzeit* supplied invaluable support for Liberatore's Thomistic synthesis, in which a theory of knowledge led to an anthropology and metaphysics that culminated in a Thomistic ethics of man and society. Kleutgen's contention that a harmonious union between an independent philosophy and a scientific theology was demanded by a proper understanding of the relation between nature and grace became a guiding principle of the whole neo-Thomistic movement.

Kleutgen's Thomism contained in embryo both of the great movements that have taken neo-Thomism in opposite directions during the twentieth century. Kleutgen's stress upon the potential intelligibility of sensible singulars as the source of the necessary intelligibility of metaphysical first principles, Kleutgen's anti-Cartesianism, his antipathy toward a subjective starting point in philosophy, and his determined hostility toward the Kantian transcendental approach to the problem of objectification and the grounding of first principles would be congenial to the Gilsonian and Maritainian Thomists. Yet, on the other hand, Kleutgen's discovery of *De veritate* I, 9, Kleutgen's exploitation of St. Thomas' metaphysics of self-consciousness, his insistence upon the moral impossibility of a real methodic doubt, and his exposition of the metaphysics of the active intellect and the unity between the metaphysics of man and nature which it entails have become fundamental theses of Maréchalian transcendental Thomism.

Nevertheless, Maréchalian transcendental Thomism would have horrified Kleutgen himself. Transcendental Thomism's openness to post-Cartesian philosophy, its subjective starting point, its denial that the contingent forms of sensible singulars can ground the necessity of "abstract" essences and metaphysical first principles, its stress upon the Divine Existence, grasped within the mind, as the necessary condition for the objectivity of human knowledge would have filled Kleutgen with dismay. Transcendental Thomism might well have appeared to Kleutgen as more akin to the modern philosophy and theology which he was trying to replace than to the Thomism which he was laboring to restore.

Kleutgen's philosophical and theological synthesis was not a permanent achievement. It was simply the first stage in a dialectical movement through which Thomism would have to pass in its relation with modern philosophy. Thomism had first to step back from modern philosophy in order to recover its own identity. Only as it recovered that identity through historical research and dialogue with contemporary thought would Thomism discover its kinship with the modern philosophy that at first appeared to be its antithesis. The dialectical movement would be long, troubled, and often painful. But it could never have been begun without the groundbreaking work of the Thomistic pioneers of whom Kleutgen may well have been the greatest.

10

DEI FILIUS AND *AETERNI PATRIS*

On 24 April 1870 the third plenary session of the First Vatican Council solemnly approved the apostolic constitution *Dei Filius*. The constitution, named after its opening words, clarified and reaffirmed the elements of the Church's traditional teaching on revelation and faith which had been obscured or called into question by nineteenth-century philosophers and theologians.[1]

The first chapter of the constitution affirmed the existence of an eternal, free, omnipotent, personal Creator, independent in his being of the spiritual and material universe, which he had produced from nothing to manifest his own perfection, and which he governed through his universal providence.[2] Pantheism and materialism were clearly the targets against which this chapter was directed, but Günther's denial that God had created the world to manifest his own perfection was also reprobated by its wording.

The constitution's second chapter declared that both God's existence and a number of the divine attributes could be known with certainty by natural reason.[3] Although atheism and agnosticism were clearly being rejected, the philosophers and theologians against whom this second chapter was principally directed were the fideists and the extreme traditionalists, both of whom declared that no knowledge of God was possible without divine revelation.[4] It was true, the chapter stated, that the ability which fallen men still possess to grasp these naturally knowable truths with ease and certitude and without error must be attributed to the influence of divine revelation. Nevertheless, revelation should not be considered absolutely necessary on that account. Revelation was absolutely necessary because God had elevated men to the supernatural order so that they might participate in divine goods that completely tran-

216

scended the natural capacity of their intellects. This indispensable historical revelation was found in Scripture and in the Church's apostolic
tradition.

The third chapter of *Dei Filius* defended the reasonableness of the
assent of faith against the "blind leap" approach to faith favored by the
Protestant pietist tradition. But, in doing so, it also insisted upon the free
and supernatural character of the act of faith which Hermes' necessary
assent of "intellectual faith" had compromised.[5] Since the assent of faith
was a reasonable one, it could be justified by rational arguments based on
"divine facts," such as miracles and prophecies. For these "divine facts"
were certain signs of revelation's divine origin, and were accommodated
to the minds of all men. And, in addition to them, the Church herself was
a powerful sign of the evident credibility of the Christian faith. The
Church's propagation, holiness, fecundity in natural and supernatural
goods, together with her unity and stability, made her a "sign rasied up
among the nations." The life and being of the Church was an invitation
to those who did not yet believe to come to her; and it confirmed her
children in their certitude that the faith which they professed rested
upon a very firm foundation.

The fourth chapter of the constitution on faith defined the proper
limits of faith and reason.[6] The constant teaching of the Church affirmed
that there were two orders of knowledge. Each order was distinguished
from the other by its principle, which in the first was natural reason and
in the second was divine faith. Each order was also distinguished from
the other by its object. For, in addition to the truths which natural reason
could discover through its own power, there were mysteries hidden in
God whose existence could never be known unless God chose to reveal
them. Nevertheless, once these mysteries had been revealed, human reason, illuminated by faith, could acquire a limited but very profitable
understanding of them through careful, pious, and sober inquiry into the
content of revelation. Human reason could acquire this fruitful understanding of the divine mysteries by observing the analogy between them
and the finite realities known to natural reason, by considering the relation between the mysteries themselves, and by reflecting upon the connection between the revealed mysteries and man's ultimate end.

Nevertheless, even after its elevation by grace and faith, human reason
could never acquire an insight into the revealed mysteries comparable to
its insight into the finite realities that constituted its own proper object.
For, even after their revelation, the divine mysteries so far exceeded the

capacity of the human mind that they always remained covered with a veil and wrapped in a cloud, as it were, during the entire course of man's life on earth. This did not mean, however, that there could be any conflict between faith and reason. No such conflict was possible, since the same God who was the author of faith was the author of reason. Far from being in conflict, faith and reason mutually supported one another. Right reason demonstrated the foundations of faith, and reason, enlightened by faith, acquired scientific knowledge of divine reality. Faith, on its side, freed reason from the errors into which it had fallen, and protected reason against further errors by the manifold truth imparted through its instruction.

Therefore the Church encouraged the progress of the arts and sciences. She declared that these disciplines were free to use their own principles and to follow their own methods within the proper sphere of their own competence. Nevertheless, she must warn philosophers and scientists not to extend their conclusions beyond the sphere of their proper competence and not to accept as valid scientific conclusions doctrinal statements which the Church had been obliged to condemn. For the revealed doctrine of faith had not been entrusted to men as a philosophical doctrine which they were to develop and improve through the use of their natural reason. On the contrary, the revealed doctrine of faith had been entrusted to the Spouse of Christ as a divine deposit, and it was her responsibility to preserve it faithfully and to expound it infallibly. An apparent conflict between the Church's teaching and the conclusions of scientific reason could only arise through an erroneous understanding of the Church's doctrinal teaching or through a false conclusion drawn by scientific reasoning.

Scholastic Influence on the Drafting of *Dei Filius*

Dei Filius therefore rejected a number of doctrinal positions attributed to nonscholastic nineteenth-century philosophers and theologians. The constitution's reaffirmation of human reason's ability to reach certain knowledge of God's existence and attributes contradicted the extreme traditionalist position which held that, in principle, divine revelation was absolutely necessary for man's knowledge of God. The constitution's defense of the free and supernatural character of the act of faith denied the orthodoxy of the distinction which Hermes had attempted to establish between the necessary conclusions reached through the "faith of the intellect" and the salutary commitment to God effected through the "faith of the heart." The constitution's own distinction between the obscure insight which the believing mind could acquire into the mysteries of faith and human reason's clear insight into the finite realities which were its proper object denied the possibility of a rationalistic "philosophy of revelation." The unconquerable obscurity of the revealed mysteries made a rationalistic deduction of their necessary connection with one another or with human experience impossible. The need of grace, faith, and pious reverence in the reflecting mind of the theologian clearly distinguished the theologizing intellect from the secular and autonomous reason of the pure philosopher. The Church's authority as the defender and infallible expounder of the deposit of faith denied to the believing theologian the personal independence which the philosopher could claim as his right within the proper sphere of his philosophical inquiry.

But the wording of the constitution also reflected the deliberate resolve of the council fathers to refrain from unnecessary determination of disputed theological questions.[7] Therefore, although the constitution declared that natural reason had the ability to know God's existence and attributes, it did not determine whether, in point of fact, natural reason ever did so.[8] Revelation and grace were morally necessary for the majority of men to acquire an adequate knowledge of God in their present fallen state. This assistance could have taken the form of God's gift of grace to every man. It could have also taken the form of a primitive divine revelation communicated to every man through the historical tradition of his community. *Dei Filius* did not exclude these possibilities, and neither did the moderate traditionalists among the council fathers who gave their approval to the constitution.[9]

Nor did *Dei Filius* specify any definite argument through which the existence and nature of God could be established. The constitution confined itself to the declaration that natural knowledge of God was possible in principle. It did not affirm that purely natural knowledge of God had ever been achieved in fact. The constitution neither recommended nor criticized any specific argument for God's existence on theological or philosophical grounds. Cardinal Pecci, the future Leo XIII, endeavored to have the council include ontologism among the doctrines which it officially condemned but he did not succeed in his endeavor.[10]

Nevertheless, despite the desire of the council fathers to avoid unnecessary intervention in theological disputes, scholastic theology had a strong influence upon the shaping of *Dei Filius*. The preparation of the first conciliar schema on faith had been entrusted to Johannes Baptist Franzelin of the Roman College.[11] Although Franzelin was not a member of the team of neo-Thomist Jesuits associated with *Civiltà Cattolica* and took no part in their campaign for the restoration of Thomism as a unitary system of philosophical and theological instruction, he was a disciple of Giovanni Perrone. Franzelin shared Perrone's scholastic views on grace and nature, faith and reason. He agreed with Perrone on the relation of apologetics to faith and theology. Franzelin therefore considered Bautain's traditionalism an erroneous opinion. Furthermore, although Franzelin was well acquainted with German theology, his evaluation of the German theologians had been influenced by the works of German theologians who judged their work from the scholastic point of view. Kleutgen's *Die Theologie der Vorzeit,* Denziger's *Vier Bücher über die religiöse Erkenntnis,* and von Schäzler's *Neue Untersuchungen über das Dogma von der Gnade und das Wesen des christlichen Glaubens,* for example, are referred to in the annotations to his schema.[12] It is not surprising therefore that the nineteenth-century theological opinions judged contrary to the orthodox Catholic position on faith in Franzelin's schema were divided, as Kleutgen had divided them, into the opposed extremes of fideism and semirationalism.

The conciliar deputation on faith, to which Franzelin's schema was submitted, approved the doctrinal content and concurred with the account of the theological opinions which the schema deemed contrary to sound Catholic teaching on faith and reason. Its style, however, was judged unsatisfactory. The length of Franzelin's schema, and the prolix, technical, pedantic style in which it was written, made it quite unsuitable for a conciliar document. Therefore the deputation on faith determined that Franzelin's draft would have to be thoroughly revised before it could be submitted to the council fathers for general discussion. Three members of the deputation on faith, Archbishop Dechamps of Malines, Bishop Pie of Poitiers, and Bishop Martin of Paderborn were designated by their colleagues to prepare a completely new schema. Franzelin's ideas would be maintained. Franzelin's account of the erroneous opinions against which the schema was directed would be preserved. The revision of his schema would completely overhaul its style but leave its doctrinal content undisturbed.[13]

Bishop Martin of Paderborn assumed the lion's share of the editing. To assist him in his work, he appointed his friend and former classmate Joseph Kleutgen to serve as his theologian. The eighteen chapters of

Franzelin's schema were reduced to nine. Of these, only the four which dealt with revelation and faith were presented to the council for general discussion on 14 March 1870 after their final revision by the deputation on faith.[14] Although the constitution was revised again in the course of the debate on the council floor, the constitution on faith, which the council approved unanimously on 24 April 1870, was in essence Martin's edited version of Franzelin's original schema.[15] Thus, in the sense that its drafters were scholastic theologians, *Dei Filius* can be considered a scholastic document, although neither its drafters nor the prelates who approved it intended the constitution to be an endorsement of the specifically scholastic point of view on faith and reason.

DEI FILIUS AND THE STATE OF "PURE NATURE"

Moreover, as Hermann-Josef Pottmeyer has pointed out in his masterly study on *Dei Filius*, the post-Reformation scholastic theologoumenon concerning the possible state of "pure nature" strongly influenced the approach to grace and nature taken at Vatican I. And a post-Reformation scholastic position on the state of pure nature had immediate consequences for the theology of faith and reason. Pottmeyer has shown that the baroque scholastic theologoumenon defending the possibility of a state of pure nature, which did not represent the thought of St. Thomas himself, not only influenced the theology of faith and reason which governed the drafting of the constitution, but also influenced the interpretation of its meaning by many of the council fathers. For a great many, perhaps most, of the prelates who took part in the council interpreted the Catholic teaching on grace and nature according to the baroque scholastic theologoumenon.[16]

The baroque scholastic theology of the state of "pure nature" not only affected the wording of *Dei Filius* and its interpretation by the prelates who approved it; it also encouraged the development of a nonhistorical Aristotelian scientific theology in the post-conciliar Church. The theology of "pure nature" focused attention upon the metaphysical possibilities of an abstract human nature, prescinding from its elevation to its supernatural end through God's free decree. As an Aristotelian theology of nature, it was not concerned with the historical order in which concrete man actually encountered the personal God of creation and revelation. Human knowledge was considered *in abstracto* and divided into two distinct metaphysical orders according to the ontological capacities of abstract "nature" and abstract "supernature." According to the Aristotelian theology of "pure nature," philosophy should concern itself with the knowledge of God which "pure nature" could acquire. Theology, on the other hand, would deal with the knowledge of God which the believing mind, elevated to the supernatural order through the ontological habits of grace and faith, could acquire through historical Christian revelation. On this view, human knowledge fell into two clear divisions, "natural" and "revealed," which corresponded to the ontological levels of "nature" and "supernature" in the human knower.

Therefore the theologoumenon of the state of pure nature also affected the understanding of the relation of apologetics to faith and to theology proposed in the text of the constitution on faith. Apologetics concerned itself with the signs, miracles, and prophecies through which "natural reason" could vindicate its rational assent to the "credibility" of revelation. The supernatural assent to revelation's "truth," on the other hand, could only be made under the influence of grace on the authority of the revealing God. Once the act of faith had been made, the believing theologian could proceed to acquire a speculative knowledge of the Christian mysteries through his careful, pious, and sober reflection upon them under the influence of grace.[17]

It was not difficult therefore for theologians who accepted the scholastic theologoumenon of the state of pure nature to read the text of *Dei Filius* in such a way that the relation between apologetics, faith, and speculative theology proposed in the constitution appeared to be the same relation which Kleutgen had proposed before the council in his *Die Theologie der Vorzeit.* "Natural reason" established the existence and attributes of the revealing God through its philosophical arguments. The philosophical and historical arguments of scientific apologetics established the credibility of Christian revelation through the evidence of the signs, miracles, and prophecies accessible to natural reason. Historical examination of Scripture and tradition manifested the positive evidence which supported the claim of the Catholic Church to be the church Christ founded. The supernatural assent of faith provided speculative theology with its revealed first principles and grounded the supernatural firmness of its theological conclusions. The Aristotelian theologian's sober awareness of the limits of his abstractive intellect preserved him from the intellectual arrogance of post-Cartesian rationalism.

DEI FILIUS AND DECHAMPS' "SUBJECTIVE" APOLOGETICS

Nevertheless, there were other elements in the text of *Dei Filius* which militated against the identification of its theology of faith and reason with the Aristotelian synthesis of philosophy, apologetics, and theology presented in Kleutgen's *Die Theologie der Vorzeit.* Perhaps the most important of these was the clear reference made in the text of the constitution to Victor Dechamps' "apologetics of providence."

The constitution's designation of the Church as "the sign raised up among the nations,"[18] a powerful living sign of the credibility of Christian faith, had been inspired by the apologetics of Victor Dechamps. This archbishop of Malines was one of the leading apologetes of the nineteenth century. Dechamps' apologetic method differed markedly from the scholastic method of establishing the credibility of revelation through proofs from miracles and prophecies and through historical arguments taken from Scripture. Besides these external divine "facts," Dechamps insisted, the apologete must also consider the "internal fact," man's interior longing for truth and goodness and the deeper longing stirred up in his heart by the Holy Spirit. The power of the Christian faith to satisfy these inner needs and the personal experience which countless Christian souls possessed of the Church's sanctity, spiritual strength, and goodness moved these simple souls to embrace the Church's faith, even though they had neither the time nor the ability to make their way through the arid reasoning of the scholastic apologetics. Its appeal to the correspondence between the concrete reality of the Church and the "interior fact" of man's subjective needs was the distinctive trait of Dechamps' apologetics.[19] The interior fact of man's subjective needs grounded his "method of providence," which he contrasted to the objective apologetic "method of the schools."

Through its reference to the Church as a sign of Christian revelation's credibility Franzelin's original schema had drawn explicitly upon Dechamps' apologetics of providence.[20] The important position which Dechamps occupied on the conciliar deputation on faith enabled the archbishop of Malines to exert a constant and significant influence upon the drafting of the revised schema which the deputation submitted to the council fathers on 14 March 1870.

Dechamps' apologetics of the "interior fact," however, presupposed a subjective and historical approach to apologetics which was more akin to the Augustinianism of the ontologists and the subject-centered method of post-Kantian philosophy than it was to the objective approach recommended by Kleutgen and the early neo-Thomists. Maurice Blondel would discover and exploit the possibilities of Dechamps' apologetics at the end of the nineteenth century, and when he did, the effect upon Catholic philosophy and theology would be explosive. Dechamps' apologetics of interiority could then be linked to the Thomistic metaphysics of self-consciousness which Kleutgen had discovered but which his anti-Cartesian animus had prevented him from exploiting fully. Blondel and Dechamps would become the bridge between the early neo-Thomism of Kleutgen and Liberatore and the subject-oriented Thomism of the Maréchalian school. But, although the transition would be made eventually, it would not be an easy one. The two apologetic methods which lay peacefully side by side in the text of *Dei Filius* would find themselves opposed in open and bitter conflict. Blondel's concrete apologetics would address itself to the mind and will of concrete historical man. The "action" of concrete man's spiritual dynamism would reveal a subjective "need" whose source was "more" than abstract human nature and which only the historical revelation mediated through the living community of the Catholic Church could satisfy.[21]

Dei Filius and the Speculative "Understanding" of the Christian Mysteries

The constitution's description of speculative theology could also be interpreted as an endorsement of the Aristotelian speculative theology which Kleutgen had defended in his *Die Theologie der Vorzeit*. Human reason acquired its fruitful understanding of the revealed mysteries through its reflection upon the analogy between the mysteries and the finite intelligibilities accessible to natural reason, the connection between the mysteries themselves and the relation between the complexus of the revealed mysteries and man's ultimate end. Certainly the careful, pious, and sober inquiry described in the text of *Dei Filius* reminds its reader of Kleutgen's Aristotelian scientific theology, whose unifying supreme subject was the triune God, the alpha and omega of the natural and the supernatural order.

As Johannes Beumer has pointed out in his revealing study on this section of the constitution, *Dei Filius*' description of the task of Catholic speculative theology profoundly influenced the development of that discipline in the postconciliar Church. Catholic theologians endeavored to acquire a fruitful understanding of the Christian mysteries through an Aristotelian science of God. Their effort to do so, Beumer observes, led to a tension in Catholic theology between its effort to acquire an understanding of faith *(Glaubenverständnis)* and its effort to develop an Aristotelian science of faith *(Glaubenswissenschaft).* [22]

The syllogisms of an Aristotelian deductive science move from its self-evident first principles to its derived conclusions. In an Aristotelian "science of faith" the Catholic theologian can proceed from his revealed first principles through his naturally known minor premises to his theologically certain conclusions. This is not the only function of an Aristotelian science of faith but, as Beumer has shown, in the post–Vatican I Church speculative theologians devoted most of their attention to its development. Catholic speculative theology became a "conclusion theology," whose aim was to derive an increasing number of theologically certain conclusions from its revealed first principles. [23]

As a result, Catholic "conclusion theology" became a sterile speculative enterprise. Its conclusions became more and more remote from the ordinary Christian's concrete life of prayer and action. Speculative theology ceased to provide the fruitful understanding of the revealed mysteries of which *Dei Filius* spoke. Theology no longer furnished the necessary help to the life of contemplation through which the life of Christian action must be nourished and enlightened. Hence the strong reaction against the pastoral sterility of Catholic speculative theology in the period between the two world wars. [24]

After World War II Thomistic speculative theology ceased to be a "conclusion theology." Thomistic speculative theology directed its attention to acquiring a deeper understanding of the revealed mysteries themselves rather than drawing an ever increasing number of theologically certain conclusions from them. This change in the orientation of Catholic speculative theology manifested itself in the "return to the mystery" recommended in the speculative theology of Karl Rahner and the emphasis upon "understanding" of the divine mysteries rather than deductive expansion of their content advocated by Bernard Lonergan. In contemporary transcendental Thomism speculative theology is considered a science of understanding rather than a science of conclusions. And, in this sense, contemporary Thomistic speculative theology has done more justice to the task assigned to speculative theology by *Dei Filius* than the "conclusion theology" of the earlier Thomistic theologians.

But can a speculative science whose aim is the understanding of the revealed mysteries still be an Aristotelian science of God? Kleutgen certainly thought so, but not all contemporary Thomists would agree with him. One of the most distinguished contemporary theologians in the Thomistic tradition is Bernard Lonergan. Lonergan has reflected deeply on the meaning of *Dei Filius,* and he has meditated more profoundly on the act of insight, St. Thomas' fundamental act of understanding, than any other Thomistic philosopher or theologian. As the result of his long reflection on the nature of theological science and on the nature of the act of understanding which is its epistemological foundation, Lonergan has reached a clear and uncompromising conclusion. A scientific theology, whose aim is the fruitful understanding of the revealed mysteries of which *Dei Filius* speaks, cannot be an Aristotelian science. For once the epistemology of St. Thomas' act of understanding has been properly appreciated, the deductive logic of Aristotelian science is seen to be inadequate to the demands of historical Christian revelation mediated to concrete man through the culture of his modern scientifically oriented society.[25]

Thus contemporary Thomists are no longer committed to the baroque scholastic theology of "pure nature," the objective apologetics of signs, miracles, and prophecies, and the Aristotelian speculative theology which the neo-Thomists considered the hallmarks of a sound and orthodox Catholic theology in the years immediately following the First Vatican Council. But the harmony which the early Thomists believed to exist between the theology of the Vatican I constitution of faith and their own understanding of St. Thomas' philosophy and theology is clearly evident in the text of Leo XII's *Aeterni Patris,* the *magna carta* of official neo-Thomism in Catholic philosophy and theology.

BACKGROUND OF *AETERNI PATRIS*

On 20 February 1878 Cardinal Gioacchino Pecci, archbishop of Perugia, succeeded Pius IX on the Chair of Peter. Pecci had been a convinced Thomist since his student days at the Roman College. As a young seminarian there, he had been one of Taparelli's most promising disciples when the latter was conducting his unsuccessful campaign to introduce Thomism into the College's faculty of philosophy. Pecci came to share Taparelli's vision of Thomism as a unified system of philosophical instruction. His brother Giuseppe shared the same vision also, for Giuseppe had come under the influence of Serafino Sordi when he was a young teacher at the Jesuit College in Modena.[26]

After Giuseppe Pecci left the Society of Jesus in 1851, he joined his brother at Perugia. Working together, the two brothers transformed the diocesan seminary into a center of Thomistic studies. The archbishop of Perugia was in contact with all the major currents in Italian neo-Thomism.[27] He invited the Dominicans to undertake the philosophical instruction of his seminarians, and he himself ordained the great Dominican neo-Thomist Tommaso Zigliara to the priesthood. Through his brother Giuseppe he kept in close touch with the team of Jesuit neo-Thomists on *Civiltà Cattolica*, and after his accession to the papacy he would invite Monsignor Salvatore Talamo, Sanseverino's disciple and successor at Naples, to come to Rome and assist him in his work of restoring the philosophy of St. Thomas to its proper place of honor in the Catholic schools.

By 1875 the neo-Thomist movement was well established in Italy and Germany. In Belgium two of the dioceses were ruled by bishops who had been educated at the Roman College.[28] Another alumnus of the College occupied a chair of theology at the University of Louvain and, in the town of Louvain, the Italian Dominican Alberto Lepidi had won his justified reputation as one of Europe's leading neo-Thomists. Lepidi had been professor of philosophy at the Dominican scholasticate in Louvain from 1863 to 1868. He was appointed its regent of studies in 1873 and occupied that post until 1885. Lepidi's *Examen philosophico-theologicum de Ontologismo* was one of the most complete and telling critiques of ontologism to be published in the nineteenth century.[29] Living in the same town as the ontologist professors of the University of Louvain, Lepidi had both the opportunity and the motivation to study ontologism thoroughly; and, as one of the most erudite among the early Dominican neo-Thomists, he was well equiped to criticize it from the viewpoint of St. Thomas' epistemology and metaphysics.

Leo XIII's first encyclical, *Inscrutibili Dei*, published on 21 April 1878, alluded to the importance of philosophy, and especially the philosophy of St. Thomas, for the Christian reconstruction of society and culture. Other indications of Leo's intention to work energetically for the restoration of Thomism in Catholic education during his pontificate soon followed. Leo prescribed that the Cartesian manual designated for the philosophy courses in the Roman diocesan seminary be replaced the following year by Sanseverino's Thomistic manual or by Zigliara's *Summa philosophica in usum scholarum*. At Leo's direction, Joseph Kleutgen was appointed prefect of studies at the Gregorian University and Leo made it clear that he desired to see the philosophy and theology of the Angelic Doctor given a more prominent place in the instruction at the Gregorian. Leo's brother, Giuseppe, and the Dominican neo-Thomist Zigliara were both elected to the cardinalate as a sign of Leo's intention to foster and promote neo-Thomism as a matter of official policy.[30]

Giuseppe Pecci, Matteo Liberatore, and, in all likelihood, Salvatore Talamo urged Leo XIII to issue an encyclical expressing his earnest desire to see the philosophy of St. Thomas reinstated as the single system employed in Catholic seminaries and faculties. Leo decided to do so and several months were devoted to the preparation of the encyclical, which was published on 4 August 1879. Liberatore prepared a preliminary schema for the encyclical and quite probably Kleutgen prepared one also.[31] It is virtually certain that Kleutgen was deeply involved in the writing of *Aeterni Patris*. And, indeed, the nonhistorical approach to philosophy and theology which characterizes the encyclical is very similar to the approach taken in Kleutgen's *Die Theologie der Vorzeit*. Furthermore, the connection which *Aeterni Patris* makes between the teaching of *Dei Filius* on the proper relation between faith and reason and the epistemology and metaphysics of St. Thomas as the philosophy necessary to that teaching represents Kleutgen's approach to nineteenth-century philosophy and theology. For the neo-Thomists *Aeterni Patris* was simply the Church's practical application of the lessons she had learned from the history of Catholic theology from the beginning of the nineteenth century until the Vatican Council.

THE CONTENT OF *AETERNI PATRIS*

An analysis of *Aeterni Patris* reveals quite clearly Leo XIII's commitment to the neo-Thomist ideal of scholastic philosophy as the necessary means to equip the Church's ministers for their apostolate in the modern world.[32] Although post-Cartesian philosophy had been used in Catholic schools by worthy men for worthy motives, Leo believed that St. Thomas' Christian philosophy was the only one capable of meeting the Church's intellectual and apostolic needs in the nineteenth century.

Philosophy must serve three functions in the Church. The first was apologetic. Philosophy could establish by natural reason both the existence of God and the divine attributes upon which the possibility of revelation depended. It could also prove that Christian revelation was credible by vindicating the possibility of signs and miracles through which the divine origin of Christian revelation could be established. Finally it could undergird the apologetic arguments through which the one, holy, Catholic, and apostolic Church manifested herself as a sign among the nations. Philosophy's second function was to invest and endow sacred theology with the nature, habit, and character of a genuine science. Using Aristotelian science as its model, *Aeterni Patris* described philosophy as the organizing structure through which the various parts of theology were unified into a single, interrelated body of knowledge. Philosophy furnished the principles through which revelation's diverse and scattered data "may be joined together in appropriate connection and all and singular confirmed by the same unanswerable arguments." The third function which philosophy served in the Church was to provide her with solid arguments to use in her controversies with her opponents.[33]

Philosophy would not be able to perform any of these functions, the encyclical continued, unless it followed the path laid out by the Vatican Council. It must never doubt or deny revealed truths, judge them by its own standards, or interpret them according to its own caprice. Philosophy's highest honor was to be admitted into familiarity with the heavenly doctrines in the capacity of their handmaid. Although philosophy should employ its own methods, principles, and arguments when dealing with truths accessible to human reason, the Christian philosopher must never reject divine authority. For the philosopher who knowingly embraced a position contrary to revealed doctrine was doing violence to the rights of faith and reason alike.

"Those therefore are the best philosophers," the encyclical asserted in what has become a classic text, "who combine the pursuit of philosophy with dutiful obedience to the Catholic faith, for the splendor of the divine truths irradiating the soul is a help to the intelligence; it does not deprive it of the least degree of its dignity, but even brings it an increase of nobility, acuteness and strength." In principle, the Christian philosopher is a better philosopher than the "separated" philosopher who ignores the light of revelation. The Christian philosopher's life of faith not only enlightens his mind through an objective grasp of revealed truth, it strengthens his power of intellectual penetration through the influence of the infused virtue of faith.[34]

Christian philosophy had served the Church well in her defense and exposition of revealed truth. The Fathers of the Church, who were distinguished Christian philosophers, were succeeded in their task by the scholastic doctors of the Middle Ages. These scholastic doctors, in the words of the encyclical, "undertook the immense task of diligently gathering together the abundant and fruitful harvest of doctrine scattered in the voluminous writings of the Holy Fathers, and of laying them up, once gathered, in one place for the use and convenience of generations to come." The praise which Sixtus V lavished on the theology of St. Thomas and St. Bonaventure in the papal bull *Triumphalis*, issued in 1588, should be extended to their philosophy as well. For scholastic philosophy possessed the same admirable qualities which made scholastic theology so formidable to the enemies of truth: coherent causal reasoning, clear definitions, sharp distinctions, strength in argument, and subtlety in controversy.[35]

St. Thomas Aquinas, however, towered above the other scholastic doctors. Without exaggeration the Angelic Doctor could be called the leader and master of them all. His great sixteenth-century commentator, Cardinal Cajetan, described St. Thomas' relation to the other Christian philosophers quite accurately when he said that Thomas "had the utmost reverence for the doctors of antiquity, [and] seems to have inherited the intellect of all." For Thomas, the encyclical continued in another classic text, "gathered their doctrines together—they had long lain dispersed like scattered limbs of a body—and knitted them into one whole."[36] Furthermore, the scholastic philosophy which made it possible for St. Thomas to absorb the heritage of patristic thought and integrate it into an enduring system, would enable Thomas' modern disciples to absorb and integrate what was best in the thought and culture of their own age. For the Angelic Doctor "considered philosophical conclusions in the reasons and principles of things, which, as they are infinite in extent, so also contain the seeds of almost infinite truths for succeeding masters to cultivate in the appropriate season and to bring forth an abundant harvest of truth." Human reason "soared to its loftiest heights on the wings of Thomas and can scarcely rise any higher, while faith can expect no further and more reliable assistance than such as it has already received from Thomas."[37]

New systems of philosophy had been introduced here and there in place of the ancient scholastic doctrine but they had not produced the same wholesome fruit for the Church and for civil society. Under the influence of the sixteenth-century Reformers men began to philosophize in complete disregard of the faith. Catholics later followed the example of Protestant philosophers with unfortunate results. A proliferation of systems based on the shifting foundation of the authority and personal judgment of individual philosophers replaced the solid and substantial philosophy of the scholastics. With all due respect to the industry and erudition of modern philosophers, industry and erudition was not the whole nor even the principal end of philosophy. The same must be said of sacred theology. While it was right to support theology with copious learning, the encyclical insisted that "it is absolutely essential that it be treated according to the severe customs of the Schoolmen."[38]

Those bishops were to be commended therefore who had given their support to the revival of scholasticism. The other bishops of the Church should follow this excellent example in their own dioceses. Attacks on the faith, dangers to the family and civil society, confused ideas about liberty and authority, which menaced the tranquility of the state and the public safety, had become sources of grave concern to the Church. The pastoral problems which they posed could not be solved without the use of sound scholastic philosophy.

The growth of natural science, which had meant so much for the progress of industry and culture in the nineteenth century, had also led to empiricism, rationalism, and skepticism, due to a faulty appreciation of the true relationship of science to philosophy and theology. Therefore natural science would derive singular advantage from the restoration of scholastic philosophy, which had escaped contamination by empiricism and rationalism. For the scientist must rise to a higher order than the order of the natural sciences in order to truly understand the nature and ordering principles of the corporeal world.[39]

Therefore, although every sagacious observation, every useful invention made by anyone was to be gratefully welcomed, the bishops of the Church were earnestly exhorted to restore the precious wisdom of St. Thomas and to propagate it as far as possible. Nevertheless, *Aeterni Patris* continued—in a qualification which profoundly influenced the later history of neo-Thomism—"if there is any proposition too subtly investigated or too inconsiderately taught by the Doctors of the School, any tenet of theirs not strictly in conformity with subsequent discoveries or in any way improbable in itself, it is no part of our intention to propose that for the imitation of our time."[40]

Bishops were to choose teachers for their seminaries who would inculcate the philosophy of St. Thomas into the minds of the Church's future priests, clearly demonstrating its solidity and value in comparison with other systems. Academies were to be founded for the scientific study of

St. Thomas, since it was most important that "the wisdom of St. Thomas be drawn from the spring itself or at any rate from streams which, flowing from that spring, still, in the certain and unanimous opinion of learned men run pure and undefiled." The minds of future priests must be preserved from contamination by "streams which, while said to flow from that spring, are in reality swollen with alien and unhealthy matter."[41]

The "Wisdom of St. Thomas" in *Aeterni Patris*

The "wisdom of St. Thomas" which *Aeterni Patris* praised so highly represented the nineteenth-century neo-Thomists' ideal model of philosophy and its relation to theology. The relation of speculative theology to philosophy and apologetics described in the encyclical is the relationship proposed by Kleutgen in his *Die Theologie der Vorzeit*. The need of a sound scholastic philosophy to overcome the dangers to public order and to religious and moral life, created by false modern notions of liberty and authority, had been one of the major themes developed in Liberatore's *Istituzioni di Etica e Diritto naturale*.[42] Scholastic philosophy's ability to provide a higher synthesis for scientific knowledge was the major theme developed in the cosmology of Giovanni Cornoldi, another member on the team of Jesuit neo-Thomists associated with *Civiltà Cattolica*.[43] In all honesty the leaders of the neo-Thomist movement identified their own philosophy with the authentic thought of the Angelic Doctor, and the text of *Aeterni Patris* reflected that conviction.

The scholastic philosophy described in the encyclical was a highly objective discipline. Its realistic epistemology prepared the way for a vindication of God's existence and attributes through causal arguments grounded on Aristotle's metaphysics. Its Aristotelian metaphysics laid the groundwork for the impersonal apologetics of signs and miracles, which would become the object of Blondel's trenchant criticism before the end of the nineteenth century. As in Kleutgen's *Die Theologie der Vorzeit*, scholastic positive theology was credited with the ability to order and unify the scattered data of revelation and subsume them under its developed concepts; and scholastic speculative theology could acquire a fruitful understanding of the Christian mysteries though its Aristotelian science of God.

Objective universality was one of the great contributions which philosophy made to theology. Scholastic philosophy dealt with the universal.

It was an impersonal science whose strength lay in its Aristotelian conceptual form, logical techniques, and metaphysical principles. One of the most important sources of its power was its respect for the objective truth of revelation and for the public and authoritative teaching of the universal Church. The weakness of modern philosophy, on the other hand, could be traced to its subjectivity and individualism. Borrowing from the traditionalists and the post-Kantian theologians, *Aeterni Patris* linked the individualism of modern philosophy to the religious individualism of the Protestant reformers who had rejected the public authority of the modern Church.[44] Since it had nothing to rest on but the authority of individual human reason, modern philosophy split into the plurality of competing systems which ultimately led to skepticism. Objectivity and antiquity were to be preferred to subjectivity and modernity as they had been preferred to them in Kleutgen's *Die Theologie der Vorzeit.*

Aeterni Patris also expressed the serene conviction of the nineteenth-century neo-Thomists that scholastic philosophy was a single metaphysical system, common to all the scholastic doctors, and that scholastic philosophy could gather up, preserve, and represent the essence of the patristic thought which it had superseded. Like every Aristotelian science, scholastic philosophy was independent of history. It was unaffected by the personality and the cultural milieu of individual thinkers. Differences in time, historical outlook, and cultural expression were accidental. The encyclical saw no essential difference between the scholasticism of St. Thomas and St. Bonaventure and perceived no appreciable diversity between their philosophies and the philosophies of baroque scholastics like Cardinal Cajetan and Pope Sixtus V. In interpreting St. Thomas, modern scholastics could safely recur either to the text of St. Thomas himself or to the "streams which, flowing from that spring, still in the certain and unanimous opinion of learned men run pure and undefiled."[45]

The norm for determining whether or not a doctrine was authentically Thomistic was not, as we would expect today, the careful study of St. Thomas' text in its historical context. On the contrary, the norm proposed by *Aeterni Patris* was the unanimous agreement of Thomas' recognized commentators. These commentators, scholastics of the late Middle Ages and of the baroque period, approached St. Thomas as metaphysicians and not as historians. In other words, they engaged in the logical and metaphysical analysis of philosophical positions that Suarez practiced brilliantly in his *Disputationes Metaphysicae,* and which, despite his great erudition and scrupulous fair-mindedness, led Suarez to misunderstand the positions which he was analyzing through his failure to consider historical context and doctrinal evolution.[46] Kleutgen had taken the same metaphysical approach to the history of theology in his *Die Theologie der Vorzeit*. According to Kleutgen's norm of philosophical evaluation, and according to the norm proposed by *Aeterni Patris*, the metaphysics of Francis Suarez could be considered one of the pure "streams flowing from [Thomas'] spring," and the reality of the act of existence, which Suarez denied and Cajetan affirmed, was reduced to the status of an accidental point on which modern scholastics could agree or disagree without compromising the purity of their Thomistic philosophy and theology. In fact, St. Thomas' metaphysics of the act of existence, which contemporary Thomists consider to be the Angelic Doctor's most distinctive and important contribution to philosophy and theology, is not even mentioned in the text of *Aeterni Patris*.

The same air of timelessness pervades the encyclical's treatment of scientific theology. Like Kleutgen's *Die Theologie der Vorzeit*, *Aeterni Patris* shows no awareness that Thomas' speculative theology and the positive theology modeled on Melchior Cano's *Loci Theologici* were different disciplines, had come into existence at different times, and were shaped by different historical and cultural preoccupations.[47] Despite the problems presented to Catholic theology by the development of historical exegesis in Germany, nothing was said in *Aeterni Patris* about the relation of scholastic theology to Scripture and patristics beyond a passing reference to their integration into the scientific theology of Bonaventure and Thomas. And that reference was taken from the papal bull of Sixtus V *Triumphalis*, issued in 1588.

In short, *Aeterni Patris* reflected the strengths and weaknesses of nineteenth-century neo-Thomism. Neo-Thomism's confidence in the integrating power of its unified synthesis of epistemology, anthropology, and metaphysics appears in the encyclical's confidence in the capacity of St. Thomas' philosophy to handle the problems of modern science, culture, and society. Neo-Thomism's awareness of the necessity of distinguishing the orders of grace and nature is reflected in the encyclical's care to distinguish philosophy from theology while steadfastly refusing to condone a rationalistic separation of the two disciplines. The importance of tradition and the necessity of contact with revelation in a Christian philosophy, upon which all the great nineteenth-century Catholic theological traditions insisted, is one of the most useful lessons taught by

Aeterni Patris. But the limitations of the encyclical are also evident. The neo-Thomist hostility to modern philosophy and the neo-Thomist blindness to subjectivity and history not only distorted the encyclical's understanding of the nature of theology but led to its mistaken interpretation of St. Thomas' own philosophical thought. The authors of *Aeterni Patris* were the initators of a movement. In the hands of their successors the possibilities of the philosophy and theology which they had rediscovered would be developed. The Thomistic synthesis, which the nineteenth-century neo-Thomists were convinced was required to defend and explain *Dei Filius'* teaching on faith and reason, would change and evolve from within until its epistemology, metaphysics, and philosophical method had ceased to be the epistemology, metaphysics, and philosophical method which, in the minds of the drafters of *Aeterni Patris,* distinguished the timeless, universal Aristotelian science of the Angelic Doctor from the individual, subjective, and historical thought of the modern philosophers.

Nevertheless, disturbing as that internal evolution might be to the drafters of *Aeterni Patris,* it would be a continuation of the work which they themselves had inaugurated. For it would be the outcome of the historical rediscovery and systematic development of the genuine possibilities of the Angelic Doctor's own thought. Historical rediscovery of St. Thomas' thought and the systematic development of its latent potentialities through a Thomistic dialogue with the modern world was the work which *Aeterni Patris* invited Catholic philosophers and theologians to undertake. The drafters of *Aeterni Patris* did not anticipate that the work which they invited their colleagues to undertake would inevitably result in the evolution and radical revision of their own Thomistic synthesis because they did not think historically. For them a radical change in St. Thomas' Aristotelian method or the sanctioning of a post-Cartesian subjective starting point in Thomistic epistemology and metaphysics would have been inconceivable. Neither of these "modern" approaches would have been compatible with their own conception of Thomism as an Aristotelian *Philosophie der Vorzeit.* Yet, despite the limitations and inaccuracies in their understanding of St. Thomas' thought, the sturdy confidence which the neo-Thomist pioneers placed in the soundness and the fruitfulness of the Angelic Doctor's epistemology and metaphysics turned out to be amply justified.

Their Thomistic descendants, whose own thought has evolved far beyond the nineteenth-century Thomism of *Aeterni Patris,* still owe a debt of gratitude to the drafters of Leo XIII's encyclical. For without their confidence in the possibilities of St. Thomas' philosophy and theology, and without the firm leadership of Leo XIII himself in the Thomistic revival, it is hardly likely that the vast historical scholarship and the remarkable systematic development that characterized the Thomistic movement in the century after the publication of *Aeterni Patris* would have taken place. Certainly the history of twentieth-century Catholic philosophy and theology would have followed an entirely different course. The twentieth century would not have been the age of Rousselot, Mercier, de Raeymaeker, Grabmann, Gilson, Maritain, Garrigou-Lagrange, Journet, de Lubac, Bouillard, Rahner, and Lonergan. Less than a decade after *Dei Filius*, the practical interpretation of its teaching by Leo XIII in *Aeterni Patris* gave a decisive and irreversible orientation to Catholic philosophy and theology. The highest authority in the Catholic Church had directed her official institutions to effect their apostolic approach to the modern world through the rediscovery, purification, and development of St. Thomas' philosophy and theology. Catholic speculative theology would evolve in its dialogue with the modern world, but, for decades, its intellectual evolution would take place within a Thomistic framework. The achievements, reverses, and painful conflicts of Thomistic theology's dialectical development would become the leitmotif of the history of Catholic theology during the decades between *Aeterni Patris* and the Second Vatican Council.

THE AFTERMATH OF *AETERNI PATRIS*

Leo XIII made it evident that it was his firm intention to take whatever measures might be needed to make sure that the philosophy and theology of the Angelic Doctor was restored to its place of honor in the Catholic schools. A number of vigorous measures followed the publication of his encyclical. The Roman Academy of St. Thomas was reactivated and the Jesuit neo-Thomist Giovanni Cornoldi was invited to assume its direction. The Dominican neo-Thomist Tommaso Zigliara, whom Leo XIII had elevated to the cardinalate, was appointed prefect of the Congregation of Studies. A shake-up in the faculties of the Propaganda and the Apollinaire removed a number of professors whose devotion to the "wisdom of St. Thomas" was deemed insufficient.[48]

It was at the Gregorian University of the Roman College, however, that the full impact of Leo's determined effort to restore the philosophy and theology of St. Thomas was felt most painfully. The professors of the Gregorian University had never shared the enthusiasm of their neo-Thomist confreres for neo-Thomism as a unitary system. Perrone, Passaglia, and Franzelin were fundamentally positive theologians. They were scholastic in their views about faith and reason, and they employed the scholastic style of exposition in their writing. But they had little interest in scholastic speculative theology, and little conviction of its value. The faculty of philosophy at the Gregorian had been resolutely hostile to the neo-Thomist movement from the time of Taparelli's rectorship until the publication of *Aeterni Patris.* In the opinion of the philosophers at the Roman College the hylomorphic metaphysics of St. Thomas could not be reconciled with the results of modern scientific research.

Serafino Sordi, whom the philosophy professors at the Gregorian had refused to accept as a colleague during Taparelli's rectorship, was provincial of Rome in 1853 when *Civiltà Cattolica* began its campaign for the restoration of Thomism. Sordi, who as provincial was the major superior on whom the Gregorian depended, saw his chance to establish a beachhead for Thomism at the Gregorian, and tried to appoint Liberatore to its faculty as professor of epistemology. But Carlo Maria Curci, the editor of *Civiltà Cattolica,* protested the appointment on the grounds that Liberatore could not be spared and the opportunity was lost. Salvatore Tongiorgi, who received the appointment, was anti-Thomistic, as was his disciple and successor Domenico Palmieri.

In 1861 a bitter polemic broke out between the philosophy faculty of the Gregorian and the team of Jesuit neo-Thomists on *Civiltà Cattolica.* In his lectures at the Roman College Tongiorgi attacked the hylomorphic metaphysics of Liberatore's *Del composto umano* when it appeared in article form in *Civiltà Cattolica.* The controversy became so heated that the Jesuit Father General Peter Beckx arranged a conference to which Liberatore, Tongiorgi, Kleutgen, and Franzelin were invited, in the hope of arriving at a peaceful solution. When it became clear that no peaceful settlement to the controversy could be hoped for, the Jesuit general ordered that the controversy cease forthwith. Nothing more was to be said on the subject either in the pages of *Civiltà Cattolica* or in the classrooms of the Roman College, although Liberatore and Tongiorgi remained free to defend their respective positions in their books. In the light of this history, it is easy to understand why the publication of *Aeterni Patris* created little enthusiasm at the Gregorian University.[49]

Leo XIII, however, was determined to make the Gregorian University a center of Thomistic learning, and he resorted to Draconian measures to achieve his purpose. Palmieri, who by 1879 had become a professor of dogmatic theology with a reputation for vast erudition, was replaced by Camillo Mazella. Palmieri spent several years in exile in Holland as a professor of scripture and oriental languages before being recalled to the Gregorian, where he began a new and brilliant career as a moral theologian. The faculty of philosophy became the base of a new team of professors, Urraburu, De Maria, Schiffini, and Remer, whose commitment to the philosophy of the Angelic Doctor was above suspicion. De Maria was a rigid and enthusiastic Thomist, and Remer's philosophical manuals, which were used in seminaries throughout the world, became one of the most effective channels for the transmission of Thomism in the closing years of the nineteenth century.[50]

Unfortunately, however, the quality of the new professors at the Gregorian and at the other Roman institutions fell far below the quality of the professors whom they had replaced. None of the philosophers at the Roman College showed any sign of the originality and breadth of the two neo-Thomist pioneers Liberatore and Kleutgen. Nor did the Roman theologians in the years following the publication of *Aeterni Patris* continue the tradition of serious positive theology that Perrone had established at the Roman College and which Passaglia and Franzelin continued. Neither Mazzella nor Zigliara had any real understanding of modern science and culture. Zigliara, in fact, was more of a dialectician than a creative and open philosophical thinker. Cornoldi, the only member of the new generation of "Roman philosophers" who had any real knowledge of modern science, shared their ignorance of modern philosophy, and, in fact, was more vehement than most in expressing his contempt for it.[51]

In essence, the Roman professors who introduced the philosophy and theology of St. Thomas to their students in the Roman institutions in the last two decades of the nineteenth century were seminary professors rather than creative philosophers and theologians. Their published works were basically school manuals whose purpose was the clear exposition of safe "received" Thomistic doctrine rather than the stimulation of original thought. The verbalism, caution, and excessive recourse to the authority of the Angelic Doctor which characterized these manuals upset even Catholic scholars like Pierre Duhem who were sympathetic to the Thomistic revival.[52] At the conclusion of his masterly study of the epistemology of the "Roman School" in his *Epistémologie thomiste*, Georges van

Riet was obliged to admit sadly that no real progress was made in Thomistic epistemology between the publication of Liberatore's works and the publication of Joseph Gredt's *Elementa Philosophiae* in 1899.[53] Roger Aubert's evaluation of the state of Roman philosophy and theology between 1880 and the beginning of the twentieth century is equally negative. Whatever may have been the reason—the necessity of teaching and writing in Latin, the increasing number of students attending the Roman institutions, an excessive desire to preserve Thomistic orthodoxy, or the need of a new generation of Thomists to master St. Thomas' thought before they could develop it—it must be admitted that Leo XIII's hopes for a brilliant revival of Thomism in the Roman institutions were disappointed.[54]

Louis Billot, who came to the Gregorian in 1885, was a striking contrast to the drab background of mediocrity in Roman theology. Billot was a brilliant metaphysician who possessed an extensive and profound knowledge of St. Thomas. Billot could not only understand the principles of St. Thomas' metaphysical theology, but he could extend them to meet new problems through the deductive conclusions of his speculative theology. The influence which Billot exerted on Catholic theology through his published works and through the presence of his former students in seminaries and scholasticates throughout the world was enormous. Billot was the first of the great Thomistic speculative theologians.

But the trouble was that Billot was an exclusively metaphysical and speculative theologian. He had no feel for history and showed little interest in it. Scripture, exegesis, and positive theology were played down in his teaching and in his writing. This was a change in the theological tradition of the Gregorian University. Perrone, Passaglia, and Franzelin had all stressed positive theology. In their eyes, scripture, tradition, and the Church's patristic heritage deserved far more attention in theological instruction than the metaphysical speculation of the scholastic doctors. From the beginning of the neo-Thomist revival the glaring weakness of nineteenth-century Thomism had been its weakness in the areas of history and positive theology. Kleutgen had misunderstood the nature of positive theology through his insensitivity to historical thought and through his failure to appreciate the essential difference between the method of history and the method of Aristotelian metaphysical science.[55]

Billot's dominant position as a metaphysical speculative theologian, the stagnation of speculative thought, and the continued hostility to modern philosophy among the Roman professors of philosophy created a gulf between the Roman Thomists and the modern intellectual world with which, if they were to be faithful to the demands of *Aeterni Patris,* they must engage in dialogue. Catholic philosophers like Maurice Blondel who had learned their philosophy at the great secular universities found the epistemology and the apologetics of the Roman manuals totally inadequate to meet the intellectual demands of the world in which they lived. The failure of the Roman philosophers and theologians to move beyond the Thomism of Liberatore, Kleutgen, and *Aeterni Patris* would have tragic consequences for Catholic theology and for the Catholic Church. For the inability of Roman epistemology, metaphysics, and speculative theology to deal with the problems created by modern exegesis and modern historical method prevented the Roman theologians and the Roman congregations from solving, or even appreciating, the genuine questions with which modern historical science and modern philosophy confronted the Church at the time of the modernist crisis.

Despite the obvious weakness of Roman Thomism, however, the neo-Thomist movement was putting down firm roots in the last two decades of the nineteenth century. The Institut Supérieur de Philosophie was established at Louvain under the direction of Désiré Mercier. Other important centers of Thomistic study were established at Piacenza and at Freiburg in Switzerland. Distinguished Thomist theologians like Matthias Scheeben were carrying on their work in Germany. Historical research into the texts of St. Thomas, St. Bonaventure, and the other scholastic doctors was undertaken in a serious and systematic way. The first of the great Thomistic reviews was founded. *Aeterni Patris* had accomplished its purpose. Thomism had been given the opportunity to establish itself with the help of powerful and continuous ecclesiastical support. The foundations were being laid for the historical research and systematic development that would flourish brilliantly in France, Belgium, Germany, and America in the twentieth century.

EPILOGUE:
THE REEMERGENCE OF PLURALISM

During the twentieth century the philosophical pluralism which Liberatore and Kleutgen unwittingly built into their neo-Thomistic synthesis reemerged. Philosophical pluralism led to theological pluralism. In the final quarter of the century, as the centenary of *Aeterni Patris* approaches, the Aristotelian scientific method which Kleutgen defended in his *Die Theologie der Vorzeit* has been abandoned by Bernard J. F. Lonergan, and a new theological method has been proposed whose epistemological foundation, according to Lonergan, can be discovered in the theory of knowledge of the Angelic Doctor. Neo-Thomism has evolved beyond the objective, nonhistorical philosophical and theological method which was the hallmark of neo-Thomistic philosophy and theology at the turn of the century. In the new atmosphere of theological pluralism, however, Thomism has lost its dominant position in Catholic philosophy and theology. Open as its new theological method may be to history and cultural evolution, it has been criticized by contemporary theologians who are convinced that even a subjective and historical transcendental Thomism is not historical enough to handle the problems of Catholic theology in the final quarter of the twentieth century. An evolved Tübingen theology has emerged whose theological method has been opposed to the method of transcendental Thomism as a distinct alternative for Catholic scientific theology. Thus the evolution of neo-Thomism during the century after *Aeterni Patris* has culminated in a renewed debate between an evolved and radically altered Thomistic theological method and an evolved and radically altered Tübingen theological method.

The history of twentieth-century neo-Thomism can be divided into four stages. The first is the period from the turn of the century to the outbreak of the First World War. The second is the period between the

wars. The third is the period between World War II and the Second
Vatican Council. The fourth and final period is the decade between
Vatican II and the present. Each of these periods had its own distinctive
intellectual climate, due in large part to the successive crises to which the
Church was reacting. Each was also distinguished by the emergence of
a new generation of leading philosophers and theologians. And each was
marked by bitter family feuds among the scholastic philosophers and
theologians over the major theses in epistemology and metaphysics that
form the core of neo-Thomistic philosophy and theology. These scholastic wars, and the official Church's often heavy-handed intervention in
them, mark the successive stages in neo-Thomism's transformation from
the static and closed conceptualism of the early 1900s to the open intellectualism of present-day transcendental Thomism.

TURN-OF-THE-CENTURY SCHOLASTICISM

By the turn of the century the scholastic revival was well under way.
Both the Church's hierarchy and her major religious orders had responded obediently to Leo XIII's vigorous directives.[1] The Jesuit
Gregorian University at Rome had become a stronghold of scholastic
philosophy and theology. Bismarck's attempt to break the Gregorian's
hold on the education of German seminary professors had been successfully resisted. Désiré Mercier had established the Institut Supérieur de
Philosophie at Louvain[2] and won it an international reputation through
his firm and imaginative leadership. Distinguished Dominican scholars
were staffing their order's theological faculties in France, Belgium, and
Switzerland and its pontifical university in Rome, the Angelicum. Jesuits
staffed the theological faculty at Innsbruck, manned a famous German
theologate at Valkenburg in Holland, and furnished a number of distinguished scholars to the Catholic institutes in France. French Dominicans
like Ambroise Gardeil and French Jesuits like Louis Billot had shown the
fruitfulness of scholastic philosophy as the structuring element of a speculative theology. Scholastic authors were reaching an influential audience of clerics and educated laymen through a number of philosophical
and theological reviews published in Italy, France, Germany, Belgium,
and Switzerland.

Historical research into scholasticism's medieval sources, which Leo
XIII had included in his program for a scholastic revival, was also proceeding at an encouraging pace. The Leonine Commission, which the

pontiff himself had established in 1880,[3] had begun to prepare the definitive edition of Thomas' corpus. At Quaracchi, a group of Franciscan scholars edited the definitive edition of St. Bonaventure during the last two decades of the nineteenth century.[4] Clemens Baeumker was bringing out the celebrated collection of medieval texts and monographs in the *Beiträge* edited under his direction.[5] The pioneering work of Heinrich Denifle, O.P., Franz Ehrle, S.J., and Maurice de Wulf was laying the foundations for the revolutionary historical studies of Grabmann, Landgraf, Lottin, and Gilson in the next generation. Scholasticism had begun to clarify its own intellectual self-possession through its renewed dialogue with contemporary philosophy. It was gradually regaining internal coherence and consistency by purging itself of extraneous accretions.

Nevertheless, a great deal of work had still to be done before scholasticism's self-possession or internal coherence could be called adequate. For one thing, scholasticism and the philosophical theology of St. Thomas had yet to be clearly distinguished from each other. Leo XIII had practically identified the two in *Aeterni Patris*. St. Bonaventure's Franciscan editors had failed to see any essential difference between the theologies of the Seraphic and the Angelic Doctors. That in reality an unbridgeable diversity divided St. Thomas' theology from the Franciscan theologies of St. Bonaventure and Duns Scotus had not occurred to them. And that another essential difference distinguished St. Thomas' epistemology and metaphysics from those of his great baroque commentators Cajetan and John of St. Thomas was not suspected by the turn-of-the-century Dominican Thomists.

Deficient historical awareness was a cause of confusion in the scholastics' own speculative thought. Any scholastic theology is a tightly woven system. The central theses on the Trinity, the Incarnation, and grace, around which it is constructed, must be coherent with the epistemological and metaphysical bases on which a given scholastic system rests. Thus, if the specific philosophical presuppositions of a given scholastic system are not clearly understood, the intrinsic coherence and cogency of the system's theology cannot be understood either. Seventy-five years ago scholastic theologians were in no position to comprehend the specific starting point and intrinsic consistency of any of the great thirteenth-century scholastic systems. Much less could they distinguish between Thomas' own theology and the theologies of his baroque commentators. In their minds Thomism was simply another name for the theology of Cajetan or John of St. Thomas. Or else it was equated with a generic

scholasticism of Suarezian or Scotistic hue. Underlying the second view
was the belief that a basically logical or metaphysical analysis would
enable a theologian to distinguish the essential theses, which were common to all the doctors, from the free opinions about which they could
differ.[6] This was the line of thought which had characterized Joseph
Kleutgen's approach to history, and we have already seen its influence
upon Kleutgen's own writings and upon the encyclical *Aeterni Patris.*

Besides producing intellectual confusion, historical ignorance had another deleterious effect on turn-of-the-century scholastic authors. It
caused them to give a misleading account of St. Thomas' thought in their
manuals. The radical uniqueness of Thomas' metaphysics of existence
was largely ignored. As a result, the distinctive character of Thomas'
philosophy of man and God was also missed. The special role which
abstraction and the judgment play in Thomas' epistemology was not
appreciated. Neither was the significant distinction between *ratio* and
intellectus in Thomas' metaphysics of knowledge.[7] Consequently the vital
role which Thomas' metaphysics of knowledge plays in his theology of
the Trinity, the Incarnation, and grace—which has been brilliantly exploited by Rahner and Lonergan in our generation—escaped theologians
of even Billot's stature.[8] Furthermore, the intelligible connection which
links Thomas' metaphysics of God to his personal religious experience
was not observed, much less exploited. In this misleading presentation
Thomism could not fail to give the impression of being a highly rationalistic system. It was, in fact, an impersonal Aristotelian science. Its arguments moved deductively to their conclusions from conceptual first
principles. Its epistemology confined itself to the discursive understanding. Little appreciation was shown for the vital role of personal experience and nonconceptual intuition in religious knowledge of God.

An unfortunate consequence of the scholastic authors' failure to understand the historical uniqueness of St. Thomas was the false impression
of St. Thomas which their misleading presentation of his thought gave
to the philosophical and theological community. The writing and teaching of scholastic philosophers and theologians displayed a markedly negative attitude toward anything like a philosophy of intuition. Yet
philosophies of intuition were the spearhead of the philosophical revolt
against positivistic scientism in the early 1900s. Maurice Blondel had
transformed German post-Kantian idealism into his powerful Christian
Philosophy of Action.[9] Bergson was also exercising a profound influence
on Catholic philosophers and theologians. Although philosophies of intu-

ition had strongly influenced Catholic Romantic theology at Tübingen, their intellectual roots were older in the history of French philosophy. The descendants of the great Oratorian Augustinians Bérulle and Malbranche included the nineteenth-century spiritualist philosophers influenced by Maine de Biran. And Bérulle's Augustinian tradition was the dominant one in the French School of Spirituality.

Understandably then, many of the best thinkers among French Catholics were ill at ease with the rationalistic theology of the scholastic revival. Their uneasiness sometimes received violent expression. Lucien Laberthonnière, for example, called for the total rejection of Aristotelian scholasticism.[10] Scholasticism was a Greek metaphysics, totally at odds with Christian experience. Scholastic theology simply could not be squared with the Christian soul's dynamic life under grace. Yet the patristic tradition gives eloquent testimony to this awareness. Other Catholics made a valiant, though sometimes painful, effort to reconcile scholasticism with their own philosophical experience. The career of Maurice Blondel is a sad example of one such struggle. Blondel's own interior agony—to say nothing of the savagely unjust attacks to which he was subjected—testify to the cost in human pain of scholasticism's deficient understanding of its own history and nature.

By the turn of the century, however, historical study of St. Thomas' text had begun to focus on the areas of epistemology and metaphysics in which St. Thomas' thought was much closer to German idealism and Bergsonianism than either scholastic or nonscholastic philosophers suspected at that time. If it had been able to proceed in a tranquil atmosphere, rapprochement between scholasticism and modern philosophy might have been achieved, though not without difficulty, much earlier in the century. As it was, however, prospects for any early rapprochement were dimmed by the storm clouds of the modernist crisis.

Twentieth-Century Scholasticism's First Stage

The modernist crisis brings us to the first period in twentieth-century scholasticism. Leo XIII had been succeeded by the saintly, pastoral, but less intellectual Pius X. The Dreyfus affair, the expulsion of the religious orders and the blatantly anticlerical legislation of the French Republic had polarized the political right and left in France. They had also divided the Catholic community in that country. Leo XIII had never excluded the possibility of a rapprochement between the Church and the nineteenth-century parliamentary governments. By the turn of the century, however, many, perhaps even most, Catholics in France had dismissed rapprochement as a dangerous illusion. They rejected the secular republic and its parliamentary constitution as fundamentally anti-Catholic institutions. The political tensions of prewar France drove Catholic laymen, clerics, and theologians to the right. Some of them, including the great Cardinal Billot, became sympathizers of the radical Action Française, which, although rightist enough, turned out in the end to be fundamentally anti-Christian.

Catholic democrats had a thin time. The embattled Catholics of the right regarded them with irritated suspicion. If their own imprudence made them vulnerable, they were promptly delated and often condemned by Rome. Lucien Laberthonnière and Marc Sagnier both fell under ecclesiastical censure. Even the saintly Blondel, although never condemned, was delated more than once. Troubled times were forging an alliance between integralist theology and right-wing politics. The alliance would remain a powerful force in the Roman curia and in the Catholic faculties of theology. Its influence would affect the course of scholasticism in the years to come.

Aeterni Patris had recommended scholasticism as the *optimus modus philosophandi*. Although scholastic philosophers were careful to observe the method and the norms of evidence proper to philosophy, the encyclical argued, no artificial barrier was erected between their philosophical reflection and Christian revelation. Scholasticism was the philosophy best equiped to thematize the data of scriptural revelation in a systematic theology. Furthermore, the scholastic metaphysics of man and being were protected from pernicious errors through the influence of the scholastics' Christian faith.

As a philosophy then, scholasticism offered a sounder view of man and society than the positivism and Kantianism espoused by the anticlerical liberals. Scholasticism could provide the theoretical foundation for a sounder and more truly human education than the truncated secular education provided by the "lay" schools and universities of the anticlerical governments. Scholastic social ethics could lay the philosophical groundwork of a broad and sane social program for Europe's new industrial civilization—a wiser, more humane, and juster social program, we must admit, than the "laissez-faire" individualism of the positivist or Kantian liberals.

The Modernist Threat

Thus, when the modernists attacked scholasticism they were striking at the heart of Leo XIII's program for theological, educational, and social reform. The modernists denied that scholastic theology was an apt instrument to thematize revelation. The positive sciences alone could determine the authorship and objective meaning of the sacred books. Furthermore, scholastic theology was an impediment to the proper appreciation of the Bible's religious meaning. Scholastic epistemology was an epistemology of changeless concepts. Its single, changeless conceptual framework was, it was claimed, an unrevisable map of reality. Scholastic epistemology defined truth as conformity of the judgment to reality. Post-Kantian German philosophy, however, had shown that concepts and conceptual frameworks were mutable and revisable. Concepts and frameworks were no more than inadequate objectivizations of the evolving mind's constant expansion of its inner experience. Furthermore, as Bergsonian philosophy had shown, the concept's function was not to conform the mind to static reality. The concept's function was merely to enable the moving, temporal mind to cope with its practical needs. And, as Schleiermacher saw early in the nineteenth century, the greatest practical need of the religious mind is a thematization of its inner experience of God. Truth in the scholastic sense, however, is not the purpose of the religious mind's thematization of its experience. On the contrary, this thematization merely serves to stimulate man's affective encounter with God through religious practice. Truth is not the conformity of a judgment to reality. Truth is the conformity of a revisable objectivation to the evolving soul's vital exigence.

Modernism's attack on scholastic epistemology had revolutionary repercussions in Catholic theology. Traditional natural theology was undermined. Causal proofs for God's existence and valid statements about God's nature, made on the basis of the analogy of being, went by the board. Modernism's rejection of natural theology undercut the form of apologetics which, since the eighteenth century, had formed the backbone of scholastic fundamental theology. Its radically different understanding of the nature and function of concepts and judgments entailed a revolutionary reevaluation of Catholic dogmatic statements. Its theory of truth implied that no unrevisable statements could be made about God or about the world. Nor indeed were any such statements called for. The function of religious dogmas was not to make immutable assertions about God or God's creation. Their purpose was simply to thematize and promote the religious quality of the individual soul's practical encounter with God. The norm of a dogma's truth was nothing more than its ability to satisfy man's religious needs.[11]

Epistemology and the Concept and Metaphysics of Being

The official Church reacted strongly to modernism's revolutionary approach to exegesis, theology, and dogma. The Biblical Commission issued severe decrees restricting the use of modern scientific methods in determining the authorship of the sacred books. A distrust of the positive sciences in the textual, historical, and cultural analysis of Old and New Testament literature hampered Catholic exegesis for several decades. The decree of the Holy Office *Lamentabili* and the encyclical *Pascendi* were strong condemnations of modernist theology and its philosophical foundations. To insure their elimination from the Church an antimodernist oath was required of every professor in ecclesiastical faculties and of every candidate for academic degrees from these institutions.

Adversaries of the modernists saw two pernicious errors at the heart of the modernist system. The first was the metaphysics of "becoming." The modernists had abandoned the metaphysics of being, in which God is the changeless Pure Act and substances owe their perduring natures to stable Aristotelian forms. They had replaced it with the evolutionary temporality of Hegel and Bergson. The modernists' second pernicious error was connected with their first. They had given up the scholastic notion of truth. Truth for the scholastic is found in the judgment. Through the judgment the mind unites a stable universal to a changing singular by the "is" of the objective affirmation. The scholastic epistemology of the conceptual judgment not only discloses that truth is the conformity of the mind to reality, it also shows that being, *esse*, is the efficient and exemplary cause of truth. By doing these three things, scholastic epistemology establishes the truth of Aristotle's metaphysics of substance and accident, matter and form and the four causes. It also confirms the truth of Thomas' metaphysics of essence and existence, on which the Angelic Doctor had built his causal proofs for God's existence, and through which he had validated his conceptual statements about God's changeless attributes. For Thomas' distinction between essence and existence is the ground of his celebrated proportional analogy of being. And, given that analogy of being, Thomas can justify the statements he makes about the infinite and changeless God through the data derived from his existential judgments about mutable sensible reality.

In the aftermath of the modernist crisis Thomism appeared to be the Church's firmest protection against dangerous modern errors in epistemology and metaphysics.[12] Thomism now deliberately defined itself against positivism, German idealism, and Bergsonian philosophy. The vital points of disagreement between Thomism and these modern philosophies were held to be the metaphysics of being and the epistemology of the concept. One immediate effect of Thomism's more aggressive stance against modern philosophy was the enhanced importance given to Thomas' commentators Cajetan and John of St. Thomas. Dominican theologians like Ambroise Gardeil who had previously shown themselves rather sympathetic to philosophies of intuition retreated to a more conventional epistemology of the concept.[13] The young convert Jacques Maritain, who had become a Catholic largely through the influence of Bergson, now abandoned Bergson's philosophy of intuition for the conceptual Thomism of the great commentators. Hard-line Dominican Thomists like Garrigou-Lagrange acquired a position of influence in their order and in the Church which they would occupy for many years.

The epistemology, metaphysics, and dogmatic theology of Cajetan and John of St. Thomas won widespread approval as the sound basis for a priestly education. The commentators' metaphysics and natural theology, which Garrigou-Lagrange presented in his famous treatise *Dieu, son Existence et sa Nature,* gave firm support to fundamental theology's traditional apologetics.[14] Their three degrees of abstraction, which Maritain would develop in the period between the wars, justified the Aristotelico-Thomistic division of philosophical science into physics, mathematics, and metaphysics. That division in its turn justified the dominant role of an Aristotelian scientific theology in the interpretation of revelation. Once a student understood the Aristotelian three-fold division of the philosophical sciences, he was immune to the assaults of modern philosophy on Catholic theology. And he could also see through the unjustified pretensions of positivistic scientism in the area of exegesis.

Blondel and Rousselot

Despite the favor enjoyed by the Thomism of the great commentators, there remained an important unconverted group of scholastic thinkers. Some were unreconstructed Suarezians, whose influence would continue even after World War I. For others Blondel's Christian Philosophy of Action still held a great attraction. The condemnation of overeager Bergsonians like Edouard LeRoy did not drive all Bergsonian Catholics into the traditional Thomist camp, as it had Maritain. Blondel's phenomenology of the human spirit and the contrast which he drew between the implicit dynamism of the human will and the explicit objects of its deliberate choices fascinated Catholic philosophers in a country where St. Augustine's influence had always been strong. Blondel's apologetics of immanence presented Christian revelation as the only meaning-giving answer to the dynamic exigencies of the human will. Thus, it provided a point of contact with a philosophical community whom the Church's traditional apologetics could not even interest. Nevertheless, the epistemology of the great commentators, focused almost entirely on the intelligibility of the concept abstracted from sense experience, was hostile to the intuitive, intramental starting point of Blondel's philosophical reflection. At best, Blondel was an Augustinian. At worst, he was a post-Kantian idealist. In any case, he was not and could not be a Thomist.

The Thomist's "philosophical excommunication" of Blondel did not pass unchallenged. One of the most important books published during the prewar period showed that it was without historical foundation. Pierre Rousselot's masterly *L'Intellectualisme de S. Thomas*[15] showed that St. Thomas' own epistemology was not the rationalistic conceptualism which it appeared to be in the scholastic manuals. The intuition which the *intellectus*, the intuitive mind, possessed of its own dynamic motion was an essential element in St. Thomas' own epistemology and metaphysics. Far from being the highest object of human knowledge, the concept of the *ratio*, the discursive intellect, in St. Thomas' opinion was no more than the deficient substitute for a missing intuition. Rousselot was convinced that a correct understanding of Thomas' metaphysics of the intellect would overcome the seeming contradiction between deductive scholastic metaphysics and the Catholic theology of the act of faith. The manuals' deductive apologetics established the preambles of faith with an objective, almost scientific, certainty. Nevertheless, the Christian's act of faith, for which the free submission of his will is a necessary condition, is the source of a more certain knowledge than the mind's objective grasp of faith's preambles. In his famous *Les Yeux de la foi*,[16] Rousselot attempted to solve this problem through an application of St. Thomas' metaphysics of the *intellectus*. The intentionality of the moving *intellectus* can be modified freely antecedently to an individual judgment on the level of the *ratio*. A free modification of the mind's intentionality can profoundly influence its ability to allow an intelligibility to appear to it on the level of the judgment. St. Thomas' epistemology was much more subtle and complex than the rationalist authors of the manuals realized. And, if St. Thomas believed that a conscious movement of the mind antecedent to abstraction and judgment was a vital element in the judgment's ability to grasp reality, the gap between Thomas' own philosophy and the modern philosophies of intuition was narrower than the Thomists were willing to admit.

Rousselot's tragic death at the age of thirty-seven in World War I put an end to his promising career. Some of his own religious brethren, notably Joseph de Tonquédec, showed little sympathy toward his intuitive approach to St. Thomas' epistemology.[17] The postwar general of Rousselot's own order Wladimir Ledóchowski took a very dim view of his theology of the act of faith. Nevertheless the influence of Blondel and Rousselot remained a powerful force among the French Jesuits. After the war it would surface again in the epistemology of the great Belgian scholastic Joseph Maréchal. After Maréchal and Rousselot there would be two irreducibly opposed Thomisms, their transcendental Thomism and the Thomism of the great commentators.

SCHOLASTICISM'S SECOND STAGE: BETWEEN THE WARS

The period between the wars saw the flowering of the scholastic revival. The changed political climate of postwar Europe and the excesses of the antimodernist vigilantes had weakened, at least for the moment, the influence of the political right wing at Rome. Pius XI's condemnation of the Action Française meant the end of reactionary royalism as a political force within the Church. Don Luigi Sturzo had begun to make Christian Democracy an acceptable option for Catholics in Italy. And, just as the condemnation of modernism had made Maritain a convinced Thomist, the condemnation of the Action Française confirmed him in his passionate attachment to democracy. The openness toward parliamentary democracy which the new generation of Thomists displayed was accompanied by a similar openness toward secular culture. Gilson and Maritain were laymen and former students at the Sorbonne, although Maritain had interrupted his formal study at the University of Paris before receiving his doctorate. Both wrote with a secular audience in mind. Although Maréchal was a Jesuit, he too was a university man with a degree in experimental psychology and a thorough grasp of contemporary philosophy. In professional training, historical knowledge, and breadth of vision the postwar generation of scholastics were on a par with the leading academic philosophers of Europe.[18]

As a group they were admirably prepared for the work which lay ahead of them. Their contribution to scholasticism can be summarized as follows: the enrichment and development of the commentators' traditional Thomism, the historical recovery of St. Thomas' own philosophy, and the establishment of transcendental Thomism. Although many distinguished scholastics worked at these tasks, a single name has become associated with each one of them. Maritain's name is associated with the first, Gilson's with the second, and Maréchal's with the third.

Jacques Maritain

Traditional Thomism has had no greater representative in this century than Jacques Maritain. Although Maritain attached himself to the Thomism of Cajetan and John of St. Thomas, he displayed a breadth, urbanity, and flexibility which other great representatives of that tradition, Garrigou-Lagrange for example, did not. As a traditional Thomist, Maritain was convinced that Thomism's epistemology of the concept and its metaphysics of being accounted for its singular ability to clarify and integrate human experience. Maritain's master work, *The Degrees of Knowledge,*[19] is a "defense and illustration" of eidetic intuition, through which the notion of being is obtained, and of the three degrees of abstraction, which justify the Aristotelian division of the philosophical sciences in the commentators' Thomism.

In Maritain's hands, however, the traditional Thomistic metaphysics of abstraction acquired an explanatory power which it never had before. Maritain's brilliant *Creative Intuition*[20] was an in-depth study of the role of the imagination in a Thomistic theory of knowledge. It gave a fascinating account of the distinction and interrelation between the abstract concept and the concrete intuition of the creative artist. Maritain's *Art and Scholasticism*[21] drew on Thomistic epistemology and metaphysics to forge an original philosophy of art. *The Situation of Poetry*[22] and *The Degrees of Knowledge* extended Maritain's philosophy of knowledge to the areas of poetical and mystical experience. Maritain was then able to present in his *True Humanism*[23] a rich and profound theory of culture whose unifying element was scholastic philosophy and theology.

Maritain also derived from St. Thomas' social ethics a philosophy of government which made him the principal theorist of the Christian Democratic movement in postwar Europe and Latin America. His *Person and the Common Good*[24] and his *Scholasticism and Politics*[25] were milestones in Catholic political theory which the activists of a less reflective age might profit by rereading.

In Maritain's writing the Thomism of the commentators lost its old-fashioned rigidity. Although the epistemology of the concept was still respected, the nonconceptual knowledge of the artist and the mystic was respected too. No other Thomist, before Maritain or after him, realized more completely Leo XIII's hopes for scholasticism as a unifier of human experience. Catholic education and politics benefited immensely from the range, profundity, and originality of his contribution to twentieth-century Thomism.

Etienne Gilson

Always an ardent Catholic, Etienne Gilson discovered scholasticism almost by accident when an agnostic professor suggested that he look into the scholastic antecedents of Descartes' philosophy. A direct realist by temperament and by conviction, Gilson was fascinated by medieval philosophy. Kantianism had never interested him. He felt that its transcendental method was a trap. The philosopher who begins inside his own mind will never work his way out of it by logic, even transcendental logic. Gilson would never admit that idealism was intrinsically contradictory. It was simply wrong. Thus, since the medievals were direct realists, the success with which medieval philosophy avoided the dead ends of modern thought could be a useful object lesson in the fruitfulness of direct realism.[26]

Gilson therefore devoted his career to the history of medieval philosophy in the golden age of medieval studies between the wars. He had many distinguished colleagues in that field: Grabmann, Landgraf, Chenu, Lottin. But he became the most widely known of all of them. Gilson's range, mastery of the texts, synthetic power, charm, and urbanity of expression won him worldwide popularity in Catholic intellectual circles. There is still no finer introduction to medieval speculative thought than his charming *Spirit of Medieval Philosophy*.[27]

After years of research Gilson came to the conclusion that a common scholastic philosophy had never existed in the Middle Ages. Scholastic scientific theology did not really begin until the thirteenth century. And, even in the thirteenth century, the unbridgeable opposition of their epistemology and metaphysics made the syntheses of Bonaventure, Thomas, and Duns Scotus irreducibly distinct. Gilson's *Philosophy of St. Bonaventure*,[28] *The Christian Philosophy of St. Thomas*,[29] and *Jean Duns Scot*[30] marshaled the evidence to support his thesis. All that the scholastic doctors had in common was their Christian faith and a vague Aristotelianism. Clearly then a common scholasticism could only be an eclectic hodgepodge devoid of intellectual coherence.

Gilson's personal philosophical allegiance was to St. Thomas. And, for Gilson, that meant that he must philosophize as St. Thomas had done, following the theological order of descent from God to creatures within the framework of an Aristotelian scientific theology.[31] For like generic scholasticism, generic Thomism was an incoherent hodgepodge. St. Thomas' epistemology is significantly different from the epistemology of the great commentators. St. Thomas held that the mind's contact with being occurs in the judgment's affirmation of the contingent *esse* of a concrete sensible existent. The *esse* grasped in the judgment's existential affirmation is an intelligibility of a completely different order from the intelligibility abstracted by the mind in its formation of the concept. That is why, in his *In Boethium de Trinitate,* St. Thomas called the abstraction of being a *separatio.* In other words, the notion of being is acquired through a negative judgment, which denies that the *esse* grasped in a prior existential judgment must be identical with any given essential intelligibility.

Since the notion of being is acquired through a double operation of the judgment, it cannot be grasped through an eidetic intuition as Maritain believed. The object of an eidetic intuition would be a formal intelligibility, abstracted, like any other concept, after the manner of a form. Thus Maritain—and the commentators—had failed to understand the epistemology of Thomas' *In Boethium de Trinitate.* Understandably enough then, they had also misunderstood Thomas' three-fold division of philosophy, which was grounded by that epistemology. Traditional Thomism —and Maritain's *Degrees of Knowledge*—grounded the distinct intelligibilities of physics, mathematics, and metaphysics on the three successive grades of formal abstraction that follow the intellect's prior abstraction of a conceptual essence *(abstractio totalis).* Unfortunately, however, these celebrated three degrees of abstraction are a complete distortion of Thomas' own thought. Thomas' *In Boethium de Trinitate* accounts for the sciences' distinct intelligibilities in a completely different way. The intelligibility of physics is derived from the mind's abstraction of a material essence *(abstractio totius).* The intelligibility of mathematics is due to the mind's abstraction of the form of quantity *(abstractio formae).* Both of these operations are abstractions of a form. The intelligibility of *esse,* however, can be grasped only by the *separatio* which follows a prior judgment of existence. For *esse* is not a form. It is the act which confers reality upon form.

The commentators' failure to grasp the unique intelligibility of *esse* in Thomas' philosophy impeded their understanding of his philosophy. They failed to appreciate the essential role played by the name of God and the existential judgment in Thomas' metaphysics. The name of God, "I Am Who Am," convinced Thomas that *esse*—not form—was the supreme perfection of being. The existential judgment enabled him to understand how *esse* could be the highest perfection in the sensible realities with which human experience must begin. Thus Thomas' baroque commentators failed to grasp the specific character and metaphysical uniqueness of Thomas' Aristotelian proofs for God's existence. Thomas' God was not Aristotle's Pure Form. In Thomas' metaphysics of *esse* the sensible world was not Aristotle's physical world of form and matter. The intelligibility of its contingent *esse* was not the intelligibility of form. The commentators' failure to appreciate this difference hampered their ability to grasp the radical difference between the metaphysics of Thomas and the metaphysics of Aristotle. So Cajetan could not understand how Thomas could claim that he had proved the immortality of the human soul when Aristotle could not. And Bañez could not believe that Thomas' proofs for God's existence were valid unless the natural world was the world described in Aristotle's *Physics*.[32]

Clearly then, Gilson believed, Thomas' own philosophy cannot be the Aristotelian act and potency metaphysics described in Manser's *Das Wesen des Thomismus*.[33] Thomism is not a Christianized Aristotelianism. It is an irreducibly distinct metaphysics of existence.[34] The rationalistic Aristotelianism of the scholastic manuals, which separated Thomas' philosophy from his theology, was simply not Thomism. For, although Thomas' metaphysics of *esse* has its own independence as a subalternate science, it remains an integral part of a theology which must begin with the Christian God and descend to his universe following the theological order.

Joseph Maréchal

Gilson's Thomism was fundamentally opposed to the traditional Thomism of Maritain. But it was even more fundamentally opposed to Blondelian philosophy. Blondel's philosophical starting point was a phenomenology of the human spirit. An immanent starting point of this sort, in Gilson's opinion, was a trap that condemned to Idealism the philosopher who used it. Blondel was trying to show that the dynamic exigence of the human spirit must lead a philosopher to affirm God's existence. For should he deny it, his very denial would entail a lived contradiction between his verbal denial and the vital drive of the human spirit. Gilson denied that any such lived contradiction could be proved. Idealism could not be overcome by trying to establish a nonexistent intrinsic contradiction. Idealism could only be overcome by the direct grasp of being in the mind's immediate existential judgments about the material singulars given in sense experience.

Thus Gilson declared his uncompromising opposition to the third important current in between-the-wars scholasticism, the transcendental Thomism of Joseph Maréchal. Under the influence of Blondel and Rousselot, Maréchal had begun a dialogue with Kantian philosophy. The five volumes of his massive *Le Point de départ de la métaphysique*[35] locate that dialogue in the whole history of Western philosophy. The fifth volume —the famous *Cahier Cinq*—is devoted to a face-to-face confrontation between St. Thomas and Kant. Maréchal's thesis is that Kant became a critical idealist because he was not consistent in his own transcendental reflection on the *a priori* conditions of human knowledge. Kant accounted for the mind's *a priori* unification of the object of its affirmation in terms of matter and form alone. Sensations, the forms of space and time, the schemata of the imagination, and the categories were fitted together statically to form the purely immanent object of experience. In the account of knowledge given in *The Critique of Pure Reason* Kant forgot, as the post-Kantians did not, that the mind's act of knowledge was not static. Knowing is an operation, a motion. Furthermore, a dynamic motion is a tendency toward an end. But the only possible end of an intellectual movement, which transcends every limited object in the very recognition of its limitedness, is Unlimited Being. Thus, if Kant had been coherent in the use of his own method, he would have realized that the existence of the Unlimited Being is an *a priori* condition of possibility for every object of the speculative reason. Instead of bringing him to Idealism, his transcendental method would have brought him to the starting point of a realistic metaphysics.

Furthermore, a Kantian realistic metaphysics would have been identical with the metaphysics of St. Thomas. For the *a priori* condition of possibility for every speculative judgment is the existence of the Infinite Pure Act of *esse* as the term of the mind's dynamism. And, in every judgment a universal form is united to a sensible singular and then placed in existence by the objective affirmation. Consequently the extramental correlate of the objective judgment must be matter, form, and existence. But matter, form, and existence are the metaphysical constituents of the sensible singular in the philosophy of St. Thomas.

Three Thomisms

Thus in the period between the wars three irreducibly distinct Thomisms emerged: the traditional Thomism of Maritain, the historical Thomism of Gilson, and the transcendental Thomism of Maréchal.[36] Each one disagreed with the others about the role of the judgment in Thomas' epistemology, the abstraction of being, and the nature of Thomas' philosophical theology. Which of these three Thomisms was the genuine scholasticism which Leo XIII envisioned? Or could it be that, even within Thomism, an unbridgeable philosophical pluralism was an inevitable necessity? In Germany, the brilliant, erratic Jesuit scholastic Erich Przywara had already suggested as much.[37] In the postwar years his suggestion would be taken up with interesting consequences.

SCHOLASTICISM'S THIRD STAGE: WORLD WAR II TO VATICAN II

After World War II the intellectual climate of Europe changed. The growing tension between Catholic exegetes and scholastic theologians had become acute. The point at issue between them was the ability of a nonhistorical discipline like scholastic theology to provide an accurate interpretation of Scripture's meaning. Exegetes were encouraged in their discontent with scholastic theology by the results of historical research in other fields. Medieval and patristic studies had brought to light the profound difference in method between scholastic theology, which was modeled on Aristotle's *Posterior Analytics*, and the older patristic theology, whose symbolic approach to Scripture dominated Christian thought and piety until the end of the twelfth century.

The New Theology

The older patristic theology was much more open in many ways to modern thought than the dominant scholastic theology. In fact, the dialectic of the mind and the cosmic symbolism that characterize the patristic approach to God had a profound, although indirect, effect on Hegel. And Hegel, through Marx, had become the most influential figure in

postwar continental thought. Might it not be possible then for Catholic
theologians to leap over the rigid scholasticism of the manuals and return
to the Fathers? And, in doing so, might they not create a new theology?
This new theology might then provide the link between the Church's
patristic heritage and contemporary neo-Hegelianism. It might also furnish a more satisfactory explanation of the way in which the saving grace
of Christ reaches millions of atheists and religious non-Christians, to
whose salvation the Church cannot be indifferent.

The Jesuit theologians whose names are associated with this movement
toward a new theology had been animated by the philosophy of Maréchal. Maréchal's metaphysics of the mind gave them the speculative principles on which their theology could be constructed. The human mind
is a drive toward Unlimited Being. Nothing short of its intuitive grasp
of God himself will satiate its natural appetite. Thus Cajetan's doctrine
of pure nature, as Henri de Lubac contended in his controversial *Surnaturel,*[38] is an illusion. God could not create a man whose mind was not a
drive for the beatific vision. Nevertheless, the beatific vision and the
elevating grace required to reach it remain gratuitous gifts of God. For
God cannot be constrained to grant a communication of his personal life
to man. Nevertheless, since the mind's drive toward the beatific vision
has been placed there by God, we know that the gift of elevating grace
cannot be just a remote possibility for man. Elevating grace is a gift which
God certainly will give. God's love for his creature is our guarantee of
that. Man is a drive toward an intuitive vision of God. Unless man
culpably excludes that vision by his own sinful action, the good and wise
God will surely grant man the grace necessary to reach it.

The Maréchalian metaphysics of the mind, which furnished de Lubac's
solution to the problem of the non-Christian's salvation, also furnished
the theoretical justification for theological pluralism. Every judgmental
affirmation is made by virtue of the intellect's natural drive toward Unlimited Being. Yet the objective content of every affirmation is confined
to the content abstracted from sense experience. Consequently every
affirmation "signifies" more than it "represents." And this difference
between "signification" and "representation" in every affirmation is the
basis of St. Thomas' proportional analogy of being.

Jean Marie LeBlond made this Maréchalian distinction the basis for a
theological pluralism.[39] Each concept can provide only a limited and
analogous representation of the Pure Act's infinite reality. And likewise
every conceptual framework can give only a limited, analogous represen-

tation of the Unlimited Divine Reality which its judgments signify. Thus several diverse, although analogous, theologies are possible. The analogy of being, based on the mind's movement toward Infinite *Esse*, will be the theologian's guarantee against relativism. The traditional Thomism of Cajetan and John of St. Thomas failed to see this possibility. One reason for its failure was that it based the analogy of being on the abstraction of the concept rather than on the affirmation of the judgment. Another reason was its disregard of the role of the dynamic movement of the mind in the abstraction of the concept and the affirmation of the judgment. Focused on the concept of the discursive *ratio*, it failed to appreciate St. Thomas' use of the intuitive *intellectus*.

Reaction Against the New Theology

The reaction of the Cajetanian Thomists to the new theology was violent. De Lubac was accused of Baianism. His *Surnaturel*, it was said, undermined the gratuity of grace and the supernatural order. In a series of trenchant articles in the *Revue Thomiste* and the *Angelicum* the Dominican theologians Labourdette, Nicholas, and Garrigou-Lagrange attacked Le Blond's suggestion that theological pluralism was possible.[40] Authentic Thomism was completely opposed to the plurality of analogous conceptual frameworks which this type of theological pluralism required. The epistemological presuppositions of its analogous conceptual frameworks were the Maréchalian metaphysics of abstraction and the Maréchalian distinction between signification and representation in the judgment. Both were without foundation in St. Thomas' thought. The authentic Thomism of the great commentators has shown that a sound metaphysics of being can have only one conceptual framework. Its fundamental concepts—being, potency, substance, and accident—may be clarified. But they cannot be essentially altered. Since only one conceptual framework is possible, and the Thomism of the commentators provides the true one, there can be only one theology. That theology is the traditional Thomistic theology associated with the Angelic Doctor.

Unfortunately the old alliance between integralism and right-wing politics had been restored at Rome. The new theology appeared to be a dangerous flirtation with modern thought and Marxist politics. The encyclical *Humani Generis* and the disciplinary measures taken by their general superiors against liberal Jesuits and Dominicans brought the movement to a sudden end. For the moment Rome's intervention gave the impression that the traditional Thomists had won the day. Actually they had lost. The new theology debate was traditional Thomism's last stand. After Vatican II Maréchal's transcendental Thomism would have complete possession of the field. And its great representatives, Rahner and Lonergan, would continue the new theologians' interrupted work.

FOURTH STAGE: VATICAN II TO THE PRESENT

The two leading Thomist theologians in the period after Vatican II are Karl Rahner[41] and Bernard Lonergan.[42] Both are transcendental Thomists who have applied Maréchal's metaphysics of the mind to the solution of theological problems. Rahner has won renown as the creator of a powerful systematic theology. Lonergan's major contribution has been in the area of theological methodology. An outline and comparison of their thought would demand more space than this chapter permits. Some points about them, however, can be made:

Both are Maréchalian epistemologists. The starting point of their philosophical reflection is a phenomenology of the human mind's dynamic movement toward Infinite Being. Each of them accounts for the abstraction of the concept and the affirmation of the judgment through the mind's conscious tendency toward its unlimited goal.

Both are Maréchalian metaphysicians. Each grounds the metaphysical structure of the concrete existent being through the *a priori* conditions of possibility of the objective judgment. The approach of both to God is based on Thomas' analogy of being. Nevertheless, there is a significant, and perhaps irreducible, difference between the Rahnerian and the Lonerganian interpretation of Thomas' matter, form, and existence metaphysics.

Both are receptive to a theological pluralism based on a plurality of conceptual frameworks. Yet each sees the mind's unobjective conscious awareness of its infinite goal as the theologian's protection against relativism. This grasp is exploited brilliantly by Lonergan in his *Method in Theology*.[43] There, as in much of Lonergan's later work, it has become the ground of a new theological method. This new method, modeled on the empirical sciences but freed from the restrictions of empiricism through the mind's *a priori* drive to infinite being, will enable the theologian to thread his way safely through the diverse historical and theoretical frameworks with which he has to deal. This method, rather than the outmoded deductive rationalism of Aristotle's *Posterior Analytics*, Lonergan believes, is the method which a contemporary scientific theology must employ.

Rahner and Lonergan are both open to the theological possibilities of diverse philosophical systems. Rahner has drawn on the metaphysics of Bonaventure and Hegel for the creation of his own peculiar interpretation of Thomas' metaphysics of being. And that unique interpretation of Thomas' metaphysics of being is the basis of Rahner's whole theological synthesis. Lonergan too has displayed a constantly increasing openness to continental phenomenology and Anglo-American linguistic philosophy.

In the hands of these two great theologians neo-Thomistic theology has given up its claim to theological imperialism. It recognizes itself as one system among many. Neo-Thomism has become conscious of the intrinsic deficiency of the Aristotelian model of scientific method which Gilson and Maritain both thought was an essential element of Thomistic theology. Thomists now concede that the complaints of the exegetes were justified. A theology structured on the method of the *Posterior Analytics* cannot adequately thematize an historical revelation. Neither can it cope with the problems presented to the theologian by the diverse conceptual frameworks whose existence he must admit today. Gilson was wrong. We cannot theologize, as St. Thomas did, within the framework of an Aristotelian scientific theology. Maritain was wrong. The eidetic intuition of being and the three degrees of abstraction do not furnish the one true and unrevisable conceptual framework that is a reliable basic map of reality.

Contemporary Transcendental Thomism and Theological Method
Transcendental Thomism has come a long way from the neo-Thomism of Liberatore and Kleutgen. After the revolutionary historical and doctrinal studies of de Lubac, Bouillard, Rahner, and Lonergan, the theology of grace and nature proposed by the transcendental Thomist theologians is no longer the baroque scholastic theology of grace and nature which Liberatore and Kleutgen took for granted.[44] Gilson's historical research has shown that neither Kleutgen's Suarezianism nor the Thomism of the commentators can be identified with the philosophy and theology of the Angelic Doctor. A common scholasticism never existed in the Middle Ages.[45] The common scholasticism of the baroque period was not in fact the coherent synthesis of positive, speculative, moral, and spiritual theology which Kleutgen thought it was.[46] Baroque scholasticism, which in essence was Kleutgen's "old theology," can no longer impose itself, even in a revised form, upon contemporary Catholic theology as a single unitary system. Its scientific method has been explicitly repudiated by Bernard Lonergan. Its endeavor to impose a "ready-made" philosophical

system upon theology has been rejected by Karl Rahner.[47] Its objective, nonhistorical approach to thought and being has been abandoned by both these transcendental Thomist theologians.

At the end of a century of internal evolution neo-Thomism has become remarkably similar to the "modern" theological systems against which the neo-Thomist pioneers directed their philosophical and theological criticism. Contemporary transcendental Thomism has proclaimed its affinity to the subjective starting point of Descartes.[48] Like the nineteenth-century post-Kantian philosophers, transcendental Thomists have endeavored to ground their metaphysics of thought and being by developing the possibilities of Kantian transcendental method which Kant himself failed to recognize. In Lonergan's later writings a theological method, modeled on modern empirical scientific method, has replaced Kleutgen's Aristotelian theological method. And, in an even more radical development, the Aristotelian anthropology of substance, faculty, and act, which Kleutgen considered essential to the defense of Catholic teaching on grace and nature, faith and reason, has been jettisoned in favor of a contemporary anthropology of the conscious intentional subject.[49]

Transcendental Thomism no longer accepts an established theological method as a given. Rahner and Lonergan have both embarked upon the quest for a new theological method, although Lonergan has made the quest the major preoccupation of his theological activity while Rahner has not. To date, the two major transcendental Thomist theologians of this generation have failed to reach an agreement on the validity and significance of the results which they have achieved.[50] Nevertheless, despite their disagreement, Rahner and Lonergan are in accord concerning a number of basic principles. First, theological method must be grounded upon a transcendental reflection upon the unitary action of sense and intellect in the conscious knowing subject. Second, the metaphysics of the active intellect can ground the causal metaphysics and the analogy of being without which contemporary historical metaphysics and theology would sink into relativism. Despite the abandonment of the baroque scholastic theology of grace and nature, the Catholic teaching on faith and reason still requires that the Catholic theologian respect the distinction between philosophical and theological knowledge of God and recognize the distinction between apologetics, or fundamental theology, and systematic speculative theology, notwithstanding the significant difference between the function which fundamental theology must serve today and the role assigned to it in the nineteenth-century manuals.[51] It can be argued then that, theologically and metaphysically, even a highly evolved transcendental Thomism is still in the tradition of Liberatore and Kleutgen and that its theological method is irreducibly distinct from the theological method of contemporary Catholic Tübingen theology.

Contemporary Catholic Tübingen Theology as an Alternative Method

The suggestion that a restored and evolved Catholic Tübingen theology might present itself as a distinct alternative to the transcendental Thomism of Rahner and Lonergan was provoked by Walter Kasper's brilliant contribution to *Theologie im Wandel,* the *Festschrift* published in 1967 to commemorate the hundred and fiftieth anniversary of the founding of the Catholic faculty of theology at the University of Tübingen.[52] Kasper observed accurately that the specific intelligibility of history was the leitmotif of Drey's Tübingen theology. Drey's positive theology was not an assemblage of *dicta probantia* as Kleutgen's positive theology was; and, unlike Kleutgen's Aristotelian speculative theology, Drey's speculative theology was built upon the intelligibility of history. Nevertheless, Drey, whose inspiration came from the early Schelling, could not overcome the ambiguity between freedom and necessity, historical event and eternal idea which was the fatal weakness of post-Kantian idealism. Drey's ideal reconstruction of historical tradition was built upon the "ideal essences" contained within it and, above all, on the eternal architectonic idea of the Kingdom of God. Drey's theological reconstruction of history, in other words, was a metahistory, supported by an outmoded metaphysic.[53]

Nevertheless, Tübingen historical theology does not rise or fall with Drey's metahistory and metaphysic. Franz Anton Staudenmaier abandoned Drey's necessary ideas. For Staudenmaier, God's freedom became the fundamental condition for the realization of God's Kingdom. God's providence became the ground of God's active intervention in the causally linked system of world events. Consequently Christianity became the intelligibly linked system of divine freedom and divine personality in their exterior expression. There was an intelligibility in sacred history, but its ground was the undeducible divine freedom and not the metaphysical necessity of a divine architectonic idea. Staudenmaier's abandonment of Drey's system of necessary ideas had profound metaphysical consequences. For all theological thought then became a form of experience. Freedom, although intelligible, is ultimately undeducible. Freedom can only be known through our experience of its exterior manifestation in historical action.[54]

Staudenmaier's form of Tübingen theology is more congenial to modern Catholic Tübingen theologians than Drey's metahistorical reconstruction of the mediation of revelation through the Church's living tradition. For modern theologians are more at home with the philosophy of Martin Heidegger than they are with Schelling's post-Kantian idealism. Heidegger's human subject does not attempt to "dominate" historical reality by enclosing it in a system of metaphysical ideas. The Heideggerian thinker responds to the intelligibility of his historical world through "thankful" receptive meditation upon the mysterious holy being which reveals and conceals itself in the interrelated, finite, historical universe whose horizon is not eternity but time.[55]

In Heidegger's historical world, Drey's Kingdom of God must be interpreted eschatologically rather than metaphysically, for an historical world is running toward its end. It is a temporal universe of promise and hope and not a mirror of the eternal fixed intelligibility of a motionless architectonic idea. Today, theological thought must be thoroughly historical; and, although historical thought and being has an intrinsic intelligibility, it is not an intelligibility which can be "mastered" through its definitive explication in a metaphysical system.[56]

All that the contemporary theologian can hope to do is to point to that intelligibility as it reveals itself through its historical expressions. The theologian can do no more than show how historical thought can mediate a living tradition and the institutions which carry that tradition and its spirit without ceasing to be historical. In its contemporary form, the Tübingen commitment to the intelligibility of history can help to overcome the split between exegesis and dogmatic theology and ease the tension between the positive and speculative method within dogmatic theology itself. It can do so by remembering that speculative intelligibility cannot be found beside history or above history. Speculative system must be immersed in history itself. Speculative theology is the "pre-understanding of Being" which is required to uncover the intelligibility of an historical tradition through the "circle" of a theological hermeneutic. But, like every hermeneutical pre-understanding, speculative theology itself must be tested, and, if need be, modified through its ongoing encounter with the historical intelligibility in which it is immersed.[57]

Concluding Reflection

Of the theological systems which were represented in the nineteenth century debate over theological method, two are still alive. The two survivors are Kleutgen's neo-Thomism and Drey's Tübingen theology. Both are active participants in the contemporary debate over theological method. Both of them, however, have evolved remarkably. Drey would be dismayed at the Heideggerian Tübingen theology of Walter Kasper, and Kleutgen would be appalled at the subject-oriented, historical transcendental Thomism of Rahner and Lonergan with their openness to culturally and historically diverse conceptual frameworks. Transcendental Thomism has abandoned Kleutgen's Aristotelian theological method. Kasper has abandoned the theological method which Drey devised under the inspiration of Schelling's *Discourses on the Method of Academic Study.* Whatever tradition may be in Catholic theology, it is no longer definable in terms of fidelity to an inherited theological method.

For two diverse Catholic theologies, heirs of two distinct nineteenth-century traditions, are now engaged in devising a theological method capable of mediating the Church's living tradition to a contemporary culture molded by modern natural and historical science. The complexity and difficulty of that task is more apparent to the contemporary theologians in the Thomist and Tübingen traditions than it was to their theological ancestors in the nineteenth century.

Nevertheless, these contemporary theologians must admit that the questions raised by the nineteenth-century theologians were good ones and that they retain their relevance for the contemporary debate over theological method. What is the proper relation of apologetics to positive and speculative theology in a Catholic theological synthesis? How is Catholic speculative theology related to Catholic positive theology? And how are both related to the results of scientific exegesis? And how can these fair questions be answered if the theologian does not devote his attention to the relation between grace and nature, faith and reason? Is an apologetics, which is in principle a discussion of the reasonableness of the assent of faith to Christian revelation, conducted with an intelligent, fair-minded but unbelieving dialogue partner methodologically admissible in Catholic theology? Kleutgen said yes. Drey said no. And, to that extent at least, one of the most intelligent participants in the current debate over theological method agrees with Kleutgen.[58] How does the historical work of the positive theologian who reflects upon the Church's living tradition in the ecclesial community of faith differ from the impartial historical thought of the detached unbelieving scholar? Rahner and Lonergan have both addressed themselves to that question from the transcendental Thomist point of view. Drey gave an answer to it which will still be valid, if the contemporary Tübingen theologians can work out a theory of the supernatural order which does not depend, as Drey's theory did, on the architectonic idea of the Kingdom of God. Kleutgen gave an answer too, which made sense in his baroque scholastic system but is no longer valid since, in essence, it ignores the distinctive difference between historical method and Aristotelian speculative science. Nevertheless, Kleutgen's distinction between the intelligibility of the revealed reality disclosed through the act of Christian faith and the intelligibility of the natural reality manifested through the intellect's unaided power is still maintained in the theology of the transcendental Thomists. Both Lonergan and Rahner have retained that distinction in their own endeavors to define the boundaries between philosophy and theology and to distinguish between the functions of fundamental and systematic theology in a Catholic theological synthesis.[59] In what way are the reflections of a Catholic speculative theology ruled normatively by the living tradition of the Church? In what sense is it meaningful to say today that Catholic theology "proceeds from the habit of faith" but "adds something to it"? Rahner and Lonergan have faced these questions and Kasper must face them too, as must any theologian who addresses himself seriously to the problem of defining the method of Catholic theology.

A Catholic speculative theology must seek a deeper understanding of the Christian mysteries through the use of analogous concepts. Without analogy there can either be no speculative theology at all or speculative theology will fail to respect the holy mystery of the triune God. But is a truly analogous concept possible without an abstractive intellect and the metaphysics of man and being that is required for the union of sense and intellect in the act of judgment? Rahner and Lonergan have answered these questions.[60] Kasper will have to answer them as well.

The nineteenth-century debate is on again and the nineteenth-century theologians still have a lot to tell us. They are worth revisiting. Their work was only the first stage in the Church's dialectical development of her theology in her long reaction to the challenge that modern thought and culture threw down in the Enlightenment. Reflecting upon the accomplishments and the limitations of their predecessors, contemporary Catholic theologians can be reassured when they realize how far Catholic theology has come in its evolution since the beginning of the nineteenth-century restoration. Hopefully, that reflection will give them the calm courage which they need to confront the work that still remains.

NOTES

CHAPTER I

1. Edgar Hocedez, *Histoire de la théologie au xixe siècle*, 3 vols. (Paris: Desclée, 1948), 1:8–9.

2. Although the neo-Thomists exploited these themes in favor of their own philosophical system, most of them, as we shall see, were commonplaces among the traditionalist philosophers and theologians. They were expressions of the Romantic reaction against the individualistic "pure reason" of Enlightenment rationalism.

3. Pierre Thibault's *Savior et pouvoir: philosophie thomiste et politique cléricale au xixe siècle* (Québec: Les Presses de l'Université Laval, 1972) presents the Thomistic revival as almost exclusively a political event. According to Thibault, the root cause of the neo-Thomist movement was the fear of modern political and intellectual freedom on the part of the Roman clerical establishment. The independence of the universities and their faculties of philosophy and theology was viewed as a grave threat to clerical dominance over the Church's intellectual and cultural life. In essence, the Thomistic revival was a triumph of clerical power over university learning. Suppression rather than open discussion was the tactic used by the neo-Thomists and their clerical allies in their contention with their opponents within the Church.

4. The greatest of the Jesuit neo-Thomists, who were the spearhead of the neo-Thomistic movement, were Matteo Liberatore and Joseph Kleutgen. Their major works will be considered at length in chapters 7, 8, and 9.

5. The inhibiting effect of their antimodern prejudice upon the philosophy of Liberatore and upon the theology of Kleutgen will be seen in chapters 7, 8, and 9.

6. Hocedez, 1:93–97.

7. Ibid., 1:146–49.

8. Ibid., 1:149–51.

9. This was particularly true of Johann Michael Sailer. See Alexander Dru, *The Contribution of German Catholicism* (New York: Hawthorn Books, 1963), pp. 41–47. It was also true of the Catholic Tübingen School. See Joseph R. Geiselmann, *Die katholische Tübinger Schule* (Freiburg: Herder, 1964), pp. 566–68.

10. Roger Aubert, *Le Pontificat de Pie IX (1846–1878)* (Paris: Bloud et Gay, 1952), pp. 132–36. See also Dru, pp. 77–85.

11. Liberatore developed these ideas in his *Istituzioni di Etica e Diretto naturale.* See chapter 7.

12. Dru, pp. 17–22.

13. Aubert, pp. 72–97.

14. Hocedez, 1:9.

15. Aubert, pp. 262–311.

16. Ibid., pp. 229–36, 303–5, 314–20.

17. See especially G. F. Rossi, *La Filosofia nel Collegio Alberoni e il neotomismo* (Piacenza: Collegio Alberoni, 1961). See also Rossi's article, "Al Collegio Alberoni ebbe inizio il neotomismo piacentino nella secunda metà del '700," *Divus Thomas* 62 (1959): 537–58. Also Thomas J. A. Hartley, *Thomistic Revival and the Modernist Era* (Toronto: University of St. Michael's College, 1971), pp. 22–29.

18. J. Bellamy, *La Théologie catholique au xixe siècle* (Paris: Beauchesne, 1904), pp. 14–16.

19. Paul Poupard, *L'Abbé Louis Bautain* (Paris: Desclée, 1961), p. 139. See also Dru, pp. 77–78.

20. Roger Bauer, *Der Idealismus und seine Gegner in Österreich* (Heidelberg: Winter, 1966), pp. 11–16. See also Kurt Erschweiler, *Die Zwei Wege der neueren Theologie: Georg Hermes–Math. Jos. Scheeben* (Augsburg: Filser, 1926), pp. 59–61.

21. For the Wolffian scholasticism of the last great eighteenth-century Jesuit scholastic, Benedict Stattler, see Bauer, pp. 16 ff. Sailer, whose Romantic traditionalism influenced the theology of the Catholic Tübingen School, began his intellectual career under the tutelage of Stattler. See Dru, p. 41. Sailer later reacted vigorously against Stattler's rationalism. It is interesting to observe that the rationalist opponent of the Tübingen theologians, Georg Hermes, was deeply influenced in his student days by his professor, Ferdinand Überwasser, who like Stattler was a member of the Society of Jesus at the time of its suppression. See Erschweiler, p. 87.

22. James E. Gurr, *The Principle of Sufficient Reason in Some Scholastic Systems 1750–1900* (Milwaukee: The Marquette University Press, 1959), pp. 11–92, esp. pp. 51–70. Bernhard Casper claims that the philosophical system of Joseph Kleutgen, the greatest of the early German neo-Thomists, was a thoroughly Wolffian system, even though Kleutgen himself was not conscious of that fact. See Bernhard Casper, "Der Systemgedanke in der spätern Tübinger Schule und in der deutschen Neuscholastik," *Philosophisches Jahrbuch* 72 (1964–65): 176–79. For the principle of sufficient reason in the philosophies of Kleutgen and Liberatore, see Gurr, pp. 121–41.

23. Hocedez, 1:147–49. For the moralism and rationalism of Bernard Bolzano, who was a professor at the University of Prague during Anton Günther's student days, see Bauer, pp. 38–60. The rationalist teaching at the University of Prague under the Josephinist régime so shook the faith of the pious young Günther that he abandoned his theological studies. See Joseph Pritz, *Glauben und Wissen bei Anton Günther* (Vienna: Herder, 1963). For the influence of Enlightenment rationalism upon theological instruction in Swabia, its effect upon the young Johann

Adam Möhler and Möhler's later reaction against it, see Geiselmann, pp. 534–605.
  24. Dru, pp. 17–22.
  25. Ibid., pp. 77–79. See also Hocedez, 1:210–11.
  26. Hartley, pp. 30–34.

CHAPTER 2

  1. Edgar Hocedez, *Histoire de la théologie au xixe siècle,* 3 vols. (Paris: Desclée, 1948), 1:105.
  2. J. Bellamy, *La Théologie catholique au xixe siècle* (Paris: Beauchesne, 1904), p. 13.
  3. Henri Moulinié, *De Bonald* (Paris: Alcan, 1915), pp. 411–14.
  4. Pierre Thibault, *Savoir et pouvoir: philosophie thomiste et politique cléricale au xixe siècle* (Québec: Les Presses de l'Université Laval, 1972), pp. 22–23.
  5. Hocedez, 1:98–99. De Maistre not only emphasized the Romantic organic notion of society and tradition. In his *Du Pape,* Book I, chapter 4, he defended the necessity of doctrinal development. Furthermore doctrinal development cannot be reduced to logical deduction. See Hocedez, loc. cit. The organic notion of society and the nonlogical, but intelligible historical development of ideas were commonplaces in the systems of the French traditionalists and in the traditionalist theology of the Catholic Tübingen School.
  6. *Examen de la philosophie de Bacon* (Part II, chapter 1), cited in Hocedez, 1:106. See also Hocedez, 1:106–107.
  7. *Soirées de Saint-Pétersbourg* (2e et 3e entretiens), cited in Hocedez, 1:106.
  8. Hocedez, 1:97.
  9. Bellamy, p. 13. See also Moulinié, p. 199.
  10. Hocedez, 1:105.
  11. Moulinié, pp. 249–54; also F. J. Thonnard, *A Short History of Philosophy* (Paris: Desclée, 1955), pp. 728–29. See also Walter M. Horton, *The Philosophy of the Abbé Bautain* (New York: New York University Press, 1926), pp. 10–12.
  12. Moulinié, pp. 268–69; Horton, pp. 12–15.
  13. *La Législation primitive* (Discours I), cited in Hocedez, 1:109.
  14. Moulinié, p. 268.
  15. Hocedez, 1:109–11. Moulinié claims that there is an intrinsic contradiction in de Bonald's system. De Bonald makes all truth dependent on revelation. At the same time he consistently endeavors to establish the principles of his philosophical system by rigorous rational arguments. If individual reason is incapable of philosophical certitude, Moulinié asks, by what right does de Bonald appeal to it in his rigorous arguments? See Moulinié, pp. 265–67.
  16. Moulinié, pp. 266–267.
  17. De Bonald's approach to philosophy is very similar to the approach of Johann Adam Möhler, one of the great theologians of the early Catholic Tübingen School. Once knowledge of God and of the first principles had been brought to actuality through the word of revelation and tradition, philosophical reasoning was possible. See Joseph R. Geiselmann, *Die katholische Tübinger Schule* (Freiburg: Herder, 1964), pp. 135–41. Despite Moulinié's accusation of self-contradiction (see

note 15), the traditionalist position is consistent enough. Moderate traditionalism did not deny the possibility of philosophical reasoning but it demanded an act of primitive revelation in order to actualize the first principles upon which philosophical reasoning depends.

18. Thonnard, pp. 729–30; Bellamy, pp. 14–15; also Hocedez, 1:113–15.

19. Hocedez, 1:112–13.

20. Thonnard, p. 730.

21. Ibid.

22. Hocedez, 1:102–3, 120–21. See also Horton, pp. 27–29.

23. Horton, p. 26.

24. Hocedez, 1:118–19.

25. DB 1613–1615; DS 2730–2732 (34th ed. of *Enchiridion Symbolorum*, H. Denzinger and A. Schönmetzer, eds. [Barcelona: Herder, 1967]).

26. Horton, pp. 89–91; also Paul Poupard, *L'Abbé Louis Bautain* (Paris: Desclée, 1961), pp. 189–209.

27. Paul Poupard, *L'Abbé Louis Bautain: Introduction et choix de textes* (Paris: Bloud et Gay, 1964), pp. 7–12.

28. Hocedez, 2:70; also Poupard, *Bautain: Introduction et choix de textes*, pp. 61–66.

29. Poupard, *L'Abbé Louis Bautain*, pp. 287–90; also Horton, pp. 173–80.

30. *De l'enseignement de la philosophie en France au xixe siècle* (Paris: Dérivaux, 1833). For a complete list of Bautain's works, see Poupard, *Bautain: Introduction et choix de textes*, pp. 53–54.

31. Geiselmann, pp. 129–35.

32. Poupard, *Bautain: Introduction et choix de textes*, pp. 13–17; Poupard, *L'Abbé Louis Bautain*, pp. 171–81.

33. Horton, pp. 159–62, 170–72; also Roger Aubert, *Le Problème de l'acte de foi* (Louvain: Warny, 1950), p. 115.

34. Geiselmann, p. 130.

35. Aubert, p. 115. Kant and Jacobi were among Bautain's favorite authors. See Poupard, *Bautain: Introduction et choix de textes*, pp. 73–74; and Poupard, *L'Abbé Louis Bautain*, pp. 140–59.

36. Poupard, *L'Abbé Louis Bautain*, pp. 369–70.

37. Ibid., pp. 370, 372–73. See also Horton, p. 169.

38. In the letter which Möhler addressed to Bautain in an effort to mediate between Bautain and his bishop, the Tübingen theologian indicated the need to distinguish between man's knowledge of God as the author of nature and man's knowledge of God as the revealer of supernatural life. See Poupard, *L'Abbé Louis Bautain*, p. 373. Möhler remarked that natural man, "left to himself" and therefore without the aid of grace, can have knowledge of God through an act of "intuitive faith" *(Vernunftglaube)*. Although this intuitive knowledge of God is dependent upon God's act of primitive revelation and upon the mediation of God's primitive revelation by society, it does not presuppose any contact with historical Mosaic or Christian revelation. Möhler points out that this natural "intuitive faith" *(Vernunftglaube)* must be distinguished from the knowledge of God derived from an act of faith in God's historical Mosaic or Christian revelation made under the influence of grace. Bautain had failed to make this distinction clearly. This dis-

tinction is important for the historian of theology. It marks the difference between Bautain's traditionalism and the more nuanced traditionalism of Johann Adam Möhler. See Geiselmann, pp. 130–35. For Möhler's strong support of the general plan of Bautain's *Philosophie du christianisme,* see Poupard, *Bautain: Introduction et choix de textes,* pp. 24–25. The Catholic Faculty of Theology at Tübingen conferred an honorary doctorate upon Bautain.

39. For the incorporation of Lessing's conception of God as the educator of the human race into the traditionalism of the Tübingen School, see Geiselmann, pp. 41, 110, 192, 350, 364, 556. Revelation, tradition, and the development of doctrine are linked together in the Tübingen theology of the education of the human race under the direction of divine providence.

40. Geiselmann, pp. 132–35. Geiselmann points out that in the philosophy of both Bautain and Möhler Jacobi's *Vernunftglaube* has been united with the ideas of French traditionalism. According to Geiselmann, the Jacobian inspiration of Bautain's philosophy of faith is undeniable. Bautain's critique of the proofs for God's existence was also inspired by Jacobi. See Geiselmann, loc. cit. For an excellent summary of the different senses of the word "faith" in Bautain's system, see Hocedez, 2:77–79.

41. Like the Tübingen theologians, who were influenced by Schelling, Bautain believed that a single architectonic idea expressed itself through the subordinated intelligibilities of an ideal system. In Bautain's philosophy of Christianity, Christianity itself was such an *idée-mère.* See Poupard, *L'Abbé Louis Bautain,* pp. 113–14. For the four main Ideas in Bautain's system, see ibid., pp. 125–41. For Bautain's Idea of God, see ibid., pp. 293–96.

42. Bautain's apologetics is found in his *Philosophie du christianisme,* 2 vols. (Paris: Dérivaux, 1835). For a brief and clear exposition of Bautain's apologetics see Roger Aubert, *Le Problème de l'acte de foi,* pp. 113–22.

43. Poupard, *Bautain: Introduction et choix de textes,* pp. 41–42.

44. *Philosophie du christianisme,* 1:310–11. See also Aubert, p. 115.

45. Poupard, *L'Abbé Louis Bautain,* pp. 292–93.

46. Ibid., pp. 171–77.

47. Aubert, pp. 115–17. Also Poupard, *Bautain: Introduction et choix de textes,* pp. 36–38. Bautain's rejection of scholasticism as a "separated philosophy" implied the identification of philosophy and theology in his "Christian wisdom." Like the dogmatic theology of the Tübingen School, Bautain's philosophy of Christianity was a "philosophy of faith." See Poupard, *L'Abbé Louis Bautain,* pp. 238–49.

48. Poupard, *Bautain: Introduction et choix de textes,* pp. 31–47, esp. pp. 43–46. See also Aubert, pp. 115–16.

49. For Bautain's apologetics of the heart, see Horton, pp. 209–14.

50. There is an historical connection between Bautain's philosophy of Christianity and Blondel's apologetics of immanence. Alphonse Gratry was one of Bautain's devoted disciples at Strasbourg, although he later turned against his master. Gratry's own philosophy was derived from Bautain's philosophy of Christianity. Gratry in turn influenced Léon Ollé-Laprune. Ollé-Laprune was one of Blondel's respected and admired professors during the latter's student days at the Ecole Normale Supérieure. Ollé-Laprune's influence on Blondel's *L'Action* is clearly discernible. See Horton, pp. 287–90.

51. Hocedez, 2:72–73
52. Poupard, *L'Abbé Louis Bautain*, pp. 208–26, esp. 233–26. See also Aubert, pp. 115–22.
53. Hocedez, 2:73–74. See also Aubert, pp. 120–22. Aubert points out (p. 121, n. 43). that Rome never formally approved the formula which Räss submitted to Bautain for his signature. The Roman propositions submitted to Bautain for his signature by the Congregation of Bishops and Regulars in 1844 was more nuanced.

CHAPTER 3

1. Edgar Hocedez, *Historie de la théologie au xix' siècle*, 3 vols. (Paris: Desclée, 1948), 1:177.
2. Ibid., 1:178. Kurt Erschweiler, *Die zwei Wege der neueren Theologie: Georg Hermes–Math. Jos. Scheeben* (Augsburg: Filser, 1926), pp. 87–90.
3. *Einleitung in die christkatholische Theologie:* I Teil, *Philosophische Einleitung* (Münster, 1819); II Teil, *Positive Einleitung* (Münster, 1829).
4. Hocedez, 1:178.
5. *Christkatholische Dogmatik*, 3 vols. (Münster: Coppenrath, 1834).
6. In the papal brief *Dum acerbissimas*, 26 September 1835 (DB 1619–1620; DS 2738). See also Roger Aubert, *Le Problème de l'acte de foi* (Louvain: Warny, 1950), pp. 108–11.
7. Hocedez, 1:195–201.
8. Aubert, 103–4; also Hocedez, 1:179. See also Franz Lakner, "Kleutgen und die kirchliche Wissenschaft Deutschlands im 19 Jahrhundert," *Zeitschrift für katholische Theologie* 57 (1933): 173.
9. Erschweiler, pp. 121–30. See also L. Gillen, "Kleutgen und der hermesianische Zweifel," *Scholastik* 33 (1938): 1–31. Also the introduction to Hermes' *Philosophische Einleitung*, cited in Joseph Kleutgen, *Die Philosophie der Vorzeit*, 2 vols. (Innsbruck: Rausch, 1878), 1:185.
10. See Hermes, *Philosophische Einleitung*, cited in Joseph Kleutgen, *Die Theologie der Vorzeit*, 5 vols. (Münster: Theissing, 1865), 5:567. See also Kleutgen, ibid., 5:592–93; and Erschweiler, pp. 95–99.
11. Erschweiler, pp. 99–104. Also Hocedez, 1:184–86. See also Aubert, p. 104.
12. Erschweiler, pp. 99–100. Lakner, pp. 173–75. For a detailed exposition of Hermes' epistemology and the controversy over his epistemology of faith, see Pierre Charles, "Le Concile du Vatican et l'acte de foi," *Nouvelle Revue Théologique* 52 (1925): 513–36. See also Hermann-Josef Pottmeyer, *Der Glaube vor dem Anspruch der Wissenschaft* (Vienna: Herder, 1968), pp. 288–95.
13. Erschweiler, pp. 101–4.
14. Ibid., pp. 90–96, 124–25.
15. Hocedez, 1:185–86.
16. Erschweiler, pp. 104–8.
17. Ibid., pp. 109–13. See also Kleutgen, *Theologie der Vorzeit*, 5:566–67.
18. Aubert, pp. 109–12.
19. Kleutgen, *Theologie der Vorzeit*, 4:218–23. See also Pottmeyer, pp. 295–300.
20. In this chapter we will refer particularly to J. R. Geiselmann's *Die katholische Tübinger Schule* (Freiburg: Herder, 1964 [hereafter KTS]) and to his article "Die

Glaubenswissenschaft der katholische Tübinger Schule in ihrer Grundlegung durch Johann Sebastian von Drey," *Theologische Quartalschrift* III (1930): 49–117.

21. Geiselmann, KTS, pp. 18, 290–91.

22. Ibid., pp. 17–19.

23. Ibid., pp. 22–26.

24. Reprinted in Geiselmann's *Geist des Christentums und des Katholizismus: Ausgewählte Schriften katholischer Theologie im Zeitalter des deutschen Idealismus und der Romantik* (Mainz, 1940), pp. 85–97. For a brief outline of Drey's *Kurze Einleitung*, see Hocedez, 1:217. Hocedez follows Brosch's interpretation of Drey's theology which Geiselmann criticizes severely. See Geiselmann, KTS, pp. 1–48.

25. For Drey's use of this Romantic Idea of Life in the structuring of his theology, see Geiselmann, KTS, pp. 282–83.

26. For Drey's use of these Romantic ideas, see Geiselmann, KTS, pp. 54–66, 283–88. See also Hermann Josef Brosch, *Das Übernatürliche in der katholischen Tübinger Schule* (Essen: Hubert Wingen, 1962), pp. 79–82.

27. Geiselmann, KTS, pp. 17–19.

28. For the influence of Schelling's philosophy of nature and history on Drey, see Geiselmann, KTS, pp. 284–90. See also Walter Kasper, *Glaube und Geschichte* (Mainz: Matthias-Grünewald, 1971), pp. 15–16; and Bernhard Casper, "Der Systemgedanke in der spätern Tübinger Schule und in der deutschen Neuscholastik," *Philosophisches Jahrbuch* 72 (1964–65): 162–63.

29. Geiselmann, KTS, pp. 295–302. See also Brosch, pp. 45–48; and Geiselmann, art. cit., pp. 78–88.

30. For the Idea of the Kingdom of God in Drey's theology, see Geiselmann, KTS, pp. 192–223. See also Brosch, pp. 72–79.

31. For the traditionalism of the Catholic Tübingen School and its relation to Bautain, see Geiselmann, KTS, pp. 129–41. See also Brosch, pp. 88–93.

32. Geiselmann, KTS, pp. 210–14.

33. Brosch, pp. 39–40.

34. Geiselmann, KTS, pp. 297–302.

35. For Drey's dialectic of history, see Geiselmann, KTS, pp. 370–78.

36. Geiselmann, KTS, p. 372.

37. For Schelling's dialectic of individual freedom and communal rationality, see F. C. Copleston, *A History of Philosophy*, vol. 5 (London: Burns and Oates, 1965), pp. 116–18. For Drey's dialectic of freedom and necessity, see Geiselmann, KTS, pp. 283–88. For its influence on the development of doctrine, see Geiselmann, KTS, pp. 58–60.

38. Brosch, pp. 73–76. See also Geiselmann, KTS, pp. 193–94.

39. Geiselmann, KTS, pp. 194, 202–3, 294, 297.

40. Ibid., pp. 26–31.

41. Ibid., pp. 31–32.

42. Ibid., pp. 29–30; see also ibid., pp. 102–3.

43. Ibid., p. 31.

44. Ibid., p. 32; see also Geiselmann, art. cit., p. 101; and Kasper, KTS, pp. 15–16.

45. Geiselmann, KTS, pp. 28–29; see also ibid., p. 104.

46. Ibid., pp. 33, 105–7. See also Brosch, pp. 61–62. Brosch attributes the method

which he describes in these pages to Drey's disciple, Hirscher. Geiselmann claims, however, that the method described by Brosch is actually Drey's method. See Brosch, p. 33.

47. For an outline of Drey's *Apologetik* (1838–1847), see Hocedez, 1:217–20.

48. Geiselmann, pp. 105, 107–8.

49. Drey's modal conception of the supernatural is explained in Geiselmann, KTS, pp. 426–36. Drey's notion of the supernatural is considered in the discussion of Hirscher's moral theology in chapter 9.

50. Thomas J. A. Hartley, *Thomistic Revival and the Modernist Era* (Toronto, University of St. Michael's College, 1971), pp. 18–24.

51. Hocedez, 1:197.

52. Ibid., 1:199.

53. Ibid., 2:72–73.

54. Pottmeyer, pp. 109–10. Perrone's apologetics greatly influenced the teaching of Vatican I on faith and reason. See Pottmeyer, loc. cit.

55. Hartley, pp. 30–31.

56. Roger Aubert, *Le Pontificat de Pie IX (1846–1878)* (Paris: Bloud et Gay, 1952), pp. 187–88.

57. Auguste Kerkevoorde, "La Formation théologique de M.-J. Scheeben à Rome (1852–1859)," *Ephemerides Theologicae Lovanienses* 22 (1946): 174–93.

58. Ibid.

59. Ibid.

60. Hartley, p. 40.

61. Hartley, p. 32.

62. For Serafino Sordi's career, see Paolo Dezza, *Alle origini del neotomismo italiano* (Milan: Fratelli Bocca, 1940), pp. 29–64.

63. Ibid., pp. 32–33, 49–52.

64. Ibid., pp. 50–51.

65. Hartley, p. 30.

66. Ibid., p. 65. See also Georges van Riet, *L'Epistémologie thomiste* (Louvain: Editions de l'Institut Supérieur de Philosophie, 1946), pp. 34–35.

67. Van Riet, pp. 34–35.

68. Hartley, pp. 17–18.

69. Van Riet, pp. 56–60.

70. Dezza, pp. 55–56.

71. Hartley, pp. 1–4.

72. Ibid., pp. 31.–32.

CHAPTER 4

1. For Günther's biography, see Joseph Pritz, *Glauben und Wissen bei Anton Günther* [an introduction to Günther's thought with a selection of texts] (Vienna: Herder, 1963), pp. 15–67; also Theo Schäfer, *Die Erkenntnis-theoretische Kontroverse Kleutgen-Günther* (Paderborn: Schöningh, 1961), pp. 28–36; and Hocedez, *Histoire de la théologie au xix⁰ siècle*, 2:40–41.

2. Franz Lakner, "Die Idee bei Anton Günther," *Zeitschrift für katholische Theologie* 59 (1935): 1–56, 197–245, esp. pp. 24–30. See also Pritz, *Glauben und Wissen*, p. 80.

3. Pritz, *Glauben und Wissen*, pp. 48–65, esp. pp. 49–52.

4. For a complete list of Günther's works, see Pritz, *Glauben und Wissen*, pp. 7–8.

5. Paul Wenzel, *Das wissenschaftliche Anliegen des Güntherianismus* (Essen: Hubert Wingen, 1961); Joseph Pritz, *Glauben und Wissen*, and *Wegweisung zur Theologie* (Vienna: Wiener Domverlag, 1971); Karl Beck, *Offenbarung und Glaube bei Anton Günther* (Vienna: Herder, 1967).

6. Pritz, *Wegweisung zur Theologie*, pp. 34–46, esp. p. 46.

7. "Protestantismus und Philosophie," *Lydia* I (1849): 37–39; also "Ein Wort über Modephilosophie," *Lydia* II (1852): 310–16. See also Pritz, *Wegweisung zur Theologie*, pp. 28–30; and Wenzel, pp. 47–52.

8. For Günther's metaphysics of *Vernunft* and *Verstand*, see Pritz, *Glauben und Wissen*, pp. 82–85; also Beck, pp. 18–19; and Wenzel, pp. 156–57.

9. *Peregrins Gastmahl* (Vienna: PP. Mechitaristen, 1830), pp. 60–61; Wenzel, pp. 15–19, 204–14; Beck, pp. 55–56. See also Günther's texts in Pritz, *Glauben und Wissen*, pp. 138–42. See especially Lakner, pp. 44–48. Günther's *Janusköpfe für Philosophie und Theologie* was extremely critical of scholastic philosophy.

10. Lakner, pp. 242–45.

11. *Thomas a Scrupulis* (Vienna: Wallishauser, 1835), pp. 154–55. See also Wenzel, pp. 192–201; Pritz, *Glauben und Wissen*, pp. 23–26; and Beck, pp. 18, 58–59.

12. Lakner, pp. 54–55; also Pritz, *Glauben und Wissen*, p. 74.

13. Lakner, p. 47. See also Wenzel, pp. 192–93, 208–11.

14. *Peregrins Gastmahl*, pp. 175–80, 479–81; Wenzel, pp. 77–78. also Lakner, pp. 222–24.

15. *Peregrins Gastmahl*, pp. 140–45, 311–13. See also Beck, pp. 18–21; and Pritz, *Wegweisung zur Theologie*, pp. 34–35. See also Günther's texts in Pritz, *Glauben und Wissen*, pp. 188–95.

16. See Günther's texts in Pritz, *Glauben und Wissen*, pp. 149–52. See also Lakner, pp. 49–52; Pritz, *Wegweisung zur Theologie*, pp. 34–36; and Wenzel, pp. 154–55.

17. See Günther's texts in Pritz, *Glaube und Wissen*, pp. 164–86. See also Wenzel, pp. 145–46, 152–54.

18. Beck, pp. 48–49.

19. Wenzel, p. 158.

20. Pritz, *Wegweisung zur Theologie*, pp. 34–35. See also Günther's texts in Pritz, *Glauben und Wissen*, pp. 188–95.

21. Wenzel, pp. 158–62; also Pritz, *Glauben und Wissen*, pp. 74–75; and Hocedez, 2:41–42.

22. See Günther's texts in Pritz, *Glauben und Wissen*, pp. 177–79, 187–94. Also *Peregrins Gastmahl*, pp. 140–42.

23. "Die Religion unserer Zeit, Eine blaue Epistel," *Lydia* I (1849): 351–52; *Janusköpfe für Philosophie und Theologie* (Vienna: Wallishauser, 1834), pp. 251–57, 266–93. See also Beck, pp. 169–73.

24. *Peregrins Gastmahl*, pp. 145–49. See also Beck, pp. 19–20.

25. See Günther's texts in Pritz, *Glauben und Wissen*, pp. 168–75. See also Beck, pp. 20–21, 55–56; and Wenzel, pp. 166–70.

26. See Günther's texts in Pritz, *Glauben und Wissen*, pp. 201–9. See also Beck, pp. 22–24.

27. See Günther's texts in Pritz, *Glaube und Wissen*, pp. 144–49.

28. Beck, pp. 38–52.

29. See Günther's texts in Pritz, *Glaube und Wissen*, pp. 149–88.

30. Wenzel, p. 163; also Beck, pp. 62–64.

31. Pritz, *Wegweisung zur Theologie*, p. 30.

32. Beck, pp. 52–53.

33. Pritz, *Wegweisung zur Theologie*, pp. 22–26. See also Günther's texts in Pritz, *Glaube und Wissen*, pp. 316–34, 357–68. Also Beck, pp. 34–36, 87–99.

34. Pritz, *Glaube und Wissen*, pp. 68–73. See also Beck, pp. 65–72; and Schäfer, pp. 156–57.

35. Beck, pp. 20–22; Wenzel, pp. 163–70.

36. *Peregrins Gastmahl*, pp. 395–98. See also Beck, pp. 24–27, 180–81. Also Günther's texts in Pritz, *Glaube und Wissen*, pp. 237–68.

37. Beck, pp. 74–75; also Pritz, *Wegweisung zur Theologie*, pp. 36–42.

38. Beck, pp. 68–74; also Pritz, *Glaube und Wissen*, pp. 93–96.

39. Beck, pp. 81–86. See also Günther's texts in Pritz, *Glaube und Wissen*, pp. 124–30.

40. Beck, pp. 87–90; Pritz, *Wegweisung zur Theologie*, pp. 42–47.

41. Beck, pp. 90–98. See Günther's texts in Pritz, *Glaube und Wissen*, pp. 275–79, 301–2, 312–16, 331–36.

42. See Günther's texts in Pritz, *Glaube und Wissen*, pp. 128–31.

43. Beck, pp. 59–66; also Pritz, *Glaube und Wissen*, pp. 86–91.

44. Wenzel, pp. 163–64.

45. Ibid., 164–67. See also Beck, pp. 61–62.

46. Wenzel, pp. 165–70; also Beck, pp. 59–64.

47. See Günther's texts in Pritz, *Glaube und Wissen*, pp. 237–68; also Beck, pp. 74–75.

48. Beck, p. 52; see also pp. 80–81, 124, 157–58.

49. See note 6.

50. For Günther's christocentric conception of revelation, see Beck, pp. 183–84. See also Pritz, *Wegweisung zur Theologie*, pp. 39–42.

51. See especially Günther's texts in Pritz, *Glaube und Wissen*, pp. 240–42 and particularly pp. 256–57. The latter text, taken from *Der Letzte Symboliker*, explains the relation of man to the whole human race through his bodily nature and man's transcendence through his spiritual *Geist*. Man is an individual member of a species through his bodily nature. Man is a person through his *Geist* or spirit.

52. See Günther's texts in Pritz, *Glaube und Wissen*, pp. 117–32. See also Pritz, *Wegweisung zur Theologie*, pp. 29–30; and Wenzel, pp. 147–52.

53. Pritz, *Wegweisung zur Theologie*, pp. 28–30.

54. Ibid., pp. 32–34, pp. 47–55. For Günther's texts, see Pritz, *Glaube und Wissen*, pp. 117–18, 125–31.

55. Pritz, *Wegweisung zur Theologie*, pp. 26–28.

56. Ibid., pp. 20–22.

57. Ibid., pp. 22–28. See Günther's texts in Pritz, *Glauben und Wissen*, pp. 311–12, 325–27.

58. Pritz, *Glaube und Wissen*, pp. 84–89; also Beck, 66–67.

59. Wenzel, pp. 170–72.

60. The fourth tractatus in Volume I of Kleutgen's *Die Theologie der Vorzeit* (Münster: Theissing, 1857). Although Günther was not named in the first edition, the tractatus was directed principally against his theology. In the *Brevis Synopsis Errorum Qui Leguntur in Scriptis Antonii Günther* (Brief Synopsis of the Errors in the Works of Anton Günther) which Wenzel discovered in the Vatican Archives (see Wenzel, pp. 248–54) Günther's failure to respect the freedom of creation is noted. This failure is also listed among the errors attributed to Günther by the Sacred Congregation of the Index. See the Congregation's letter of 8 January 1857 to Johann Cardinal Geisel, Archbishop of Cologne (DB 1655; DS 2828).

61. This error is explicitly mentioned in the apostolic letter *Dolore haud mediocri*, addressed to Melchior Cardinal Dipenbrock, Archbishop of Breslau on 30 April 1860 (DS 2833). For Kleutgen's criticism of Günther's anthropology in the memorandum which he prepared for the Congregation of the Index, see Schäfer, pp. 143–51.

62. See the papal brief *Eximiam tuam* (DB 1655; DS 2828). For other difficulties with Günther's trinitarian theology, see Beck, pp. 86–87; also Pritz, *Glaube und Wissen*, pp. 89–90.

CHAPTER 5

1. Edgar Hocedez, *Histoire de la théologie au xixᵉ siècle*, 2:100–106,111–12.

2. Fortuné Palhoriès, *Rosmini* (Paris: Alcan, 1908), pp. 42–52. See also Hocedez, 2:140–41.

3. Gioberti's *Introduzione allo studio della filosofia* has been published in the Edizione nazionale delle opere edite e inedite di Vincenzo Gioberti, vols. 4 and 5 [Giovanni Calò, ed.] (Milan: Fratelli Bocca, 1939–1941).

4. See Calò's introduction to the *Introduzione*, in Edizione nazionale (hereafter EN), 4:lxviii–lxxi.

5. *Introduzione allo studio della filosofia*, EN, 5:1–8.

6. Ibid., 5:143–49. See also Giovanni Gentile, *Gioberti e Rosmini* (Florence: Sansoni, 1955), pp. 294–96.

7. See Calò's introduction to the *Introduzione*, EN, 4:lxv–lxvii. See also Gentile, pp. 251–59.

8. Gioberti defends his own ontologistic account of the origin of ideas in *Introduzione*, EN, 5:148–63. See also Hocedez, 2:141–44.

9. Gioberti's *Degli errori filosofici di Antonio Rosmini* is published in vols. 8, 9, and 10 of the Edizione nazionale [Ugo Radanò, ed.] (Milan: Fratelli Bocca, 1939). For the controversy between Gioberti and Rosmini, see Radanò's introduction to *Degli errori*, EN, 8:xiv–xix. See also Gentile, pp. 123–62; and Hocedez, 2:145–50.

10. *Degli errori*, EN, 8:69–84.

11. *Introduzione*, EN, 5:166–73.

12. Ibid., 5:149–54, 169–70. See also Hocedez, 2:116.

13. *Introduzione*, EN, 5:181–91, esp. p. 189.

14. Ibid., 5:9–11. See also Fortuné Palhoriès, *Gioberti* (Paris: Alcan, 1929), pp. 168–75.

15. *Introduzione*, EN, 5:41–45. See also Gentile, pp. 266–71; and Hocedez, 2:116–17.

16. *Introduzione*, EN, 5:176–85, esp. p. 184, and 5:232–33. See also *Degli errori*, EN, 8:168–92.

17. Hocedez, 2:122.

18. Palhoriès, *Gioberti*, pp. 147–50. See also Etienne Gilson, *The Christian Philosophy of St. Augustine* (New York: Random House, 1960), pp. 77–112.

19. *Introduzione*, EN, 5:187–96. See also Hocedez, 2:117–18.

20. *Introduzione*, EN, 5:4–7. See also Giulio Bonafede, *Gioberti e la Critica* (Palermo: Mori, 1950), pp. 184–87.

21. *Teorica del sovranaturale*, Edizione nazionale delle opere edite e inedite di Vincenzo Gioberti, vols. 24 and 25 [Arnaldo Cortese, ed.] (Padua: Cedam, 1970). See especially "Parte Prima: Convenienza della religione rivelata colla mente umana" in vol. 25.

22. *Teorica del sovranaturale*, EN, 25:27–35. See also Palhoriès, *Gioberti*, pp. 213–315; and Giulio Bonafede, *Gioberti*, 2 vols. (Palermo: Unione Tipografica, 1941), 1:139–46, 156–58.

23. Palhoriès, *Gioberti*, pp. 226–27.

24. Ibid., pp. 290–325. See also Bonafede, *Gioberti e la critica*, pp. 170–203. Although Liberatore, the great Italian neo-Thomist, was convinced that Gioberti's system was radically pantheistic, Bonafede defends Gioberti's Catholic orthodoxy. See *Gioberti e la critica*, pp. 134 ff.

25. *Nuovo saggio sull'origine delle idee*, Edizione nazionale delle opere edite e inedite di Antonio Rosmini, vols. 3, 4, and 5 [Francesco Orestano, ed.] (Rome: Anonima romana editoriale, 1934).

26. *Nuovo saggio*, EN, 4:12–18. See Orestano's introduction, EN, 3:xlix. See also Carlo Giacon, *L'Oggetività in Antonio Rosmini* (Milan: Silva, 1960), pp. 29–32, 91–93.

27. *Nuovo saggio*, 4:24–30; also *La teosofia* (vols. 7–11 in the Edizione nazionale, Carlo Gray, ed., EN, 11:46–47. See also Gray's introduction to *La teosofia*, EN, 7:xlv–lii.

28. *Nuovo saggio*, EN, 4:34–35, 49–50; *La teosofia*, EN, 8:125, 11:230–35. See also Giacon, pp. 104–5.

29. *La teosofia*, EN, 7:149–55, 8:128–38.

30. Ibid., EN, 8:149–50, 9:14–18.

31. Ibid., EN, 9:210.

32. *Nuovo saggio*, EN, 4:15–16.

33. Ibid., EN, 4:16–18.

34. Ibid., EN, 4:57–63; *La teosofia*, EN, 8:19.

35. *Nuovo saggio*, EN, 4:57–70.

36. *Ibid.*, EN, 4:57–58, 73–74, 116–38.

37. *Ibid.*, EN, 4:109–15.

38. *Principi della scienza morale*, EN, 21:81–85, 104–7.

39. Ibid., EN, 21:101.

40. *Storia comparative e critica dei sistemi intorno al principio della morale*, EN, 21:129–47. See also *Compendio di Etica*, EN, 21:62.

41. See Ugo Radanò's introduction to Gioberti's *Degli errori di Antonio Rosmini*, EN di Vincenzo Gioberti, 8:xvi-xvii.

42. *La teosofia*, EN, 7:211–14.

43. For French ontologism, see Hocedez, 2:126–40.

44. Ibid., 100–101.

45. Ibid., 101–3.

46. Ibid., 103–6.

47. For the traditionalism of Bonnetty and Ventura, see Hocedez, 2:83–100.

48. Roger Aubert, *Le Pontificat de Pie IX (1846–1878)* (Paris: Bloud et Gay, 1952), pp. 192–93.

CHAPTER 6

1. DB 1634–1639; DS 2775–2786 (34th ed. of *Enchiridion Symbolorum*, Denziger-Schönmetzer [Barcelona: Herder, 1967]).

2. DB 1649–1652; DS 2811–2814. For a description of Bonnetty's traditionalism and an account of the controversy leading up to the intervention of the Congregation of the Index, see Hocedez, *Histoire de la théologie au xixᵉ siècle*, 2:17–100. Liberatore and Passaglia both reviewed and approved Chastel's *De la valeur de la raison ou ce que peut la raison par elle-même*, a polemical work which their Jesuit confrere directed against the traditionalism of Bonnetty. Chastel's work was published in 1854. The approval given to the work by both Liberatore and Passaglia is an indication of the common opposition to traditionalism on the part of the theologians of the Roman College and the Jesuit neo-Thomists.

3. DB 1655–1658; DS 2828–2831.

4. DB 1655; DS 2833.

5. DB 1651–1665; DS 2841–2847. For the controversy following the decree of the Holy Office, see Hocedez, 2:129–40.

6. DB 1668–1676; DS 2841–2861.

7. DB 1701–1780; DS 2901–2980. See also Roger Aubert, *Le Pontificat de Pie IX (1846–1878)* (Paris: Bloud et Gay, 1952), pp. 254–59.

8. Hocedez, 2:100–110. See also Aubert, *Pontificat*, pp. 192–93.

9. Aubert, *Pontificat*, pp. 205–9. See also Alexander Dru, *The Contribution of German Catholicism* (New York: Hawthorn, 1963), pp. 86–91.

10. Aubert, *Pontificat*, pp. 140–44. See also Dru, pp. 79–85.

11. Aubert, *Pontificat*, pp. 295–96.

12. Ibid., pp. 200–201. Rauscher and Günther had both belonged to the Hofbauer circle. After the death of St. Clement Mary Hofbauer his disciples broke into two hostile groups. Rauscher belonged to the conservative and Günther to the liberal group of Hofbauer's former disciples. Rauscher had been hostile to Günther for more than twenty years. In fact Rauscher had endeavored to secure the condemnation of Günther's works in the 1830s. The political alliance between a number of Günther's followers and the Austrian liberals who were

agitating for the repudiation of the Concordat intensified Rauscher's hostility to Günther.

13. Pierre Thibault, *Savoir et pouvoir: philosophie thomiste et politique cléricale au xixe siècle* (Québec: Les Presses de l'Université Laval, 1972), pp. 95–99, 151–58, 229–31. For the influence of the Jesuits at the court of Pius IX, see Aubert, *Pontificat* p. 286.

14. Giovanni Gentile, *Gioberti e Rosmini* (Florence: Sansoni, 1955), p. 252. See also Hocedez, 2:153; and Aubert, *Pontificat*, pp. 237–40.

15. Auguste Kerkevoorde, "La Formation théologique de M.-J. Scheeben à Rome (1852–1859)," *Ephemerides Theologicae Lovanienses* 22 (1946): 174–93, esp. pp. 176–77.

16. Paolo Dezza, *Alle origini del neotomismo italiano* (Milan: Fratelli Bocca, 1940), pp. 52–55.

17. Thomas J. A. Hartley, *Thomistic Revival and the Modernist Era* (Toronto: University of St. Michael's College, 1971), pp. 31–32. See also Robert Jacquin, *Taparelli* (Paris: Lethielleux, 1943), pp. 110–15; and idem, "Taparelli et le néo-thomisme," *Aquinas* 5 (1962): 421–30. See also Thibault's lively and interesting account, *Savoir*, pp. 43–46.

18. Hartley, p. 32. See also Franz Lakner, "Kleutgen und die kirchliche Wissenschaft Deutschlands im 19 Jahrhundert," *Zeitschrift für katholische Theologie* 57 (1933): 196.

19. The second volume, *Dell'anima umana*, was published in 1875.

20. Paolo Dezza, *I neotomisti italiani del xix secolo* (Milan: Fratelli Bocca, 1942), pp. 1–16. This was the strategy employed by both Liberatore and Kleutgen, as will appear in the following chapters.

21. Bernhard Welte, "Zum Strukturwandel der katholischen Theologie im 19 Jahrhundert," *Auf der Spur des Ewigen* (Freiburg: Herder, 1965), pp. 380–409.

CHAPTER 7

1. Auguste Pelzer, "Les initiateurs italiens du néo-thomisme contemporain," *Revue néo-scholastique de philosophie* 18 (1911): 230–54, esp. pp. 244–46. See also Amato Masnovo, "Le Père Liberatore fut-il thomiste de 1840–1850?" *Revue néo-scholastique de philosophie* 15 (1908): 518–26. See also Paolo Dezza, *Alle origini del neotomismo* (Milan: Fratelli Bocca, 1940), pp. 69–73.

2. Georges van Riet, *L'Epistémologie thomiste* (Louvain: Editions de l'Institut Supérieur de Philosophie, 1946), pp. 32–37.

3. These articles were soon published in book form. Liberatore's articles on theory of knowledge appear in the two volumes of his *Della conoscenza intellettuale* (Naples: Stamperia e Cartiere del Fibreno, 1857–1858). Liberatore's articles on philosophy of man were published in his *Del composto umano* (Rome. Coi Tipi della Civiltà Cattolica, 1862) and in his *Dell' anima umana* (Rome: Belfani, 1875). In 1874–1875 Belfani brought out Liberatore's philosophy of knowledge and man in a new edition under the general title, *Dell' uomo. Del composto umano* (1874) was the first volume. *Dell' anima umana* (1875) was the second. An excellent selection of

texts from these two volumes can be found in the first volume of Paolo Dezza's *I neotomisti italiani del xix secolo* (2 vols.; Milan: Fratelli Bocca, 1942).

4. *Della conoscenza intellettuale,* 2:36–38.

5. Ibid., 2:39–43.

6. Ibid., 2:48–52.

7. Ibid., 2:24–25.

8. Ibid., 2:36–38

9. Ibid., 2:68–69. See also van Riet, pp. 52–53.

10. *Della conoscenza intellettuale,* 2:48–52.

11. Ibid., 2:211–18.

12. *Del composto umano,* pp. 236–41, 267–72. See also Dezza, *I neotomisti italiani,* 1:11–13.

13. *Della conoscenza intellettuale,* 2:41–43, 48–50.

14. Ibid., 2:301–5, 317–22.

15. Ibid., 1:49–53, 230–31.

16. Ibid., 2:195–205. See also van Riet, pp. 52–53.

17. *Della conoscenza intellettuale,* 2:286–93.

18. Ibid., 2:289.

19. Ibid., 2:290. For Liberatore's understanding of the idea of being, see ibid., 2:279–83. For his identification of essences with possible being, see ibid., 2:283–86.

20. Ibid., 2:291–92.

21. Ibid., 1:49–53. See also van Riet, p. 56.

22. *Della conoscenza intellettuale,* 2:290–91. For Liberatore's critique of Rosmini's Ideal Being, see ibid., 1:303–36. The entire fourth section of the first volume (pp. 255–336) is devoted to Liberatore's discussion of Rosmini's philosophy.

23. For Liberatore's critique of Gioberti, see ibid., 1:54–61.

24. Ibid., 2:268–74.

25. Ibid., 2:363–65.

26. Ibid., See also van Riet, p. 48. Van Riet's reference is to the 1845 edition of Liberatore's *Institutiones Logicae et Metaphysicae.* Thus Liberatore's commitment to the analytico-synthetic method antedates his conversion to Thomism.

27. *Del composto umano,* pp. 17–33, 234–44, 311–15.

28. Ibid., pp. 514–24.

29. *Della conoscenza intellettuale,* 2:49–50.

30. *Dell' anima umana,* pp. 324–31. The citation is taken from the 1875 edition of *Dell' unomo,* of which *Dell' anima umana* is the second volume. For the spirituality of the human soul, see *Dell' anima umana,* pp. 120–27.

31. *Dell' anima umana,* pp. 59–65. See also *Del composto umano,* pp. 244–52.

32. *Istituzioni di Etica e Diretto naturale* (Turin: Marietti, 1865). For a brief and clear account of Italian neo-Thomist ethics, see Dezza, *I neotomisti italiani,* 2:1–7. A fine selection of Liberatore's ethical texts can be found in the same volume.

33. *Istituzioni di Etica e Diretto naturale,* pp. 23–37, 42–44.

34. Ibid., pp. 49–53.

35. Ibid., pp. 99–107, 115–17. See also Dezza *I neotomisti italiani,* 2:5–6.

36. *Istituzioni di Etica e Diretto naturale,* pp. 133–40. See also *Institutiones Ethicae et Juris Naturae,* 7th ed. (Prato: Giachetti, 1880), pp. 89–94.

37. *Istituzioni di Etica e Diretto naturale,* pp. 238–42, 250–66.
38. Ibid., pp. 148–50, 156–58, 161–65.
39. *Della conoscenza intellettuale,* 2:288–89.
40. Ibid., 2:287. See also van Riet, pp. 54–55.

CHAPTER 8

1. Theo Schäfer, *Die Erkenntnis-theoretische Kontroverse Kleutgen-Günther* (Paderborn: Schöningh, 1961), pp. 25–26, 131–32.
2. Edgar Hocedez, *Histoire de la théologie au xixe siècle,* 2:135–36.
3. Roger Aubert, *Le Problème de l'acte de foi* (Louvain: Warny, 1950), pp. 132–33, 149–50.
4. Franz Lakner, "Kleutgen und die Kirchliche Wissenschaft Deutschlands im 19 Jahrhundert," *Zeitschrift für katholische Theologie* 57 (1933): 161–214, esp. p. 199, n. 4. See also Schäfer, p. 51.
5. Lakner, pp. 184–85. See also A. Kerkevoorde, "La Formation théologique de M.-J. Scheeben à Rome (1852–1859)," *Ephemerides Theologicae Lovanienses* 22 (1946): 174–93.
6. Both *Die Theologie der Vorzeit* and *Die Philosophie der Vorzeit* were first published by Theissing of Münster. The second edition of *Die Philosophie der Vorzeit* (1878) was published by Rausch of Innsbruck. Citations in this chapter and the next are taken from the second edition of *Die Philosophie der Vorzeit* and from the first edition of *Die Theologie der Vorzeit,* with the exception of the first volume. Citations from the first volume are taken from the second edition (1867), also by Theissing.
7. Bernhard Casper, "Der Systemgedanke in der spätern Tübinger Schule und in der deutschen Neuscholastik," *Philosophisches Jahrbuch* 72 (1964–65): 161–79, esp. p. 174.
8. *Die Theologie der Vorzeit,* 4 (marked "Letzter Band" in the first edition), pp. 5–31, 77–102.
9. *Die Theologie der Vorzeit,* 1:3–8; *Die Philosophie der Vorzeit,* 1:1–22. See also Schäfer, pp. 65–75, 93–97; and Bernhard Welte, "Zum Strukturwandel der katholischen Theologie im 19 Jahrhundert," *Auf der Spur des Ewigen* (Freiburg: Herder, 1965), pp. 380–409.
10. The full title of *Die Theologie der Vorzeit* is *Die Theologie der Vorzeit vertheigt* (defended). In his introduction to the first volume of the second edition Kleutgen states that his work is intended to be a defense of scholastic theology against the criticisms levelled against it by Hermes, Günther, and Hirscher (pp. 25–36) and describes the plan of his proposed defense (pp. 36–45).
11. The second part of *Die Theologie der Vorzeit,* which is concerned with theological methods *(Lehrweise),* is a protracted comparison between the scholastic theological method and Hermes' method in dogmatic theology (5:591–626), Hirscher's method in practical theology (5:627–87) and Günther's method in speculative theology (5:688–841).
12. *Die Theologie der Vorzeit,* 1:36–45. Kleutgen was right. Hermes, Günther and

Hirscher did not understand scholastic theology. Hirscher's prejudice against scholasticism was well known and his ignorance of scholasticism is generally admitted. See J. R. Geiselmann, *Die katholische Tübinger Schule* (Freiburg: Herder, 1964), p. 16. Kleutgen complained (5:685) that when he verified the theologically erroneous statements which Hirscher asserted were contained in Canisius' "Small Catechism" not one of them could be found in Canisius' book. The German theologians' ignorance of scholasticism served Kleutgen well in his controversy with them. Their complaints against scholasticism could be attributed to prejudice based on hearsay evidence.

13. *Die Theologie der Vorzeit,* 5:984–1022.

14. The first part of *Die Theologie der Vorzeit,* devoted to points of doctrine *(Lehrpunkte),* contrasted the scholastic teaching with the teaching of Hermes, Günther, and Hirscher on the principal disputed questions in nineteenth-century Catholic theology. Volume 1 dealt with the norm of faith, the divine essence, the Trinity, the freedom and the final goal of creation. Volume 2 dealt with the supernatural order, grace, sin, and the grace and the sin of the first man. Volume 3 dealt with the Redeemer and the redemption.

15. In the first edition the second part *(Zweiter Teil)* was divided into six treatises *(Abhandlungen).* The two volumes of the second section were paginated successively. The fifth volume (1865) began with the fifth *Abhandlung* on page 545.

16. *Die Theologie der Vorzeit,* 4:139–214.

17. Ibid., 4:215–31.

18. Schäfer, pp. 46–47.

19. Hocedez, 2:325.

20. *Die Theologie der Vorzeit,* 5:545–55.

21. Ibid., 5:548–53, 565–67.

22. Ibid., 5:841–46.

23. Ibid., 5:554–55.

24. Ibid.

25. Ibid., 4:457–61.

26. Ibid., 5:553–54.

27. Ibid., 5:618–22.

28. Ibid., 5:555–63.

29. Ibid., 5:563.

30. Ibid.

31. Aubert, *Le Problème de l'acte de foi,* p. 132, n. 3. See also Hermann-Joseph Pottmeyer, *Der Glaube vor dem Anspruch der Wissenschaft* (Freiburg: Herder, 1968), pp. 26, 38, 59–61, 75–81, 83–88.

32. *Die Theologie der Vorzeit,* 5:565–81.

33. Ibid., 5:586–90.

34. Ibid., 4:390–91.

35. Ibid., 5:597–98, 607–10, 616–22.

36. Ibid., 4:217–331.

37. Ibid., 1:341–57.

38. Ibid., 5:567.

39. Ibid., 5:587.

40. Ibid., 5:591–92.
41. Ibid., 5:594–95.
42. Ibid., 5:622–26.
43. Ibid., 5:567, 592–93, 597.
44. Ibid., 5:565–81.
45. Ibid., 5:616–22.
46. Ibid., 5:557, 618–19.

CHAPTER 9

1. Edgar Hocedez, *Histoire de la théologie au xixe siècle*, 2:71–73, 320–21. See also Roger Aubert, *Le Problème de l'acte de foi* (Louvain: Warny, 1950), pp. 117–21; and Alexander Dru, *The Contribution of German Catholicism* (New York: Hawthorn, 1963), pp. 77–79.
2. J. R. Geiselmann, *Die katholische Tübinger Schule* (Freiburg: Herder, 1964), pp. 129–41.
3. For a complete list of Hirscher's books, see Hermann Josef Brosch, *Das Übernatürliche in der katholische Tübinger Schule* (Essen: Hubert Wingen, 1962), p. xiii.
4. Hocedez, 1:221–26.
5. For Hirscher's Idea of the Kingdom of God, see Geiselmann, pp. 224–62; and Brosch, pp. 71–85. For Geiselmann's severe criticism of Brosch's scholastic evaluation of the Catholic Tübingen School, see *Die Katholische Tübinger Schule*, pp. 15–43.
6. *Die Theologie der Vorzeit*, 5:632–33.
7. Ibid., 5:628–29.
8. Ibid.
9. Ibid., 5:633–38.
10. Hocedez, 1:224–25; also *Die Theologie der Vorzeit*, 5:636–37.
11. Geiselmann, pp. 426–50.
12. *Die Theologie der Vorzeit*, 5:638–56.
13. Ibid., 5:640–46.
14. Ibid., 5:638–39, 656–57.
15. Ibid., 5:662–63.
16. Ibid., 5:669–71.
17. Ibid., 5:669–75.
18. Ibid., 5:670–71, 681.
19. Ibid., 5:629–35.
20. Ibid., 5:670.
21. Ibid., 5:656–57.
22. Ibid., 5:670–71.
23. Ibid., 5:634–35, 670, 678.
24. Ibid., 5:673–75.
25. Ibid., 5:608–13, 628–34.
26. Ibid., 5:646–48, 634–35.
27. Ibid., 5:665–67.

28. Ibid., 5:652–56.

29. Ibid., 5:664–67.

30. Geiselmann, p. 16. See also *Die Theologie der Vorzeit*, 2:547–51; and Brosch, pp. 136, 139–40.

31. *Die Theologie der Vorzeit*, 5:637–38.

32. Ibid., 5:642–45.

33. Ibid., 5:658–61.

34. Ibid., 5:673–84.

35. Ibid., 5:671–75.

36. Ibid., 5:682–84.

37. See note 5.

38. For the role of the Holy Spirit, see Brosch, pp. 107–21; also Geiselmann, pp. 155–61.

39. See Bernard J. F. Lonergan, "Theology in Its New Context," *A Second Collection* (Philadelphia: Westminster, 1974), pp. 55–67.

40. *Die Theologie der Vorzeit*, 5:586–88, 688–95.

41. Ibid., esp. 689–92.

42. Ibid., 5:695–714.

43. Ibid., 5:716–32.

44. Ibid., 5:722–23.

45. Ibid., 5:725–28.

46. "Die ideale Probe des realen Facit," cited from Günther's *Eurysthes und Heracles*, p. 325 (also from *Lydia* II [1852]: 310), in *Die Theologie der Vorzeit*, 5:722.

47. *Die Theologie der Vorzeit*, 5:739–44, 746–50.

48. Ibid., 5:787–801.

49. Ibid., 5:767–87.

50. Karl Rahner, "The Concept of Mystery in Catholic Theology," *Theological Investigations* IV (Baltimore: Helicon, 1966): 52–54.

51. Joseph Pritz, *Wegweisung zur Theologie* (Vienna: Wiener Domverlag, 1971), pp. 34–47.

52. Karl Rahner, "The Theological Notion of Concupiscentia," *Theological Investigations* I (Baltimore: Helicon, 1965): 300–302, 310–15.

53. *Die Philosophie der Vorzeit*, 1:587–98.

54. Theo Schäfer, *Die Erkenntnis-theoretische Kontroverse Kleutgen-Günther* (Paderborn: Schöningh, 1961), pp. 67–70.

55. *Die Philosophie der Vorzeit*, 1:344–48.

56. Ibid., 1:376–96.

57. Georges van Riet, *L'Epistémologie thomiste* (Louvain: Editions de l'Institut Supérieur de Philosophie, 1946), pp. 79–80. See also *Die Philosophie der Vorzeit*, 1:173–79, esp. 175 n. 1; 1:521–30. Also Schäfer, pp. 116–18.

58. Van Riet, pp. 79–80.

59. Schäfer, pp. 100–106.

60. Ibid., pp. 107–13.

61. Ibid., pp. 170–74. See also *Die Philosophie der Vorzeit*, 1:439–43.

62. *Die Philosophie der Vorzeit*, 1:23–31.

63. Ibid., 1:502–14.

64. Ibid., 2:46–58.

65. See Kleutgen's un-Thomistic explanation of the distinction between essence and existence, in *Die Philosophie der Vorzeit,* 2:59–74.

66. See Etienne Gilson, *Being and Some Philosophers* (Toronto: Pontifical Institute of Medieval Studies, 1952), pp. 105–7.

CHAPTER 10

1. For a brief and clear account of Vatican I, see Roger Aubert, *Le Pontificat die Pie IX (1846–1878)* (Paris: Bloud et Gay, 1952), pp. 311–67, esp. pp. 335–38. For a detailed account of the background and content of the Dogmatic Constitution on Faith, *Dei Filius,* see the excellent treatise of Hermann-Josef Pottmeyer, *Der Glaube vor dem Anspruch der Wissenschaft* (Freiburg: Herder, 1968). See also the detailed account in Roger Aubert, *Le Problème de l'acte de foi* (Louvain: Warny, 1950), pp. 132–222.

2. DB 1782–1784, 1801–1805; DS 3001–3003, 3021–3025 (34th ed. of *Enchiridion Symbolorum,* Denziger–Schönmetzer [Barcelona: Herder, 1967]).

3. DB 1785–1788, 1801–1805; DS 3004–3007, 3021–3025.

4. For the references to traditionalism in the *votum* which Franzelin prepared for the pre-conciliar Dogmatic Commission, see Pottmeyer, *Anhang,* pp. 31–35.

5. DB 1789–1794, 1810–1815; DS 3008–3014, 3031–3036. See also Pottmeyer, p. 256.

6. DB 1795–1800, 1816–1818; DS 3015–3020, 3041–3043.

7. Aubert, *Le Problème de l'acte de foi,* p. 45. See also Pottmeyer, pp. 112–13.

8. See Pottmeyer, pp. 168–204. For a masterly exposition of the teaching of Vatican I concerning the natural knowledge of God, see Bernard J. F. Lonergan, "Natural Knowledge of God," *A Second Collection* (Philadelphia: Westminster, 1974), pp. 117–33, esp. 118–19.

9. Pottmeyer, pp. 179–88.

10. Hocedez, *Histoire de la théologie au xixe siècle,* 2:137.

11. Aubert, *Problème de l'acte de foi,* p. 132. For the full text of the *votum* which Franzelin prepared for the Consultors of the pre-conciliar Dogmatic Commission, see Pottmeyer, *Anhang,* pp. 28–89. For the full text of Franzelin's schema, see Pottmeyer, *Anhang,* pp. 90–105. The essential elements of Franzelin's *votum* were preserved in the schema which he was authorized to draw up after the presentation of his *votum,* and which he submitted to the Commission on 5 August 1869.

12. Aubert, *Le Problème de l'acte de foi,* p. 132, n. 3. For Franzelin's dependence on Perrone, see Pottmeyer, pp. 109–10.

13. Aubert, *Le Problème de l'acte de foi,* pp. 145–52.

14. Ibid.

15. For a comparison between Franzelin's schema and Kleutgen's re-edited version, see Pottmeyer, pp. 478–88. For a comparison between the final version of the schema and the final text approved by the Fathers of the Vatican Council, see *Pottmeyer,* pp. 488–98. See also, Aubert, *Le Problème de l'acte de foi,* pp. 157, 164–65, 177.

16. Pottmeyer, pp. 82–107.

17. Ibid., pp. 107–9, 259–60.

18. *Dei Filius,* chapter 3, DB 1794; DS 3014.

19. Aubert, *Le Problème de l'acte de foi,* pp. 142–45, 149–52.

20. See the letter of Cardinal Billot, the President of the pre-conciliar Dogmatic Commission, to Dechamps, cited in Aubert, *Le Problème de l'acte de foi,* p. 142.

21. For the Blondelian "rediscovery" of Dechamps' apologetics, see Aubert, *Le Problème de l'acte de foi,* pp. 323–25. Aubert cites the series of articles on apologetics published under the name of Abbé Mallet. Although these articles were published under Mallet's name, it is now known that their real author was Blondel himself. See Henri Bouillard, *Blondel et le christianisme* (Paris: Editions du Seuil, 1961), p. 280.

22. Johannes Beumer, *Theologie als Glaubensverständnis* (Würzburg: Echter, 1953), pp. 13–24. See also the penetrating analysis of Beumer's book by Bernard J. F. Lonergan, "Theology and Understanding," *Collection* (New York: Herder and Herder, 1967), pp. 121–41.

23. Beumer, pp. 228–29.

24. Ibid., pp. 237–44.

25. Bernard J. F. Lonergan, "Theology in Its New Context," *A Second Collection,* pp. 55–67, and "Insight Revisited," ibid., pp. 263–78.

26. Paolo Dezza, *Alle origini del neotomismo* (Milan: Fratelli Bocca, 1940), p. 56.

27. Thomas J. A. Hartley, *Thomistic Revival and the Modernist Era* (Toronto: University of St. Michael's College, 1971), pp. 1–7.

28. Aubert, *Le Pontificat de Pie IX,* p. 192.

29. Hocedez, 2:138–39.

30. Roger Aubert, *Aspects divers du néo-thomisme sous le pontificat de Léon XIII* (Rome: Edizioni 5 Lune, 1961), pp. 7–9.

31. Aubert, *Aspects divers du néo-thomisme,* p. 10. Also Franz Lakner, "Kleutgen und die kirchliche Wissenschaft Deutschlands im 19 Jahrhundert," *Zeitschrift für katholische Theologie* 57 (1933); 199. Also Theo Schäfer, *Die Erkenntnis-theoretische Kontroverse Kleutgen-Günther* (Paderborn: Schöningh, 1961), p. 51.

32. For an English translation of *Aeterni Patris,* see Jacques Maritain, *The Angelic Doctor* (New York: Dial Press, 1931), pp. 224–62. Citations in this chapter are from that translation.

33. *Aeterni Patris,* in Maritain, *The Angelic Doctor,* pp. 228–34.

34. Ibid., pp. 235–39.

35. Ibid., pp. 239–46.

36. Ibid., p. 247.

37. Ibid., pp. 247–48.

38. Ibid., pp. 253–54.

39. Ibid., pp. 254–58.

40. Ibid., pp. 259–60.

41. Ibid., pp. 250–61.

42. See Paolo Dezza, *I neotomisti del xix secolo* (Milan: Fratelli Bocca, 1942), pp. 2–5.

43. See Paolo Dezza, *Alle origini del neotomismo* (Milan: Fratelli Bocca, 1940), pp. 85–124. Also Aubert, *Aspects divers du néo-thomisme,* pp. 24–25.

44. *Aeterni Patris*, in Maritain, *The Angelic Doctor*, p. 253.

45. Ibid., p. 260.

46. See Robert F. Harvanek, "The Unity of Metaphysics," *Thought* 28 (1953): 382–84.

47. See Bernard J. F. Lonergan, "Theology in Its New Context."

48. Aubert, *Aspects divers du néo-thomisme*, pp. 10, 31–32.

49. Hartley, *Thomistic Revival and the Modernist Era*, pp. 32–33.

50. Aubert, *Aspects divers du néo-thomisme*, pp. 30–31. See also Georges van Riet, *L'Epistémologie thomiste* (Louvain: Editions de l'Institut Supérieur de Philosophie, 1946), pp. 81–107.

51. Aubert, *Aspects divers du néo-thomisme*, pp. 38–40; Hocedez, 3:48–49; Hartley, pp. 37–38.

52. Edouard Lecanuet, *La Vie de l'Eglise sous Léon XIII* (Paris: Alcan, 1930), pp. 478–79, n. 1.

53. Van Riet, p. 125.

54. Aubert, *Aspects divers du néo-thomisme*, pp. 33–41.

55. Hartley, pp. 40–45. See also Jules Lebreton, "Son Eminence le Cardinal Billot," in *Etudes* 129 (1911): 514–25.

EPILOGUE

1. The encyclical *Aeterni Patris* was issued on 4 August 1879. The papal letter *Jampridem*, 15 October 1879, proclaimed Leo's intention to restore the Roman Academy of St. Thomas. The papal brief *Cum hoc sit*, 4 August 1880, designated St. Thomas as the universal patron of Catholic schools. The brief *Gravissime Nos*, December 1892, invited the members of the Society of Jesus to follow the teachings of St. Thomas. On 25 November 1898, the same invitation was extended to the Franciscans.

2. The institute was established by a pontifical brief of Leo XIII in 1889. In 1894 its famous review, *La Revue néo-scholastique de philosophie*, began to appear. In 1946 the name of the review was changed to *La Revue philosophique de Louvain*.

3. Through the motu proprio *Placere Nobis*, 18 January 1880.

4. Doctoris Seraphici S. Bonaventurae, *Opera omnia ed. studio et cura PP. Collegii a S. Bonaventura ad plurimos codices mss. emendata anecdotis aucta, praelegomonis scholiis notisque illustrata*, 10 vols. in folio. (Quarrachi, 1882–1902).

5. *Beiträge zur Geschichte der Philosophie des Mittelalters*, ed. G. von Hertling and C. Baeumker (Münster: Aschendorff, 1891–1973).

6. This type of presupposition lay beneath the endless debate carried on between the authors of the Suarezian and Thomistic manuals over the real distinction between essence and existence, the analogy of being etc. Suarez' own *Disputationes Metaphysicae* provide a remarkably extensive canvas of the diverse philosophical opinions held by the Greek and Scholastic philosophers. Nevertheless, in his discussion of these diversities of opinion, Suarez seems unaware of the different historical perspectives which gave rise to them.

7. One of the classical studies on this distinction is J. Pégaire's *Intellectus et Ratio selon S. Thomas* (Paris: Vrin, 1936).

8. Bernard J. F. Lonergan has shown that Thomas' Trinitarian theology cannot be understood until the intelligible procession of the verbum from the act of insight has been clearly grasped. See *Verbum: Word and Idea in Aquinas* (Notre Dame, Ind.: Notre Dame University Press, 1967). The conceptualist theologians of Billot's generation were not aware of St. Thomas' metaphysics of the act of insight.

9. Blondel's master work was *L'Action* (Paris: Alcan, 1893). For a fine exposition of Blondel's philosophy, see James M. Somerville, *Total Commitment: Blondel's "L'Action"* (Washington: Corpus Books, 1968). For the influence of German Idealism on Blondel see John J. McNeill, S.J., *The Blondelian Synthesis* (Leyden: E. J. Brill, 1966).

10. See Etienne Gilson, *The Philosopher and Theology* (New York: Random House, 1962), pp. 43–61.

11. For a clear account of the Modernists' theological program see John J. Heaney, *The Modernist Crisis: von Hügel* (Washington: Corpus Books, 1968).

12. Three years after the publication of his strong condemnation of Modernism in the encyclical *Pascendi*, Pius X issued the motu proprio *Doctoris Angelici*, dated 1 September 1910. *Doctoris Angelici* again recommended the philosophy and theology of the Angelic Doctor. On 17 October 1914 the Congregation of Seminaries and Universities issued its famous 24 Thomist theses as safe guides for the philosophical education of future priests. The new Code of Canon Law (1917) prescribed that teachers "shall adhere religiously to the methods, doctrine and principles" of St. Thomas (Can. 1366, sec. 2).

13. See the excellent summary of Gardeil's epistemology in Georges van Riet, *L'Epistémologie thomiste* (Louvain: Editions de l'Institut Supérieur de Philosophie, 1946), pp. 244–62.

14. *Dieu, son Existence et sa Nature* (Paris: Beauchesne, 1915); English trans., *God: His Existence and His Nature*, 2 vols. (St. Louis: B. Herder, 1934–36). For a synthesis of Garrigou-Lagrange's metaphysics, see *Reality: A Synthesis of Thomistic Thought* (St. Louis: B. Herder, 1950).

15. *L'Intellectualisme de S. Thomas* (Paris: Beauchesne, 1908); English trans., *The Intellectualism of St. Thomas* (London: Sheed and Ward, 1935).

16. "Les Yeux de la foi," *Recherches de science religieuse* 1 (1910): 241–59, 444–75.

17. For an outline of de Tonquédec's epistemology, see van Riet, pp. 314–38.

18. Gilson and Maritain both continued their publication into the period following World War II. As a matter of fact, the English translations of a number of their important works appeared at this time and their influence in North America remained significant. From the chronological point of view, therefore, the fourfold division of this essay is subject to criticism. Nevertheless it does represent with reasonable accuracy the internal movement of the scholastic revival. In the scholastic theology of the postwar period transcendental Thomism assumed the leadership which it has retained up to the present.

19. *Distinguer pour Unir ou Les Degrés du Savoir* (Paris: Desclée de Brouwer, 1932); English trans., *Distinguish to Unite or The Degrees of Knowledge* (New York: Scribner, 1946). For Maritain's reaction to Bergson's philosophy, see his *Bergsonian Philosophy and Thomism* (New York: Philosophical Library, 1955).

20. *Creative Intuition in Art and Poetry* (New York: Meridian Books, 1955).
21. *Art and Scholasticism* (New York: Scribner, 1962).
22. *The Situation of Poetry* (New York: The Philosophical Library, 1955).
23. *True Humanism* (New York: Scribner, 1938).
24. *The Person and the Common Good* (Notre Dame, Ind.: University of Notre Dame Press, 1966).
25. *Scholasticism and Politics* (New York: Macmillan, 1940). See also *Man and the State* (Chicago: University of Chicago Press, 1951).
26. Gilson has given an account of his epistemology in his *Réalisme thomiste et critique de connaissance* (Paris: Vrin, 1939). See also van Riet, pp. 494–517.
27. *The Spirit of Mediaeval Philosophy* (New York: Scribners, 1940).
28. *The Philosophy of St. Bonaventure* (New York: Sheed and Ward, 1938).
29. *The Christian Philosophy of St. Thomas* (New York: Random House, 1956).
30. *Jean Duns Scot* (Paris: Vrin, 1957).
31. See *The Philosopher and Theology*, pp. 174–214. For a Thomistic rejoinder to Gilson's thesis see James M. Collins, *Three Paths in Philosophy* (Chicago: Regnery, 1962), pp. 280–99.
32. In his *Elements of Christian Philosophy* (New York: Doubleday, 1960) Gilson gives an exposition of how Thomas' metaphysics of *esse*, inspired by the name of God and grounded by the judgment of existence, develops into a coherent metaphysics within Thomas' theology.
33. Gallus M. Manser, O.P., *Das Wesen des Thomismus* (Freiburg in der Schweiz: Divus Thomas, 1932).
34. For the distinctiveness of Thomas' metaphysics of *esse* see Gilson's *Being and Some Philosophers* (Toronto: Pontifical Institute of Mediaeval Studies, 1952).
35. *Le Point de départ de la métaphysique* (Paris: Alcan, 1922–26). For an outstanding translation and abridgement of Maréchal's major work, see Joseph Donceel, S.J., *A Maréchal Reader* (New York: Herder and Herder, 1970).
36. For a clear presentation of the points at issue between Gilsonian and Maréchalian Thomism, see Joseph Donceel, S.J., "A Thomistic Misapprehension?" *Thought* 32 (1957): 189–98.
37. Erich Przywara, S.J., *Polarity* (London: Oxford University Press, 1935).
38. Henri de Lubac, S.J., *Surnaturel* (Paris: Aubier, 1946). For a brief summary of de Lubac's position, see William C. Shepherd, *Man's Condition* (New York: Herder and Herder, 1969), pp. 70–80.
39. Jean Marie LeBlond, S.J., "L'Anologie de la Vérité," *Recherches de science religieuse* 34 (1947): 129–41. For a clear discussion of the new theology debate over theological pluralism, see Robert F. Harvanek, S.J., "The Unity of Metaphysics," *Thought* 28 (1953): 375–412. See also James Collins, pp. 255–79.
40. Robert F. Harvanek has carefully summarized these articles in his "Philosophical Pluralism and Catholic Orthodoxy," *Thought* 25 (1950): 21–52. See also Gustave Weigel, S.J., "The Historical Background of the Encyclical *Humani Generis*," *Theological Studies* 12 (1951): 208–30.
41. Rahner's major philosophical works are *Spirit in the World* (New York: Herder and Herder, 1968) and *Hearers of the Word* (New York: Herder and Herder, 1969). His principal theological essays have been collected in *Theological Investiga-*

tions, 14 vols. to date (London: Darton, Longman & Todd, 1961–76; New York: Seabury Press, 1974–76). For a one volume collection of Rahner's selected texts, see the author's *A Rahner Reader* (New York: Seabury Press, 1974).

42. Lonergan's major philosophical work is his *Insight* (New York: Philosophical Library, 1957).

43. *Method in Theology* (New York: Herder and Herder, 1972).

44. Henri de Lubac, *Surnaturel;* Henri Bouillard, *Conversion et grâce chez S. Thomas d'Aquin* (Paris: Aubier, 1944); Karl Rahner, "Concerning the Relationship Between Nature and Grace," *Theological Investigations* I (Baltimore: Helicon, 1965): 297–317; idem, "Nature and Grace," *Theological Investigations* IV (Baltimore: Helicon, 1966): 165–88; "Reflections on the Experience of Grace," *Theological Investigations* III (Baltimore: Helicon, 1967): 86–90; idem, *The Christian Commitment* (New York: Sheed and Ward, 1963), pp. 38–74; Bernard J.F. Lonergan, *Grace and Freedom* (New York: Herder and Herder, 1971).

45. Etienne Gilson, *Elements of Christian Philosophy* (New York: New American Library, 1963), pp. 228–40.

46. See Bernard J. F. Lonergan, "Theology in Its New Context," *A Second Collection* (Philadelphia: The Westminster Press, 1974), pp. 55–67.

47. See Karl Rahner, "Philosophy and Philosophizing in Theology," *Theological Investigations* IX (New York: Herder and Herder, 1972): 46–63.

48. Johannes B. Metz, *Christliche Anthropozentrik* (Munich: Kösel, 1962). See also Rahner's introductory essay to this volume, pp. 9–20.

49. Bernard J. F. Lonergan, "The Subject," *A Second Collection,* pp. 69–86.

50. See Karl Rahner, "Some Critical Thoughts on 'Functional Specialties in Theology,'" in Philip McShane, ed., *Foundations of Theology* (Notre Dame, Ind.: Notre Dame University Press, 1972), pp. 194–97.

51. Karl Rahner, "Reflections on Methodology in Theology," *Theological Investigations* XI (New York: The Seabury Press, 1974): 68–114, esp. pp. 91–92. See also idem, *Hearers of the Word* (New York: Herder and Herder, 1969); Bernard J. F. Lonergan, "Natural Knowledge of God," *A Second Collection,* pp. 117–34; and idem, *The Philosophy of God and Theology* (Philadelphia: The Westminster Press, 1973).

52. Walter Kasper, *Glaube und Geschichte* (Mainz: Grünewald, 1970), pp. 9–32.

53. Ibid., pp. 15–16.

54. Ibid., pp. 16–18.

55. Ibid., pp. 18–19.

56. Ibid., pp. 19–21. See also Kasper's *The Methods of Dogmatic Theology* (Glen Rock: The Paulist Press, 1968), esp. pp. 33–44.

57. Kasper, *Glaube und Geschichte,* pp. 19–21; *The Methods of Dogmatic Theology,* pp. 52–60.

58. See David Tracy, *Blessed Rage for Order* (New York: The Seabury Press, 1975). Tracy clearly distinguishes between a Catholic fundamental theology, which in principle does not include among its presuppositions the specific intelligibility of the Christian mysteries which is accessible only through the explicit assent of Christian faith, and a Catholic systematic theology, which in principle does include this specific intelligibility in its presuppositions.

59. Karl Rahner, "Philosophy and Theology," *Theological Investigations* VI (Baltimore: Helicon, 1969): 71–81, and "Reflections on the Contemporary Intellectual Formation of Future Priests," ibid., pp. 113–38, esp. pp. 130–31. Also Bernard J. F. Lonergan, *Method in Theology*, esp. pp. 125–45.

60. Karl Rahner, *Hearers of the Word*, pp. 45–52; Bernard J. F. Lonergan, *Insight*, pp. 348–74, esp. pp. 360–62.

INDEX

Abstraction 10f., 14; and Liberatore 150, 153ff.; metaphysics of, in Kleutgen 212; three degrees of 249; and Maritain 252; and judgment of existence 254; the Maréchalian metaphysics of 259.

Adam: first and second in Günther 98–104; Kleutgen on Hirscher's theology of Adam's state 197f.

Aeterni Patris 1ff., 14f., 83f., 128, 241, 246; background and preparation 167, 226ff; three functions of philosophy 228f; on scholastic philosophy 229ff.; recommendation of 230ff.; weakness and strengths 234f., unhistorical conception of philosophy and theology 234f.; aftermath 236–239.

Analogy 10; of being 238, 259; and supernatural concepts 206ff., 266; in Hermes 184; in *Dei Filius* 217, 224.

Apologetics 7f., 13ff., 18, 34, 47, 52f.; in Drey 78ff.; of immanence 13, 54; in *Dei Filius* 223f.; of Victor Deschamps 223f.; and Gioberti 119; in Kleutgen 178, 210.

Aristotle: need to explain original justice 199.

Aristotelian: scholasticism 57, 115, 128, 199ff.; metaphysics 8f., 14, 29, 136, 266; in Kleutgen 199–202, 262; scientific method of 14, 241; division of sciences 200; in Maritain 249; science of faith 181, 221f., 225f., Hirscher's critique of 195; theology of nature in Vatican I 221f.

Ascetical and mystical theology in Kleutgen's system 200f.

Aubert, Roger 239, 269, 271ff., 275, 280, 283ff., 287ff.

Augustinianism 44, 111, 113, 127, 223; of Gioberti 114–118; of Rosmini 122–125; and intuition 55, 114, 116, 121.

Baader, Franz von 31.

Baeumker, Clemens 243.

Bautain, Louis 46–54: Jacobi's influence on 48ff., 55; faith and reason in 47ff., 51–54; epistemology 48–51; first principles and tradition 51f.; on scholastic apologetics 53; apologetics of immanence 54; reaction against 46f., 54f.; retraction 54.

Beatific Vision 19, 170.

Beck, Karl 90, 276ff.

Beckx, Peter 137, 237.

Bergson, Henri 244f., 247.

Beumer, Johannes 224f., 288.

Billot, Louis 3, 83, 239, 242.

Blondel, Maurice 54, 119, 224, 244f., 255.

Bonald, Louis de 40–43: and Cartesianism 40ff.; faith and reason 42f., revelation and tradition 41ff.; language, thought, society and first principles 40–42; knowledge of God 42; universal consent-criterion for religious truth 41.

Bonaventure, St. 124f., 185, 261; and Rosmini 124f.; and Rahner 124f.

Bonnetty, Auguste 128f., 137, 280.

Bouillard, Henri 3, 236, 261.

Brosch, Hermann Josef 201, 274f., 285f.

Cajetan 13, 175, 234, 243, 249, 259.

Cano, Melchior 9, 175, 179, 182, 186, 203, 234.

Cartesian: philosophy 28f., 40f., 156f.; innatism 114; method 139f., 156f.; difference from Catholic theology 156f., 168.

Cartesianism 17, 47.

Casper, Bernard 269, 274, 283.

Casuistry: Kleutgen's defense of 200.

Christian philosophy: in *Aeterni Patris* 229f.

Church and state: 21–27; relations 21ff., 27; tensions 23, 25f.; and grace/nature debate 21.

Christology: Drey's: 72, 76, 189f, 192f.; Günther's second Adam 99–105, 207f.; Kleut-